IPSpecialist

D1749981

cisco

[Document Control]

Proposal Name	:	CCNA Service Provider – Workbook
Document Version	:	1.0
Document Release Date	:	1st August 2017
Reference	:	IPSpecialist_WB_CCNA_SP_v_1.0

Copyright © 2018 IPSpecialist LTD.

Registered in England and Wales

Company Registration No: 10883539

Registration Office at: Office 32, 19-21 Crawford Street, London W1H 1PJ, United Kingdom

www.ipspecialist.net

All rights reserved. No part of this book may be reproduced or transmitted in any form or by any means, electronic or mechanical, including photocopying, recording, or by any information storage and retrieval system, without written permission from IPSpecialist LTD, except for the inclusion of brief quotations in a review.

Feedback:

If you have any comments regarding the quality of this book, or otherwise alter it to better suit your needs, you can contact us through email at info@ipspecialist.net

Please make sure to include the book title and ISBN in your message

About IPSpecialist

IPSPECIALIST LTD. IS COMMITTED TO EXCELLENCE AND DEDICATED TO YOUR SUCCESS.

Our philosophy is to treat our customers like family. We want you to succeed, and we are willing to do anything possible to help you make it happen. We have the proof to back up our claims. We strive to accelerate billions of careers with great courses, accessibility, and affordability. We believe that continuous learning and knowledge evolution are most important things to keep re-skilling and up-skilling the world.

Planning and creating a specific goal is where IPSpecialist helps. We can create a career track that suits your visions as well as develop the competencies you need to become a professional Network Engineer. We can also assist you with the execution and evaluation of proficiency level based on the career track you choose, as they are customized to fit your specific goals.

We help you STAND OUT from the crowd through our detailed IP training content packages.

Course Features:

- Self-Paced learning
    - Learn at your own pace and in your own time
- Covers Complete Exam Blueprint
    - Prep-up for the exam with confidence
- Case Study Based Learning
    - Relate the content with real life scenarios
- Subscriptions that suits you
    - Get more pay less with IPS Subscriptions
- Career Advisory Services
    - Let industry experts plan your career journey
- Virtual Labs to test your skills
    - With IPS vRacks, you can testify your exam preperations
- Practice Questions
    - Practice Questions to measure your preparation standards
- On Request Digital Certification
    - On request digital certification from IPSpecialist LTD.

About the Authors:

This book has been compiled with the help of multiple professional engineers. These engineers specializes in different fields e.g Networking, Security, Cloud, Big Data, IoT etc. Each engineer develops content in its specialized field that is compiled to form a comprehensive certification guide.

About the Technical Reviewers:

Nouman Ahmed Khan

AWS-Architect, CCDE, CCIEX5 (R&S, SP, Security, DC, Wireless), CISSP, CISA, CISM is a Solution Architect working with a major telecommunication provider in Qatar. He works with enterprises, mega-projects, and service providers to help them select the best-fit technology solutions. He also works closely as a consultant to understand customer business processes and helps select an appropriate technology strategy to support business goals. He has more than 14 years of experience working in Pakistan/Middle-East & UK.

He holds a Bachelor of Engineering Degree from NED University, Pakistan, and M.Sc. in Computer Networks from the UK.

Abubakar Saeed

Abubakar Saeed has more than twenty-five years of experience, Managing, Consulting, Designing, and implementing large-scale technology projects, extensive experience heading ISP operations, solutions integration, heading Product Development, Presales, and Solution Design. Emphasizing on adhering to Project timelines and delivering as per customer expectations, he always leads the project in the right direction with his innovative ideas and excellent management.

Muhammad Yusuf

Muhammad Yousuf is a professional technical content writer. He is Cisco Certified Network Associate in Routing and Switching, holding bachelor's degree in Telecommunication Engineering from Sir Syed University of Engineering and Technology. He has both technical knowledge and industry sounding information, which he uses perfectly in his career.

Table of Contents

About this Workbook 12
Cisco Certifications 12
About the CCNA Exam 14
    How to become CCNA Service Provider? 15
Chapter 1: IP Network 17
    Technology Brief 17
    Network Hierarchy 18
        The Core Layer 19
        The Distribution Layer 19
        The Access Layer 19
    OSI Layers 21
    TCP/IP Model 22
    Common Network Applications 23
    Troubleshooting networking using the OSI model 23
    Types of networks 25
        Local Area Network (LAN) 25
        Metropolitan Area Network (MAN) 26
        Wide Area Network (WAN) 27
    IP Addressing 29
        IPv4 Address 29
        IPv4 Address Classes 31
        Variable Length Subnet Mask (VLSM) 32

Route summarization (Route Aggregation) 33

Subnetting 33

IPv6 Address 38

Chapter 2: IP NGN Architecture 43

Technology Brief 43

Features of NGN Network 44

IP NGN Architecture 44

Troubleshooting NGN using the OSI model 45

Different types of ISP 47

Number resources 50

Chapter 3: Network Management 55

Network Time Protocol 55

Logging 58

Simple Network Management Protocol 61

Lab 3-1 : Troubleshoot SNMP v3 Logging and NTP 63

Net Flow 74

Lab 3.2 Configuration of NetFlow Exporter on Cisco Routers. 75

CDP 80

Cisco IP SLA 82

Lab 3-3 : IP SLA 82

Cisco IOS Call Home Feature 85

Technical Assistance Center (TAC) 86

Cisco Support Tools 87

Implementation of Management Access Techniques 88

SSH 88

Telnet 91

Out-of-Band Management 92

Implement ERSPAN 94

SPAN 94

RSPAN 97

File Transfers using FTP, SCP, TFTP, SFTP, and RCP 98

Chapter 4: Switched Network Technology -1 100

Technology Brief 100

Bridging Concept and Layer 2 Ethernet Frames 100

Types of Bridges 101

The Basic Ethernet Frame Format 101

Spanning Tree Protocol 103

    STP Configuration 106

Basic Switch Security 107

    Port Security 107

    How to Secure Unused Ports 108

Cisco Switch Verification Commands 109

    Show command 109

    Debug Command 109

Ethernet Link bundling Aggregation (LAG) 110

    What is LACP 111

    What is PAgP 111

Chapter 5: Switched Network Technologies II 113

Configuration of Enhanced Switching Technologies 113

    Lab 5-1 : RSTP Lab Configuration 113

    Lab 5-2 : PVST Lab Configuration 115

    Lab 5-3 : Multiple Spanning Tree (MST) 118

What are VLAN's? 126

    VLAN Lab Configuration 128

VTP Lab Configuration 129

InterVLAN Routing 132

    Lab 5-4 : Inter VLAN Configuration 132

REP (Resilient Ethernet Protocol) Lab Configuration 138

802.1Q Tunneling (Q-in-Q) 142

Chapter 6: Routed Network Technology- I 147

Technology Brief 147

Classful Versus Classless Routing Protocols 147

Types of Routes 147

RIP (Routing Information Protocol) 150

    RIPv1 151

    RIPv2 151

    RIPng (RIP Next Generation) 152

Route Redistribution 152

VRF (Virtual routing and forwarding) 154

GRE (Generic Routing Encapsulation) 157

EIGRP (Enhanced Interior Gateway Protocol) 159

    Lab 6-1 : EIGRPv4 167

    Lab 6-2 : EIGRP IPv6 Configuration 171

Chapter 7: Routed Network Technologies II 177

Technology Brief 177

OSPF Features 177

    Lab 7-1 : OSPFv2 Single Area 185

    Lab 7-2 : OSPFv3 (OSPF for IPv6) Configuration 188

IS-IS Network Protocol 193

    Basic IS-IS Configuration 199

    IS-IS Troubleshooting 200

    Lab 7-3 : ISIS Configuration 201

Static v/s Dynamic Routing 205

    Static Routing 205

    Dynamic Routing Categories 207

BGP (Border Gateway Protocol) 208

    Lab 7-4 : BGP Configuration 214

Address Family 223

IPv6 Transitioning Technologies 225

    Dual Stack 225

ISATAP 226

6to4 226

Teredo 227

Securing Tunnels 229

PortProxy Interface 230

First Hop Router Redundancy Protocol 231

Hot Standby Router Protocol (HSRP) 231

Lab 7-5 : Hot Standby Router Protocol (HSRP) 234

Virtual Router Redundancy Protocol (VRRP) 238

Lab 7-6 : Virtual Router Redundancy Protocol (VRRP) 239

Gateway Load Balancing Protocol (GLBP) 242

Lab 7-7 : Gateway Load balancing Protocol 244

Access Control Lists (ACLs) 248

Wild Card Masks 249

Multiprotocol Label Switching 253

Configuring Basic MPLS 258

MPLS functions in the SP IP NGN 259

Network Address Translation 261

Carrier Grade NAT (CGN) 261

NAT64 261

CDP (Cisco Discovery Protocol) 261

Chapter 8: Cisco Operating Systems and Platforms I 263

Basic Operation of Cisco Internetwork OS 263

CLI and Configuration 264

Chapter 9: Cisco Operating Systems and Platforms II 277

Technology Brief 277

IOS XR software packages 277

Cisco IOS XE Software Packaging 279

Cisco SP router platforms, their operating system and placement in the SP IP NGN
.... 282

Cisco SP router platforms 282

Operating system 282

Placement in the SP IP NGN 284

Chapter 10: Transport Technologies 285

SONET and SDH 285

DWDM 288

IPoDWDM 288

ROADM 288

Implement 10/40/100 gigabit Ethernet interfaces on Cisco IOS-XR routers 289

Frame relay 290

ATM 291

Metropolitan Ethernet (Metro Ethernet) 292

DSL 293

Leased lines (T1, T2, T3) 294

Cable (DOCSIS) 294

BRAS and BNG routers 295

Passive optical network (PON) 296

Chapter 11: Security in a Network 297

Technology Brief 297

What Is IPsec? 301

RADIUS 302

Basic AAA Configuration on IOS 303

Lab 11.1: Configuring Administrative Access On A Cisco Router Using TACACS+ And ACS Server 306

Lab 11.2: Configuring Administrative Access On A Cisco Router Using RADIUS And ISE Server 320

Routing Protocol Security 334

Common Types of Network Attacks 336

Users, user groups, tasks groups and task IDs in IOS-XR 339

Chapter 12: IP Services 343

Technology Brief 343

Internet Control Message Protocol (ICMP) 343

    ICMP4 344

    ICMP6 344

Domain Name Servers (DNS) 345

Network Address Translation 345

    Lab 12-1 : Static Network Address Translation: 345

    Lab 12-2 : Dynamic Network Address Translation: 350

    Lab 12-3 : Port Address Translation: 356

    Lab 12-4 : Configuring DHCP Server, Relay and Client. 362

About this Workbook

This workbook covers all the information you need to pass the Cisco CCNA 640-875 and 640-878 exam. The workbook is designed to take a practical approach of learning with real life examples and case studies.

- ☐ Covers complete CCDP Architecture blueprint
- ☐ Summarized content
- ☐ Case Study based approach
- ☐ Ready to practice labs on GNS3/VM
- ☐ Pass guarantee
- ☐ Mind maps

Cisco Certifications

Cisco Systems, Inc. specializes in networking and communications products and services. A leader in global technology, the company is best known for its business routing and switching products that direct data, voice, and video traffic across networks worldwide.

Cisco also offers one of the most comprehensive vendor-specific certification programs in the world, the *Cisco Career Certification program*. The program has six (6) levels, which begins at the Entry level and then advances to Associate, Professional, and Expert levels. For some certifications, the program closes at the Architect level.

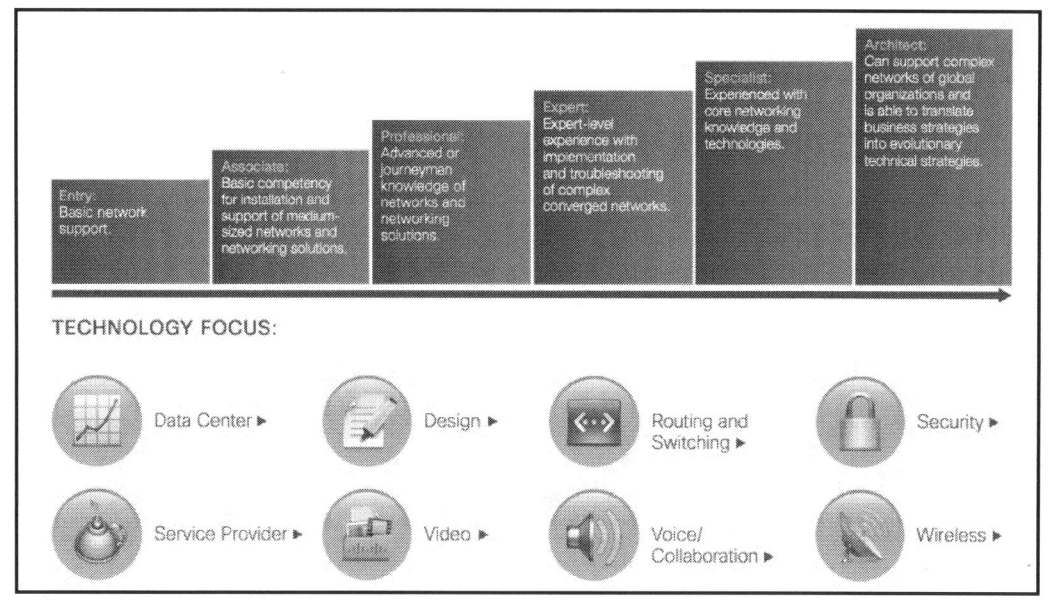

Figure 1 Cisco Certifications Skill Matrix. Copyright 2013 by Cisco and/or its affiliates.

How does Cisco Certifications help?

Cisco certifications are a de facto standard in networking industry, which helps you boost your career in the following ways:

1. Gets your foot in the door by launching your IT career
2. Boosts your confidence level
3. Proves knowledge which helps improve employment opportunities

As for companies, Cisco certifications is a way to:

1. Screen job applicants
2. Validate the technical skills of the candidate
3. Ensure quality, competency, and relevancy
4. Improve organization credibility and customer's loyalty
5. Meet the requirement in maintaining organization partnership level with OEMs
6. Helps in Job retention and promotion

Cisco Certification Tracks

Certification Tracks	Entry	Associate	Professional	Expert	Architect
Collaboration				CCIE Collaboration	
Data Center		CCNA Data Center	CCNP Data Center	CCIE Data Center	
Design	CCENT	CCDA	CCDP	CCDE	CCAr
Routing & Switching	CCENT	CCNA Routing and Switching	CCNP	CCIE Routing & Switching	
Security	CCENT	CCNA Security	CCNP Security	CCIE Security	
Service Provider		CCNA Service Provider	CCNP Service Provider	CCIE Service Provider	
Service Provider Operations	CCENT	CCNA Service Provider Operations	CCNP Service Provider Operations	CCIE Service Provider Operations	
Video		CCNA Video			
Voice	CCENT	CCNA Voice	CCNP Voice	CCIE Voice	
Wireless	CCENT	CCNA Wireless	CCNP Wireless	CCIE Wireless	

Figure 2 Cisco Certifications Track

About the CCNA Exam

- **Exam Number:** 640-875 SPNGN1 & 640-878 SPNGN2
- **Associated Certifications:** CCNA Service Provider
- **Duration:** 90 minutes (65-75 questions)
- **Exam Registration:** Pearson VUE

The "Building Cisco Service Provider Next-Generation Networks (SPNGN1), Part 1" (640-875) exam is associated with the CCNA® SP certification. This exam tests a candidate's basic knowledge and skills necessary to support a service provider network.

The following topics are general guidelines for the content likely to be included on the 90 minute, 65-75 question based exam:

- ☐ IP Networks   12%
- ☐ IPv4 and IPv6 Addressing   13%
- ☐ Switched Network Technologies I   12%
- ☐ Routed Network Technologies I   10%
- ☐ IP services   10%
- ☐ Cisco Operating Systems and Platforms I   15%

- Transport Technologies 9%
- Security in the Network 10%
- Network Management 9%

The "Building Cisco Service Provider Next-Generation Networks (SPNGN2), Part 2" (640-875) exam is associated with the CCNA® SP certification. This exam tests a candidates' knowledge and skills necessary to implement and support a service provider network.

The following topics are general guidelines for the content likely to be included on the on the 90 minute, 65-75 question based exam:
- IP NGN Architecture 21%
- Switched Network Technologies II 23%
- Routed Network Technologies II 24%
- Cisco Operating Systems and Platforms II 32%

Complete list of topics covered in the CCNA SP exam can be downloaded from here:

https://learningnetwork.cisco.com/community/certifications/ccna_service_provider/spngn1_exam/exam-topics

How to become CCNA Service Provider?

Step 1: Pre-requisites
There are no prerequisites for this exam.

Step 2: Prepare for the CCNA Service Provider Exam
Exam preparation can be accomplished through self-study with textbooks, practice exams, and on-site classroom programs. This workbook provides you all the information and knowledge to help you pass the CCDA Exam. Your study will be divided into two distinct parts:

- Understanding the technologies as per exam blueprint
- Implementing and practicing the technologies on Cisco hardware

IPSpecialist provides full support to the candidates in order for them to pass the exam.

Step 3: Register for the exam
Certification exams are offered at locations throughout the world. To register for an exam, contact the authorized test delivery partner of Cisco, contact *Pearson VUE*, who will administer the exam in a secure, proctored environment.

Prior to registration, decide which exam to take, note the exam name and number. For complete exam details, refer to the "Current Exam List" from the Cisco website.

Other important details to note are the following:

1. Your personal information prior to exam registration
    a. Legal name (from government issued ID)
    b. Cisco Certification ID (i.e. CSCO00000001) or Test ID number
    c. Company name
    d. Valid email address
    e. Method of payment
2. If you have already taken a Cisco exam before, please locate your Cisco Certification ID (i.e. CSCO00000001) before continuing with your registration to avoid duplicate records and delays in receiving proper credit for your exams.
3. A valid email is required during exam registration. Cisco requires this in order to send email reminders when a candidate's certification is about to expire, confirm the mailing address before shipping out the certificate, and to inform candidates if their certificate was returned due to an incorrect address.

4. Pearson VUE is the authorized test delivery partner of Cisco. You may register online, by telephone, or by walk in (where available).

How much does an exam cost?
Computer-based certification exam prices (written exam) depend on scope and exam length. You may refer to the "Exam Pricing" page on the Cisco website for complete details.

Step 4: Getting the Results
After you complete an exam at an authorized testing centre, you'll get immediate, online notification of your pass or fail status, a printed examination score report that indicates your pass or fail status, and your exam results by section.

Congratulations! You are now CCNA Service Provider Certified.

Chapter 1: IP Network

Technology Brief

A data network is a group of computers or host connected to one another by communication paths, as well as the standards that permit communication. A network can connect to other networks, permitting virtually worldwide communication between two endpoints. Many networks share information among one another, creating larger networks. Figure 3 is an example of a segment of a network.

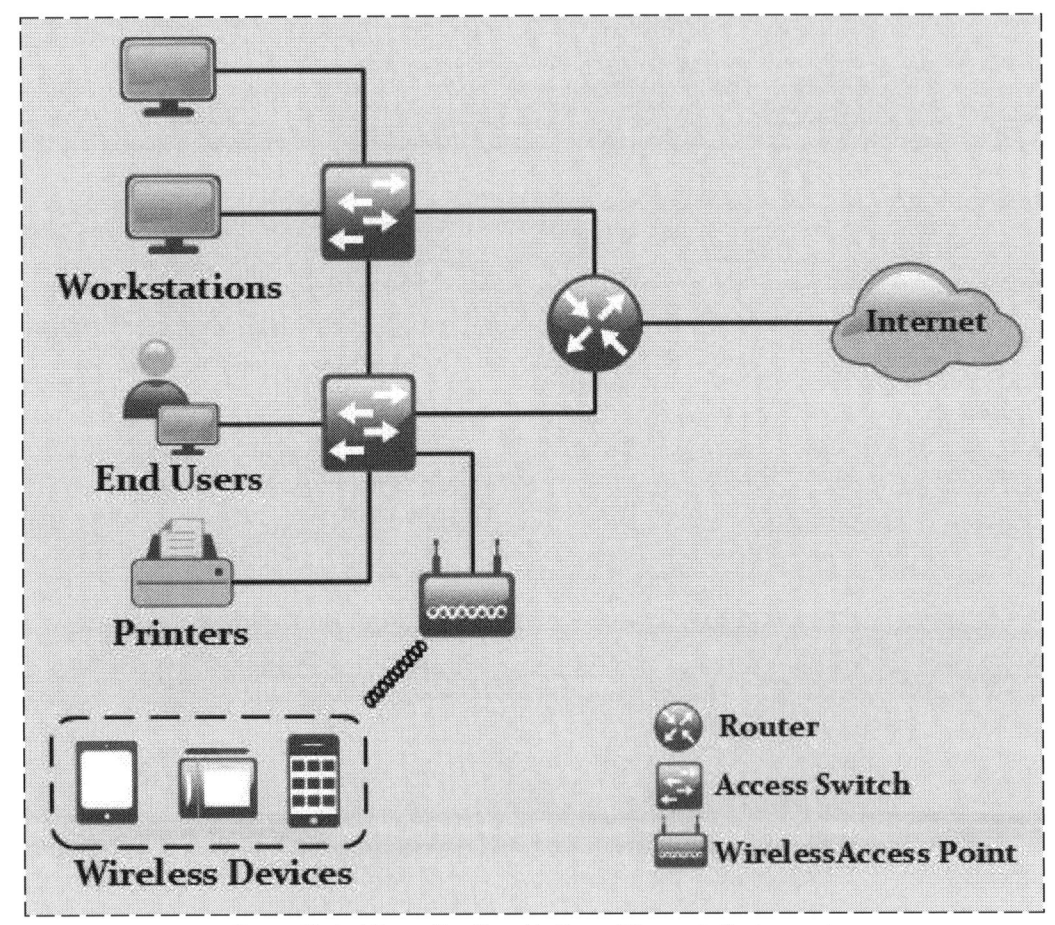

Figure 3 Typical Networking Found in General Corporate Environment

Many things are shared on a network. Networks permit users to share applications which are saved on servers on the network (e-mail applications, word-processing applications, databases, and many others). They allow communication between end users. Data can be shared or forwarded between companies, individuals for business or personal purposes.

The ability to share information over dissimilar networks is known as internetworking. By using a set of standards, nodes in two or more data networks can share information reliably between one another. In a bridged network, the term does not really apply as the data is not shared with multiple segments and no internetworking protocol is required to transfer the data. Internetworking was designed for the specific purpose of providing an avenue for sharing data among different nodes on the network and among different system software and operating systems.

Network Hierarchy

A hierarchical network design model converts the complex problem of network design into smaller, more manageable problems. Every level, or tier in the hierarchy addresses a various set of problems. This helps the network designer for optimizing network hardware and software to perform specific roles. For example, devices at the lowest tier are optimized to accept traffic into a network and pass that traffic to the higher layers. Cisco offers a three-tiered hierarchy as the preferred approach to network design.

In the three-layer network design model, network devices and links are grouped according to three layers:

- Core
- Distribution
- Access

The three-layer model is a conceptual framework. It is an abstract picture of a network similar to the concept of the Open System Interconnection (OSI) reference model.

Layered models are very much useful as they facilitate modularity. Devices on every layer have similar and well-defined functions. This permits administrators to easily add, replace, and remove individual pieces of the network. This kind of flexibility and adaptability makes a hierarchical network design more scalable and manageable.

At the same time, layered models can be difficult to comprehend because the exact composition of every layer varies from network to network. Each layer of the three-tiered design model may include the following:

- A Layer 3 device (for example router)
- A Layer 2 device (for example switch)
- A link
- A combination of these

Some networks may combine the function of two layers into a single device or omit a layer entirely. The following sections discuss each of the three layers in detail.

The Core Layer

The core layer provides an optimized & reliable transport structure by sending traffic at very high speeds. The core layer switches packets as fast as possible. Devices at the core layer should not be burdened with any processes that stand in the way of switching packets at top speed. This includes the following:

- Access-list checking
- Data encryption
- Address translation

The Distribution Layer

The distribution layer is situated between the access and core layers and helps differentiate the core from the rest of the network. The purpose behind this layer is to provide boundary definition by using access lists and other filters to restrict or limit what gets into the core. Thus, this layer set policy for the network. A policy is an approach to handling certain kinds of traffic, including the following:

- Routing updates
- Route summaries
- VLAN traffic
- Address aggregation

Utilize these policies in order to make networks secure and to preserve resources by preventing unnecessary traffic. If a network has two or more routing protocols, such as Routing Information Protocol (RIP) and Interior Gateway Routing Protocol (IGRP), information between the different routing domains is shared, or redistributed, at the distribution layer.

The Access Layer

The access layer forwards traffic to the network and performs network entry control. End users can access network resources by way of the access layer. Acting as the front door to a network, the access layer employs access lists designed to prevent unauthorized users from gaining entry or access. The access layer can also give remote sites access to the network by way of a wide-area technology, such as Frame Relay, ISDN, or leased lines.

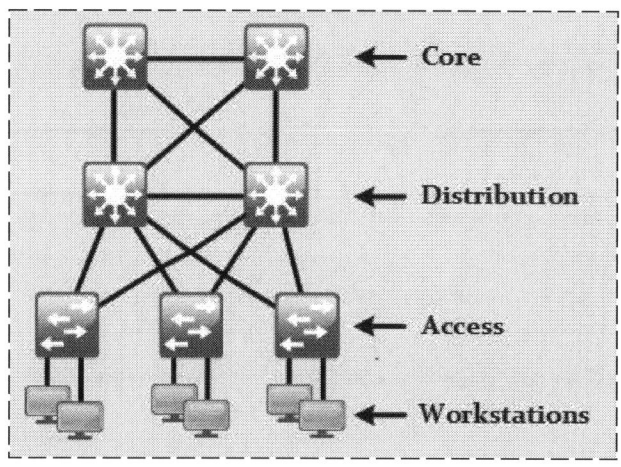

Figure 4 Three Layered based Hierarchical Network Design

The following table summarizes the features of the explained hierarchical network design:

Access	Distribution	Core
Layer 2 Switching	Redundancy and Load Balancing	Fast Switching
High Availability	Aggregation of Access Switches	High Reliability
Port Security	Aggregation of WAN Connections	Redundancy
Broadcast Suppression	QoS	Fault Tolerance
QoS Classification Marking Trust Boundaries	Policy Enforcement for e.g. Source and Destination Address based Filtering, Port based Filtering etc.	Low Latency
Rate Limiting/Policing	Summarization	Simplicity
Address Resolution Protocol (ARP) Inspection	Broadcast or Multicast Domain	
Virtual Access Control Lists (VACLs)	Routing between Virtual LANs (VLANs)	
Spanning Tree	Media Translations for e.g. between Ethernet and Fiber	
Power over Ethernet (PoE)	Redundancy between Routing Domains	
Network Access Control		

Table 1 Features of Hirarchiel Network Design

Benefits Of Hierarchical Network Design

- Better Performance
- Better management & troubleshooting

- Better Filter/Policy creation and application
- Better Scalability
- Better Redundancy

OSI Layers

The main concept of OSI is that the process of communication between two endpoints in a telecommunication network can be divided into seven distinct layers. Each communicating user or program is at a computer that can provide those seven layers of function. So in a given message between users, there will be a flow of data down through the layers in the source computer, across the network and then up through the layers in the receiving computer. The seven layers of function are provided by a combination of applications, operating systems, network card device drivers and networking hardware that enable a system to put a signal on a network cable or over Wi-Fi or other wireless protocol.

The following table explains the different functions available at each layer of OSI model:

OSI Layer	Description	Examples and Terminologies
Application Layer	Interface to End-User. Interacts directly with Software Application	FTP, HTTP, SMTP, TELNET, DNS, TFTP, NFS
Presentation Layer	Formats the data to be presented between Application-Layer Entities.	ASCII, JPEG, MPEG, GIF, MIDI, Data Translation, Compression, Encryption/Decryption, Formatting.
Session Layer	Manages connections between Local and Remote Applications	Session Establishments/Teardown, SQL, RPC, NFS
Transport Layer	Ensures the Integrity of Data Transmission	Data Segmentation, Reliability, Flow Control, Sequencing, Error Checking, TCP, UDP, SPX, Apple Talk
Network Layer	Determines how data gets from one Host to another	Routing, Subnetting, IP, IPX, ICMP, ARP, PING, Traceroute
Data Link Layer	Defines the Format of data on the Network	MAC Addresses, CRC Error Checking, Frame Traffic Control, Switches, Bridges, Frames, PPP/SLIP, Ethernet
Physical Layer	Transmits Raw Bit Stream over Physical Medium	Binary Transmission, Bit Rates, Voltage Levels, Hubs.

Table 2 OSI Layer Model

TCP/IP Model

Like OSI, TCP/IP also has a network model. TCP/IP was on the path of development when the OSI standard was published and there was interaction between the designers of OSI and TCP/IP standards. The TCP/IP model is not same as OSI model. OSI is a seven-layered standard, but TCP/IP is a four-layered standard.

Application Layer

This is the top- most layer of the four-layer TCP/IP model. Application layer is present on the top of the Transport layer. Application layer defines TCP/IP application protocols and how host programs interface with Transport layer services to use the network.

Application layer includes all the higher-level protocols like DNS (Domain Naming System), HTTP (Hypertext Transfer Protocol), Telnet, SSH, FTP (File Transfer Protocol), TFTP (Trivial File Transfer Protocol), SNMP (Simple Network Management Protocol), SMTP (Simple Mail Transfer Protocol), DHCP (Dynamic Host Configuration Protocol), X Windows, RDP (Remote Desktop Protocol) etc.

Transport Layer

This is the third layer of the four-layer TCP/IP model. The position of the Transport layer is between Application layer and Internet layer. The purpose of Transport layer is to permit devices on the source and destination hosts to carry on a conversation. Transport layer defines the level of service and status of the connection used when transporting data.

The main protocols included at Transport layer are TCP (Transmission Control Protocol) and UDP (User Datagram Protocol).

Internet Layer

This is the second layer of the four-layer TCP/IP model. The position of Internet layer is between Network Access Layer and Transport layer. Internet layer pack data into data packets known as IP datagrams, which contain source and destination address (logical address or IP address) information that is used to forward the datagrams between hosts and across networks. The Internet layer is also responsible for routing of IP datagrams.

Packet switching network depends upon a connectionless internetwork layer. This layer is known as Internet layer. Its job is to allow hosts to insert packets into any network and have them to deliver independently to the destination. At the destination side data packets may appear in a different order than they were sent. It is the job of the higher layers to rearrange them in order to deliver them to proper network applications operating at the Application layer.

The main protocols included at Internet layer are IP (Internet Protocol), ICMP (Internet Control Message Protocol), ARP (Address Resolution Protocol), RARP

(Reverse Address Resolution Protocol) and IGMP (Internet Group Management Protocol).

Network Access Layer
This is the first layer of the four-layer TCP/IP model. Network Access Layer defines details of how data is physically sent through the network, including how hardware devices that interface directly with a network medium, such as coaxial cable, optical fiber, or twisted pair copper wire electrically or optically signal bits.

The protocols included in Network Access Layer are Ethernet, Token Ring, FDDI, X.25, Frame Relay etc.

Common Network Applications

A network is a collection or set of computing devices connected to one another to establish communication and share available resources. A network will comprise of software and hardware devices. You can have a network even if you are not connected to the internet. Computer networks make it possible for people to transfer files from one place to another and to communicate taking the shortest time possible.

The following are some examples of network-based applications:

- E-mail
- Web Instant messaging
- Remote login
- P2P file sharing
- Multi-user network games
- Streaming stored video clips
- Internet telephone
- Real-time video conference

Troubleshooting networking using the OSI model

When trying to troubleshoot a network, it is always sensible to approach the problem from the perspective of the OSI model. The OSI (Open System Interconnection) model defines a networking framework for implementing protocols in 7 layers. The beauty of this model is the fact that you can individually troubleshoot each layer by using simple methods. Its good working from layer 1 upwards until you find the problem.

Troubleshooting Physical Layer
Always check Physical media first to avoid making troubleshoot complicated. You can use cable testers to check cables, or use some common sense when swapping things round to isolate the cause of the problem. Making sure your operating system can see the hardware (and shows that it is functional) is also covered at this layer.

Troubleshooting Data Link Layer

Most problems at this layer can be diagnosed with the ARP command (in windows anyway). MAC addresses are supposedly globally unique to a device, but some people like to play around which can cause problems (google for Arp poisoning / spoofing). Using "arp –a" will show you which MAC addresses are mapped to which IP addresses locally which is sometimes helpful. You could also setup a network sniffer to look at the frames being sent across your hubs / switches.

Troubleshooting Network Layer

It covers the routing protocols (RIPv1 and v2, OSPF, EIGRP and others) as well as the routed protocols (most notably IP). You can verify IP with ICMP packets. Utilities like PING and TRACERT use ICMP packets in order to get responses back from hosts.

Troubleshooting Transport Layer

Most of the troubleshooting here can be done with a packet sniffer. TCP is used with IP as a means to ensure that the data within the packets is sent and received without any loss. If there is an error, packets are re-sent with the correct sequence number so that no data is lost, it ensures complete data transfer. You can use packet sniffers to examine the tcp/udp packet headers to see what is happening at layer 4.

Packet sniffers work by intercepting and logging network traffic that these can see via the wired or wireless network interface to the computer in use.

On a wired network, what can be captured depends on the structure of the network. A packet sniffer might be able to see traffic on an entire network or only a certain segment of it, depending on how network switches are configured, placed, etc.

On a wireless network, a packet sniffer can usually only capture one channel at a time, unless the host computer has multiple wireless interfaces that allow for multichannel capture.

Once raw packet data is captured, packet-sniffing software must analyses it and present it in human-readable form so that the person using the software can make sense of it. The person analyzing the data can view details of the conversations happening between two or more nodes on the network.

Troubleshooting Session Layer

The most likely thing you would be troubleshooting at this layer would be NetBIOS over TCP/IP. Windows has some very useful utilities like NBTSTAT and the group of 'net' commands, which will help you. Other protocols like DNS, LDAP (this is used for most of the active directory replication), NFS, SQL, RPC and X-Windows can also be diagnosed at this layer.

Troubleshooting Presentation Layer

This layer looks at things like JPEG, MPEG, MIDI, QUICKTIME and other files of the same nature. Most of your troubleshooting will be with the applications that create them (at layer 7) but be aware that you can edit hex files to look at the structure and change them.

Troubleshooting Application Layer

If all other layers are working properly and have been tested, then this is usually just a matter of applying patches to software or reinstalling. Telnet is an excellent tool for connecting to virtually any port to check to see if the above layers are working properly.

Types of networks

Computer Networks fall into three classes based on the size, distance, and the structure namely:

- LAN (Local Area Network)
- MAN (Metropolitan Area Network)
- WAN (Wide Area Network)

Local Area Network (LAN)

A local area network or LAN is consists of a computer network at a single site, typically an individual office building. A LAN is very useful for sharing resources, such as data storage and printers. LANs can be built with relatively inexpensive hardware, such as hubs, network adapters and Ethernet cables as shown in figure 5.

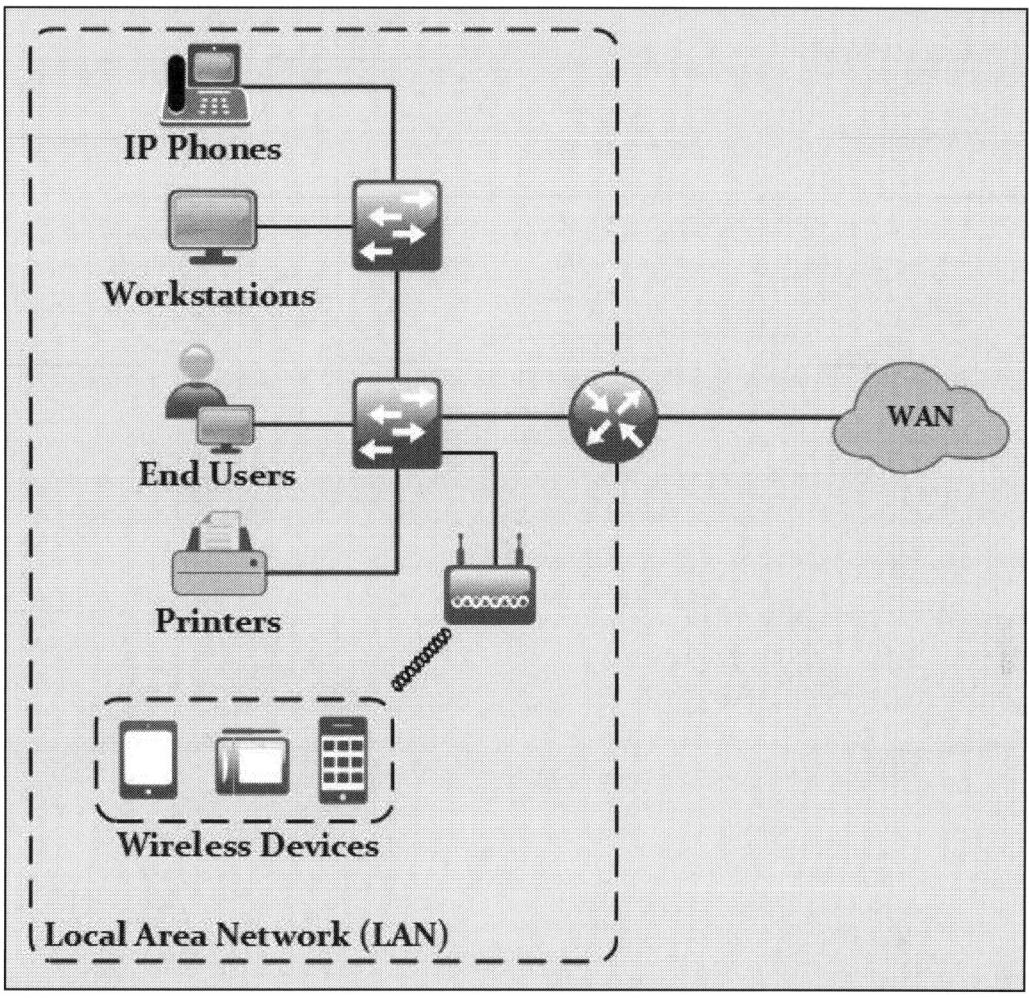

Figure 5. Example of Local Area Network

Metropolitan Area Network (MAN)

MAN (metropolitan area network) is consists of a computer network across an entire city, college campus or small region. A metropolitan area network is larger than a local area network (LAN), which is typically limited to a single building or site. Depending on the configuration, this type of network can cover an area from several miles to tens of miles. Connect several LANs together to form a bigger network as shown in figure 6.

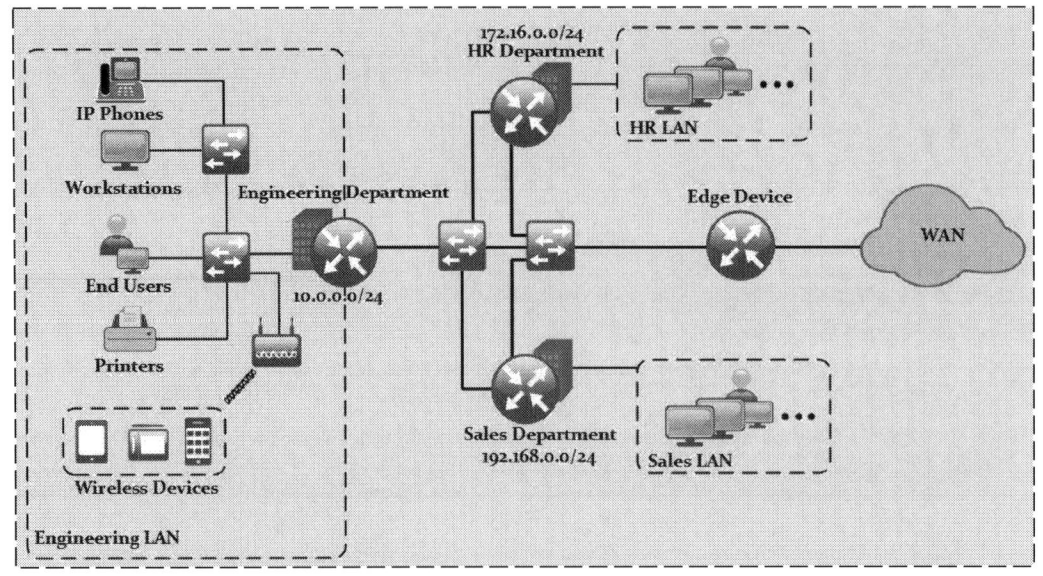

Figure 6 Example of Metropolitan Area Network

Wide Area Network (WAN)

A wide area network (WAN) covers a very large area, such as an entire country or the entire world. A WAN may be consists of multiple smaller networks, such as LANs or MANs. The Internet is the best example of a public WAN as shown in figure 7.

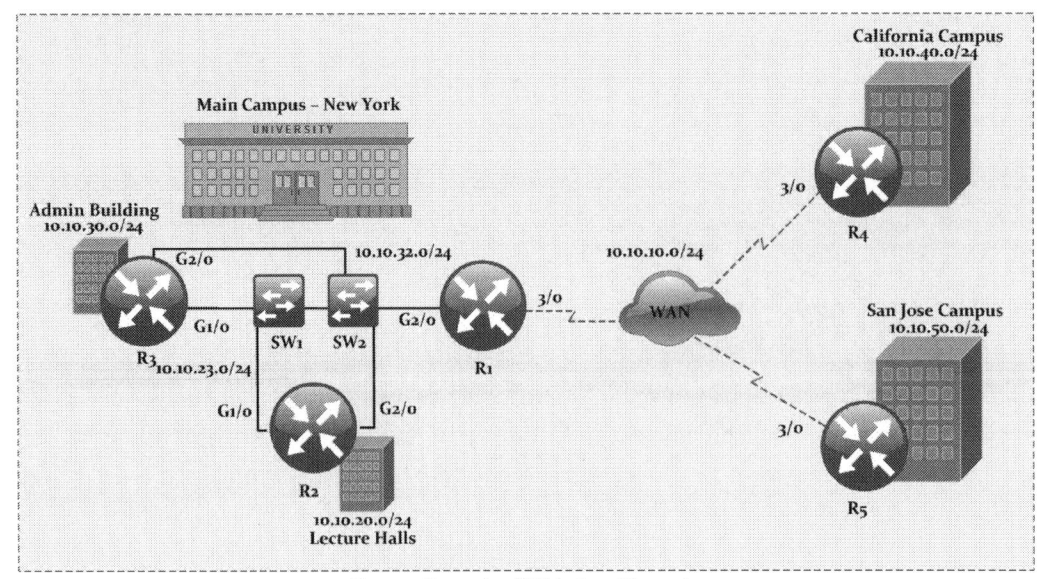

Figure 7 Example of Wide Area Network

Difference between LAN, MAN and WAN

The following table summarizes and compares different features of LAN, MAN and WAN:

Features	LAN	MAN	WAN
Range	A communication network linking a number of stations in same local area. Range is 1-10 km	This network shares the characteristics of packet broadcasting networks. Range is 5km-50km	Range is beyond 50km
Media Used	Uses guided media	Uses guided as well as unguided media	Uses unguided media
Speed	A high speed i.e. 100kbps to 1000mbps	Optimized for a large geographical area than LAN 1mbps to 150mbps	Long distance communication, which may or may not be provided by public packet network Up to 600mbps
Cost/Equipment Needed	Cheaper NIC, Switch and HUB	Costly Modem and router	Expensive Microwave, Radio, Infra-red laser
Protocols	Attached resource computer network (ARCNET), Ethernet, token ring	Frame relay, ATM and MPLS	ATM, FDDI and SMDS

Table 3 Comparision of LAN, WAN and MAN

IP Networks Mind Map

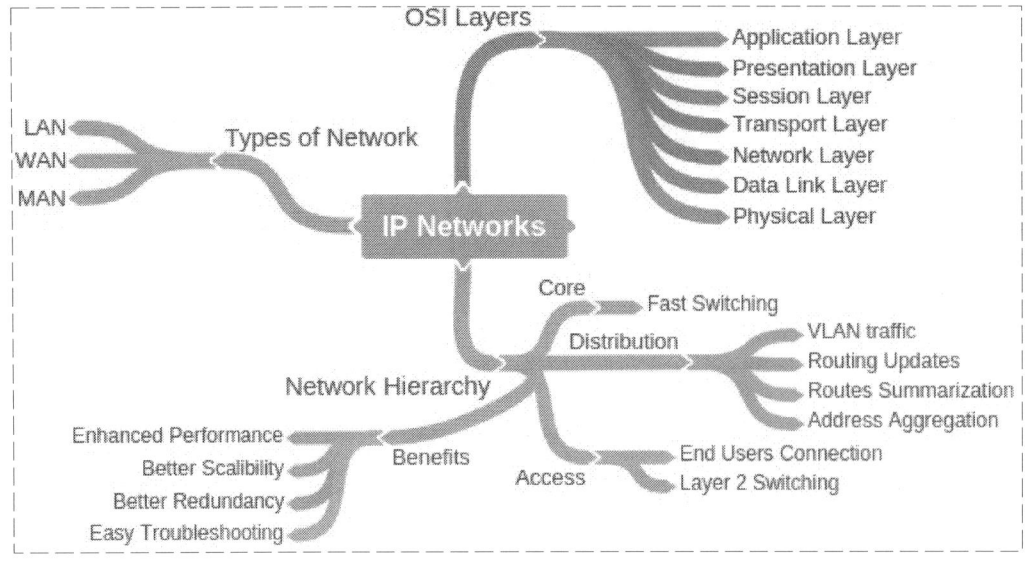

Figure 8 IP Networks Mind Map

IP Addressing

Internet Protocol is the major protocols in the TCP/IP protocols suite. This protocol functions at the network layer of the OSI model and at the Internet layer of the TCP/IP model. Thus, this protocol has the responsibility to identify hosts based upon their logical addresses and routing data among them over the underlying network. IP offers a mechanism to uniquely identify hosts by an IP addressing scheme. IP uses best effort delivery, i.e. it does not ensures that packets would be delivered to the destined host, but it will do its best to reach the destination from source.

There are two types of IP addressing, namely IPv4 and IPv6.

IPv4 Address

Internet Protocol version 4 uses 32-bit logical address. Internet Protocol being a layer-3 protocol (OSI) takes data Segments from layer-4 (Transport) and divides it into packets. IP packet encapsulates data unit received from above layer and add to its own header information.

IP Header	Layer – 4 Data
(IP Encapsulation)	

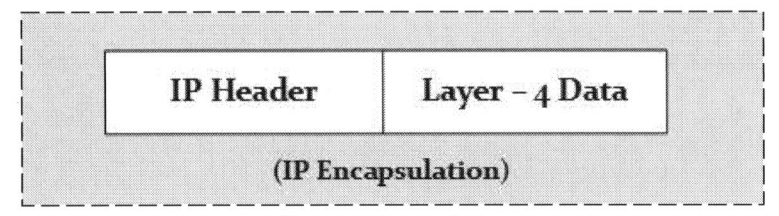

Figure 9 IP Encapsulation

The encapsulated data is referred to as IP Payload. IP header contains all the necessary information to deliver the packet at the other end.

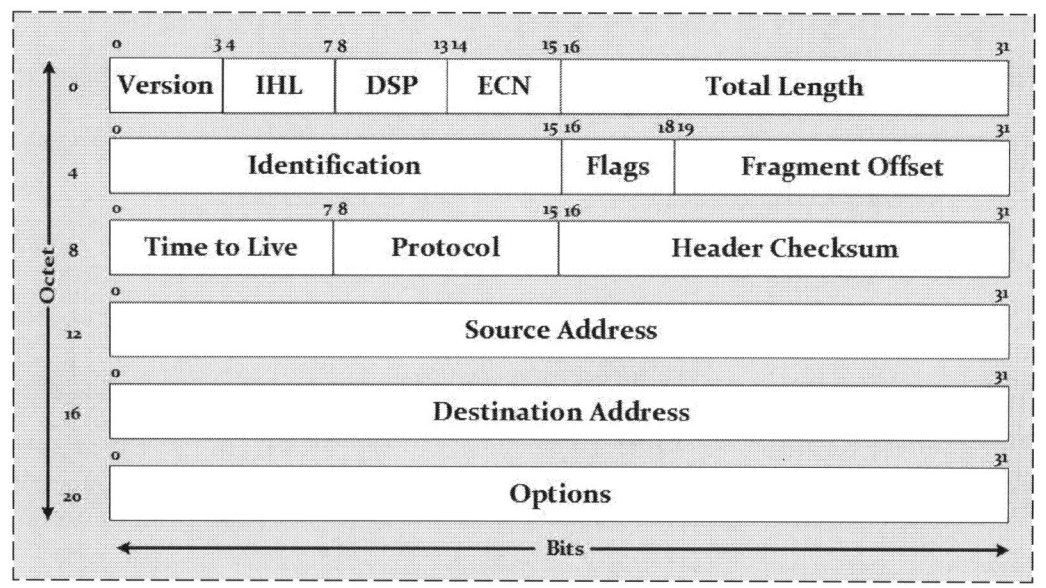

Figure 10 IPv4 Header Details

IP header includes much relevant information including Version Number, which, in this context, is 4. Other details are as follows:

- **Version:** Version no. of Internet Protocol used (e.g. IPv4).
- **IHL:** (Internet Header Length), Length of entire IP header.
- **DSCP:** (Differentiated Services Code Point), this is Type of Service to set QOS.
- **ECN:** (Explicit Congestion Notification), It carries information about the congestion seen in the route.
- **Total Length:** Length of entire IP Packet (including IP Header and IP Payload).
- **Identification:** If IP packet is fragmented during the transmission, all the fragments contain same identification number, to identify original IP packet they belong to.
- **Flags:** As required by the network resources, if IP Packet is too large to handle, these 'flags' tells if they can be fragmented or not. In this 3-bit flag, the MSB is always set to '0'.
- **Fragment Offset:** This offset tells the exact position of the fragment in the original IP Packet.
- **Time to Live:** To avoid looping in the network, every packet is sent with some TTL value set, which tells the network how many routers or hops this packet can cross. At each hop, its value is decremented by one and when the value reaches zero, the packet is discarded.

- **Protocol:** Tells the Network layer at the destination host, to which Protocol this packet belongs to, i.e. the next level Protocol. For example, protocol number of ICMP is 1, TCP is 6 and UDP is 17.
- **Header Checksum:** This field is used to keep checksum value of entire header that is then used to check the packet is received error-free or not.
- **Source Address:** 32-bit address of the sender or source of the packet.
- **Destination Address:** 32-bit address of the receiver or destination of the packet.
- **Options:** This is optional field, which is used if the value of IHL is greater than 5. These options may contain values for options such as Security, Record Route, Time Stamp, etc.

The Subnet Mask

A Subnet mask is a 32-bit number that masks an IP address, and divides the IP address into network address and host address. Subnet mask tells you the available hosts in the specific network. In subnet mask, network bits represented by "1"s and host bits by "0"s. Within a given network, two host addresses are reserved, one for network address and second for broadcast address. The "0" address is assigned a network address and "255" is assigned to a broadcast address, and they cannot be assigned to hosts.

Looking at the below address and subnet mask in binary:

IP Address: 10011110.01010000.10100100.00000011
Subnet Mask: 11111111.11111111.00000000.00000000

IPv4 Address Classes

Class A

- In this class the network segment has 8-bits and the host segment has 24-bits.
- Its range is from 1 up to 126 and total 17millions hosts exist. 0 and 127 are reserved, 0 is an invalid address you can't connect or communicate through this network and 127 is used for loopback addresses.
- Subnet mask is 255.0.0.0

Class B

- In this class each segment (host, network) have 16-bits.
- Its range is from 128 up to 191 and total 65,534 hosts exist.
- Subnet mask is 255.255.0.0

Class C

- In this class the network segment has 24-bits and host segment has 16-bits.
- Its range is from 192 up to 223 and total host exist 254.
- Subnet mask is 255.255.255.0

Class D

- It ranges is from 224 up to 239.

Class E

- It ranges from 240 up to 255.

After the class E IPV4 addressing range ends, after that we use IPV6 addressing.

Classless Inter Domain Routing (CIDR)

CIDR is a slash notation of subnet mask. CIDR tells us number of "ON" bits in a network address.

- Class A has default subnet mask 255.0.0.0 that means first octet of the subnet mask has all on bits. In slash notation it would be written as /8, means address has 8 bits on.
- Class B has default subnet mask 255.255.0.0 that means first two octets of the subnet mask have all on bits. In slash notation it would be written as /16, means address has 16 bits on.
- Class C has default subnet mask 255.255.255.0 that means first three octets of the subnet mask have all on bits. In slash notation it would be written as /24, means address has 24 bits on.

Variable Length Subnet Mask (VLSM)

Variable Length Subnet Mask (VLSM) extends classic subnetting. VLSM is a process of breaking down subnets into the smaller subnets, according to the need of individual networks. Variable-length subnet masking (VLSM) is the more realistic way of subnetting a network to make the most efficient use of all of the bits. What you have to remember is that you need to make sure that there is no overlap in any of the addresses.

Now you can use the formula $2^2 - 2$ to calculate the available number of host.

Route summarization (Route Aggregation)

Route summarization is also called route aggregation. It is a method of minimizing or reducing the number of routing tables in an IP network. It works by consolidating/summarizing selected multiple routes into a single route advertisement, in contrast to flat routing in which every routing table contains a unique entry for each route. In order to implement route summarization in IP Version 4 (IPv4), Classless Inter-Domain Routing (CIDR) must be used. All IP addresses in the route advertisement must share identical high-order bits. The length of the prefix must not exceed 32 bits.

Route summarization offers several important advantages over flat routing as route summarization can minimize the latency in a complex network, especially when many routers are involved by reducing number of routing entries, the overhead for routing protocols is minimized. Network stability can be achieved by reducing or eliminating unnecessary routing updates after part of the network undergoes a change in topology. Route summarization reduces processor workloads, memory requirements and bandwidth demand.

Let us say we want to create the most optimal summary for the following 4 networks:

- 192.168.0.0 / 24 subnet mask 255.255.255.0
- 192.168.1.0 / 24 subnet mask 255.255.255.0
- 192.168.2.0 / 24 subnet mask 255.255.255.0
- 192.168.3.0 / 24 subnet mask 255.255.255.0

As you can see, we have 4 networks, or when we speak in 'blocks' it's a block of 4. Here is a formula you can use:

> 256 – Number of networks = subnet mask for summary address.
> For example: 256 – 4 networks = 252
> The subnet mask will be 255.255.252.0

Figure 11 Route Summarization

Subnetting

It is the process of dividing the single network ID into further various different network IDs.

There are 3 usable IP address classes:

- **Class A:** Default subnet mask 255.0.0.0
- **Class B:** Default subnet mask 255.255.0.0
- **Class C:** Default subnet mask 255.255.255.0

Class A networks have the highest number of available host and Class C has the fewest number of hosts. The subnet mask is the 32-bit number that the router uses to cover up the network address to show which bits are being used to identify the subnet.

A network has its own unique address, such as a Class B network with the address 172.16.0.0, which has all zeroes in the host portion of the address and all ones in the network portion. From the basic definitions of a Class B network & the default Class B subnet mask, this network can be created as a single network that contains 65,534 individual hosts. With the help of subnetting, the network can be furthur logically divided into subnets with fewer hosts on each subnetwork. It does not improve the available shared bandwidth only, but it cuts down on the amount of broadcast traffic generated over the entire network as well.

The two primary benefits of subnetting are:

- Fewer IP addresses, often as few as one, are needed to provide addressing to a network & subnetting.
- Subnetting usually results in smaller routing tables in routers beyond the local internetwork.

When the network administrator divides the 172.16.0.0 network into 5 smaller networks – 172.30.1.0, 172.30.2.0, 172.30.3.0, 172.30.4.0 & 172.30.5.0 – the outside world stills sees the network as 172.30.0.0, but the internal routers now break the network addressing into the 5 smaller sub networks.

Borrowing Bits to Grow a Subnet

- The key concept in subnetting is borrowing bits from the host portion of the network to create a subnetwork.
- Rules govern this borrowing, ensuring that some bits are left for a Host ID.
- The rules require that two bits remain available to use for the Host ID& that all of the subnet bits cannot be all 1's or 0's at the same time.
- For each IP address class, only a certain number of bits can be borrowed from the host portion for use in the subnet mask.

Address Class	Host Bits	Bits available for subnet
Class A	24	22

Class B	16	14
Class C	8	6

Table 4 Available host and subnetnetwork bits for IPv4 Classes

This set of formula can be used to calculate number of hosts and subnets within a network with default subnet mask:

Number of Host per Subnet: $(2^{\text{Number of bits used for Host}})-2$

Number of Subnets: $2^{\text{Number of bits used for subnet}}$

Conversion form Binary to Decimal

$$2^7 \quad 2^6 \quad 2^5 \quad 2^4 \quad 2^3 \quad 2^2 \quad 2^1 \quad 2^0$$
$$1 \quad\ 1 \quad\ 1 \quad\ 1 \quad\ 1 \quad\ 1 \quad\ 1 \quad\ 1$$
$$128 \ 64 \ 32 \ 16 \ 8 \ 4 \ 2 \ 1$$

The binary number **11111111** converts into the decimal number:

$$128+64+32+16+8+4+2+1=255$$

Byte Values								
Base^{Exponent}	2^7	2^6	2^5	2^4	2^3	2^2	2^1	2^0
Weight	128	64	32	16	8	4	2	1
Byte and Network Mask Value								
128	1	0	0	0	0	0	0	0
192	1	1	0	0	0	0	0	0
224	1	1	1	0	0	0	0	0
240	1	1	1	1	0	0	0	0
248	1	1	1	1	1	0	0	0
252	1	1	1	1	1	1	0	0
254	1	1	1	1	1	1	1	0
255	1	1	1	1	1	1	1	1

Table 5 Decimal to Binary Conversion

Subnetting Example

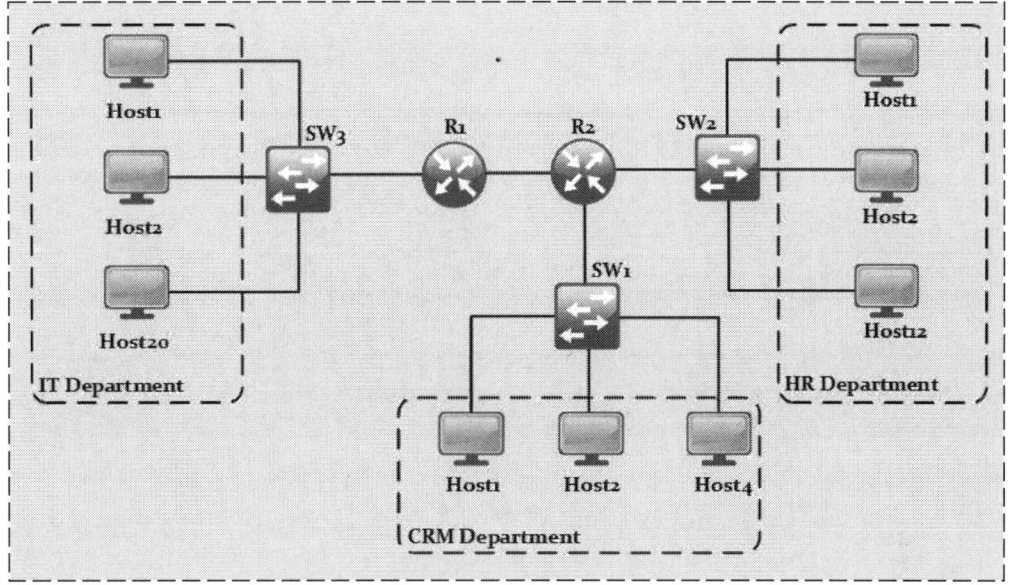

Figure 12 Subnetting Example

In a company, there are 3 departments, IT, HR and CRM. We have to design IP scheme for them. IT needs 20 hosts, HR needs 12 hosts and CRM needs 4 hosts. We have 200.10.20.0/24 network being available for this task. In this network, we have $2^8-2=254$ host available which is higher than the required host. Therefore, we have to perform subnetting for 3 departments in order to utilize IP addresses efficiently.

Required Subnets: 3

Calculation of Appropriate Subnet for IT Department

Available Network: 200.10.20.0/24
Default Subnet Mask: 255.255.255.0
Default Subnet Mask in Binary: 11111111.11111111.11111111.0000000

Apply above-mentioned formula:

$2^n-2=$ available hosts
$2^5-2 = 32-2=$ 30 Usable IPs/Hosts

Therefore, you can use 5 bits form default subnet masks

11111111.11111111.11111111.11100000

Now you are using 27 bits for Network and 5 bits for Hosts.

Converted Subnet mask:

200.10.20.0/27
255.255.255.224

Block Size: 256-224= 32

200.10.20.0 ---------Network Address
200.10.20.1 ----------Usable IP/Host
200.10.20.2
.
.
200.10.20.30 --------- Last Usable IP/Host
200.10.20.31 ---------- Broadcast Address

Therefore, you can use 20 usable IP for IT department. Now you have available **200.10.20.32** for further subnetting.

Calculation of Appropriate Subnet for HR Department

Available Network: 200.10.20.32/24
Available Subnet mask: 255.255.255.0
Available Subnet mask in binary 11111111.11111111.1111111.000000

Apply above-mentioned formula:

$$2^n-2=\text{Usable IPs}$$
$$2^4-2= 16-2=14$$

We have used 4 bits for host and remaining will be considered as network bits.

11111111.1111111.11111111.11110000

Converted subnet mask: 255.255.255.240

200.10.20.32/28
255.255.255.240

Block Size: 256-240=16

200.10.20.32-------Network Address/IP
200.10.20.33-------Usable IP/Host
200.10.20.34-------Usable IP/Host
.
.
200.10.20.46------Last Usable IP/Host
200.10.20.47------Broadcast Address/IP

Therefore, you can use 12 IPs for HR department from this range. Now you have available **200.10.20.48** for further subnetting.

Calculation of Appropriate Subnet for CRM Department

Available Network: 200.10.20.48/24
Default Subnet Mask: 255.255.255.0
Default Subnet Mask in Binary: 11111111.11111111.11111111.000000

Apply above-mentioned formula:

$$2^n-2 = \text{Usable IPs}$$
$$2^3-2 = 8-2 = 6$$

We have used 3 bits for host and remaining will be considered as network bits.

11111111.11111111.11111111.11111000
Converted subnet mask = 255.255.255.248
200.10.20.48/29
255.255.255.248

Block Size: 256-248=8

200.10.20.48-------Network Address/IP
200.10.20.49-------Usable IP/Host
200.10.20.50-------Usable IP/Host
.
.
200.10.20.56------Last Usable IP/Host
200.10.20.57------Broadcast Address/IP

Therefore, you can use 4 IPs for CRM department from this range.

IPv6 Address

This topic introduces you to the next generation of TCP/IP: IP version 6 (IPv6). Because of the many deficiencies found in IPv4, as well as the poor scalability for hierarchical addressing in IPv4, IPv6 was developed to meet the rapidly growing needs of small companies, corporations, and the explosive growth of the Internet. One of the main benefits of Internet Protocol version 6 (IPv6) over previously used Internet Protocol version 4 (IPv4) is the large address-space that contains (addressing) information to route packets for the next generation Internet. IPv6 uses 128-bit logical address. With this large address-space scheme, IPv6 has the capability to provide unique addresses to each device or node attached to the Internet.

IPv6 Features

Obviously, the replacement for IPv4 needs to support enough addresses for this growing demand, but it also needs to provide ease of use and configuration, enhanced security, and the ability to interoperate with IPv4 as the transition takes place. Here are some features built into IPv6:

Very large address space: IPv6's large address space deals with global growth, where route prefixes can be easily aggregated in routing updates. Support for multihoming to ISPs with a single address space is easily accomplished. Auto-configuration of addressing information, including the capability of including MAC addresses in the IP address, as well as plug-and-play options, simplifies address management. Renumbering and modification of addresses is easily accommodated, as well as public-to-private readdressing without involving address translation.

Security: IP security (IPsec) is built into IPv6, whereas it is an awkward add-on in IPv4. With IPv6, two devices can dynamically negotiate security parameters and build a secure tunnel between them with no user intervention.

Mobility: With the growth of mobile devices like smart phones and tablets, devices can roam between wireless networks without breaking their connections.

Streamlined encapsulation: The IPv6 encapsulation is simpler than IPv4, providing faster forwarding rates by routers and better routing efficiency. No checksums are included, reducing processing on endpoints. No broadcasts are used, reducing utilization of devices within the same subnet. QoS information is built into the IPv6 header, where a flow label identifies the traffic; this alleviates intermediate network devices from having to examine contents inside the packet, the TCP/UDP headers, and payload information to classify the traffic for QoS correctly.

Addressing capabilities: Like IPv4, addresses can be assigned statically or obtained via DHCPv6. However, unlike IPv4, IPv6 supports stateless auto-configuration, which allows a device to acquire addressing automatically without implementing a DHCP server solution.

Transition capabilities: Various solutions exist to allow IPv4 and IPv6 to successfully co-exist when migrating between the two. One method, dual stack, allows you to run both protocols simultaneously on an interface of a device. A second method, tunneling, allows you to tunnel IPv6 over IPv4 and vice versa to transmit an IP version of one type across a network using another type. Cisco supports a third method, referred to as Network Address Translation-Protocol Translation (NAT-PT), to translate between IPv4 and IPv6 (sometimes the term *Proxy* is used instead of Protocol).

IPv6 address Format

Whereas IPv4 addresses use a dotted-decimal format, where each byte ranges from 0 to 255, IPv6 addresses use eight sets of four hexadecimal addresses (16 bits in each set), separated by a colon (:), like this: **xxxx:xxxx:xxxx:xxxx:xxxx:xxxx:xxxx:xxxx** (x would be a hexadecimal value). This notation is commonly called string notation. Hexadecimal numbers range from 0 to F.

Here are some important items concerning IPv6 addresses:

- Hexadecimal values can be displayed in either lower- or uppercase for the numbers A–F.
- A leading zero in a set of numbers can be omitted; for example, you could enter either 0012 or 12 in one of the eight fields—both are correct.
- If you have successive fields of zeroes in an IPv6 address, you can represent them as two colons (::). For example, 0:0:0:0:0:0:0:5 could be represented as ::5; and 2000:C67:0:0:8888:9999:1111:0 could be represented as 2000:C67::8888:9999:1111:0.
- An unspecified address is represented as :: since it contains all zeroes.

Types of IPv6 address

IPv6 also has different types of addresses. Following are the three main types:

- **Anycast:** Very different from an IPv4 broadcast—one-to-the-nearest interface, where many interfaces can share the same address. These addresses are taken from the unicast address space but can represent multiple devices, like multiple default gateways. For example, using an anycast address as a default gateway address on your routers, user devices only have to know of one address and you do not need to configure a protocol like HSRP or VRRP.
- **Multicast:** Address of a set of interfaces. One-to-many delivery to all interfaces in the set.
- **Unicast:** Address of a single interface. One-to-one delivery to single interface.

The five types of unicast addresses are listed in below table. Interestingly enough, multiple addresses of any type can be assigned to a device's interface: unicast, multicast, and Anycast.

Address	Value	|Description
Global	2000::/3	These are assigned by the IANA and used on the public networks. They are equivalent to IPv4 global (sometime called public) address. ISPs summarize these to provide scalability in the internet

Reserved	(range)	Reserved addresses are used for specific types of Anycast as well as for future use. Currently about 1/256 of the IPv6 address space is reserved.
Private	FE80::/10	Like IPv4, IPv6 originally supported private addressing, which is used by devices that do not need to access a public network. The first two digits are FE, and the third digit can range from 8 to F
Loopback	::1	Like the 127.0.0.1 address in IPv4, 0:0:0:0:0:0:0:1, or ::1, is used for local testing function; unlike IPV4, which dedicates a complete class A block of addresses for local testing. Only one is used in IPv6
Unspecified	::	0.0.0.0 In IPv4 means "unknown" address. In IPv6, this is represented by 0:0:0:0:0:0:0:0, 0 ::, and is typically used in the source address field of the packet when an interface doesn't have an address and is trying to acquire one dynamically.

Table 6 IPv6 Unicast Address Types

IPv6 Header

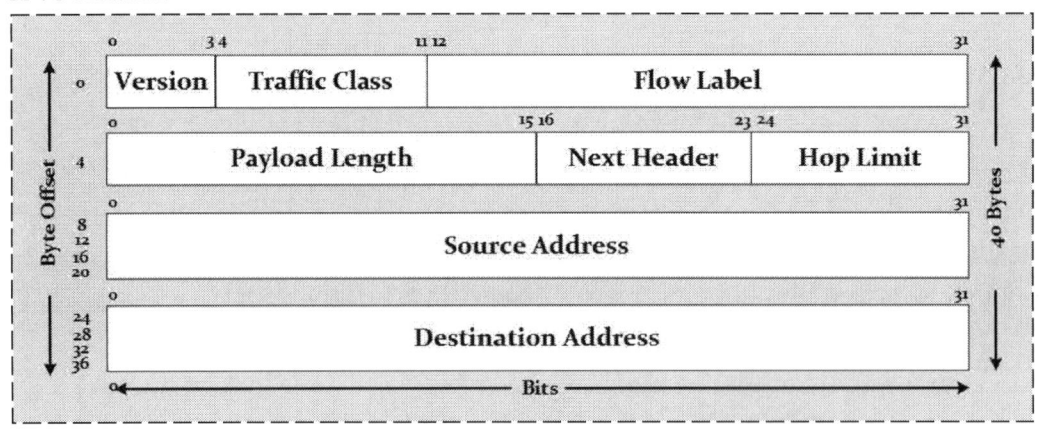

Figure 13 IPv6 Header Details

Version: Version of IP Protocol. 4 and 6 are valid. This diagram represents version 6 structure only.

Traffic Class: 8-Bit traffic field.

Flow Label: 20 bit flow label.

Payload length: 16-bit unsigned integer length of the IPv6 payload. I.e. the rest of the packet following this IPv6 header in octets. Any extension header are considered part of the payload.

Source Address: 128 bit address of the originator of the packet.

Next Header: 8-bit selector, Identifies the type of header immediately following the IPv6 header. Uses the same values as the IPv4 protocol field.

Destination Address: 128 bit address of the intended recipient of the packet (possibly not the ultimate recipient. If a routing header is present).

Hop Limit: 8-bit unsigned integer decremented by 1 by each node that forwards the packet. The packet is discarded if hop limit is decremented to zero.

Points to Remember

- IPv6 addresses are 128 bits in length.
- IPsec is built into the IPv6 protocol and allows for device roaming without losing connectivity.
- IPv6 addresses use eight sets of four hexadecimal addresses (16 bits in each set), separated by a colon (:), like this: xxxx:xxxx:xxxx:xxxx:xxxx:xxxx:xxxx:xxxx .
- If you have successive fields of zeroes in an IPv6 address, you can represent them using two colons (::), but this can be used only once in an address.
- An Anycast address represents the nearest interface to a device, where many devices can share an Anycast address. Multicast addresses begin with FF.
- Global unicast addresses begin with 2000::/3. Private addresses range from FE8 through FFF. A loopback address is ::1.
- The subnet ID is the first 64 bits and the interface ID is the last 64 bits. EUI-64 allows dynamic creation of the interface ID portion by using the MAC address on the interface.

IP Address Mind Map

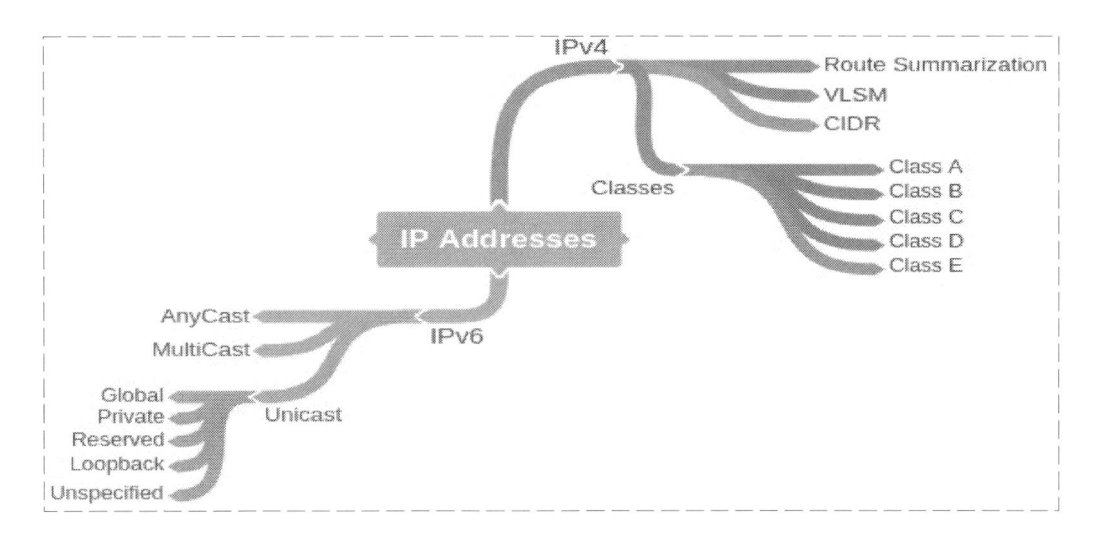

Figure 14 IP Addresses MindMap

Chapter 2: IP NGN Architecture

Technology Brief

"IP NGN is a platform for the Connected Life." Okay, what does that really mean? It is an infrastructure for voice, video, mobile, and cloud, or managed services based on Cisco products including the CRS Series, ASR Series (such as ASR 1000 running IOS-XE and ASR 9000 running IOS-XR), and different switch series, such as 6500, Metro Ethernet Series, and possibly Nexus Series. Other than some very subtle differences, IOS and IOS-XE look the same. The difference is that IOS is a monolithic operating system (OS) and IOS-XE (and IOS-XR) is a modular OS. Theoretically, a modular OS should be more stable than a monolithic OS since there is a separation of control plane and data plane, and a separation of processes. Therefore, if there is a failure in process or at the control plane, the data plane can continue to pass traffic based on last known information. Service providers agree that the Carrier Ethernet and IP/Multiprotocol Label Switching (MPLS) technology is and will be the way to next-generation networks.

Service provider challenge is to maintain growth and profitability. Service provider's needs are:

- Accommodate demand for broadband services by maintaining competitive residential and business service offerings
- Ignore service commoditization by launching new and premium services
- Strengthen profitability by increasing capital while reducing cost of ownership
- Switch existing legacy ATM/Frame Relay networks to more cost-effective Carrier Ethernet or MPLS services
- Secure and grow business services in parallel with consumer services. Cisco IP NGN carrier Ethernet design incorporates multiple networking technologies to provide optimal flexibility for current and next-generation service offerings.
- Ethernet over MPLS (EoMPLS)
- Layer 3 Protocol Independent Multicast-Source Specific Multicast (PIM-SSM)
- MPLS VPN
- IP over dense wavelength-division multiplexing (IPoDWDM)

- Hierarchal Virtual Private LAN Service (H-VPLS)
- IEEE 802.1ad; as well as emerging Ethernet, IP, and MPLS technologies.

Features of NGN Network

NGNs offer many key features when compared to older networks. These include characteristics, such as:

Packet-based transfer: Unifying all switching using different technologies, such as connectionless or connection-oriented layer 2 switching or layer 3 routing

Software-defined networking: This architecture separate the network control and forwarding functions by making network control directly programmable, means that network is more agile, scalable and centrally managed.

Unrestricted access to different service providers: NGNs allow access from various networks, including fixed line, traditional mobile and fixed wireless.

Legacy support: SS7 signaling and TDM bearers at interconnect points.

IP NGN Architecture

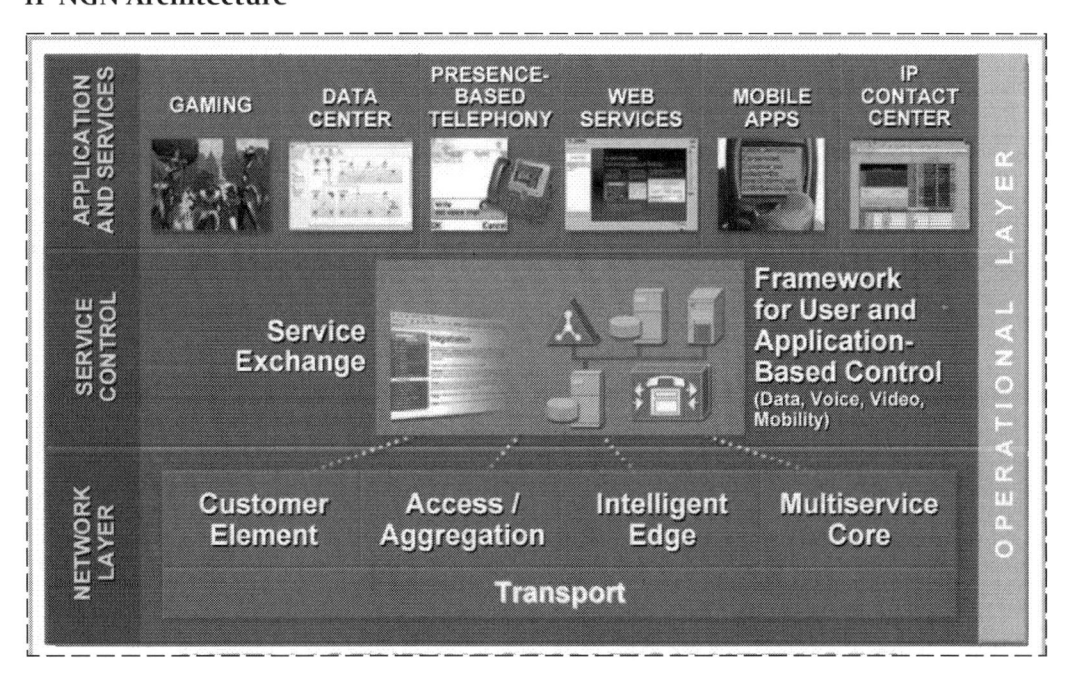

Figure 15 IP NGN Network Offerings

The goal of the IP NGN architecture is to offer rich, personalized, and value-add multimedia services. To accomplish this, service providers need a service control framework that supports the key business transition that must be made:

Application layer:

Today devices are providing a range of voice, video, and data services and yet be mobile. Called "Triple Play on the Move," these services span the communication and entertainment realms. However, delivering "service" to a "device" is a challenge that can be addressed by an ordinary network, which is - resilient, adaptive, and can support integration.

Service control layer: To deliver various services over a broad range of devices over multiple access means, the network should be able to process granular customer information. Hence, the network should be able to assess and address issues regarding user identity, device identification, access medium, usage, etc.

A service exchange framework enhances broadband and mobile IP networks with an application-aware service control point. This offers service providers the benefit of having a more controlled and efficient (facilitates the reduction of OpEx and CapEx) network which service providers can leverage to provide deliver new, tiered services.

Secure network layer:

Today the secure network layer is undergoing a dramatic change. IP/MPLS is being integrated throughout each section of the network. Edge and core areas are converging, with each adopting capabilities of the other, etc. Service providers can leverage this convergence to launch new, more, and better services.

One area in the network that is not converging is access or aggregation. More and more types of technologies are offering in the access realm - from 3G and WiFi, and Ethernet and Cable, to DSL, ATM, Frame Relay, Fiber, and TDM. This poses new challenges to the network, as it now has to adapt to whatever the access means, even multiple ones.

Another big challenge is security. Customers today consider security as an absolute necessity. As a result, security needs to be integrated throughout the network, crossing its own internal barriers to ensure that the services are delivered without compromise. For both of these challenges, and many more in the network layer, intelligence is once again the necessary solution.

To summarize, by building a network with more and more intelligence fully integrated throughout, a service provider is able to leverage a platform on which to better building its business.

Troubleshooting NGN using the OSI model

When troubleshooting any network, it is always sensible to approach the issue from the perspective of the OSI model. The OSI (Open System Interconnection) model defines a networking framework for implementing protocols in 7 layers. The beauty of this model is the fact that you can individually troubleshoot every layer using simple methods. I suggest working from layer 1 upwards until you find the problem.

Physical, Layer 1:

Always check Physical media first to avoid making troubleshoot complicated. You can use cable testers to check cables, or use some common sense when swapping things round to isolate the cause of the problem. Making sure your operating system can see the hardware (and shows that it is functional) is also covered at this layer.

Data Link, Layer 2:

Most issues can be troubleshot with the Arp command (in windows anyway). MAC addresses are globally unique to a device, but some people like to play around which can cause problems (google for Arp poisoning / spoofing). Using 'arp -a' will show you which MAC addresses are mapped to which IP addresses locally, which is sometimes helpful.

Network, Layer 3:

It contains the routing protocols (rip1 and 2, ospf, igrp and a few others) as well as the routed protocols (most notably IP). You can troubleshoot IP with icmp packets. Utilities like ping and tracert use icmp packets to get responses back from networked hosts. In this way you can also verify the connectivity and the destination host

Transport, Layer 4:

Most of the troubleshooting here can be done with a packet sniffer. TCP is used with IP as a means to ensure that the data within the packets is sent and received without any loss. If there is an error, packets are re-sent (it would be worth googling tcp packet header structure) with the correct sequence number so that no data is lost (it ensures complete data transfer). You can use packet sniffers to examine the tcp/udp packet headers to see what is happening at layer 4.

Session, Layer 5:

The most likely thing you would be troubleshooting at this layer would be netbios over TCP/IP. Windows has some very useful utilities like nbtstat and the group of 'net' commands, which will help you. Other protocols like DNS, LDAP (this is used for most of the active directory replication), NFS, SQL, RPC and XWindows are also things that would be troubleshooted at this layer.

Presentation, Layer 6:

This layer covers the things like JPEG, MPEG, MIDI, QUICKTIME and other files of the same nature. Most of your troubleshooting will be with the applications that create them (at layer 7) but be aware that you can hex files to look at the structure and change them.

Application, Layer 7:

If all of the other layers are working fine and have been tested, then this is usually just a matter of applying patches to software or reinstalling. Everyone probably has experience troubleshooting problems in windows. Telnet is an excellent tool for connecting to virtually any port to check to see if the above layers are functioning properly.

Different types of ISP

Internet Service Providers (ISPs) have various types of connectivity options for the Internet. Each ISP is different in that the company provides a different type of connectivity protocol and speed. Most ISPs are providing cable or DSL, but other options are available for small, rural areas. It is important to analyze your individual needs before deciding on an ISP.

Dialup:

Although it is slow, dialup access is still a necessity for small, rural areas. ISPs offer dialup access in these areas. A dialup ISP requires the user to have a modem for Internet access as mentioned in figure 14. The user dials a phone connection using a telephone number, connects to a remote server, and uses the telephone connection to browse websites.

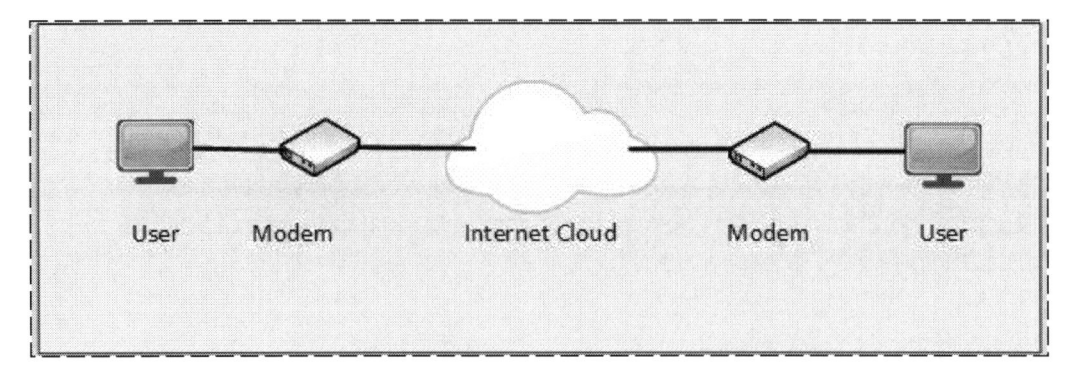

Figure 16 Dialup

DSL

The local phone company normally provides DSL. DSL is a technology that uses the "extra" signals not used by telephone signals. These "extra" signals make DSL usage available even during times when the phone is ringing or people are using the telephone access. DSL uses a DSL router that connects using a telephone cable to a phone jack as shown in Figure 15.

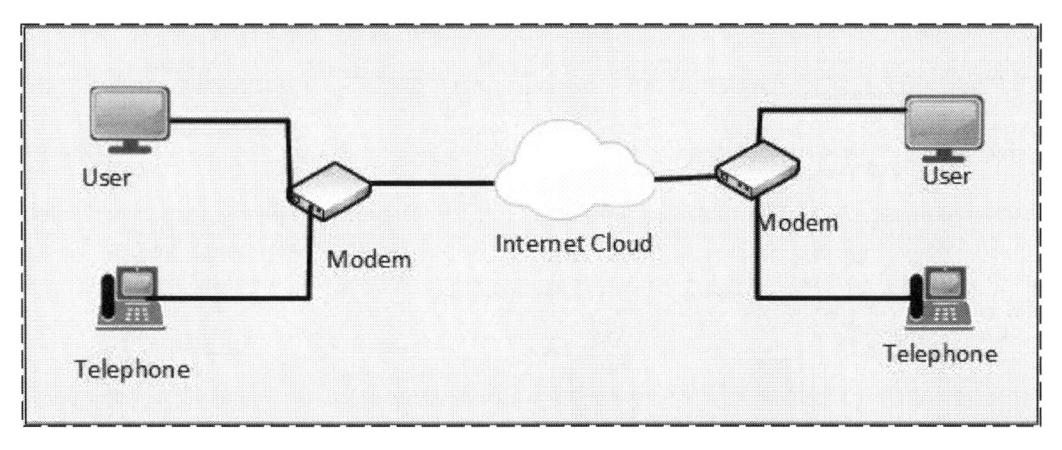

Figure 17 DSL

Cable

The local cable company in the user's neighborhood provides Cable. Cable Internet access is available by connecting a cable router to the computer via switch as shown in figure. Cable ISPs are usually faster, especially in areas where there is not much consumption. Neighbors share Cable connections, which differs from DSL, so cable access speed is dependent on the amount of traffic from other neighborhood users.

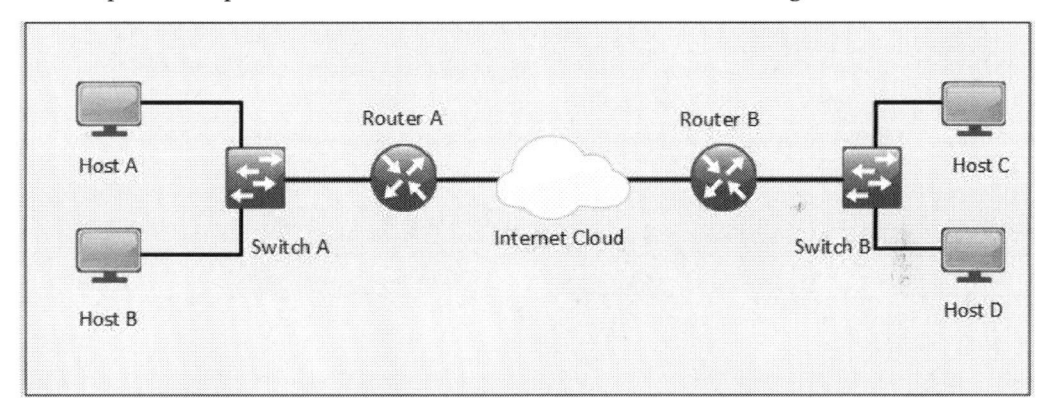

Figure 18 Cable

WiFi Access

WiFi is wireless Internet connection. It is used by laptops and offered freely by many hotels and coffee shops. WiFi can be installed in the home for people who have desktops and laptops. WiFi is not as quick as DSL or Cable, but it is a more convenient ISP service.

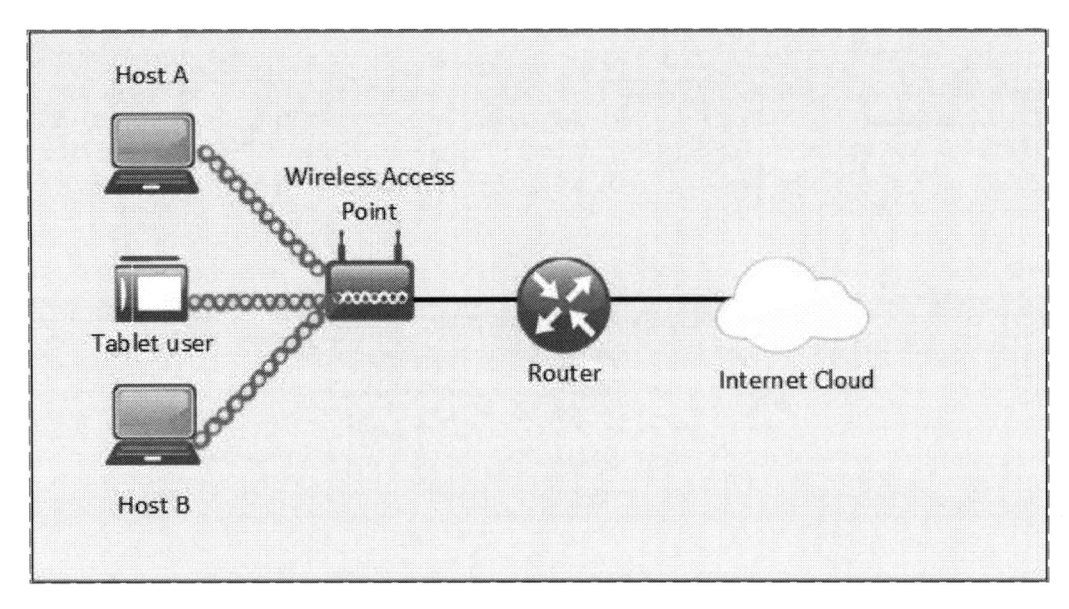

Figure 19 Wifi Access

Satellite

Satellite connection is offered for people who are not able to receive DSL or Cable options. Satellite access has very quick download speeds, but upload speeds are used through a modem, which is very slow. People in very rural areas who have no other broadband connection uses satellite connection.

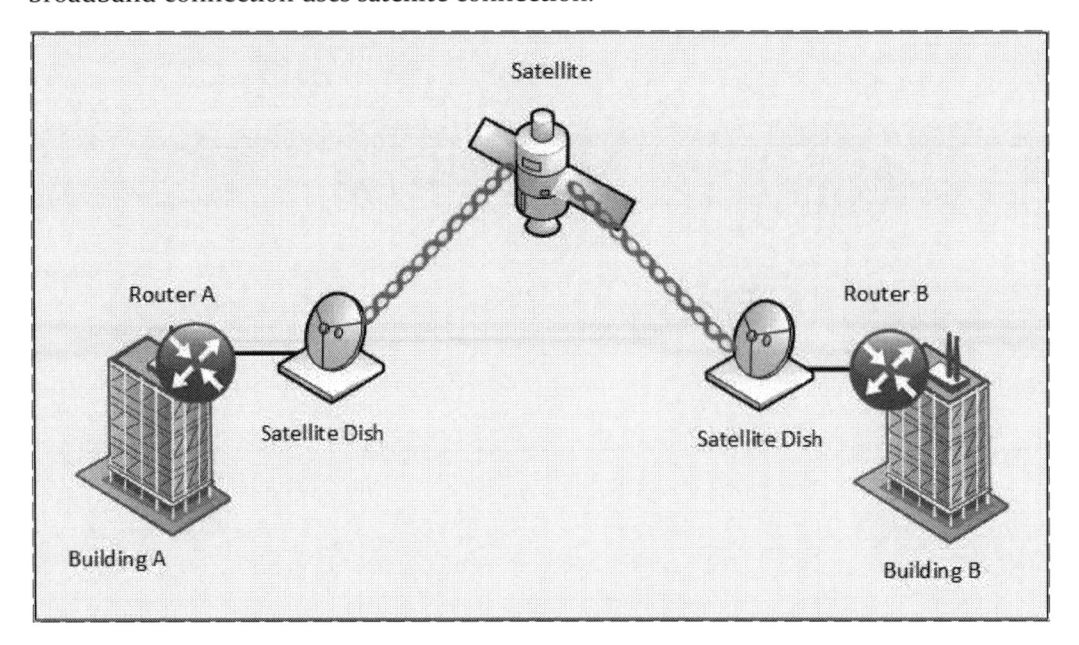

Figure 20 Satellite Connection

Number resources

IANA is responsible for global coordination of the Internet Protocol addressing systems, as well as the Autonomous System Numbers used for routing Internet traffic.

Currently, there are two types of Internet Protocol (IP) addresses in active use: IP version 4 (IPv4) and IP version 6 (IPv6). IPv4 was initially deployed on 1 January 1983 and is still the most commonly used version. IPv4 addresses are 32-bit numbers often expressed as 4 octets in "dotted decimal" notation (for example, 192.0.2.53). Deployment of the IPv6 protocol began in 1999. IPv6 addresses are 128-bit numbers and are conventionally expressed using hexadecimal strings (for example, 2001:0db8:582:ae33:29).

Both IPv4 and IPv6 addresses are generally assigned in a hierarchical manner. Users are assigned IP addresses by Internet service providers (ISPs). ISPs obtain allocations of IP addresses from a local Internet registry (LIR) or National Internet Registry (NIR), or from their appropriate Regional Internet Registry (RIR).

Registry	Area Covered
AFRINIC	Arica Region
APNIC	Asia/Pacific Region
ARIN	Canada, USA, and some Caribbean Islands
LACNIC	Latin America and some Caribbean Islands
RIPE NCC	Europe, the Middle East, and Central Asia

Table 7 Different Registry with their associated area

Internet Assigned Numbers Authority (IANA) Policy for Allocation of IPv4 Blocks to Regional Internet Registries

This topic describes the policy governing the allocation of IPv4 address space from the IANA to the Regional Internet Registries (RIRs). This topic does not stipulate performance requirements in the provision of services by IANA to an RIR in accordance with this policy. Such requirements should be specified by appropriate agreements among the RIRs and ICANN.

1. **Allocation Principles**
    ❖ The IANA will allocate IPv4 address space to the RIRs in /8 units.

- The IANA will allocate sufficient IPv4 address space to the RIRs to support their registration needs for at least an 18-month period.
- The IANA will allow the RIRs to apply their own respective chosen allocation and reservation strategies in order to ensure the efficiency and efficacy of their work.

2. **Initial Allocations**

    Every new RIR shall, now of recognition, be allocated a new /8 block by the IANA. This allocation will be done regardless of the newly formed RIR's projected utilization figures and shall be independent of the IPv4 address space that may have been transferred to the new RIR by the already existing RIRs as part of the formal transition process.

3. **Additional Allocations**

    A RIR is eligible to receive additional IPv4 address space from the IANA when either of the following conditions is met.

    - The RIR's AVAILABLE SPACE of IPv4 addresses is less than 50% of a /8 block.
    - The RIR's AVAILABLE SPACE of IPv4 addresses is less than its established NECESSARY SPACE for the following 9 months.

In this case, the IANA shall make a single allocation of a whole number of /8 blocks, sufficient to satisfy the established NECESSARY SPACE of the RIR for an 18 month period.

3.1 Calculation of Available Space

The Available Space of IPv4 addresses of a RIR shall be determined as follows:

AVAILABLE SPACE = CURRENTLY FREE ADDRESSES + RESERVATIONS EXPIRING DURING THE FOLLOWING 3 MONTHS - FRAGMENTED SPACE

Fragmented Space is determined as the total amount of available blocks smaller than the RIR's minimum allocation size within the RIR's currently available stock.

3.2 Calculation of Necessary Space

If the applying Regional Internet Registry does not establish any special needs for the period concerned, Necessary Space shall be determined as follows:

NECESSARY SPACE = AVERAGE NUMBER OF ADDRESSES ALLOCATED MONTHLY DURING THE PAST 6 MONTHS * LENGTH OF PERIOD IN MONTHS

- If the applying RIR anticipates that due to certain special needs the rate of allocation for the period concerned will be different from the previous 6 months, it may determine its NECESSARY SPACE as follows:

- Calculate NECESSARY SPACE as its total needs for that period according to its projection and based on the special facts that justify these needs.

- Submit a detailed justification of the above-mentioned projection. If the justification is based on the allocation tendency prepared by the Regional Internet Registry, data explaining said tendency must be enclosed. If the justification is consist on the application of one or more of the Regional Internet Registry's new allocation policies, an impact analysis of the new policy/policies must be enclosed.

- If the justification is based on external factors such as new infrastructure, new services within the region, technological advances or legal issues, the corresponding analysis must be enclosed together with references to information sources that will allow verification of the data.

- If IANA does not have, elements that clearly question the Regional Internet Registry's projection than the special needs projected for the following 18 months and shall be considered valid.

4. Announcement of IANA Allocations:

When address space is allocated to a RIR, the IANA will send a detailed announcement to the receiving RIR. The IANA will also make announcements to all other RIRs, informing them of the recent allocation. The RIRs will coordinate announcements to their respective membership lists and any other lists they deem necessary. The IANA will make appropriate modifications to the "Internet Protocol V4 Address Space" page of the IANA website and may make announcements to its own appropriate announcement lists. The IANA announcements will be limited to which address ranges, the time of allocation and to which Registry they have been allocated.

Internet Assigned Numbers Authority (IANA) Policy for Allocation of IPv6 Blocks to Regional Internet Registries | (Ratified 7 September 2006)

Policy statement

This document briefly defines the policy governing the allocation of IPv6 address space from the IANA to the Regional Internet Registries (RIRs). This document does not stipulate performance requirements in the provision of services by IANA to an RIR in accordance with this policy. Such requirements will be specified by mutual agreements between ICANN and the NRO.

1. Allocation Principles:

The unit of IPv6 allocation from IANA to an RIR is a /12.

The IANA will allocate sufficient IPv6 address space to the RIRs to support their registration needs for at least an 18-month period.

The IANA will allow the RIRs to apply their own respective chosen allocation and reservation strategies in order to ensure the efficiency and efficacy of their work.

2. Initial Allocations:

On inception of this policy, each current RIR with less than a /12 unallocated address space, shall receive an IPv6 allocation from IANA

Each new RIR shall, on recognition by ICANN receive an IPv6 allocation from the IANA.

3. Additional Allocations:

An RIR is able to receive additional IPv6 address space from the IANA when either of the following conditions is met.

The RIR's AVAILABLE SPACE of IPv6 addresses is less than 50% of a /12.

The RIR's AVAILABLE SPACE of IPv6 addresses is less than its established NECESSARY SPACE for the following 9 months.

In either case, IANA shall make a single IPv6 allocation, sufficient to satisfy the established NECESSARY SPACE of the RIR for an 18-month period.

3.1 Calculation of AVAILABLE SPACE

The AVAILABLE SPACE of IPv6 addresses of a RIR can be determined as follows:

> **AVAILABLE SPACE = CURRENTLY FREE ADDRESSES + RESERVATIONS EXPIRING DURING THE FOLLOWING 3 MONTHS - FRAGMENTED SPACE**

FRAGMENTED SPACE is determined as the total amount of available blocks smaller than the RIR's minimum allocation size within the RIR's currently available stock.

3.2 Calculation of NECESSARY SPACE

If the applying Regional Internet Registry does not establish any special needs for the period concerned, NECESSARY SPACE can be determined as follows:

> **NECESSARY SPACE = AVERAGE NUMBER OF ADDRESSES ALLOCATED MONTHLY DURING THE PAST 6 MONTHS * LENGTH OF PERIOD IN MONTHS**

If applying RIR anticipates that due to certain special needs the rate of allocation for the period concerned will be distinguished from the previous 6 months, it may determine its NECESSARY SPACE as follows:

- Calculate NECESSARY SPACE as its total needs for that period according to its projection and based on the special facts that justify these needs.
- If the justification is made on the allocation tendency prepared by the Regional Internet Registry, data explaining said tendency must be enclosed.
- If the justification is based on the application of one or more of the Regional Internet Registry's new allocation policies, an impact analysis of the new policy/policies must be enclosed.
- If the justification depends on external factors such as new infrastructure, new services within the region, technological advances or legal issues, the corresponding analysis must be enclosed together with references to information sources that will allow verification of the data.
- If IANA does not have, elements that clearly question the Regional Internet Registry's projection, the special needs projected for the following 18 months and shall be considered valid.

4. Announcement of IANA Allocations:

The IANA, the NRO, and the RIRs will make announcements and update their respective web sites regarding an allocation made by the IANA to an RIR. ICANN and the NRO will establish administrative procedures to manage this process.

Mind Map

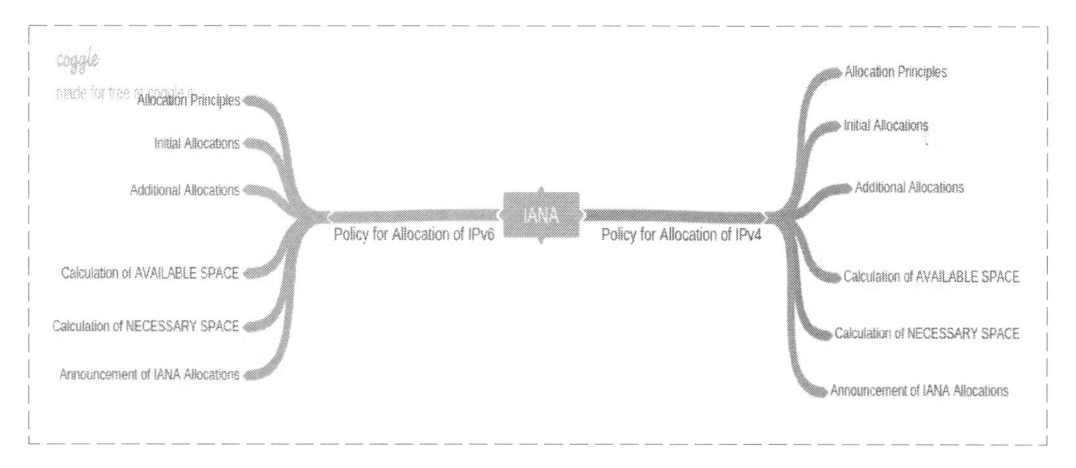

Figure 21 Mind Map of Address allocation Policy for IPv4 and IPv6

Chapter 3: Network Management

Overview

A network management system (NMS) is consists of hardware and/or software tools that allow an IT professional to supervise the individual components of a network within a larger network management framework.

Network management system components assist with:

- Network device discovery, identifying what devices are present on a network

- Network device monitoring, monitoring at the device level to determine the health of network equipment's and the extent to which their performance matches capacity plans and intra-enterprise service-level agreements (SLAs)

- Network performance analysis, tracking performance indicators such as bandwidth utilization, packet loss, latency, availability and uptime of routers, switches and other Simple Network Management Protocol (SNMP) -enabled devices

- Intelligent notifications, configurable alerts that will respond to specific network scenarios by paging, emailing, calling or texting a network engineer or an administrator

Network Time Protocol

NTP is an open standard that allows you to synchronize your router's time with a centralized timeserver, where your device periodically polls the NTP server for the current date and time. NTP uses the User Datagram Protocol (UDP) on port 123. NTP can get the correct time for an internal or external server. The reliability of the server refers to its stratum level of clock source. The most accurate is an atomic clock, but most networks typically do not need that kind of precision and instead obtain time from a GPS source.

NTP has three basic methods of delivering time messages between the timeserver and the NTP client:

- **Broadcast** The NTP server periodically announces the time using a broadcast message. This method assumes that all clients are in the local subnet.

- **Multicast** The NTP server periodically announces the time using a multicast message. In most cases, multicast routing must be set up to disseminate the time across the network (multicast routing is beyond the scope of this book).

- **Unicast** the NTP client periodically (commonly, every 10 minutes) queries the NTP server for the correct time.

NTP Configuration Example

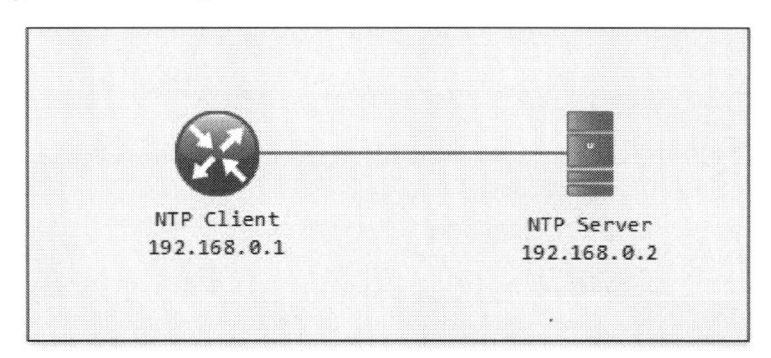

Figure 22 Configuration of NTP

The router on the top is called "Core Router" and it's the edge of my network. It is connected to the Internet and will use one of the NTP servers from pool.ntp.org to synchronize its clock. The network also has two internal switches that require synchronized clocks. Both switches will become NTP clients of the Core Router, thus making the Core Router a NTP server.

NTP Server Configuration:

```
NTP-SERVER(config)#ntp master 10
```

This command will make the device as an authoritative NTP device.

Router configuration

First, we will configure the Router on top. We will use NTP server for this example. Make sure that the routers are ping able

```
Router(config)#ntp-server 192.168.0.2
```

This commands defines the NTP server address on the Client device.

```
Router#(config)ntp update-calendar
```

Just one command and we will synchronize our clock with the public server. We can verify our work like this:

```
Router#show ntp associations
       address         ref clock      st   when  poll reach  delay  offset   disp
*~192.168.0.2       127.127.7.1       10    33    64   377    16.2   -4.13    7.5
 * master (synced), # master (unsynced), + selected, - candidate, ~ configured
```

Above, we see the show ntp associations command that tells us if our clock is synchronized or not. The ~ in front of the IP address tells us that we configured this server but we are not synchronized yet. You can see this because there is no * in front of the IP address and the "st" field (stratum) is currently 10.

There is one more command that gives us more information about the NTP configuration:

```
Router(config)#do show ntp status
Clock is synchronized, stratum 11, reference is 192.168.0.2
nominal freq is 250.0000 Hz, actual freq is 250.0000 Hz, precision is 2**18
reference time is C029441E.07463F9B (00:04:46.028 UTC Fri Mar 1 2002)
clock offset is -7.2275 msec, root delay is 14.45 msec
root dispersion is 21.84 msec, peer dispersion is 14.57 msec
```

The router tells us that we are unsynchronized and that there is no reference clock. we will just wait a couple of minutes and look at these commands again:

```
NTP-SERVER#show ntp associations
      address         ref clock      st   when  poll reach  delay   offset    disp
*~127.127.7.1      127.127.7.1        9    48    64   377    0.0     0.00     0.0
 * master (synced), # master (unsynced), + selected, - candidate, ~ configured
NTP-SERVER#
```

Cisco routers have two different clocks, they have a software clock and a hardware clock and they operate separately from each other. Here's how to see both clocks:

```
Router#show clock
12:41:25.197 UTC Mon Jul 7 2017
Router#show calendar
12:43:24 UTC Mon Jul 7 2017
```

The show clock command shows me the software clock while the show calendar command gives me the hardware clock. The two clocks are not in sync so this is something we should fix; you can do it like this:

```
NTP-SERVER#clock set 12:22:00 14 aug 2017
.Aug 14 12:22:00.003: %SYS-6-CLOCKUPDATE: System clock has been updated from 12:22:20 UTC Tue Aug 15 2017 to 12:22:00 UTC Mon Aug 14 2017, configured from console by console.
```

```
Router#(config)ntp update-calendar
```

The ntp update-calendar command will update the hardware clock with the time of the software clock, here is the result:

```
Router#show clock
*01:57:39.511 UTC Tue Aug 15 2017
Router#show calendar
02:22:34 UTC Tue Aug 15 2017
```

That is all to configure on the Router for now. We still have to configure two switches to synchronize their clocks.

Logging

An event is something that happens (someone logging in) while an incident is an issue with what happened (an unauthorized login access was detected). Logging plays a key role in your management and security solution. Even though SNMP supports traps, the number of traps is limited: logging supports many more types and kinds of messages than do SNMP traps. Logging to a syslog server makes it easier to manage and keep a historical record of your logging information from a multitude of devices. Syslog uses UDP and runs on port 514. However, all logging information is sent in clear text, has no packet integrity checking, and is easy for a hacker to send false data to the syslog server. Therefore, it is highly recommended that you encrypt information between your networking devices and the syslog server, as well as set up a filter on the syslog server to accept only logging information from particular IP addresses.

By default, logging messages are sent to the router's console port; however, the following locations are also supported: terminal lines, internal memory buffer, SNMP traps, and a syslog server. Common destinations used by administrators are the logging buffer (RAM), the console terminal, and syslog servers. Syslog is the most common, since it allows you to easily centralize (aggregate) logging messages on a server. The advantage of using syslog is that messages can be stored on a hard drive on the syslog server instead of on the router itself, freeing up router resources. The following sections introduce you to logging as well as how to configure logging from the CLI.

Logging Messages

All of Cisco's log messages can contain the following information:

- **Timestamp:** The date and time of the occurrence (this is optional)
- **Log message name:** The name of the message
- **Severity level:** The severity level of the log message, embedded in the log name, like %SYS-5-CONFIG_I, where 5 is the severity level

- **Message text:** A very brief description of the event

Here is an example of a log message:

```
Nov 19 12:30:00 EST: %SYS-5-CONFIG_I: Configured from
    console by vty0 (10.0.11.11)
```

Figure 23 Log Message

In this example, the timestamps have been enabled (they are disabled by default). This is followed by the category of logging (SYS indicates a system message), the severity level (5), and the subcategory (CONFIG indicates a change on the router). Last is the message text.

Logging Severity Levels

Level	Name	Description
0	Emergency	The router is unusable (IOS cant load).
1	Alerts	The router needs immediate attention; for instance, the temperature is too high.
2	Critical	There is a critical condition; for instance, the router is running out of memory
3	Errors	An error condition exists, such as an invalid memory size.
4	Warnings	A warning condition exists; for instance, a crypto operation failed.
5	Notification	A normal event occurred, an interface changed state
6	Informational	A router dropped a packet because of ACL filter.
7	Debug	Output of debug command

Table 8 Logging Levels

Logging Configuration

```
IOS(config)# logging [host] {hostname | IP_address}
IOS(config)# logging trap level_name_or_#
IOS(config)# logging console level_name_or_#
IOS(config)# logging buffered level_name_or_#
IOS(config)# logging monitor level_name_or_#
IOS(config)# logging facility facility_type
IOS(config)# logging source-interface interface_name
IOS(config)# logging on
```

Figure 24 Configuration of logging

Logging Commands

- The logging host command defines a syslog server to send log messages to.

- The logging trap command defines the severity level at which to log messages: this must specify the name or number of the level. The level indicates any message at that level or higher. For example, if you set the level to three, messages from levels 1 to 3 would be logged.

- The logging console command defines the logging level for the console line.

- The logging buffered command defines the logging level for the log messages stored in the router's RAM and the logging monitor command defines the logging level for log messages sent to the router's other lines, like the VTYs.

- The logging facility command is used to direct logging information to the appropriate file on the syslog server. The default is local7, but this can be changed. The facility type allows you to keep different log files for different devices on the same syslog server, making it easier to find log messages.

- The logging source-interface command specifies which interface on the router will be used to reach the syslog server—by default, the router will use its routing table to determine what interface, and thus what source IP address to use, when sending a log message. You might want to configure this command if the router has multiple interfaces it can use to reach the log server, and thus the possibility of multiple source IP addresses to use, but the syslog server is only allowing log messages from one of the router's IP addresses.

- Last, you must enable logging with the logging on command—this is not necessary for log messages sent to the console, which is enabled by default.

Please note that there are many other parameters to the logging command. By default, Cisco IOS devices do not include the local timestamp (date and time) with the syslog messages sent to the syslog server: they rely on the server attaching it is time to the message. To have the IOS device include its own local time, configure the following command:

IOS(config)# **service timestamps {log| debug} datetime [msec]**

You can add timestamps to log messages or the output of debug commands. The msec parameter specifies to include the current millisecond value in the router's time stamped log message.

Logging CLI Example

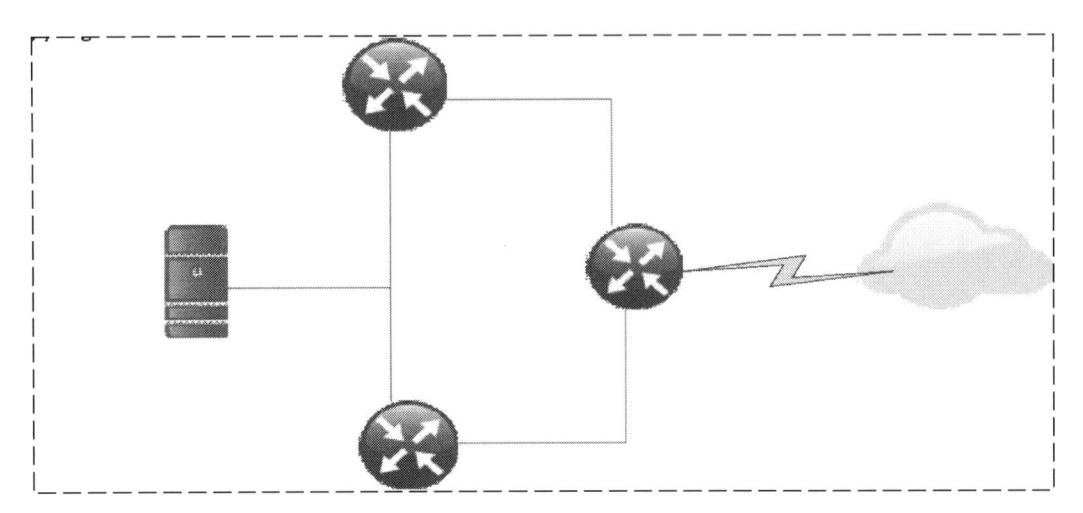

Figure 25

R1(config)#logging 10.0.0.1
R1(config)#logging trap 5
R1(config)#logging source-interface fa0/0
R1(config)#logging on

Notice that the router will only send log messages from level 5 and lower and that the router sources log messages from the FA0/0 interface.

Simple Network Management Protocol

Some management of network devices requires the use of the Simple Network Management Protocol (SNMP). SNMP is commonly used to remotely manage (configure and/or monitor) a remote networking device.

SNMP is composed of three components:

- **Network Management Station (NMS)** This device manages agents, and sometimes referred to as the manager.
- **Agent** This is a device managed by an NMS.

- **Management Information Base (MIB)** this defines how information (configuration, operational, and statistical) is stored on an agent.

The interaction is between the NMS and the agent, which can involve two types of connections:

- NMS sends "get" or "set" commands to the agent; get commands are used for retrieving MIB information, and set commands are used to change MIB information.

- The agent sends "traps" or "informs" to the NMS, which are a form of log message, indicating an important condition on the device.

Information stored on an agent is located in an MIB. Each MIB is uniquely identified with an object identifier (OID). Get, send, and trap messages are based on the MIB information identified by a particular OID.

SNMP Versions

There are three main versions of SNMP: versions 1, 2c, and 3. SNMPv1 and v2c use community strings for security: read-only and read-write. The read-only community string is used to restrict the reading of MIB information, and the read-write community string is used to change MIB information. The main problem with community strings is that they are sent in clear text and thus are susceptible to eavesdropping attacks. SNMPv2c also added the support of inform requests, which allows for acknowledged notifications, and get bulk requests, which allows a management station to access multiple MIBs in one request.

SNMPv3 is an enhancement of SNMPv2c. Besides supporting the same MIB structure and gets, sets, and traps, SNMPv3 also supports authentication, message integrity, and payload encryption. Message integrity is used to ensure that SNMP messages have not been tampered with and are coming from a legitimate source; this is accomplished with the MD5 or SHA-1 HMAC functions. Payload encryption is used so that a man-in-the-middle cannot examine the get, set, and trap command information. A man-in-the-middle is basically a device that sees traffic flowing between the source and destination. Encryption can be used to defeat man-in-the-middle attacks: the attacker can still see the packets, but the content is encrypted from eavesdropping. Encryption is accomplished with the DES, 3DES, or AES encryption algorithms.

SNMP Version	Level	Authentication	Encryption	What Happens
1	NoAuthNoPriv	Community string	NO	Authentication with community string match

2c	NoAuthNoPriv	Community string	NO	Authentication with community string match
3	NoAuthNoPriv	Username	NO	Authentication with a username
3	AuthNoPriv	MD5 or SHA	NO	Provides MD5/SHA for authentication
3	AuthPriv	MD5 or SHA	DES,3DES or AES	Provides MD5/SHA for authentication and encryption via DES/3DES/AES

Table 9 SNMP Versions

SNMP Configuration

This section briefly introduces you to the configuration of SNMPv2c and SNMPv3 on IOS devices. Of the two, configuring SNMPv2c is simpler, but less secure.

SNMPv2 Configuration

Here are the basic commands to set up SNMPv2c communications:

```
R1(config)#snmp-server community ipspecialist ro
R1(config)#snmp-server community ipspecialist rw
R1(config)#snmp-server host 192.168.11.1 traps ipspecialist
R1(config)#snmp-server enable traps
```

The first command defines the community string used to allow read-only access. The second command defines the community string for read-write access. Please note that the community string is sent in clear text in the SNMP packet to restrict access. The last two commands enable the sending of SNMP traps to an SNMP management station (you also have to match the community string on the IOS device to what the NMS has configured).

SNMPv3 Configuration

The configuration of SNMPv3 is much more complicated. Here is a list of commands involved in its setup:

Lab 3-1 : Troubleshoot SNMP v3 Logging and NTP

Case Study:

In the Simple Network Management Protocol (SNMP) v2c and v3, the major difference is Authentication and Encryption. SNMP v3 is more secure than the previous versions, V1 and V2c. Version 1 is the oldest version having plain text community. It does not support 64 bit counters. V2c not only support 64 bit counter also some feature are added. Version 3 Supports ENcyption and Authentication features. In this lab, we are troubleshooting SNMP v2c and v3.

Topology:

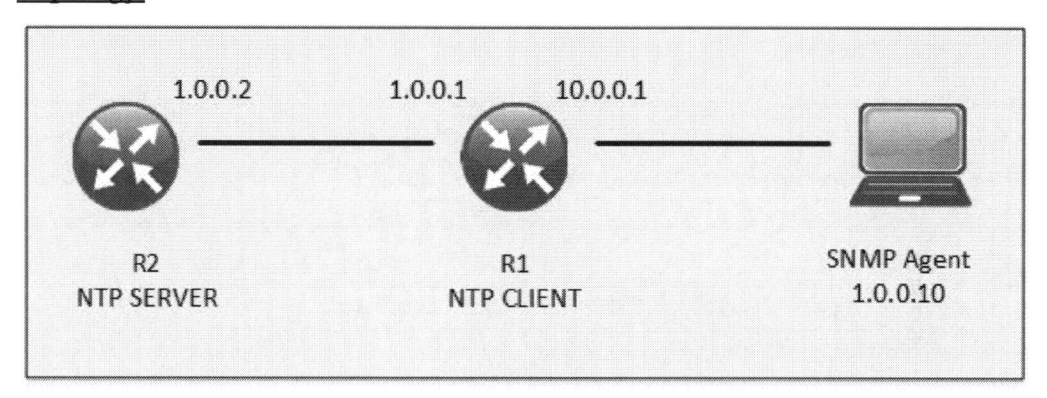

```
         1.0.0.2      1.0.0.1   10.0.0.1

          R2              R1            SNMP Agent
       NTP SERVER      NTP CLIENT         1.0.0.10
```

Configuration:

NTP-Client(config)#int eth 0/1

NTP-Client(config-if)#ip add 10.0.0.1 255.255.255.0

NTP-Client(config-if)#no sh

*Mar 1 00:00:55.355: %LINK-3-UPDOWN: Interface FastEthernet0/1, changed state to up

*Mar 1 00:00:56.355: %LINEPROTO-5-UPDOWN: Line protocol on Interface FastEthernet0/1, changed state to up

NTP-Client(config)#int eth 0/0

NTP-Client(config-if)#ip add 1.0.0.1 255.0.0.0

NTP-Client(config-if)#no sh

*Mar 1 00:01:11.387: %LINK-3-UPDOWN: Interface FastEthernet0/0, changed state to up

*Mar 1 00:01:12.387: %LINEPROTO-5-UPDOWN: Line protocol on Interface FastEthernet0/0, changed st

```
NTP-Client(config)#snmp-server group Mygroup v3 auth read Myview
NTP-Client(config)#snmp-server user MyUser Mygroup v3 auth md5 P@$$word:10
NTP-Client(config)#

*Mar 1 00:19:43.803: Configuring snmpv3 USM user, persisting snmpEngineBoots. Please Wait...

NTP-Client(config)#do show snmp engineID
Local SNMP engineID: 800000090300C2030DAD0000
Remote Engine ID       IP-addr     Port


NTP-Client(config)#snmp-server engineID remote 10.0.0.10
NTP-Client#
*Mar 1 00:21:10.575: %SYS-5-CONFIG_I: Configured from console by consoleconfig t
Enter configuration commands, one per line. End with CNTL/Z.

NTP-Client(config)#snmp-server engineID remote 10.0.0.10 800000090300C2030DAD0000
NTP-Client(config)#ntp authenticate
NTP-Client(config)#ntp authentication-key 1 md5 P@$$word:10
NTP-Client(config)#ntp trusted-key 1
NTP-Client(config)#ntp server 1.0.0.2
NTP-Client(config)#end
NTP-Client#show
*Mar 1 00:27:47.019: %SYS-5-CONFIG_I: Configured from console by console clock
*00:27:49.659 UTC Fri Mar 1 2002
NTP-Client (config)#ntp update-calender


NTP-Client#show ntp status
Clock is synchronized, stratum 11, reference is 1.0.0.2
nominal freq is 250.0000 Hz, actual freq is 250.0000 Hz, precision is 2**18
reference time is DCA7F5D4.FA7567B1 (03:56:04.978 UTC Mon Apr 24 2017)
clock offset is -0.0891 msec, root delay is 20.14 msec
```

root dispersion is 15875.14 msec, peer dispersion is 15875.02 msec

NTP-Client(config)#logging 10.0.0.10

NTP-Client(config)#logging trap debugging

NTP-Client(config)#service timestamps debug datetime msec

NTP-Client(config)#service timestamps log datetime msec

NTP-Server

NTP-Server#clock set 03:52:00 apr 24 2017

*Apr 24 03:52:00.000: %SYS-6-CLOCKUPDATE: System clock has been updated from 00:22:26 UTC Fri Mar 1 2002 to 03:52:00 UTC Mon Apr 24 2017, configured from console by console.

NTP-Server#show clock

03:52:05.919 UTC Mon Apr 24 2017

NTP-Server(config)#int eth 0/1

NTP-Server(config-if)#ip add 1.0.0.2 255.255.255.0

NTP-Server(config-if)#no sh

NTP-Server(config)#ntp master 10

NTP-Server(config)#ntp authentication-key 1 md5 P@$$word:10

SNMP verification:

Click Manage Engine pinned to task bar of provided VMware image of windows-7. Following windows will open. Click first time user to enter.

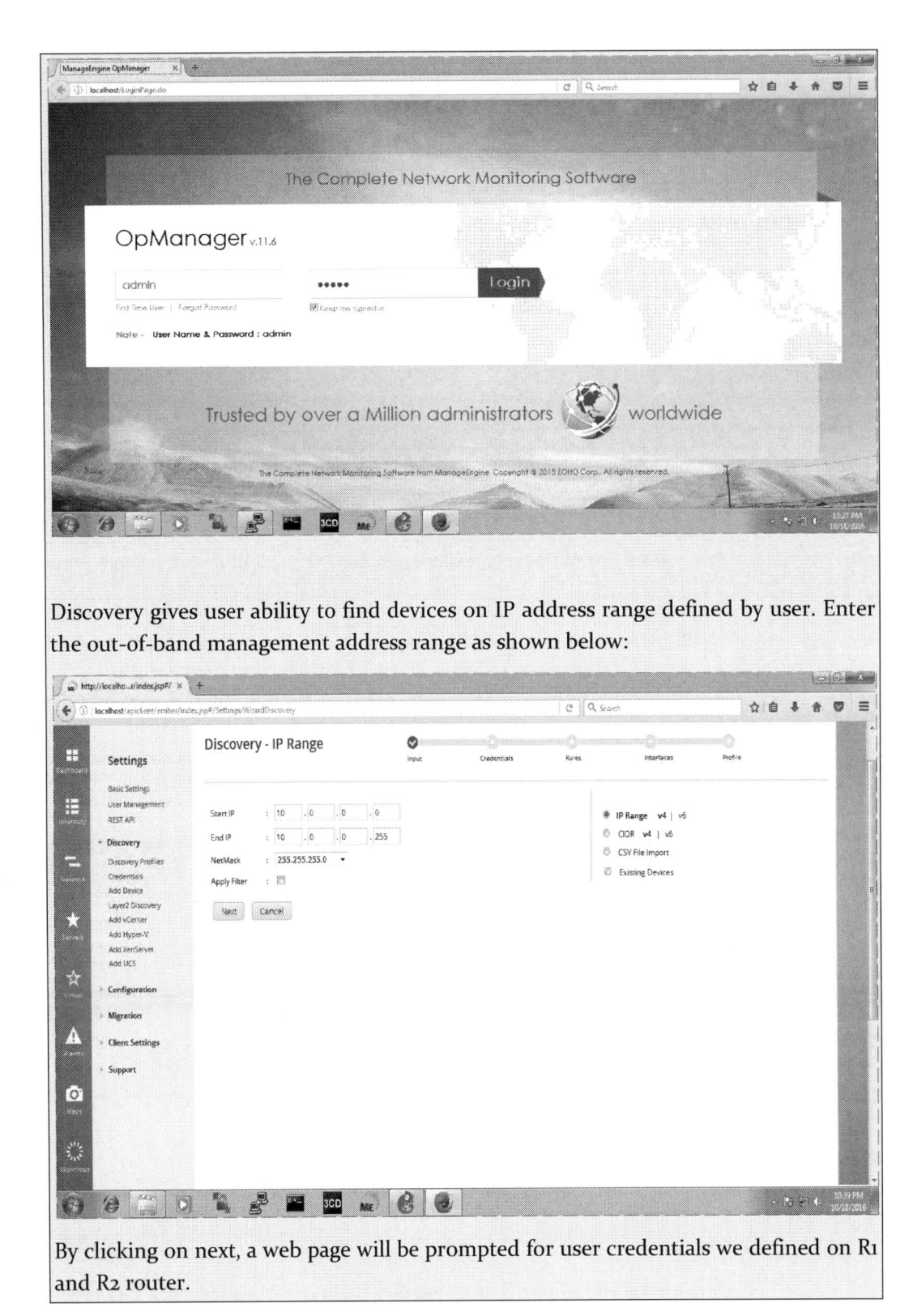

Discovery gives user ability to find devices on IP address range defined by user. Enter the out-of-band management address range as shown below:

By clicking on next, a web page will be prompted for user credentials we defined on R1 and R2 router.

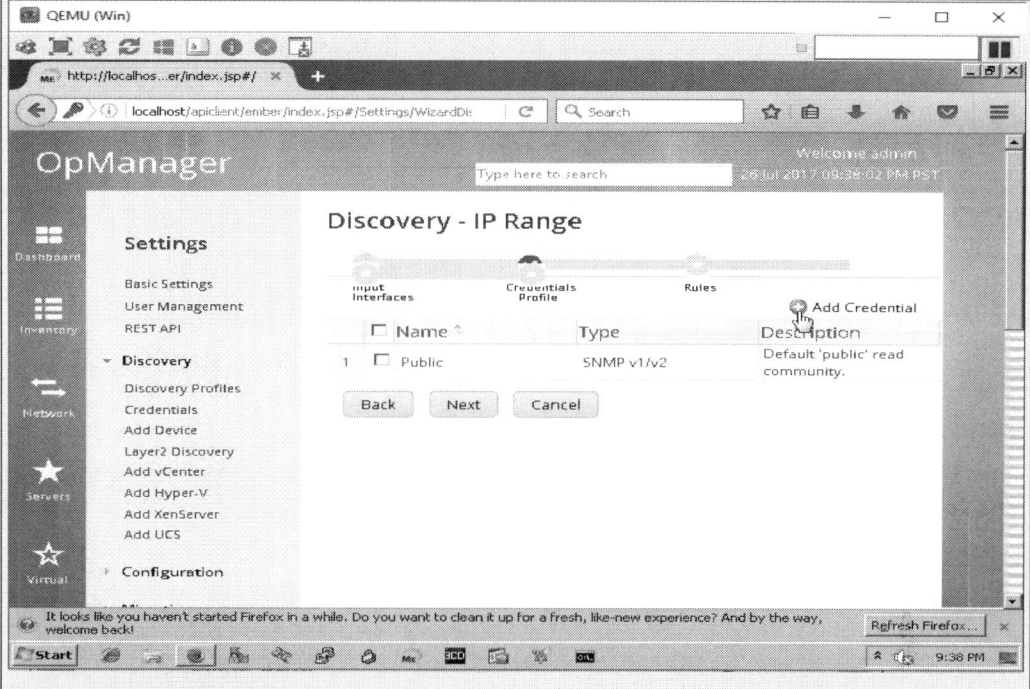

Goto "**Add Credentials**"

Enter the credentials of SNMPv3 AuthNoPriv model. Select MD5 as hashing algorithm as it has to match with R1's configuration.

Add Credential		
Credential Type	SNMP v3	
Name	MyUser	
Description	MyUser Defined on R1	
User Name	MyUser	
Context Name		
Authentication	Protocol	MD5
	Password	••••••••••
Encryption	Protocol	-
	Password	
SNMP Port	161	
SNMP Timeout (secs)	5	
SNMP Retries	0	

Save   Cancel

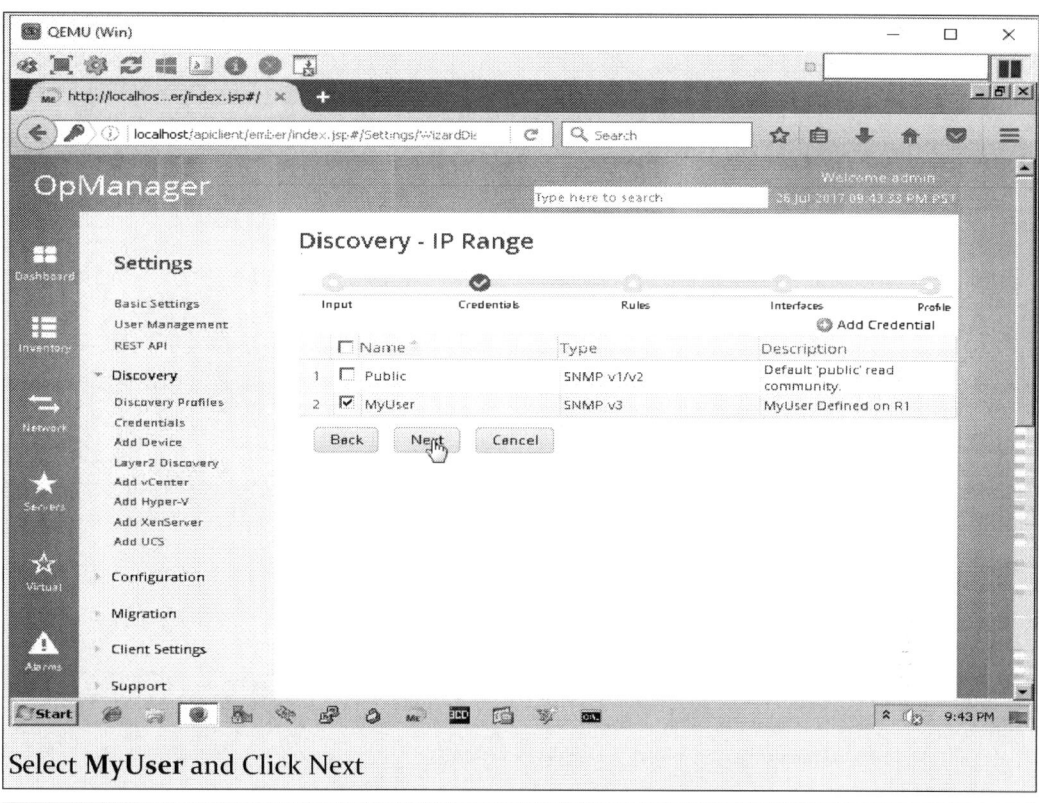

CCNA-SP Workbook

Select **MyUser** and Click Next

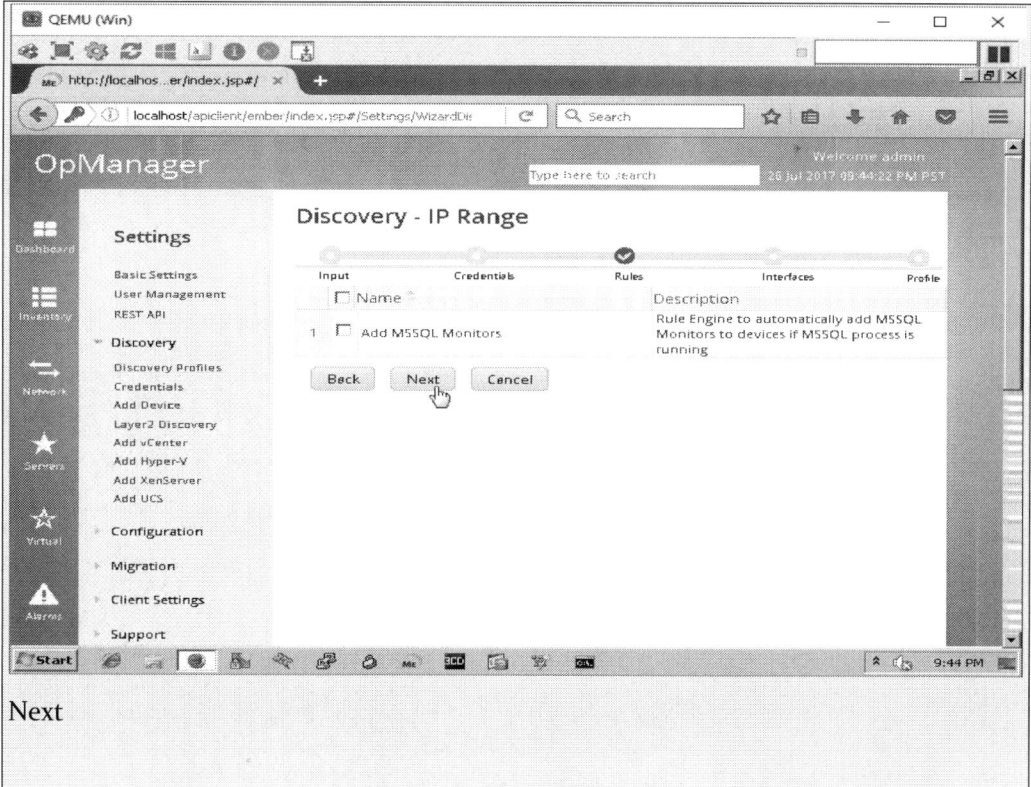

Next

IPSpecialist.net   1 August 2017

CCNA-SP Workbook

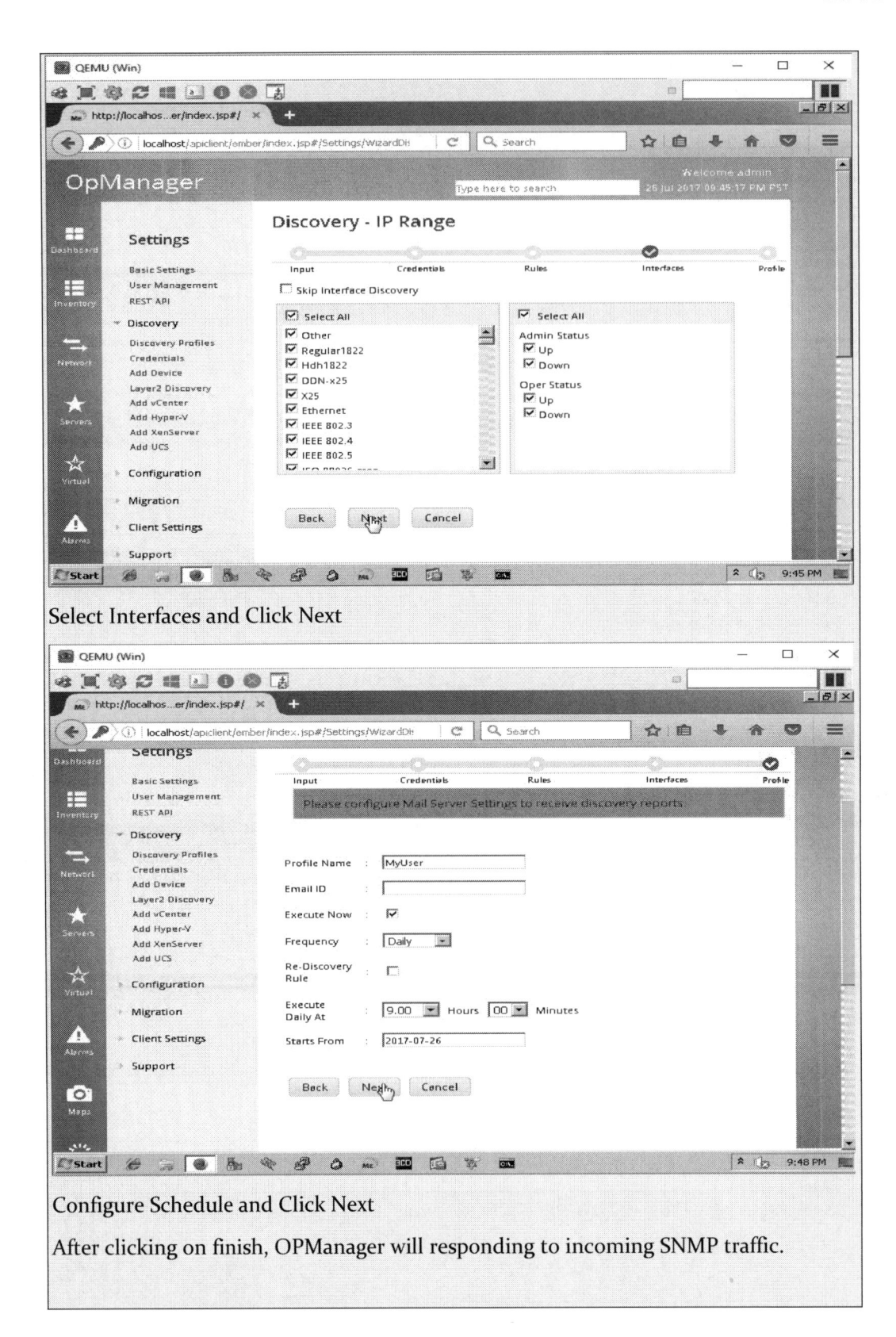

Select Interfaces and Click Next

Configure Schedule and Click Next

After clicking on finish, OPManager will responding to incoming SNMP traffic.

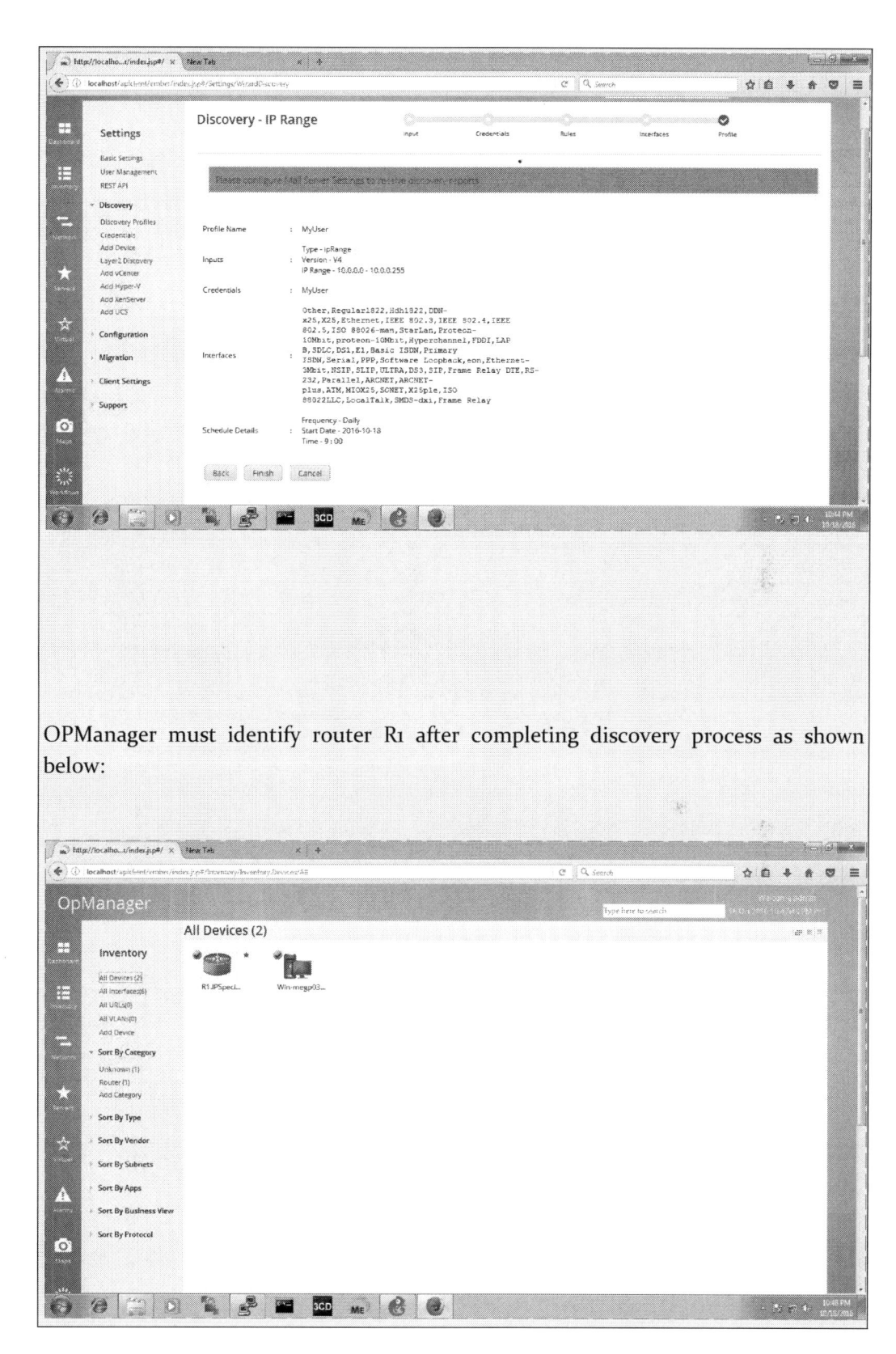

OPManager must identify router R1 after completing discovery process as shown below:

By double clicking on R1.IPSpecialist.net, it is clear that OP Manager has identified router category and its model number along with interfaces and other features.

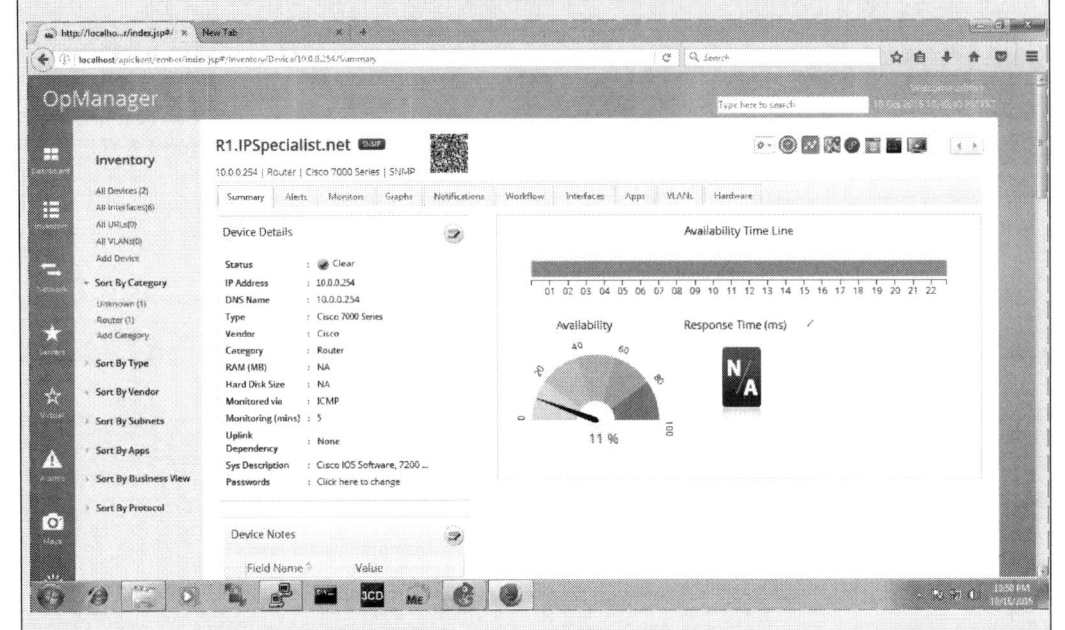

After adding every device from discovery process, Dashboard can be used to view important information. Importance of securing such important information displayed by SNMP should be clear at this stage.

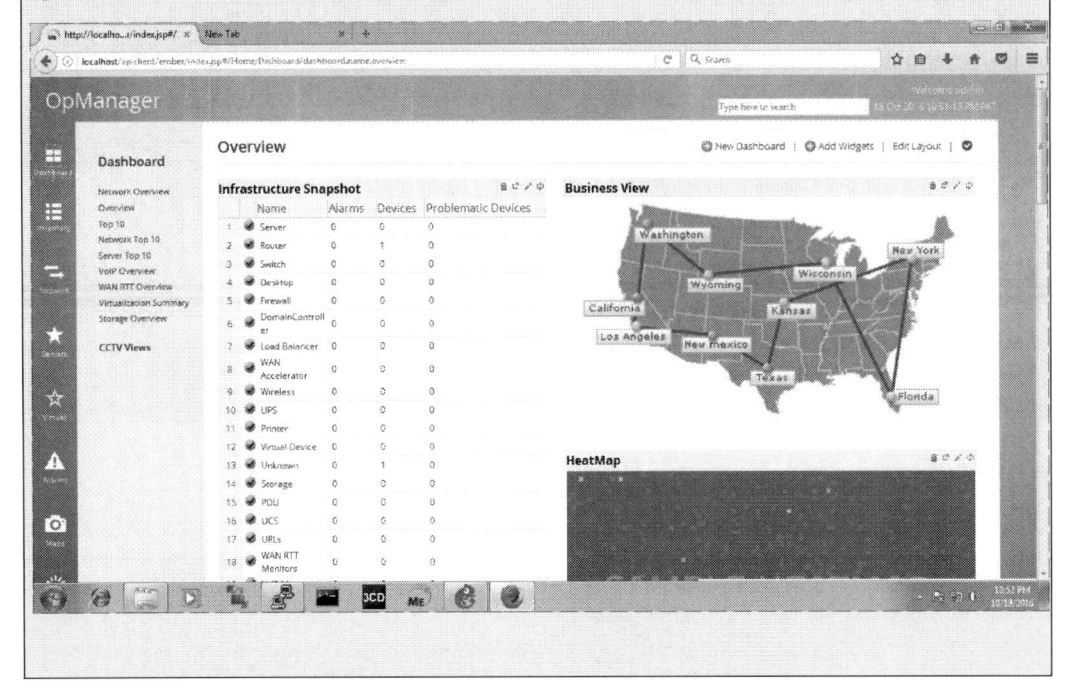

Syslog Verification:

Open source 3CDaemon server used in this lab contains Syslog server along with FTP and other servers. Click on 3CD icon on start menu to start it and view its operations. As OP Manager is also installed on same management station. We may need to stop manage engine service before starting syslog server.

To stop manage engine service, type *services.msc* in start menu and stop the *Manage Engine OPManager* service.

Following figure shows few logs received by Syslog server.

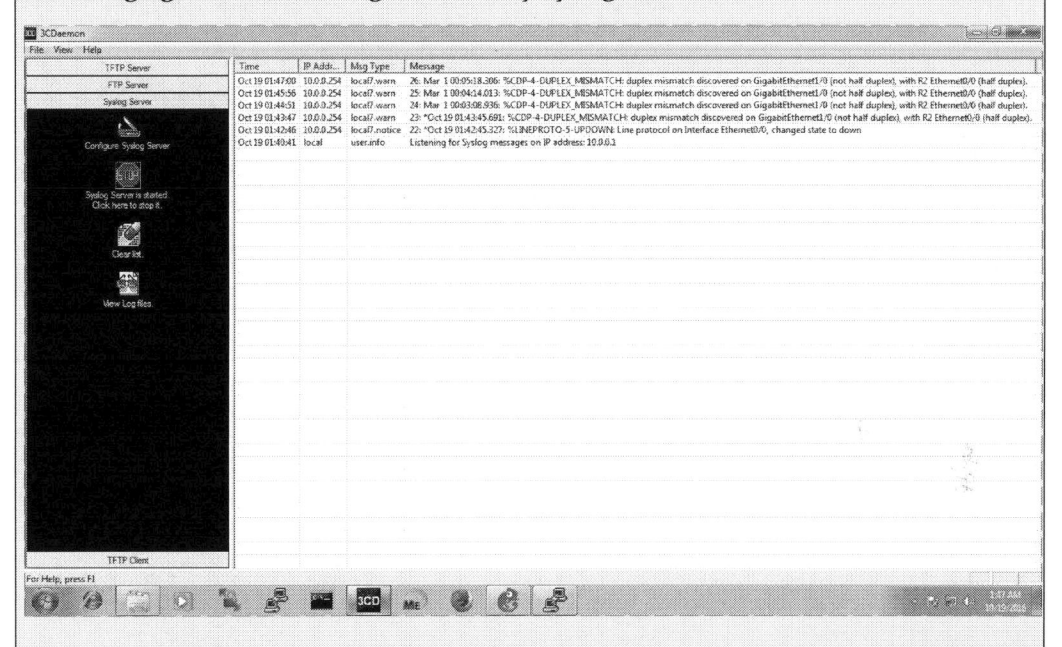

In order to use SCP for file transfer anywhere inside IOS of cisco devices, we need to enable SCP server option on cisco devices. Following command is used to make device an SCP server. SSH needs to be enabled first for SCP to work as SCP based sessions use SSH encrypted flow of data.

R2(config)#ip scp server enable.

Any scp supported software can be used from workstation to access any location within cisco IOS.

NTP Verification
NTP-Client>en
NTP-Client#config t
Enter configuration commands, one per line. End with CNTL/Z.
NTP-Client(config)#ntp update-calendar
NTP-Client(config)#end
May 12 06:16:56.468: %SYS-5-CONFIG_I: Configured from console by console
NTP-Client#show ntp status

```
NTP-Client>
NTP-Client>
NTP-Client>en
NTP-Client#config t
Enter configuration commands, one per line.  End with CNTL/Z.
NTP-Client(config)#ntp up
NTP-Client(config)#ntp update-calendar
NTP-Client(config)#end
NTP-Client#show
May 12 06:16:56.468: %SYS-5-CONFIG_I: Configured from console by console
NTP-Client#show ntp st
NTP-Client#show ntp status
Clock is synchronized, stratum 11, reference is 1.0.0.2
nominal freq is 250.0000 Hz, actual freq is 250.0000 Hz, precision is 2**10
ntp uptime is 16800 (1/100 of seconds), resolution is 4000
reference time is DCBFD1B8.59168820 (08:16:24.348 EET Fri May 12 2017)
clock offset is 0.5000 msec, root delay is 1.00 msec
root dispersion is 7942.70 msec, peer dispersion is 7938.47 msec
loopfilter state is 'CTRL' (Normal Controlled Loop), drift is 0.000000000 s/s
system poll interval is 64, last update was 38 sec ago.
NTP-Client#
```

Net Flow

Net Flow allows administrators to identify applications causing network congestion, diagnose slow performance, and verify that an application receives the appropriate amount of bandwidth based on its class of service (CoS). Benefits include network, application, and user monitoring; network planning; and accounting/billing. Minimally, a flow must contain a source IP address, a destination IP address, and an ingress interface. Traffic is considered in the same flow if the packets contain the same IP addressing, port numbers, and layer 3-protocol information. Sending flow information to a collector can be CPU-intensive. One concern with a collector is the number of devices and amount of flow information the collector will receive. Version 5 is the most common implementation of Net Flow. Flow monitors are Net Flow components that allow you to globally define Net Flow parameters, like the cache size and the number of unique flow records to collect. This configuration is then applied to a respective interface. **The show ip cache flow** command visualizes the general Net Flow data captured by an IOS device.

Net Flow Configuration

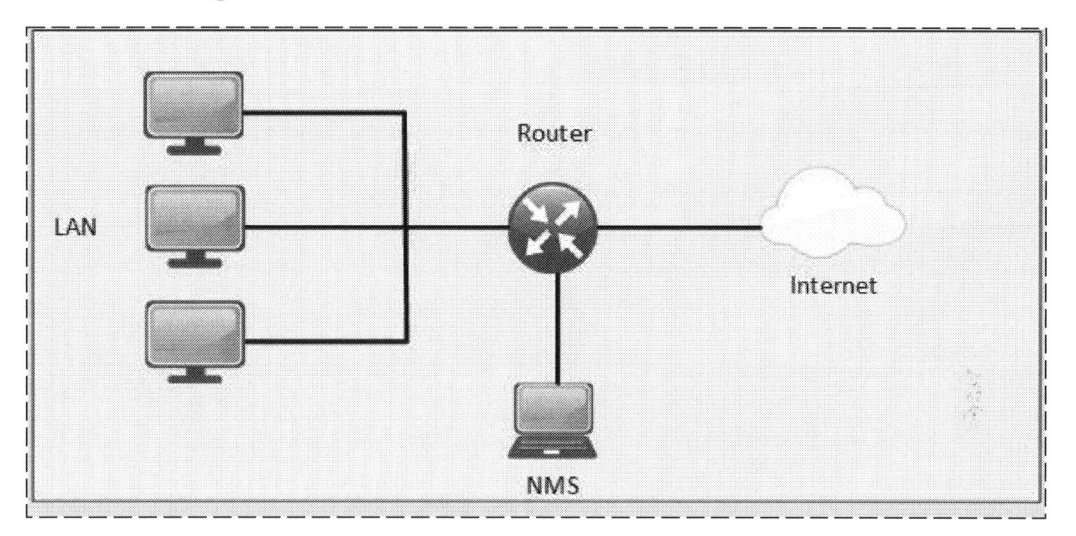

Figure 26 NetFlow configuration example

To configure NetFlow, you must perform the following four tasks:

1. Enable data capturing on an interface: ingress is incoming and egress is outgoing.
2. Define the IP address and UDP port of the NetFlow collector.
3. Optionally identify the version of NetFlow to export the flow information.
4. Verify the NetFlow configuration, operation, and statistics.

The following commands show how to enable NetFlow from the CLI and how to export the information to a NetFlow collector:

Lab 3.2 Configuration of NetFlow Exporter on Cisco Routers.

As explained in previous section of NetFlow, one of the components of NetFlow i.e. exporter needs to be configured on a device whose interface traffic needs to be analysed. Exporter will send this traffic back to the management station where dedicated NetFlow Analyzer software is running. Commercially available NetFlow softwares have their own requirements. For example, the software used in this lab discovers the NetFlow devices via SNMP. So previously, configure SNMP lab must be implemented before starting this lab.

NetFlow exporter will be configured on R1 and Firewall in this lab and then different types of traffic will be generated from management station to analyse the behaviour of NetFlow.

R1
R1(config)# snmp-server view MyView iso included
R1#sho snmp engineID
Local SNMP engineID: 800000090300C2061B750000
R1(config)#snmp-server engineID remote 10.0.0.2 800000090300C2061B750000
R1(config)#snmp-server group MyGroup v3 auth read MyView access SNMP-ACL
R1(config)#IP access-list standard SNMP-ACL
R1(config-std-nacl)#permit host 10.0.0.2
R1(config)# snmp-server user MyUser MyGroup v3 auth md5 P@$$word:10

Above commands configure SNMPv3 on Route R1 with read access to management station ! (10.0.0.1) only.

R1(config)# flow exporter EXPORT-1
R1(config-flow-exporter)# destination 10.0.0.2
R1(config-flow-exporter)#transport udp 9996
R1(config-flow-exporter)#source fastEthernet 0/0

Above commands create an exporter object with name EXPORT-1. UDP port number 9996 ! is configured for NetFlow. As of our lab scenario, all traffic from management station hits ! fastEthernet 0/0 of R1. So FastEthernet 0/0 is configured as source interface for capturing ! NetFlow statistics.

R1(config)#flow monitor MONITOR-1
R1(config-flow-monitor)#record netflow ipv4 original-input
R1(config-flow-monitor)#exporter EXPORT-1

Above commands define the record type i.e. the type if data collected by NetFlow instance. This information will be exported to management station for NetFlow

Analyzer by EXPORT-1. In the final step, go to the desired interface and apply the monitor instance in ! desired direction.

R1(config)#interface fastEthernet 0/0

R1(config-if)#IP flow monitor MONITOR-1 input

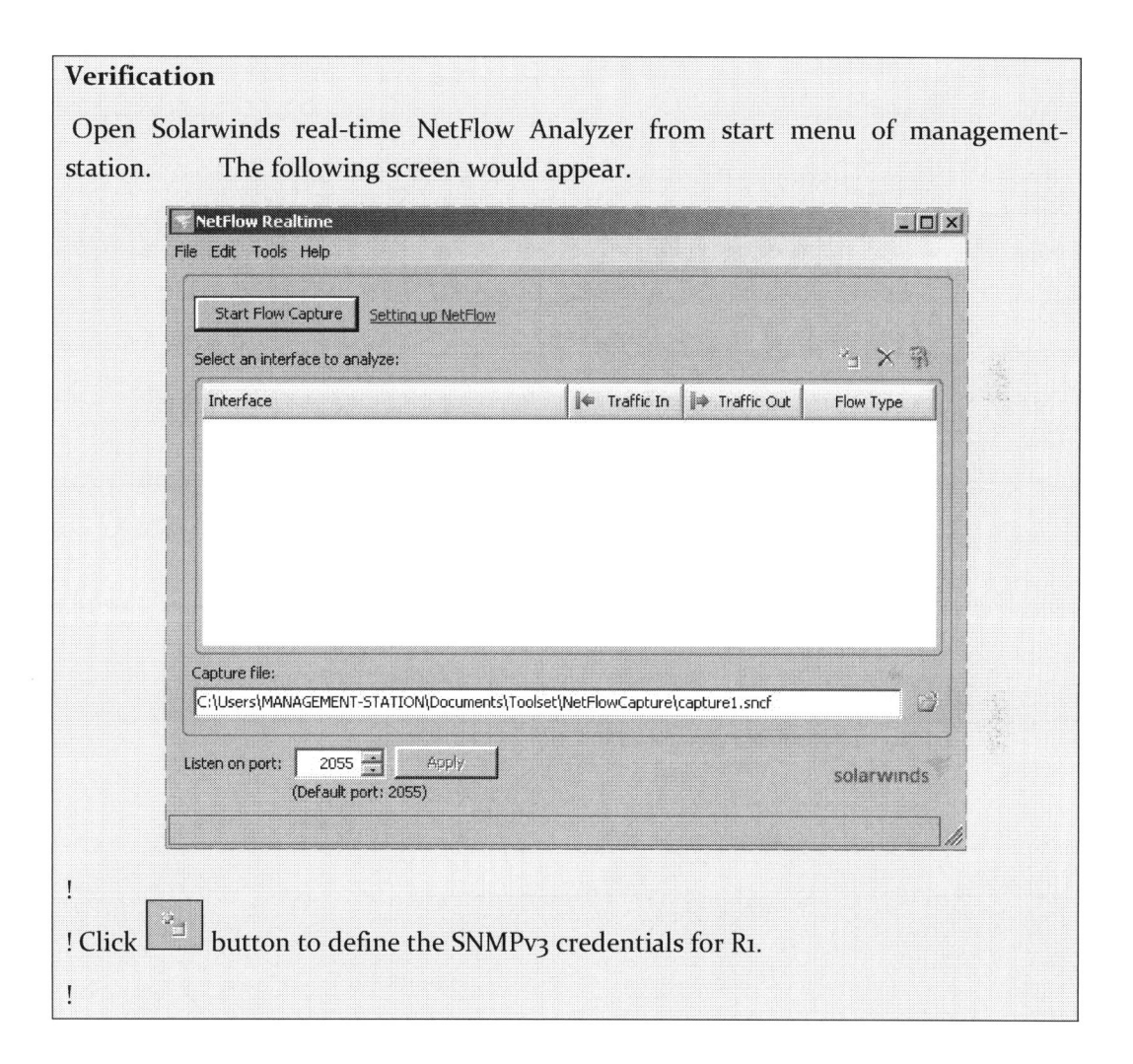

Verification

Open Solarwinds real-time NetFlow Analyzer from start menu of management-station. The following screen would appear.

!
! Click button to define the SNMPv3 credentials for R1.
!

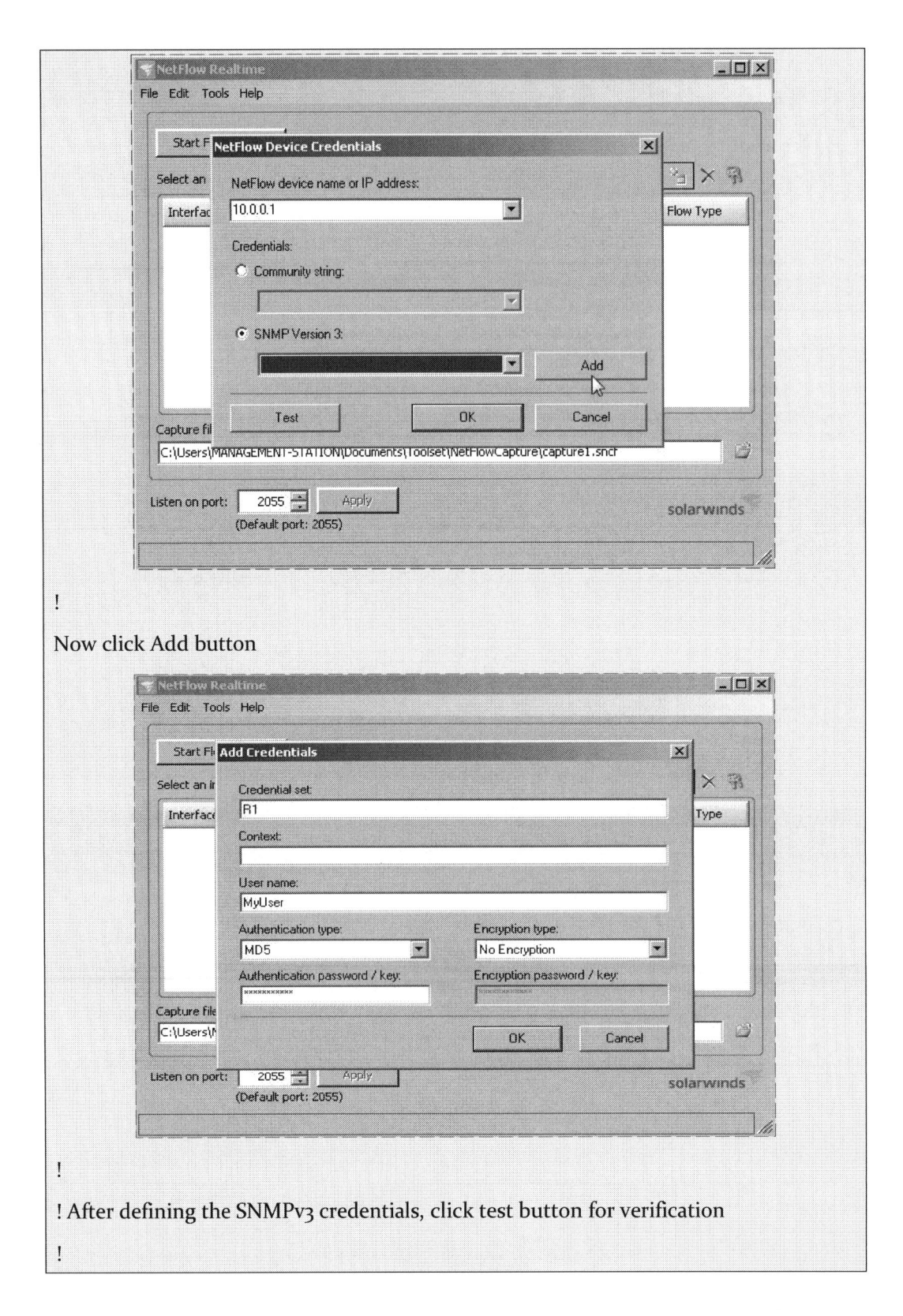

!

Now click Add button

!

! After defining the SNMPv3 credentials, click test button for verification

!

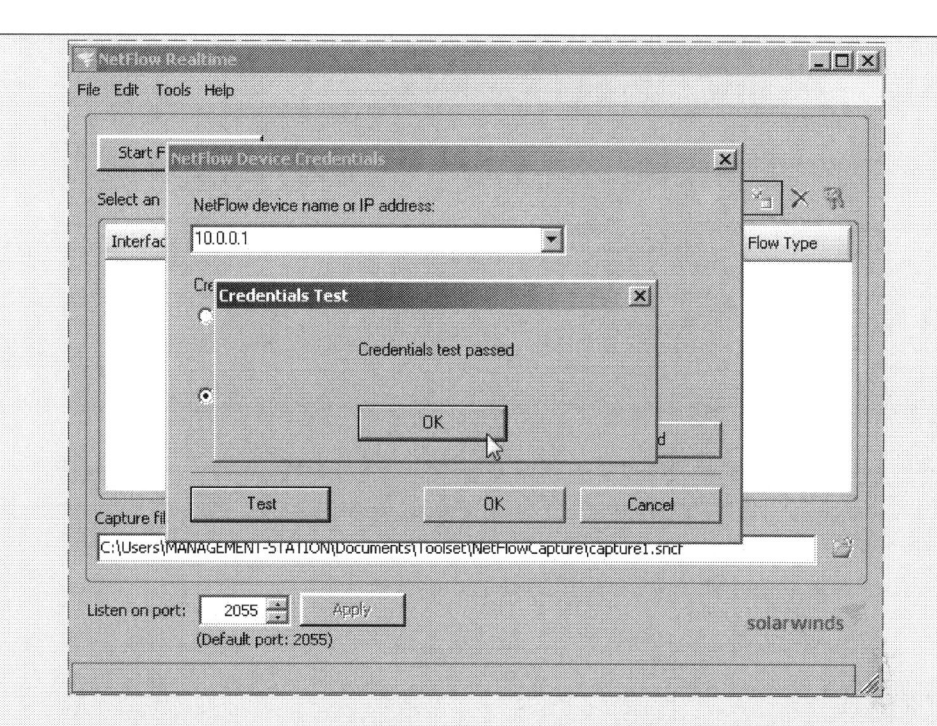

After clicking OK, R1 should appear in main window of NetFlow Analyzer. Change the port to 9996

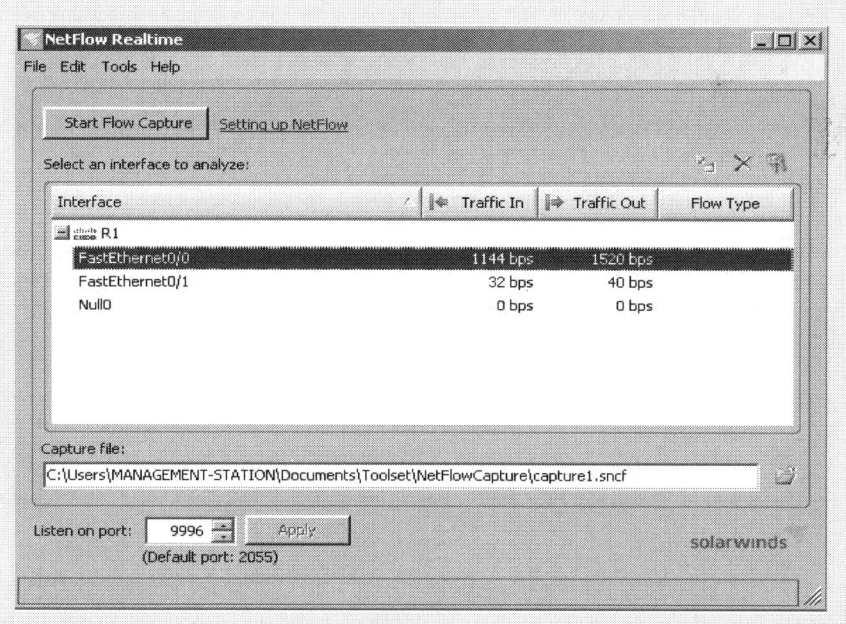

Showing Traffic in and Traffic Out over interfaces in bps

R1# show flow export EXPORT-1

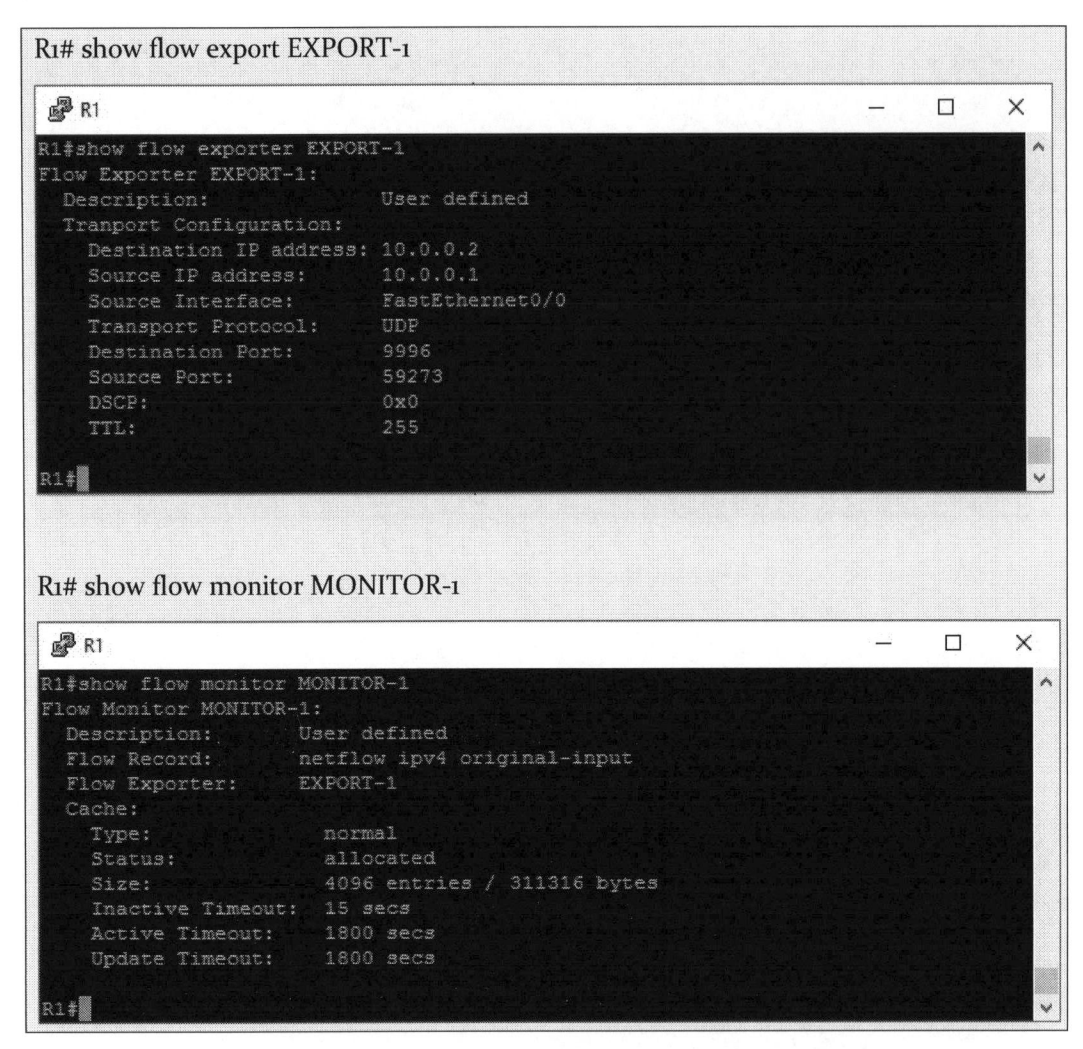

```
R1#show flow exporter EXPORT-1
Flow Exporter EXPORT-1:
  Description:           User defined
  Tranport Configuration:
    Destination IP address: 10.0.0.2
    Source IP address:      10.0.0.1
    Source Interface:       FastEthernet0/0
    Transport Protocol:     UDP
    Destination Port:       9996
    Source Port:            59273
    DSCP:                   0x0
    TTL:                    255
R1#
```

R1# show flow monitor MONITOR-1

```
R1#show flow monitor MONITOR-1
Flow Monitor MONITOR-1:
  Description:     User defined
  Flow Record:     netflow ipv4 original-input
  Flow Exporter:   EXPORT-1
  Cache:
    Type:             normal
    Status:           allocated
    Size:             4096 entries / 311316 bytes
    Inactive Timeout: 15 secs
    Active Timeout:   1800 secs
    Update Timeout:   1800 secs
R1#
```

CDP

CDP is a Cisco-proprietary protocol that works between Cisco devices at the data link layer. CDP information sends only between directly connected Cisco devices; a Cisco device never forwards a CDP frame. CDP enables systems that support different network layer protocols to communicate and enables other Cisco devices on the network to be discovered. CDP provides a summary of directly connected switches, routers, and various Cisco devices.

CDP is a media- and protocol-independent protocol that is enabled by default on each supported interface of Cisco equipment's (such as routers, access servers, and switches). The physical media must support Subnetwork Access Protocol encapsulation.

CDP Information

Information in CDP frames includes the following:

- Device ID: The name of the neighbor device and either the MAC address or the serial number of the device.

- Local Interface: The local (on this device) interface connected to the discovered neighbor.

- Hold time: The remaining amount of time (in seconds) that the local device holds the CDP advertisement from a sending device before discarding it.

- Capability List: The type of device discovered (R—Router, T—Trans Bridge, B—Source Route Bridge, S—Switch, H—Host, I—IGMP, r—Repeater).

- Platform: The device's product type.

- Port Identifier (ID): The port (interface) number on the discovered neighbor on which the advertisement is sent. This is the interface on the neighbor device to which the local device is connected.

- Address List: All network layer protocol addresses configured on the interface (or, in the case of protocols configured globally, on the device). Examples include IP, Internetwork Packet Exchange, and DECnet.

Configuring the CDP Characteristics

You can configure the frequency of CDP updates, the amount of time to hold the information before discarding it, and whether or not to send Version-2 advertisements.

Beginning in privileged EXEC mode, follow these steps to configure the CDP timer, holdtime, and advertisement type.

This example shows how to configure CDP characteristics.

```
Switch# configure terminal
Switch(config)# cdp timer 40
Switch(config)# cdp holdtime 130
Switch(config)# cdp advertise-v2
Switch(config)# end
```

CDP is enabled by default.
This example shows how to enable CDP if it has been disabled.

```
Switch# configure terminal
Switch(config)# cdp run
Switch(config)# end
```

CDP is enabled by default on all supported interfaces to send and to receive CDP information.

This example shows how to enable CDP on a port when it has been disabled.

```
Switch# configure terminal
Switch(config)# interface gigabitethernet1/0/2
Switch(config-if)# cdp enable
Switch(config-if)# end
```

Cisco IP SLA

Cisco IP SLA is a technology that actively monitors traffic to measure the performance of the network by measuring critical parameters for traffic passing Cisco IOS software devices and other network application servers. By leveraging Cisco IP SLA, it is possible to make the network sensitive to critical metrics that affect network performance and that of the associated applications. With increasing popularity of voice and data on the network, Cisco IP SLA reports provide the most vital metrics that help in building the most business-friendly network.

IP SLA Advantages:

- Embedded in Cisco IOS that rules out the need for any separate hardware or software installation
- Automated, real-time and accurate monitoring of network health
- End to end monitoring
- No additional hardware cost
- Vast extent of pervasiveness
- Measurement of critical factors like jitter, latency, packet loss, MoS and RTT
- Extreme ease of deploying

Lab 3-3 : IP SLA

IP SLA Configuration

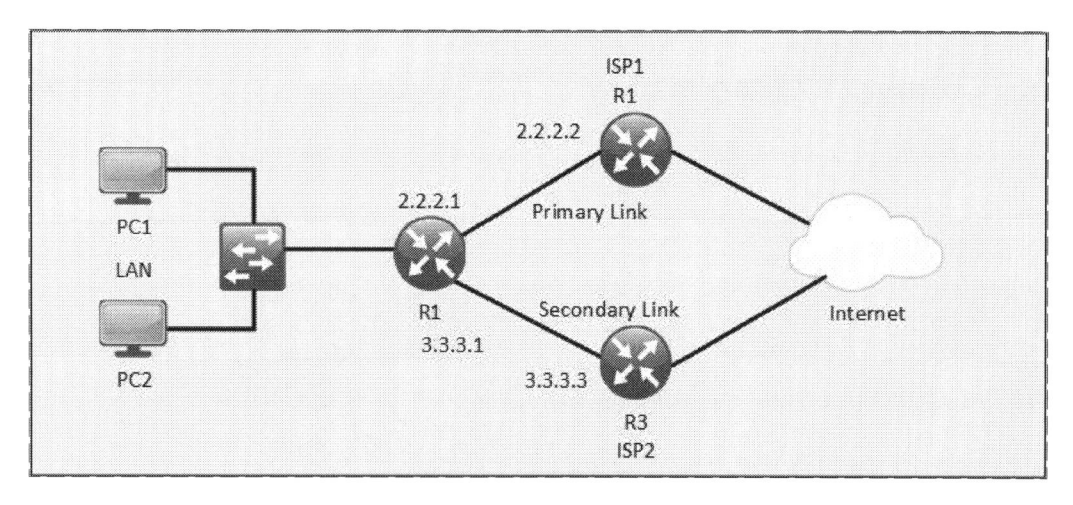

Figure 27 IP SLA Configuration Toplogy

In the above figure, the Cisco device is connected to two WAN links ISP1 and ISP2. The most common setup that we use in day-to-day life is to have to default routes configured on the Cisco router pointing to the respective next hop IPs as shown below:

```
R1(config)# ip route 0.0.0.0 0.0.0.0 2.2.2.2
R1(config)# ip route 0.0.0.0 0.0.0.0 3.3.3.3 10
```

If you notice the Administrative Distance for the secondary route, pointing to ISP2 is increased to 10 so that it becomes the backup link.

The above configuration with just two floating static routes partially accomplishes our requirement, as it will work only in the scenario where the routers interfaces connected to the WAN link are in up/down or down/down status. However, in many situations we see that even though the links remain up but we are not able to reach the gateway, this usually happens when the issue is at the ISP side.

In such scenarios, IP SLAs becomes an engineer's best friend. With around six additional IOS commands we can have a more reliable automatic failover environment.

Using IP SLA the Cisco IOS gets the ability to use Internet Control Message Protocol (ICMP) pings to identify when a WAN link goes down at the remote end and hence allows the initiation of a backup connection from an alternative port. The Reliable Static Routing Backup using Object Tracking feature can ensure reliable backup in the case of several catastrophic events, such as Internet circuit failure or peer device failure.

IP SLA is configured to ping a target, such as a publicly routable IP address or a target inside the corporate network or your next-hop IP on the ISP's router. The pings are routed from the primary interface only. Following a sample configuration of IP SLA to generate icmp ping targeted at the ISP1s next-hop IP.

```
R1(config)# ip sla 1
R1(config)# icmp-echo 2.2.2.2 source-interface FastEthernet0/1
R1(config)# timeout 1000
R1(config)# threshold 200
R1(config)# frequency 3
R1(config)# ip sla schedule 1 life forever start-time now
```

The above configuration defines and starts an IP SLA probe.

The ICMP Echo probe sends an ICMP Echo packet to next-hop IP 2.2.2.2 every 3 seconds, as defined by the "frequency" parameter.

Timeout sets the amount of time (in milliseconds) for which the Cisco IOS IP SLAs operation waits for a response from its request packet.

Threshold sets the rising threshold that generates a reaction event and stores history information for the Cisco IOS IP SLAs operation.

After defining the IP SLA operation our next step is to define an object that tracks the SLA probe. This can be accomplished by using the IOS Track Object as shown below:

```
R1(config)# track 1 ip sla 1 reachability
or
R1(config)# track 1 rtr 1 reachability
// Same function of command for Different version of Routers.
```

The Last step in the IP SLA Reliable Static Route configuration is to add the **track** statement to the default routes pointing to the ISP routers as shown below:

```
R1(config)# ip route 0.0.0.0 0.0.0.0 2.2.2.2 track 1
R1(config)# ip route 0.0.0.0 0.0.0.0 3.3.3.3 10
```

The track number keyword and argument combination specifies that the static route will be installed only if the state of the configured track object is up. Hence, if the track status is down the secondary route will be used to forward all the traffic.

The above command will track the state of the IP SLA operation. If there are no ping responses from the next-hop IP the track will go down and it will come up when the ip sla operation starts receiving ping response.

To verify the track status, use the use the show track command as shown below:

```
R1# show track
```

```
 R1                                                  —  □  ×
Router(config)#do show track
Track 1
  Response Time Reporter 1 reachability
  Reachability is Up
    2 changes, last change 00:04:36
  Latest operation return code: OK
  Latest RTT (millisecs) 31
  Tracked by:
    STATIC-IP-ROUTING 0
Router(config)#
Router#
```

The above output shows that the track status is down. Every IP SLAs operation maintains an operation return-code value. The tracking process interprets this return code. The return code may return OK, OverThreshold, and several other return codes.

Different operations may have different return-code values, so only values common to all operation types are used. The below table shows the track states as per the IP SLA return code.

Tracking	Return Code	Track State
Reachability	OK or over threshold	Up
	(all other return codes)	Down

Table 10

Cisco IOS Call Home Feature

Call Home provides email-based and web-based notification of critical system events. A versatile range of message formats is available for optimal compatibility with pager services, standard email, or XML-based automated parsing applications. Common uses of this feature may include direct paging of a network support engineer, email notification to a Network Operations Centre, XML delivery to a support website, and utilization of Cisco Smart Call Home services for direct case generation with the Cisco Systems Technical Assistance Centre (TAC). The Call Home feature can deliver alert messages containing information on configuration, diagnostics, environmental conditions, inventory, and syslog events. The Call Home feature can deliver alerts to multiple recipients, referred to as Call Home destination profiles, each with configurable message formats and content categories. A predefined destination profile (CiscoTAC-1) is provided, and you can define your own destination profiles. The CiscoTAC-1 profile is used to send alerts to the backend server of the Smart Call Home service, which can be used to create service requests to the Cisco TAC (depending on the Smart Call Home service support in place for your device and the severity of the alert). Flexible message delivery and format options make it easy to integrate specific support requirements. If multiple destination profiles are configured, and one fails, the system will try every configured profile before sending a failure message. The Call Home feature provides these functions:

- Multiple message-format options: – Short Text—Suitable for pagers or printed reports. – Plain Text—Full formatted message information suitable for human reading. – XML—Machine readable format using Extensible Mark-up Language (XML) and Adaptive Mark-up Language (AML) document type definitions (DTDs). The XML format enables communication with the Cisco Smart Call Home server. • Multiple concurrent message destinations.

- Multiple message categories including configuration, diagnostics, environmental conditions, inventory, and syslog events.

- Filtering of messages by severity and pattern matching.

- Scheduling of periodic message sending.

- Continuous device health monitoring and real-time diagnostics alerts.

- Analysis of Call Home messages from your device and, where supported, Automatic Service Request generation, routed to the appropriate TAC team, including detailed diagnostic information to speed problem resolution.

- Secure message transport directly from your device or through a downloadable Transport Gateway (TG) aggregation point. You can use a TG aggregation point in cases requiring support for multiple devices or in cases where security requirements mandate that your devices may not be connected directly to the Internet.

- Web-based access to Call Home messages and recommendations, inventory and configuration information for all Call Home devices that provides access to associated Field Notices, Security Advisories and End-of-Life Information.

Technical Assistance Center (TAC)

For all customers, partners, resellers and distributors who hold valid Cisco service contracts, Cisco provides around-the-clock, award-winning technical support services, online and over the phone. Online service request tools are available to registered Cisco.com users with a valid service contract. Start with the Cisco TAC Service Request Tool to create a service request. This tool lets you describe the issue in your own words and attach files to the service request. It will then route your service request to an appropriate engineer as fast as possible. You can also use the Cisco TAC Service Request Tool to update your service request. This tool lets you update a service request in less than half the time it takes to dictate changes to a Cisco representative over the telephone. Moreover, the tool will send an automatic alert to your Cisco TAC engineer when you submit any updates.

How to Open a TAC Case

To open a TAC case, Customers/Partners may access the TAC Service Request Tool at the following URLs:

- English: http://tools.cisco.com/ServiceRequestTool/create/launch.do
- Japanese: http://tools.cisco.com/ServiceRequestTool/create/ChangeLocale.do?locale=ja_JP&forward=/launch
- Click on the link "Create a new TAC Service Request."

The TAC Service Request Tool allows Customers/Partners to:

- Open severity 3 and 4 service requests
- Check the current status of open service requests
- Update open service requests with your own notes
- Attach files to open service requests
- View service requests closed within the last 18-months If you describe a severity 3 or 4 service request online, the tool recommends resources that it may provide a solution immediately. If you have a severity 1 or 2 network-down emergency, open your service request by telephone.

Cisco Support Tools

Cisco Support Tools is an application that contains a suite of utilities that allow you to manage and troubleshoot servers that run broad range of Cisco Unified product software components. Through Support Tools, you can troubleshoot configuration and performance problems on these systems from any machine running a supported version of Windows and Internet Explorer on your network that can access the Support Tools Server. Access to utilities in the Support Tools suite is through a browser-based interface--the Support Tools Dashboard--installed on the Support Tools Server. Levels of security control both access to the Dashboard and the ability to use specific tools once logged in. In low bandwidth conditions (for example, via dial-up access) or when Web browsing is otherwise impractical, many Support Tools utilities can also be accessed and run via command line.

Key Features

- Unified products. It also provides key new functionality including the ability to detect events and alert you to them. The Event Detection tool collects Cisco log messages and Syslog messages from various processes.
- Interrogate individual Support Tools nodes for their hardware/OS, Cisco component, third party product information, and application specific data or files.
- View, stop, and start services running on Support Tools nodes.

- View and terminate processes running on Support Tools nodes.
- Performance Monitor.
- Compare and synchronize registry settings from different Support Tools nodes.
- Pull logs from many Support Tools nodes including the following:
    - ICM call routers
    - ICM Loggers
    - ICM Peripheral Gateways (PGs)
    - ICM Admin Workstations (AWs)
    - CTI Object Server (CTIOS)
    - Cisco Collaboration Server (CCS)
    - Cisco Unified Contact Center Express (CRS)
    - Cisco Unified IP IVR (CRS)
    - Cisco Agent Desktop (CAD)
    - Cisco Security Agent (CSA)
    - Customer Voice Portal (CVP)
    - Cisco Email Manager (CEM)
    - Cisco Media Blender (CMB)
    - Cisco Call Manager (CCM)
- Create enhanced time-synchronized merged logs across different servers.
- Set trace levels trace levels on different applications for a duration of time, and then collect logs against that application.
- Run a majority of the tools in either Interactive Mode (where one system is immediately selected and queried) or Batch Mode (where several systems can be scheduled to be queried at some point in the future)

Implementation of Management Access Techniques

SSH

Secure Shell (SSH) improves network security by establishing secure connections among networking devices for management, thereby preventing hackers from gaining access.

Using Digital Certificates, in Public/Private Key Cryptography, SSH is able to authenticate clients or servers ensuring that the device or server you are about to connect to is exactly who they claim to be.

Digital Certificates can be acquired in generally 3 different ways. The most secure (and expensive) is requesting it from a trusted company called a CA - Certificate Authorities. An example of one such company is VeriSign, which is highly popular within the CA Industry for their role in providing worldwide trusted certificates; these certificates can however cost quite a bit.

There are two other ways of requesting a certificate. One is by using an internally trusted CA (trusted within a company) also called an enterprise CA or by generating a self-sign certificate on the device itself. The last one is the least secure form, but provides more than enough security to lock down your average network device. This self-signed certificate can be generated using the built in commands on your Cisco router.

By default, when you configure a Cisco device, you have to use the console cable and connect directly to the system to access it. Follow the steps mentioned below, which will enable SSH access to your Cisco devices. Once you enable SSH, you can access it remotely using Putty or any other SSH client.

- Setup Management IP

First, make sure you have performed basic network configurations on your switch. For example, assign default gateway, assign management ip-address, etc. If this is already done, skip to the next step.

In the following example, the management ip address is set as 192.168.101.2 in the 101 VLAN. The default gateway points to the firewall, which is 192.168.101.1

- Set hostname and domain-name

Next, make sure the switch has a hostname and domain-name set properly.

```
Switch#config t
myswitch(config)# hostname myswitch
myswitch(config)# ip domain-name ipspecilist.net
myswitch(config)#ip default-gateway 192.168.101.1
myswitch(config)#interface vlan 1
myswitch(config-if)# ip address 192.168.101.2 255.255.255.0
```

- Generate the RSA Keys

The switch or router should have RSA keys that it will use during the SSH process. So, generate this using crypto command as shown below.

```
myswitch(config)# crypto key generate rsa
The name for the keys will be: ipspecialist.net
```

```
Choose the size of the key modulus in the range of 360 to 2048 for your
General Purpose Keys.
Choosing a key modulus greater than 512 may take a few minutes.
How many bits in the modulus [512]: 1024
 % Generating 1024 bit RSA keys, keys will be non-exportable...[OK
```

In addition, if you are running on an older Cisco IOS image, it is highly recommended that you upgrade to latest Cisco IOS.

- Setup the Line VTY configurations

Setup the following line vty configuration parameters, where input transport is set to SSH. Set the login to local, and password to 7.

```
myswitch(config)# line vty 0 4
myswitch (config-line)# transport input ssh
myswitch (config-line)# login local
myswitch (config-line)# password 7
myswitch (config-line)# exit
```

If you have not set the console line yet, set it to the following values.

```
myswitch(config)# line console 0
(config-line)# logging synchronous
(config-line)# login local
```

Create the username password

If you do not have a username created already, do it as shown below.

```
myswitch# config t
Enter configuration commands, one per line.  End with CNTL/Z.
myswitch(config)# username ramesh password mypassword
```

Note: If you don't have the enable password setup properly, do it now.

```
myswitch# enable secret myenablepassword
```

Make sure the password-encryption service is turned-on, which will encrypt the password, and when you do "sh run", you'll see only the encrypted password and not clear-text password.

```
myswitch# service password-encryption
```

Verify SSH access

From the switch, if you do 'sh ip ssh', it will confirm that the SSH is enabled on this cisco device.

```
myswitch# sh ip ssh
SSH Enabled - version 1.99
Authentication timeout: 120 secs; Authentication retries: 3
```

After the above configurations, login from a remote machine to verify that you can ssh to this cisco switch.

In this example, 192.168.101.2 is the management ip-address of the switch.

```
remote-machine# ssh 192.168.101.2
login as: ipspecialist
Using keyboard-interactive authentication.
Password:
myswitch>en
Password:
myswitch#
```

Telnet

Configuring Cisco Routers for Telnet access

Assuming you have configured the interface IP address settings properly just entering the following commands will configure your cisco router for telnet access.

```
Router>enable
Router#configure terminal
Router(config)#enable secret password
Router(config)#service password-encryption
Router(config)#line vty 0 4
```

```
Router(config-line)#password telnetpw
Router(config-line)#login
```

The command enable secret sets a privilege mode password and stores it in an encrypted format so that it is not visible when viewing the running configuration. If you already have a privilege mode password set, ignore the command. Replace the word password with your strong password. Similarly, after the "line vty" command replace telnetpw with your telnet password. The "service password-encryption" stores the telnet password in encrypted format.

Out-of-Band Management

In a data center network, out-of-band (OOB) management means that management traffic is traversing though a dedicated path in the network. The purpose of creating an out-of-band network is to increase the security and availability of management capabilities within the data center. OOB management enables a network administrator to access the devices in the data center for routine changes, monitoring, and troubleshooting without any dependency on the network build for user traffic. The advantage of this approach is that during a network outage, network operators can reach the devices using this OOB management network.

In a data center, dedicated switches, routers, and firewalls are deployed to create an OOB network. This network is dedicated for management traffic only and is completely isolated from the user traffic. This network provides connectivity to management tools, the management port of network devices, and ILO ports of servers.

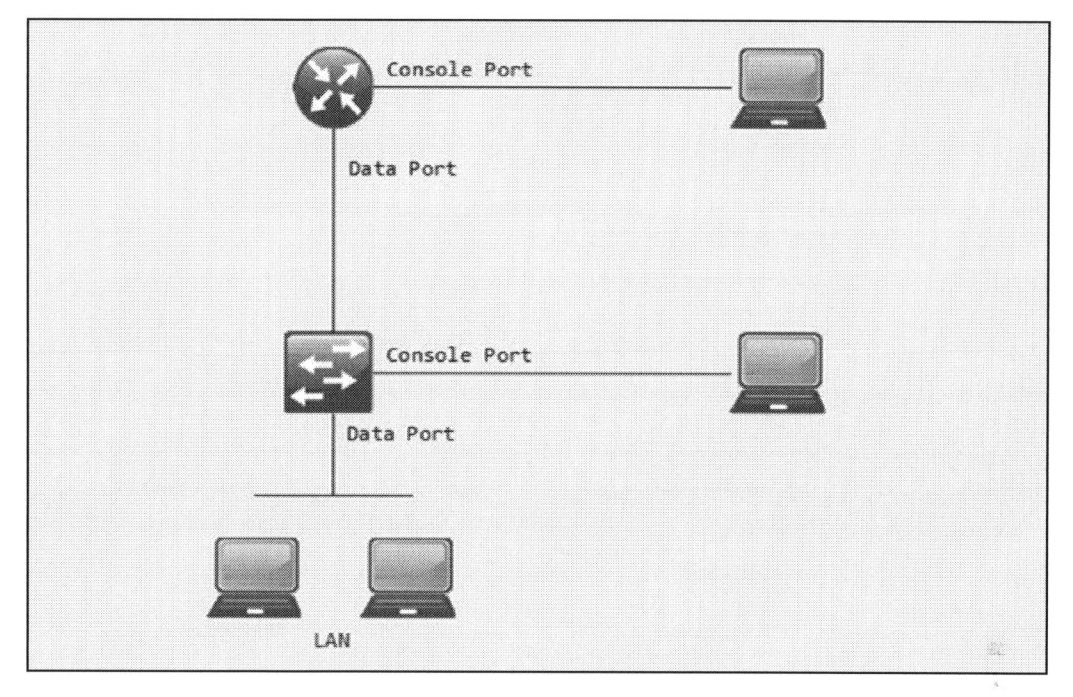

Figure 28 OOB Management

Cisco Nexus switches can be connected to the OOB management network using the following methods:

- Console port
- Connectivity Management Processor (CMP)
- Management port

Console Port

The console port is an asynchronous serial port used for initial switch configuration. It provides an RS-232 connection with an RJ-45 interface. It is recommended to connect all console ports of the devices to a terminal server router such as Cisco 2900 for remotely connecting to the console port of devices. The remote administrator connects to the terminal server router and performs a reverse telnet to connect to the console port of the device.

Connectivity Management Processor

For management high availability, the Cisco Nexus 7000 series switches have a connectivity management processor that is known as the connectivity management processor (CMP). The CMP provides OOB management and monitoring capability independent from the primary operating system.

- CMP provides a dedicated operating environment independent of the switch processor.
- It provides monitoring of supervisor status and initiation of resets.
- It provides complete visibility of the system during the entire boot process.
- It provides the capability to initiate a complete system restart.
- It provides access to critical log information on the supervisor.
- It provides the capability to take complete console control of the supervisor.

Management Port (mgmt0)

The management port of the Nexus switch is an Ethernet interface to provide OOB management connectivity. It enables you to manage the device using an IPv4 or IPv6 address. Management port is also known as mgmt0 interface. This port is part of management VRF on the switch and supports speeds of 10/100/1000 Ethernet. The OOB management interface (mgmt0) can be used to manage all VDCs. Each VDC has its own representation for mgmt0 with a unique IP address from a common management subnet for the physical switch that can be used to send syslog, SNMP, and other management information.

Implement ERSPAN

ERSPAN or Encapsulated Remote SPAN is a method of sending SPAN traffic across a layer 3 network by utilizing GRE. In the ERSPAN header, the DF bit is set and the ERSPAN packet can be up to 9202 bytes. In addition, ERSPAN on the ASR1k platform is only supported on Layer 3 ports.

This configuration will be the source router

```
router(config)#monitor session 1 type erspan-source
router(config-mon-erspan-src)#source interface g0/1/0
router(config-mon-erspan-src)#no shutdown
router(config-mon-erspan-src)#destination
router(config-mon-erspan-src-dst)#ip address 10.1.1.1
router(config-mon-erspan-src-dst)#origin ip address 10.2.2.1
router(config-mon-erspan-src-dst)#erspan-id 101
```

And this is the configuration of the destination router

```
router(config)#monitor session 1 type erspan-destination
router(config-mon-erspan-dst)#destination interface g2/0/1
router(config-mon-erspan-dst)#no shut
router(config-mon-erspan-dst)#source
router(config-mon-erspan-dst-src)#ip address 10.1.1.1
router(config-mon-erspan-dst-src)#erspan-id 101
```

SPAN

You have a user who has complained about network performance, no one else in the building is experiencing the same issues. You want to run a Network Analyser on the port like Wireshark to monitor ingress and egress traffic on the port. To do this you can configure SPAN (Switch Port Analyser). SPAN allows you to capture traffic from one port on a switch to another port on the same switch.

SPAN makes a copy of all frames destined for a port and copies them to the SPAN destination port. Certain traffic types are not forwarded by SPAN like BDPUs, CDP, DTP, VTP, STP traffic. The number of SPAN sessions that can be configured on a switch is model dependent. For example, Cisco 3560 and 3750 switches only support up to 2 SPAN sessions at once, whereas Cisco 6500 series switches support up to 16.

SPAN can be configured to capture either inbound, outbound or both directions of traffic. You can configure a SPAN source as either a specific port, a single port in an Ether channel group, an Ether channel group, or a VLAN. SPAN cannot be configured with a source port of a MEC (Multi chassis Ether channel). You also cannot configure a source of a single port and a VLAN. When configuring multiple sources for a SPAN session, you simply specify multiple source interfaces.

One thing to keep in mind when configuring SPAN is if you are using a source port that has a higher bandwidth than the destination port, some of the traffic, if the link is congested, traffic will be dropped.

Simple Local SPAN Configuration

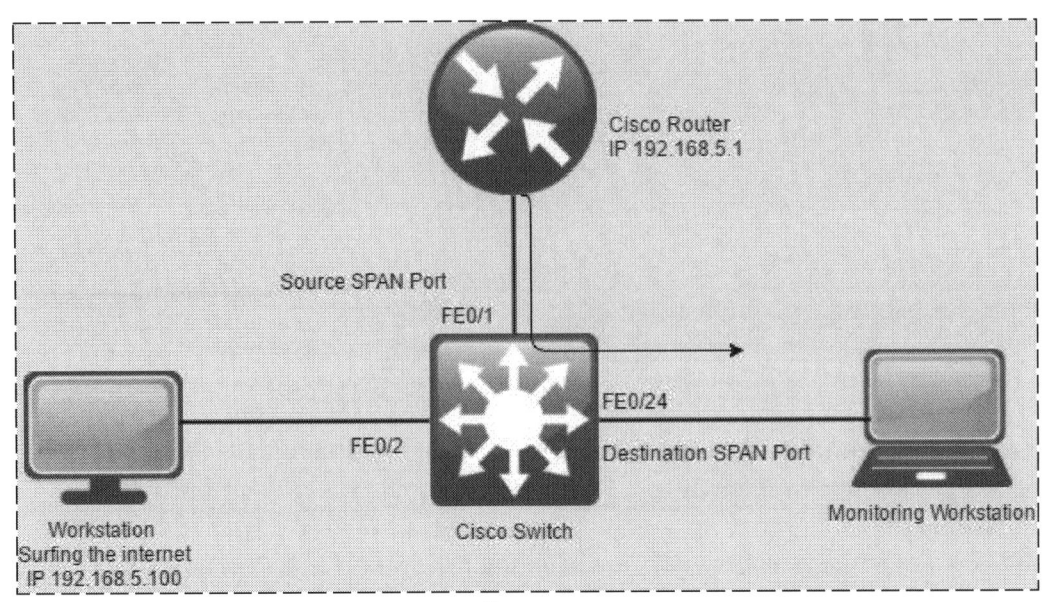

Figure 29

Since router, R1 connects to the 3550 Catalyst switch on port FE0/1, this port is configured as the Source SPAN port. Traffic copied from FE0/1 is to be mirrored out FE0/24 where our monitoring workstation is waiting to capture the traffic.

Once we have our network analyser setup and running, the first step is to configure FastEthernet 0/1 as a source SPAN port:

Catalyst-3550(config)# monitor session 1 source interface fastethernet 0/1

Next, configure FastEthernet 0/24 as the destination SPAN port:

Catalyst-3550(config)# monitor session 1 destination interface fastethernet 0/24

After entering both commands, we noticed our destination's SPAN port LED (FE0/24) began flashing in synchronisation with that of FE0/1's LED – an expected behaviour considering all FE0/1 packets were being copied to FE0/24.

Confirming the monitoring session and operation requires one simple command, *show monitor session 1*:

```
Catalyst-3550# show monitor session 1
Session 1
---------
Type                : Local Session
Source Ports        :
 Both               : Fa0/1
```

```
Destination Ports        : Fa0/24
Encapsulation            : Native
Ingress                  : Disabled
```

To display the detailed information from a saved version of the monitor configuration for a specific session, issue the show monitor session 1 detail command:

```
Catalyst-3550# show monitor session 1 detail
Session 1
---------
Type                     : Local Session
Source Ports             :
    RX Only              : None
    TX Only              : None
    Both                 : Fa0/1
Source VLANs             :
    RX Only              : None
    TX Only              : None
    Both                 : None
Source RSPAN VLAN        : None
Destination Ports        : Fa0/24
    Encapsulation        : Native
         Ingress         : Disabled
Reflector Port           : None
Filter VLANs             : None
Dest RSPAN VLAN          : None
```

Notice how the Source Ports section shows Fa0/1 for the row named both. This means that we are monitoring both RX & TX packets for Fa0/1, while the Destination Port is set to Fa0/24.

RSPAN

As a network engineer, you don't really want to get out of your seat and carry a laptop to another office or floor and have to actually talk to a user. This is why we have RSPAN or Remote SPAN. As the name suggests, RSPAN allows you to monitor a port that is on a different switch. The switches do however need to be connected over a Trunk interface meaning that you have to part of the same Layer 2 Domain in your network.

RSPAN works by configuring a special VLAN dedicated only for SPAN traffic. This traffic is copied from the source port on a switch over the Trunk interface. As with SPAN, port speed and utilization should be taken into account when configuring RSPAN. Particularly as the traffic is traversing a Trunk interface that other user VLANs are using. Too much RSPAN traffic can lead to poor performance due to link congestion.

Configuration

Configuring RSPAN is identical to SPAN. The only difference is that instead of configuring the destination port, you are configuring a destination VLAN.

First, you need to configure the RSPAN VLAN.

Next, you need to configure the RSPAN session on your source switch.

Then you configure the RSPAN session on your destination switch.

```
router(config)#vlan 999
router(config-vlan)#remote-span
router(config-vlan)#monitor session 1 source remote vlan 999
router(config)#monitor session 1 destination interface fa0/10
router(config)#end
```

That is it, RSPAN is ready to go.

Verification of RSPAN is the same as SPAN.

One thing to note is if configuring SPAN or RSPAN, you should always remove the monitor session when done. This is to ensure that no one in the future connects a PC to the network and is then able to capture confidential data.

File Transfers using FTP, SCP, TFTP, SFTP, and RCP

When it comes to managing files on your Cisco device there are many ways to do it. It is a little different on IOS-XR than it is with IOS but the same methods are available. Cisco provides the following methods of copying files to and from their devices:

- TFTP
- FTP
- SCP
- RCP

The options a Cisco device has for copying will vary depending on the model and IOS version. Unfortunately, the version of IOS-XRv only supports TFTP, FTP, and RCP. RCP (Remote Copy Protocol) is a clear text version of SCP (Secure Copy Protocol). SCP uses rsa keys to encrypt the data that is being sent while RCP simply copies everything in plain text. Configuring SCP also requires the configuration of AAA even if it is just using the local routers database. To enable SCP on Cisco IOS router use the following commands

```
router(config)#ip domain name ipspecialist.net
router(config)#crypto key gen rsa modu 2048\
router(config)#aaa new-model
router(config)#aaa authentication login default local
router(config)#aaa authorization exec default local
router(config)#ip scp server enable
router(config)#end
```

That is it, now you can use scp to copy files to and from the Cisco router using the command copy <source> scp://username:password@hostname or to copy from SCP to the local device use the command copy scp://username:password@hostname <destination>.

RCP is not something that is really used any more at all. I would almost go as far as to say that no one uses it any more but there will always be that one network that requires RCP. RCP can be enabled on IOS using the following commands

```
router(config)#ip rcmd rcp-enable
router(config)#ip rcmd remote-host ipspecialist 10.2.2.2 ipspecialist enable
router(config)#ip rcmd remote-username ipspecialist
router(config)#end
```

The above command syntax is ip rcmd remote-host <local-user> <ip address> <remote-username. After that, you can use RCP to manage files on your Cisco device using RCP.

TFTP is the most basic forms of transferring files to and from a Cisco device and requires no additional configuration. There is no encryption when transferring the files either. TFTP is probably the most commonly used form of transferring files. The commands to transfer a file using TFTP are

```
copy tftp://[ip]/[file] [dest]
Copy [source] tftp://[ip]/[file]
```

A Cisco router can also be configured as a TFTP server utilising the devices flash as a storage device. To enable a Cisco Device to serve as a TFTP server, using the command

Tftp-server flash:[filename]

FTP transfer is similar to TFTP. This can be a used transfer file to and from a Cisco device utilising FTP, which is more secure, that TFTP. Transferring files using FTP can be done as follows

Copy ftp://[username]:[password]@[ip]/[file-path] [dest]
Copy [source] ftp://[username]:[password]@[ip]/[file-path]

Chapter 4: Switched Network Technology -1

Technology Brief

Bridges and switches are communication devices that operate principally at Layer 2 of the OSI reference model. As such, they are referred to as data link layer devices. Bridges became commercially- available in the early 1980s. At the beginning, bridges connected and enabled packet forwarding between homogeneous networks. More recently, bridging between various networks has also been defined and standardized.

Several kinds of bridging have proven important as internetworking devices. Transparent bridging is found primarily in Ethernet environments, while source-route bridging occurs primarily in Token Ring environments. Translational bridging provides translation between the formats and transit principles of different media types (usually Ethernet and Token Ring). Finally, source-route transparent bridging combines the algorithms of transparent bridging and source-route bridging to enable communication in mixed Ethernet/Token Ring environments.

Today, switching technology has emerged as the evolutionary heir to bridging-based internetworking solutions. Switching implementations now dominate applications in which bridging technologies were implemented in prior network designs. Superior throughput performance, higher port density, lower per-port cost, and greater flexibility have contributed to the emergence of switches as replacement technology for bridges and as complements to routing technology.

Bridging Concept and Layer 2 Ethernet Frames

Bridging and switching occurs at the Data link layer that controls data flow, handles transmission errors, provides physical (as opposed to logical) addressing, and manages access to the physical medium. Bridges provide these functions by using various link layer protocols that dictate specific flow control, error handling, addressing, and media-access algorithms. Examples of popular link layer protocols include Ethernet, Token Ring, and FDDI.

Bridges and switches are not complicated devices. They analyze incoming frames, make forwarding decisions based on information contained in the frames, and forward the frames toward the destination. In some cases, like source-route bridging, the entire path to the destination is contained in each frame. In other cases, such as transparent bridging, frames are forwarded one hop at a time toward the destination.

Bridges are capable of filtering frames based on any Layer 2 fields. For example, a bridge can be program to reject (not forward) all frames sourced from a particular network. Because link layer information often includes a reference to an upper-layer protocol, bridges usually can filter on this parameter. Furthermore, filters can be helpful in dealing with unnecessary broadcast and multicast packets. By dividing large networks into self-contained units, bridges and switches provide several advantages. Because only a certain percentage of traffic is forwarded, a bridge or switch diminishes the traffic experienced by devices on all connected segments. The bridge and switch will act as a firewall for some potentially damaging network errors and will accommodate communication between a larger numbers of devices than would be supported on any single LAN connected to the bridge. Bridges and switches extend the effective length of a LAN, permitting the attachment of distant stations that was not previously permitted.

Types of Bridges

Three types of Bridges are used in network.

- Transparent Bridge
- Translational Bridge
- Source-route Bridge

Transparent Bridge:

Transparent Bridges is invisible to the other devices on the network. Transparent Bridge only performs the function of blocking or forwarding data based on MAC address. MAC address may also be referred as hardware address or physical address. These addresses are used to built tables and make decision regarding whether a frame should be forward and where it should be forwarded.

Translational Bridge:

Translational Bridges are useful to connect segments running at different speeds or using different protocols such as token Ring and Ethernet networks. Depending on the direction of travel, a Translational Bridge can add or remove information and fields from frame as needed.

Source-route Bridge:

IBM designed Source-route Bridges for use on Token ring networks. The sr Bridge derives the entire route of the frame embedded within the frame. This allows the Bridge to make specific decision about how the frame should be forwarded through the network.

The Basic Ethernet Frame Format

The IEEE 802.3 standard defines a basic data frame format that is required for all MAC implementations, plus several additional optional formats that are used to extend the protocol's basic capability. The basic data frame format contains the following seven fields, as shown in Figure 19.

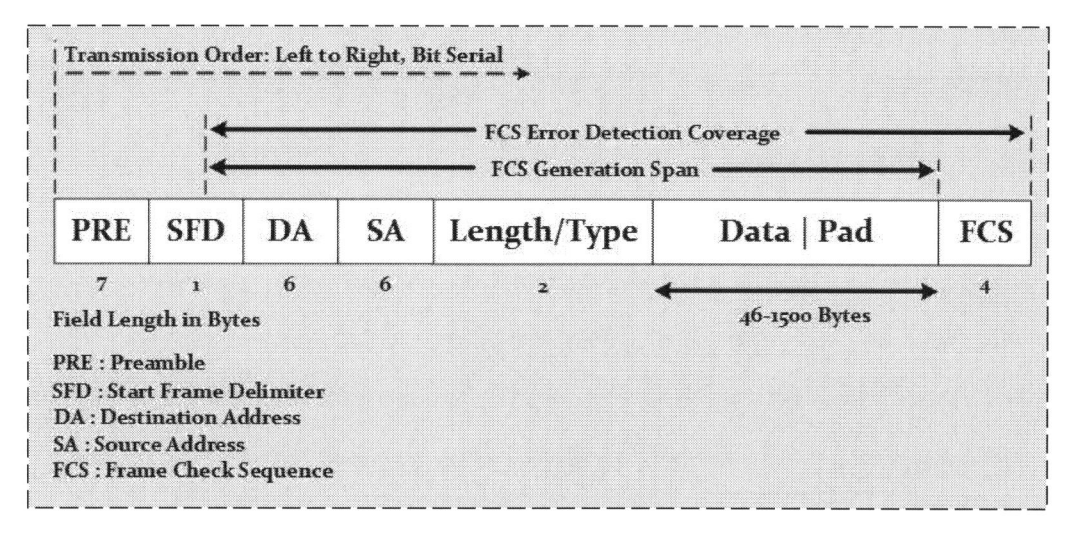

```
 _____
| Transmission Order: Left to Right, Bit Serial                  |
| - - - - - - - - - - - - - - - - - - - →                       |
|                                                                |
|         |←——————— FCS Error Detection Coverage ———————→|       |
|         |←————————— FCS Generation Span —————————→|            |
| ┌─────┬─────┬─────┬─────┬─────────────┬──────────────┬──────┐  |
| │ PRE │ SFD │ DA  │ SA  │ Length/Type │  Data | Pad  │ FCS  │  |
| └─────┴─────┴─────┴─────┴─────────────┴──────────────┴──────┘  |
|    7     1     6     6         2        ←46-1500 Bytes→    4   |
| Field Length in Bytes                                          |
|                                                                |
| PRE : Preamble                                                 |
| SFD : Start Frame Delimiter                                    |
| DA : Destination Address                                       |
| SA : Source Address                                            |
| FCS : Frame Check Sequence                                     |
|_____|
```

Figure 30 Data Frame Packet Structure

- Preamble (PRE): Consists of 7 bytes. The PRE is an alternating pattern of 1s and 0s that tells receiving stations that a frame is coming, and that provides a means to synchronize the frame-reception portions of receiving physical layers with the incoming bit stream.

- Start-of-frame delimiter (SOF): Consists of 1 byte. The SOF is an alternating pattern of 1s and 0s, ending with two consecutive 1 bits, indicating that the next bit is the leftmost bit in the leftmost byte of the destination address.

- Destination address (DA): Consists of 6 bytes. The DA field identifies which station(s) should receive the frame. In the first byte of the DA, the 2 least significant bits are used to indicate whether the destination is an individual address or group address (that is, multicast). The first of these 2 bits indicates whether the address is an individual address (indicated by a 0) or a group address (indicated by a 1). The second bit indicates whether the DA is globally administered (indicated by a 0) or locally administered (indicated by a 1). The remaining bits are a uniquely assigned value that identifies a single station, a defined group of stations, or all stations on the network.

- Source addresses (SA): Consists of 6 bytes. The SA field identifies the sending station. The SA is always an individual address, and the leftmost bit in the SA field is always 0.

- Length/Type: Consists of 2 bytes. This field indicates either the number of MAC-client data bytes that are contained in the data field of the frame, or the frame type ID if the frame is assembled using an optional format. If the Length/Type field value is less than or equal to 1500, the number of LLC bytes in the Data field is equal to the Length/Type field value. If the Length/Type field value is greater than 1536, the frame is an optional type frame, and the

Length/Type field value identifies the particular type of frame being sent or received.

- Data: Is a sequence of n bytes of any value, where n is less than or equal to 1500. If the length of the Data field is less than 46, the Data field must be extended by adding a filler (a pad) sufficient to bring the Data field length to 46 bytes.
- Note that jumbo frames up to 9000 bytes are supported on the current-generation Cisco Catalyst switches.
- Frame check sequence (FCS): Consists of 4 bytes. This sequence contains a 32-bit cyclic redundancy check (CRC) value, which is created by the sending MAC and is recalculated by the receiving MAC to check for damaged frames. The FCS is generated over the DA, SA, Length/Type, and Data fields.

Spanning Tree Protocol

High availability is a primary goal for enterprise networks, which relies on their multilayer-switched network to conduct business. One method to ensure high availability is by providing Layer 2 redundancy of devices and links throughout the network.

Network redundancy at Layer 2, however, introduces the potential for bridging loops, where packets loop endlessly between devices, crippling the network. The Spanning Tree Protocol identifies and prevents such Layer 2 loops. Multiple redundant paths among switches can cause loops in the network topology. If a loop exists, the potential for message duplication exists. When loops occur, some switches see stations appear on both sides of the switch. This condition confuses the forwarding algorithm and enables duplicate frames to be forwarded. To prevent loops while providing path redundancy, Spanning Tree Protocol (STP) defines a tree that spans all switches in an extended network. STP allow only one active path and block any redundant paths, as shown in Figure 20. In case of failure of the active path, one of the redundant paths may become the active path.

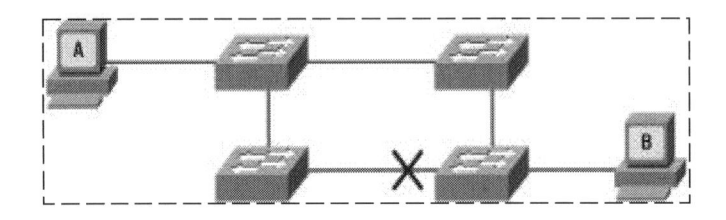

Figure 31 Spanning Tree Protocol

STP Operation

STP uses the concepts of root bridges, root ports, designated, and nondesignated ports to establish a loop-free path through the network. STP initially converges on a logically loop-free network topology by performing these steps:

Elects one root bridge:

The protocol uses a process to elect a root bridge. Only one bridge acts as the root bridge in a given network per VLAN. On the root bridge, all ports act as designated ports. Designated ports send and receive traffic and configuration messages, or BPDUs. In the sample scenario in the following figure, switch X wins the election as the root bridge because it has the lower priority parameter.

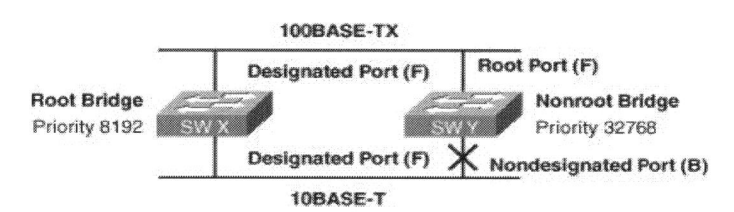

Figure 32 Root Bridge election

Selects the root port on all nonroot bridges:

The protocol establishes one root port on each nonroot bridge. The root port is the lowest-cost path from the nonroot bridge to the root bridge. Root ports send and receive traffic. If a nonroot bridge has two or more equal-cost paths to the root, the nonroot bridge selects the port that has lowest port ID. Port ID consists of a configurable priority + Port number that defaults to the lowest port number when all eligible root ports have equal priority. In the scenario in Figure 3-2, from Switch Y, the lowest-cost path to the root bridge is through the 100BASE-TX Fast Ethernet link.

Selects the designated port on each segment:

On each segment, STP establishes one designated port on the bridge that has the lowest path cost to the root bridge. In the scenario in Figure 3-2, the designated port for both segments is on the root bridge because the root bridge directly connects to both segments. The 10BASE-T Ethernet port on Switch Y is a nondesignated port because there is only one designated port per segment. The switch primarily chooses a designated port as the least-cost path to the root bridge. In the event of a tie, the bridge ID acts as the tiebreaker and if the bridge ID is same then lowest physical port number as the tiebreaker. This table summarizes the port roles in a no designated switch.

Port Role	Description
Root port	This port exists on non-root bridges and is the switch port with the best path to the root bridge. Root port forward data traffic toward

	the root bridge and the source MAC address of frames received on the root port can populate the MAC table. Only one root port is enabled per bridge
Designated port	This port exists on root and bridges. For root bridge, all switch port is designated port. For nonroot bridges, a designated port is the switch port that receives and forwards the data frames towards the root bridge as needed. Only one designated port is enabled per segment.
Non Designated Port	The non-designated port is a switch port that is not forwarding (blocking) data frames and not populating the MAC address table with the source address of frames seen on that segment
Disable Port	The disabled port is a switch port that is shutdown

Table 11 STP Ports

By examining the switch port roles on a switch, STP can determine the most desirable forwarding path for data frames.

Each Layer 2 port on a switch running STP exists in one of these five port states:

- Blocking: The Layer 2 port is a nondesignated port and does not participate in frame forwarding. The port receives BPDUs to determine the location and root ID of the root switch and which port roles (root, designated, or nondesignated) each switch port should assume in the final active STP topology. By default, the port spends 20 seconds in this state (max age).
- Listening: Spanning tree has determined that the port can participate in frame forwarding according to the BPDUs that the switch has received so far. At this point, the switch port is not only receiving BPDUs, but it is also transmitting its own BPDUs and informing adjacent switches that the switch port is preparing to participate in the active topology. By default, the port spends 15 seconds in this state (forward delay).
- Learning: The Layer 2 port prepares to participate in frame forwarding and begins to populate the CAM table. By default, the port spends 15 seconds in this state (forward delay).
- Forwarding: The Layer 2 port is considered part of the active topology; it forwards frames and also sends and receives BPDUs.
- Disabled: The Layer 2 port does not participate in spanning tree and does not forward frames.

To determine its root port (best port toward the root bridge), each switch uses a cost value. Each port link speed is associated to a cost. The cost to the root bridge is calculated using the cumulative costs of all links between the local switch and the root bridge that becomes the path cost.

Default individual port cost values are:

- 10 Gbps link: Cost 1
- 1 Gbps link: Cost 4
- 100 Mbps link: Cost 19
- 10 Mbps link: Cost 100

In the following figure, switch 0000.1111.3333 has three links that can link to the root bridge. Suppose that all links are 100 Mbps links.

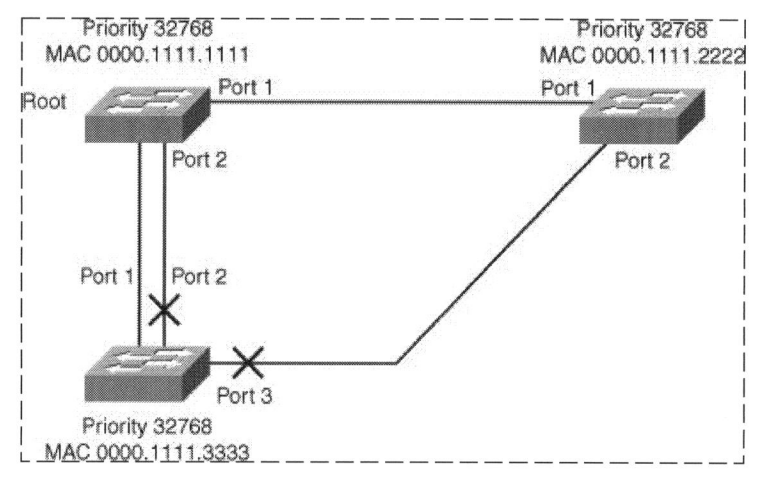

Figure 33 STP operation Example

Port 1 and Port 2 would both have a cost of 19. Port 3 would have a cost of 38, which represents the overall path cost (19+19) to reach the root. Port 1 or Port 2 would be elected as root port due to both having lower path cost to the root. When two ports have the same cost, arbitration can be done using the priority value. Priority is a combination of a default value and port number. Default value is 128. The first port will have a priority of 128.1, the second port of 128.2, and so on. With this logic, the lower port is always chosen as the root port when priority is the determining factor.

STP Configuration

Spanning Tree Protocol (STP) is enabled by default on modern switches. It is possible to disable or enable the Spanning Tree Protocol (STP) when required.

To enable Spanning Tree Protocol (STP) on an IOS based switch, use the "spanning-tree vlan vlan_number" command from global configuration mode as shown below.

```
switch01>
switch01>enable
```

```
switch01#configure terminal
Enter configuration commands, one per line. End with CNTL/Z.
switch01(config)#spanning-tree vlan 1
switch01(config)#exit
switch01#
```

To disable Spanning Tree Protocol (STP) on an IOS based switch use "no spanning-tree vlan vlan_number" command from global configuration mode as shown below.

Note: Never disable Spanning Tree Protocol (STP) if there is no valid reason to disable it. Disabling Spanning Tree Protocol (STP) can cause Broadcast Storms and Layer 2 Switching Loops, which can make your network down within a short span of time. Use with extreme care.

```
switch01>enable
switch01#configure terminal
Enter configuration commands, one per line. End with CNTL/Z.
switch01(config)#no spanning-tree vlan 1
switch01(config)#exit
switch01#
```

Basic Switch Security

Port Security

Port Security helps secure the network by preventing unknown devices from forwarding packets. When a link goes down, all dynamically locked addresses are freed. The port security feature offers the following benefits:

- You can limit the number of MAC addresses on a given port. Packets that have a matching MAC address (secure packets) are forwarded; all other packets (unsecure packets) are restricted.
- You can enable port security on a per port basis.

Port security implements two traffic filtering methods, dynamic locking and static locking. These methods can be used concurrently.

- Dynamic locking. You can specify the maximum number of MAC addresses that can be learned on a port. The maximum number of MAC addresses is platform dependent and is given in the software Release Notes. After the limit is reached, additional MAC addresses are not learned. Only frames with an allowable source MAC addresses are forwarded.

Note: If you want to set a specific MAC address for a port, set the dynamic entries to 0, then allow only packets with a MAC address matching the MAC address in the static list.

Dynamically locked addresses can be converted to statically locked addresses. Dynamically locked MAC addresses are aged out if another packet with that address is not seen within the age-out time. You can set the time out value. Dynamically locked MAC addresses are eligible to be learned by another port. Static MAC addresses are not eligible for aging.

- Static locking. You can manually specify a list of static MAC addresses for a port. Dynamically locked addresses can be converted to statically locked addresses.

How to Configure Port Security

SW1(config-if)#interface fa0/11
SW1(config-if)#switchport port-security
SW1(config-if)#switchport port-security maximum 1
SW1(config-if)#switchport port-security mac-address stick
SW1(config-if)#switchport port-security violation shutdown

In the configuration above, you have enable port security by allowing only 1 host and stick the mac address. In case of violation, port will be shutdown. You can also verify your configuration.

SW1#show port-security interface fa0/11	
Port Security	: Enabled
Port Status	: Secure-shutdown
Violation Mode	: Shutdown
Aging Time	: 0 mins
Aging Type	: Absolute
SecureStatic Address Aging	: Disabled
Maximum MAC Addresses	: 1
Total MAC Addresses	: 1
Configured MAC Addresses	: 1
Sticky MAC Addresses	: 0
Last Source Address:Vlan	: 00E0.F7B0.086E:20
Security Violation Count	: 1

How to Secure Unused Ports

Disabling unused switch ports a simple method many network administrators use to help secure their network from unauthorized access. Disabling an unused port stops traffic from flowing through the ports.

SW1(config)#interface fa0/10
SW1(config-if)#shutdown
You can also specify the range to disable
SW1(config)#interface range fa0/1-24
SW1(config-if)#shutdown

Cisco Switch Verification Commands

Show command

Here are some show commands of Cisco switches:

- **Show version:** This command displays the hardware and software status of the Cisco switch

- **Show flash:** This command displays the files and directories in the flash of the Cisco switch

- **Show interfaces:** This command displays the detailed information about all the interfaces of the Cisco switch

- **Show interfaces fast Ethernet 0/x:** This command displays the detailed information about the specific interface of the Cisco switch

- **Show interfaces VLAN 1:** This command displays the ip address configuration of VLAN 1

- **Show running-config:** This command displays the status of RAM

- **Show startup-config:** This command displays the status of NVRAM

- **Show-mac-address-table:** This command displays the MAC address of the devices that are directly connected to any switch port.

- **Show port-security:** [interface] [address]: This command displays the port security options on the interface

- **Show history:** This command displays the last ten commands that are executed in the switch configuration

- **Show line:** This command is used to view the brief information about all the Cisco switch lines

- **Show line console o:** This command is used to view the detailed information about the specific line of the Cisco switch
- **Erase startup-config:** This command is used to erase the nvram of the Cisco switch

Debug Command

First, it is important to caution readers that because debugging output is assigned high priority in the CPU process, it can render the system unusable. For this reason, use debug commands only to troubleshoot specific problems or during troubleshooting sessions with Cisco technical support staff. Moreover, it is best to use debug commands during periods of lower network traffic and fewer users.

All debug commands are entered in privileged EXEC mode, and most debug commands take no arguments. Retyping the command and preceding it with a no can turn off all debug commands. To display the state of each debugging option, enter the show debugging command in the Cisco IOS privileged EXEC mode. The no debug all command turns off all diagnostic output. Using the no debug all command is a convenient way to ensure that you have not accidentally left any debug commands turned on. To list and see a brief description of all the debug command options, enter the debug ? command. The following is a short list of useful debug options:

- debug interface interface-slot/number: Provides debug messages for specific physical ports on the device.
- debug ip icmp: Used to troubleshoot connectivity issues, from the output you can see whether the device is sending or receiving ICMP messages.
- debug ip packet: Used to troubleshoot end-to-end communication. It should always be used with an access control list (ACL).
- debug eigrp packets hello: Used to troubleshoot neighbor establishment. It shows the frequency of the sent and the received hello packets.
- debug ip ospf adjacency: Provides information about events concerning adjacency relationships with other OSPF routers.
- debug ip ospf events: Provides information about all OSPF events.
- debug ip bgp updates: Provides information about routes you have advertised/received from your BGP peer.
- debug ip bgp events: Provides information about any BGP event, such as neighbor state changes.
- debug spanning-tree bpdu receive: Used to confirm the bridge protocol data unit (BPDU) flow on switches.

debug IP packet Sample Output

```
IP: s=172.69.13.44 (Fddi0), d=10.125.254.1 (Serial2), g=172.69.16.2, forward
IP: s=172.69.1.57 (Ethernet4), d=10.36.125.2 (Serial2), g=172.69.16.2, forward
IP: s=172.69.1.6 (Ethernet4), d=255.255.255.255, rcvd 2
IP: s=172.69.1.55 (Ethernet4), d=172.69.2.42 (Fddi0), g=172.69.13.6, forward
IP: s=172.69.89.33 (Ethernet2), d=10.130.2.156 (Serial2), g=172.69.16.2, forward
IP: s=172.69.1.27 (Ethernet4), d=172.69.43.126 (Fddi1), g=172.69.23.5, forward
IP: s=172.69.1.27 (Ethernet4), d=172.69.43.126 (Fddi0), g=172.69.13.6, forward
IP: s=172.69.20.32 (Ethernet2), d=255.255.255.255, rcvd 2
IP: s=172.69.1.57 (Ethernet4), d=10.36.125.2 (Serial2), g=172.69.16.2, access denied
```

Figure 34 Debuging IP pakets

Ethernet Link bundling Aggregation (LAG)

Link aggregation (LAG) is used to describe various methods for using multiple parallel network connections to increase throughput beyond the limit that one link (one connection) can achieve. For link aggregation, physical ports must reside on a single switch. Split Multi-Link Trunking (SMLT) and Routed-SMLT (RSMLT) remove this limitation and physical ports are allowed to connect/split between two switches.

This term is also known as Multi-Link Trunking (MLT), Link Bundling, Ethernet/Network/NIC Bonding or NIC teaming.

What is LACP

Standards-based negotiation protocol, known as IEEE 802.1ax Link Aggregation Control Protocol, is simply a way to dynamically build an EtherChannel. Essentially, the "active" end of the LACP group sends out special frames advertising the ability and desire to form an EtherChannel. It is possible, and quite common, that both ends are set to an "active" state (versus a passive state). Once these frames are exchanged, and if the ports on both side agree that they support the requirements, LACP will form an Ether Channel.

What is PAgP

Cisco's proprietary negotiation protocol before LACP is introduced and endorsed by IEEE. EtherChannel technology was invented in the early 1990s. Cisco Systems later acquired them in 1994. In 2000 the IEEE passed 802.3ad (LACP), which is an open standard version of EtherChannel.

EtherChannel Negotiation

An EtherChannel can be established using one of three mechanisms:

PAgP – Cisco's proprietary negotiation protocol

LACP (IEEE 802.3ad) – Standards-based negotiation protocol

Static Persistence ("On") – No negotiation protocol is used

Any of these three mechanisms will suffice for most scenarios, however the choice does deserve some consideration. PAgP, while perfectly able, should probably be disqualified as a legacy proprietary protocol unless you have a specific need for it (such as ancient hardware). That leaves LACP and "on", both of which have a specific benefit.

PAgP/LACP Advantages over Static

Prevent Network Error

LACP helps protect against switching loops caused by misconfiguration; when enabled, an Ether Channel will only be formed after successful negotiation between its two ends. However, this negotiation introduces an overhead and delay in initialization. Statically configuring an Ether Channel, ("on") imposes no delay yet can cause serious problems if not properly configured at both ends.

Hot-Standby Ports

If you add more than the supported number of ports to an LACP port channel, it has the ability to place these extra ports into a hot-standby mode. If a failure occurs on an active port, the hot-standby port can replace it.

Failover

If there is a dumb device sitting in between the two ends of an EtherChannel, such as a media converter, and a single link fails, LACP will adapt by no longer sending traffic down this dead link. Static does not monitor this. This is not typically the case for most vSphere environments, but it may be of an advantage in some scenarios.

Configuration Confirmation

LACP will not form if there is an issue with either end or a problem with configuration. This helps ensure things are working properly. Static will form without any verification, so you have to make sure things are good to go.

To configure an EtherChannel using LACP negotiation, each side must be set to either active or passive; only interfaces configured in active mode will attempt to negotiate an EtherChannel. Passive interfaces merely respond to LACP requests. PAgP behaves the same, but its two modes are referred to as desirable and auto.

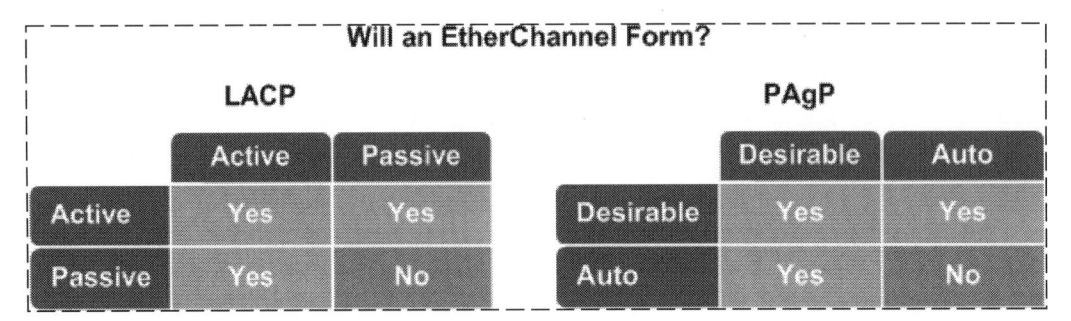

	LACP			PAgP	
	Active	Passive		Desirable	Auto
Active	Yes	Yes	Desirable	Yes	Yes
Passive	Yes	No	Auto	Yes	No

Figure 35 LAGP and PAgP Aggregation Conditions

Conclusion

EtherChannel/port trunking/link bundling/bonding/teaming is to combine multiple network interface.

PAgP/LACP is just a protocol to form the EtherChannel link. You can have EtherChannel without protocol, but not advisable.

Chapter 5: Switched Network Technologies II

Avanced switching technologies like RSTP, PVST, Inter-VLAN routing etc are inmplemented over complex and large network infrastructure to provide efficient services throughout network.

Configuration of Enhanced Switching Technologies

Lab 5-1 : RSTP Lab Configuration

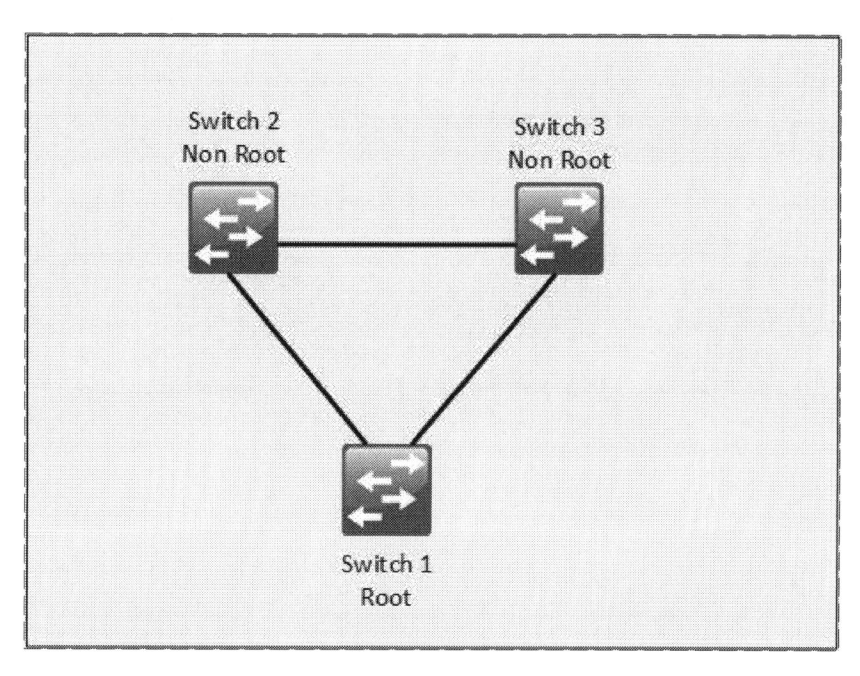

Figure 36

First, enable RSTP on switch 1

```
SW1(config)#spanning-tree mode rapid-pvst
```

Enable RSTP on switch 2

```
SW2(config)#spanning-tree mode rapid-pvst
```

Now enable RSTP on switch 3

```
SW3(config)#spanning-tree mode rapid-pvst
```

That's it. Just one command will enable rapid spanning tree on our switches. The implementation of rapid spanning tree is rapid-pvst.

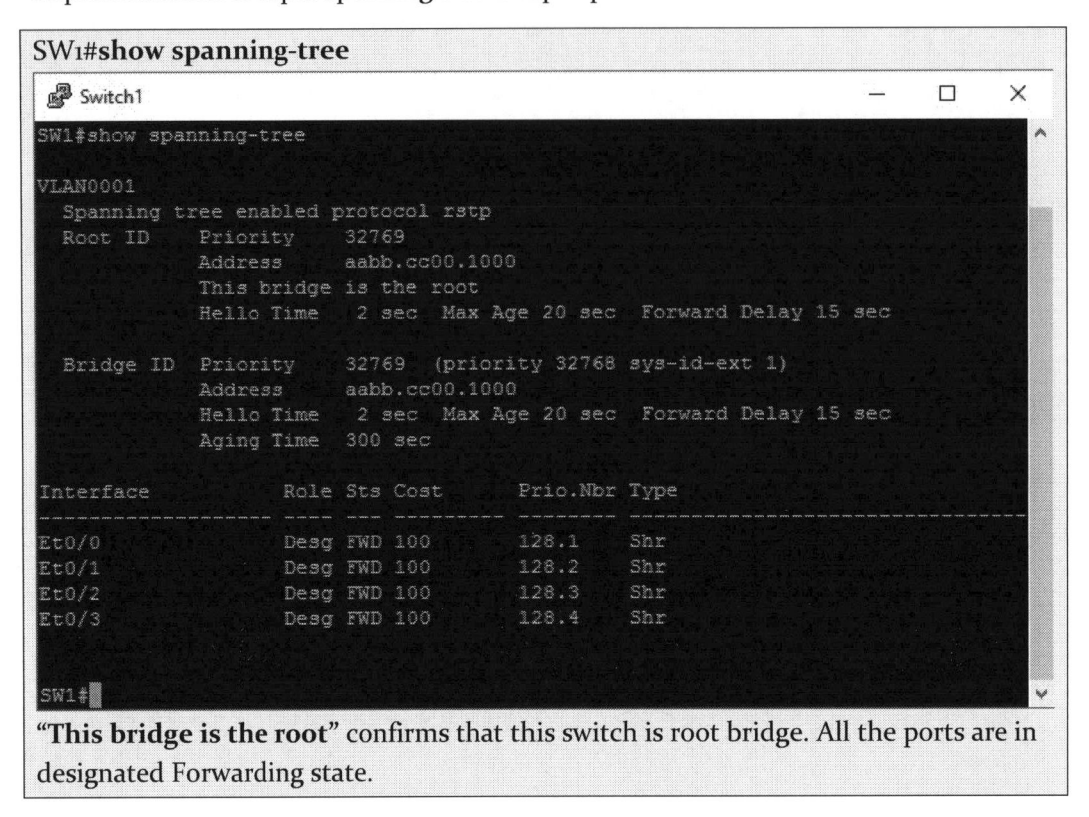

SW1#**show spanning-tree**

```
SW1#show spanning-tree

VLAN0001
  Spanning tree enabled protocol rstp
  Root ID    Priority    32769
             Address     aabb.cc00.1000
             This bridge is the root
             Hello Time   2 sec  Max Age 20 sec  Forward Delay 15 sec

  Bridge ID  Priority    32769  (priority 32768 sys-id-ext 1)
             Address     aabb.cc00.1000
             Hello Time   2 sec  Max Age 20 sec  Forward Delay 15 sec
             Aging Time  300 sec

Interface        Role Sts Cost      Prio.Nbr Type
---------------- ---- --- --------- -------- --------------------
Et0/0            Desg FWD 100       128.1    Shr
Et0/1            Desg FWD 100       128.2    Shr
Et0/2            Desg FWD 100       128.3    Shr
Et0/3            Desg FWD 100       128.4    Shr

SW1#
```

"This bridge is the root" confirms that this switch is root bridge. All the ports are in designated Forwarding state.

SW2#**show spanning-tree**

```
Switch2
SW2#show spanning-tree

VLAN0001
  Spanning tree enabled protocol rstp
  Root ID    Priority    32769
             Address     aabb.cc00.1000
             Cost        100
             Port        1 (Ethernet0/0)
             Hello Time  2 sec  Max Age 20 sec  Forward Delay 15 sec

  Bridge ID  Priority    32769  (priority 32768 sys-id-ext 1)
             Address     aabb.cc00.2000
             Hello Time  2 sec  Max Age 20 sec  Forward Delay 15 sec
             Aging Time  300 sec

Interface           Role Sts Cost      Prio.Nbr Type
------------------- ---- --- --------- -------- --------------------------------
Et0/0               Root FWD 100       128.1    Shr
Et0/1               Desg FWD 100       128.2    Shr
Et0/2               Desg FWD 100       128.3    Shr
Et0/3               Desg FWD 100       128.4    Shr

SW2#
```

Eth 0/0 is in root state.

SW3#**show spanning-tree**

```
Switch3
SW3#show spanning-tree

VLAN0001
  Spanning tree enabled protocol rstp
  Root ID    Priority    32769
             Address     aabb.cc00.1000
             Cost        100
             Port        2 (Ethernet0/1)
             Hello Time  2 sec  Max Age 20 sec  Forward Delay 15 sec

  Bridge ID  Priority    32769  (priority 32768 sys-id-ext 1)
             Address     aabb.cc00.3000
             Hello Time  2 sec  Max Age 20 sec  Forward Delay 15 sec
             Aging Time  300 sec

Interface           Role Sts Cost      Prio.Nbr Type
------------------- ---- --- --------- -------- --------------------------------
Et0/0               Altn BLK 100       128.1    Shr
Et0/1               Root FWD 100       128.2    Shr
Et0/2               Desg FWD 100       128.3    Shr
Et0/3               Desg FWD 100       128.4    Shr

SW3#
```

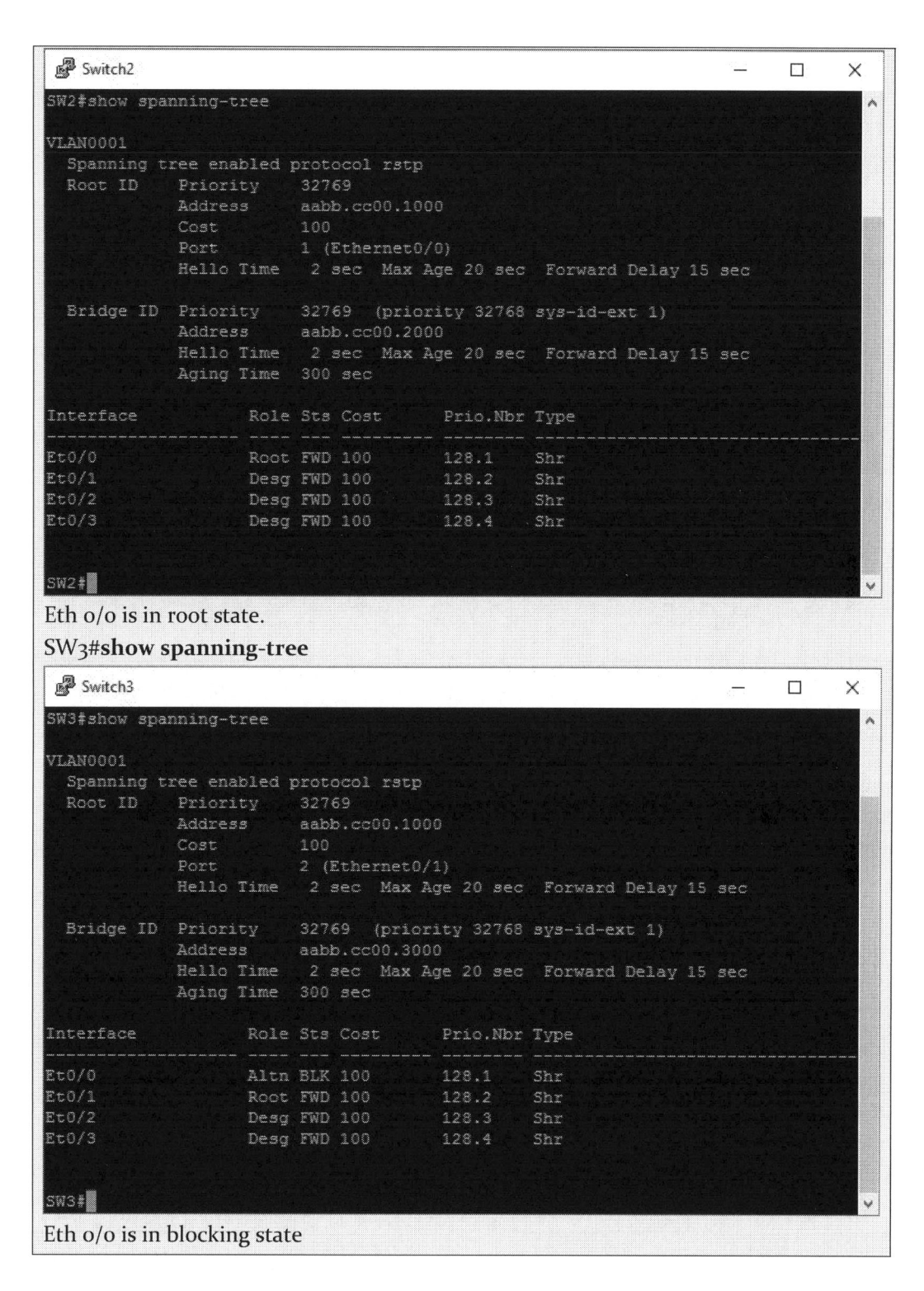

Eth 0/0 is in blocking state

Lab 5-2 : PVST Lab Configuration

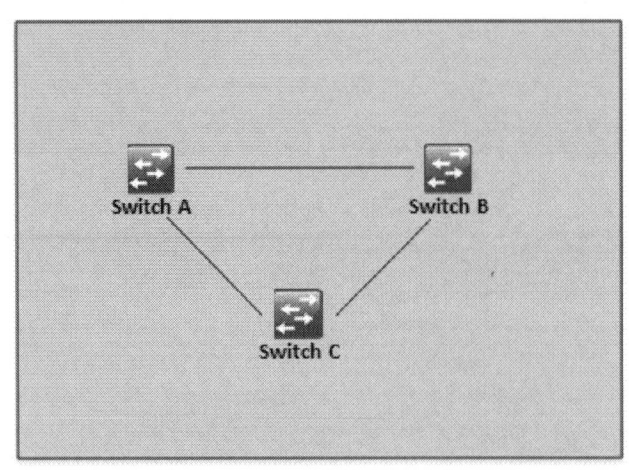

Figure 37

1. Configure SW1 as the ROOT Bridge for VLAN 1 and 10. Verify your configuration on SW2.
2. Configure SW2 as the ROOT Bridge for VLAN 20. Verify your configuration on SW1.
3. Configure SW3 as the ROOT Bridge for VLAN 30. Verify your configuration on SW1.

To configure SW1 as the ROOT Bridge for VLAN 1 and 10, you can use one of two commands. Spanning-tree vlan #root primary, which determines the best bridge priority and sets it to become the root bridge or you, can use the spanning-tree vlan # priority # which manually specifies the priority on a per vlan basis. Remember the lower the priority number the higher chance the switch will be the root bridge during an election. If the switch has the lowest priority of all switches then it will automatically become the root per that vlan. Bridge priorities can be a number 0-65535 and must use 4096 increments to abide by the IEEE standard using the sum of the bridge priority and sys-id-ext (which is the VLAN Number). Therefore, if you set a priority on vlan 1 to 4096, the sum of the bridge priority and the sys-id-ext will be 4097 and that will be the bridge priority on that switch for that vlan.

Shown below is an example root bridge configuration using the spanning-tree vlan # root primary command:

```
SW1(config)#spanning-tree mode pvst
SW1(config)#spanning-tree vlan 1 priority 0
SW1(config)#spanning-tree vlan 10 priority 0
```

```
SW2(config)#spanning-tree mode pvst
SW2(config)#spanning-tree vlan 20 priority 0
```

```
SW3(config)#spanning-tree mode pvst
SW3(config)#spanning-tree vlan 30 priority 0
```

To verify your configuration, you can use the show spanning-tree vlan # command or the show spanning-tree vlan root command as shown below;

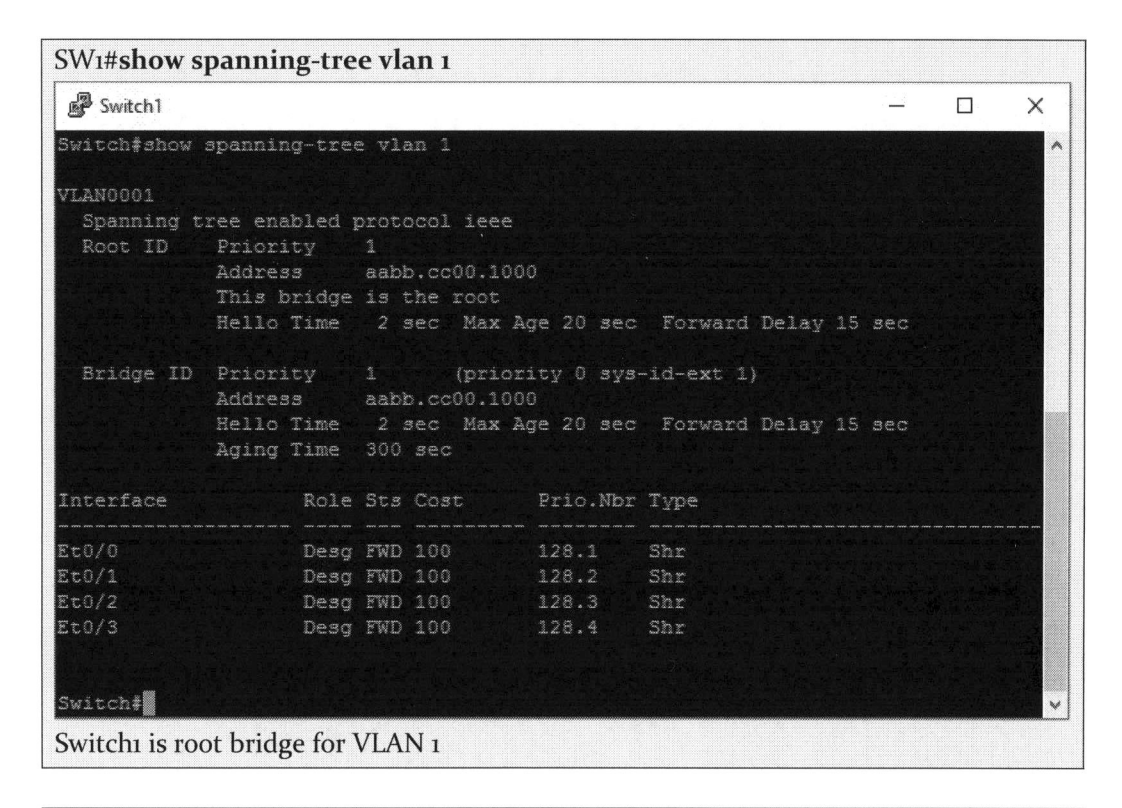

SW1#**show spanning-tree vlan 1**

```
Switch#show spanning-tree vlan 1

VLAN0001
  Spanning tree enabled protocol ieee
  Root ID    Priority    1
             Address     aabb.cc00.1000
             This bridge is the root
             Hello Time  2 sec  Max Age 20 sec  Forward Delay 15 sec

  Bridge ID  Priority    1       (priority 0 sys-id-ext 1)
             Address     aabb.cc00.1000
             Hello Time  2 sec  Max Age 20 sec  Forward Delay 15 sec
             Aging Time  300 sec

Interface           Role Sts Cost      Prio.Nbr Type
------------------- ---- --- --------- -------- --------------------
Et0/0               Desg FWD 100       128.1    Shr
Et0/1               Desg FWD 100       128.2    Shr
Et0/2               Desg FWD 100       128.3    Shr
Et0/3               Desg FWD 100       128.4    Shr

Switch#
```

Switch1 is root bridge for VLAN 1

SW1#**show spanning-tree vlan 10**

```
Switch#show spanning-tree vlan 10

VLAN0010
  Spanning tree enabled protocol ieee
  Root ID    Priority    10
             Address     aabb.cc00.1000
             This bridge is the root
             Hello Time   2 sec  Max Age 20 sec  Forward Delay 15 sec

  Bridge ID  Priority    10     (priority 0 sys-id-ext 10)
             Address     aabb.cc00.1000
             Hello Time   2 sec  Max Age 20 sec  Forward Delay 15 sec
             Aging Time  300 sec

Interface           Role Sts Cost      Prio.Nbr Type
------------------- ---- --- --------- -------- --------
Et0/0               Desg FWD 100       128.1    Shr
Et0/1               Desg FWD 100       128.2    Shr

Switch#
```

Switch1 is root bridge for VLAN 10

SW2#show spanning-tree vlan 20

```
Switch#show spanning-tree vlan 20

VLAN0020
  Spanning tree enabled protocol ieee
  Root ID    Priority    20
             Address     aabb.cc00.2000
             This bridge is the root
             Hello Time   2 sec  Max Age 20 sec  Forward Delay 15 sec

  Bridge ID  Priority    20     (priority 0 sys-id-ext 20)
             Address     aabb.cc00.2000
             Hello Time   2 sec  Max Age 20 sec  Forward Delay 15 sec
             Aging Time  300 sec

Interface           Role Sts Cost      Prio.Nbr Type
------------------- ---- --- --------- -------- --------
Et0/0               Desg FWD 100       128.1    Shr
Et0/1               Desg FWD 100       128.2    Shr

Switch#
```

Switch1 is root bridge for VLAN 20

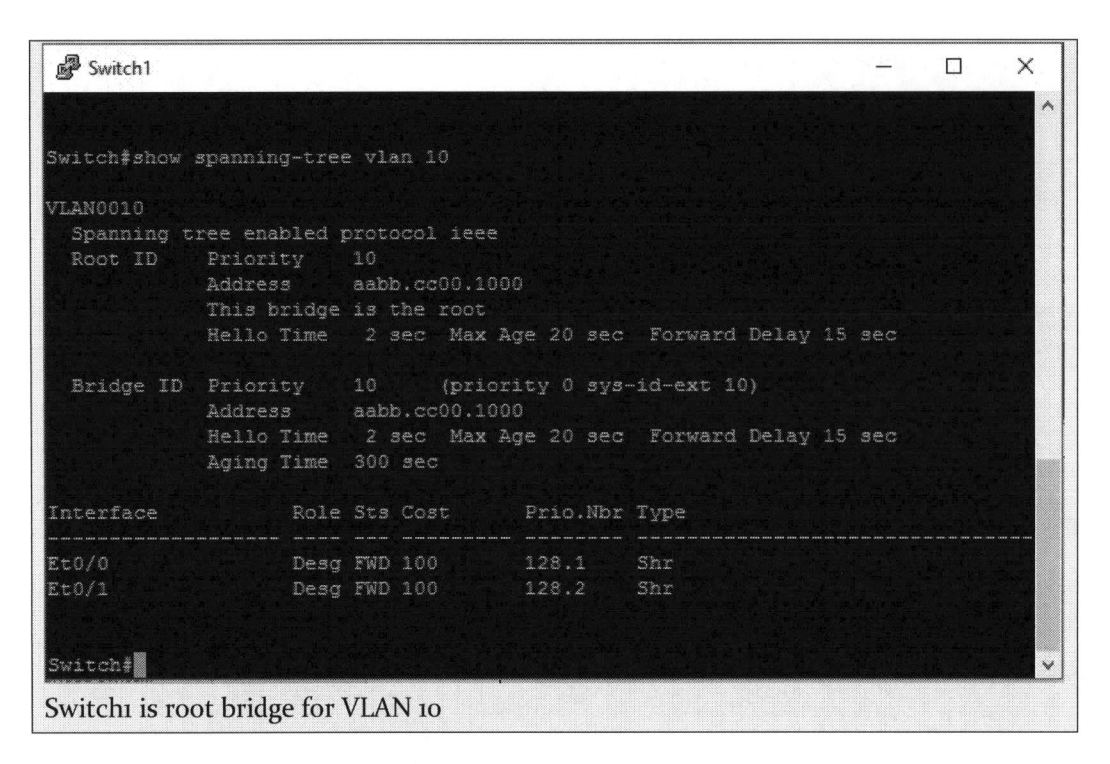

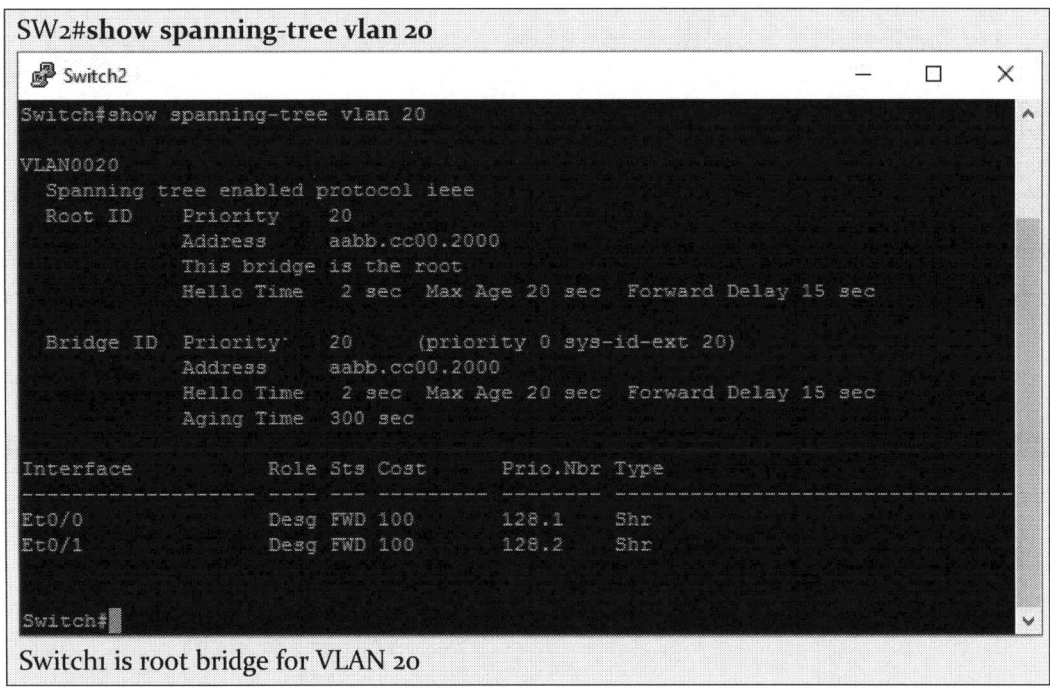

SW3#show spanning-tree vlan 30

```
Switch#show spanning-tree vlan 30

VLAN0030
  Spanning tree enabled protocol ieee
  Root ID    Priority    30
             Address     aabb.cc00.3000
             This bridge is the root
             Hello Time   2 sec  Max Age 20 sec  Forward Delay 15 sec

  Bridge ID  Priority    30     (priority 0 sys-id-ext 30)
             Address     aabb.cc00.3000
             Hello Time   2 sec  Max Age 20 sec  Forward Delay 15 sec
             Aging Time  300 sec

Interface           Role Sts Cost      Prio.Nbr Type
------------------- ---- --- --------- -------- --------------------------------
Et0/0               Desg FWD 100       128.1    Shr
Et0/1               Desg FWD 100       128.2    Shr

Switch#
```

Switch1 is root bridge for VLAN 30

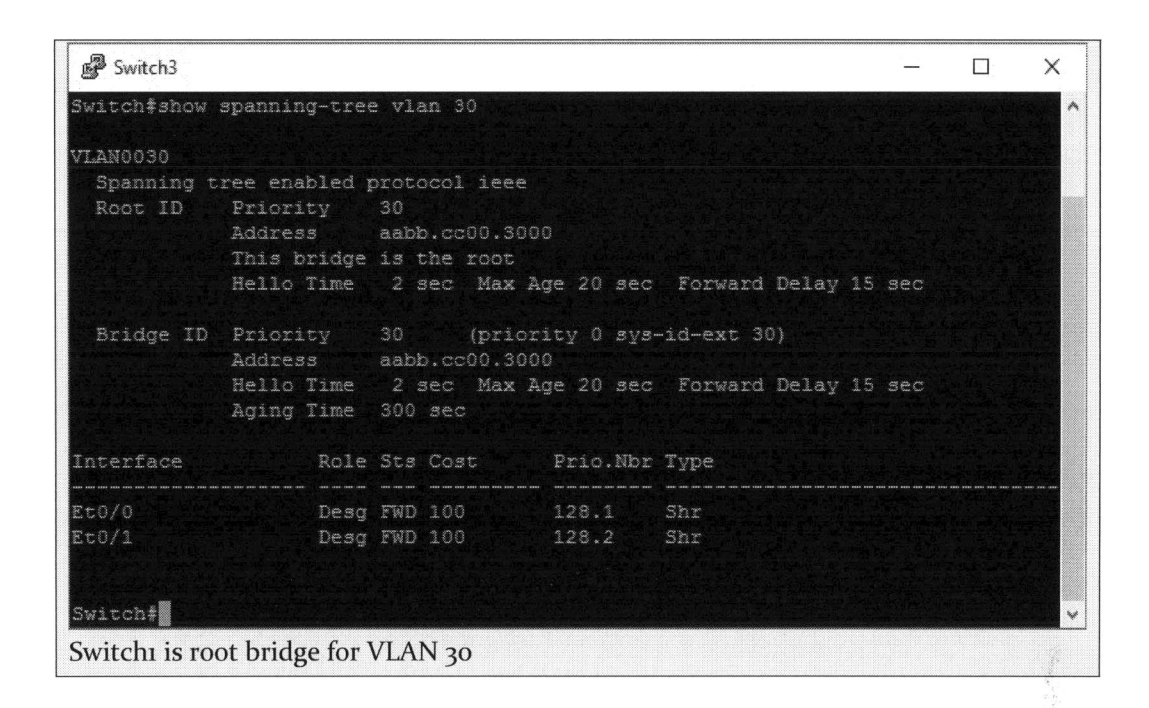

Lab 5-3 : Multiple Spanning Tree (MST)

Issue is reported that no communication is taking place between the switched using MST. Trunk is configured along with encapsulation.

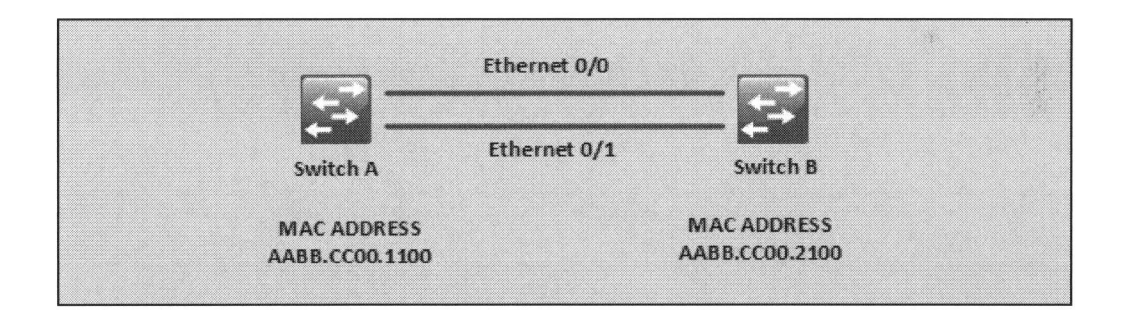

Switch A — MAC ADDRESS AABB.CC00.1100
Switch B — MAC ADDRESS AABB.CC00.2100
Connected via Ethernet 0/0 and Ethernet 0/1

Configuration:

Switch 1:

S1(config)#VLAN 10

S1(config)#VLAN 20

S1(config)#VLAN 30

S1(config)#VLAN 40

S1(config)#int range Ethernet 0/0,Ethernet 0/1

S1(config-if-range)#switchport trunk encapsulation dot1q

// First change the encapsulation from Auto to dot1Q

S1(config-if-range)#switchport mode trunk

//Change the Port from Access to Trunk

S1(config-if-range)#ex

S1(config)#spanning-tree mst configuration

S1(config-mst)#instance 1030 VLAN 10,30

//Remember Instance Number, Assign Correct VLANs

// Remember Priority (33,798) will be the sum of Default Priority (32768) andn Instance Number(1030)

S1(config-mst)#name IPS

//Requires the same Configuration on all switches

S1(config-mst)#revision 1

//Requires the same Configuration on all switches

S1(config-mst)#exit

S1(config)#spanning-tree mst 0 priority 0

//Priority for MST 0 will be 0+0 = 0 (Highest)

S1(config)#spanning-tree mst 1030 priority 32768

//Priority for MST 1030 will be (1030+32,768) = 33,798

S1(config)#spanning-tree mode mst

// Must Enable MST

Switch 2:

S2(config)#VLAN 10

S2(config)#VLAN 20

S2(config)#VLAN 30

S2(config)#VLAN 40

S2(config)#

//Make sure all VLANs are the same as in switch 1

```
S2(config)#int range Ethernet 0/0,Ethernet 0/1
S2(config-if-range)#switchport trunk encapsulation dot1q
```
// First change the encapsulation from Auto to dot1Q
```
S2(config-if-range)#switchport mode trunk
```
//Change the Port from Access to Trunk
```
S2(config-if-range)#ex
S2(config)#

S2(config)#spanning-tree mst configuration
S2(config-mst)#instance 1030 VLAN 10,30
```
//Verify Instance Number from Switch 1, Assign same VLANs
```
S2(config-mst)#name IPS
```
//Requires the same Configuration on all switches
```
S2(config-mst)#revision 1
```
//Requires the same Configuration on all switches
```
S2(config-mst)#exit

S2(config)#spanning-tree mst 0 priority 32768
```
//Priority for MST 0 will be 0+32768 = 32768
```
S2(config)#spanning-tree mst 1030 priority 0
```
//Priority for MST 1030 will be 1030+0 = 1030
```
S2(config)#spanning-tree mode mst
```
//Enable MST

Troubleshooting

```
S1#show spanning-tree mst
```

```
S1#show spanning-tree ms
S1#show spanning-tree mst

##### MST0      vlans mapped:   1-9,11-29,31-4094
Bridge          address aabb.cc00.1100  priority       0     (0 sysid 0)
Root            this switch for the CIST
Operational     hello time 2 , forward delay 15, max age 20, txholdcount 6
Configured      hello time 2 , forward delay 15, max age 20, max hops    20

Interface       Role Sts Cost      Prio.Nbr Type
---------------- ---- --- --------- -------- --------------------------------
Et0/0           Desg FWD 2000000   128.1    Shr
Et0/1           Desg FWD 2000000   128.2    Shr
Et0/2           Desg FWD 2000000   128.3    Shr
Et0/3           Desg FWD 2000000   128.4    Shr

##### MST1030 vlans mapped:   10,30
Bridge          address aabb.cc00.1100  priority      33798 (32768 sysid 1030)
Root            address aabb.cc00.2100  priority      1030  (0 sysid 1030)
                port    Et0/0           cost          2000000  rem hops 19

Interface       Role Sts Cost      Prio.Nbr Type
---------------- ---- --- --------- -------- --------------------------------
Et0/0           Root FWD 2000000   128.1    Shr
Et0/1           Altn BLK 2000000   128.2    Shr
Et0/2           Desg FWD 2000000   128.3    Shr
Et0/3           Desg FWD 2000000   128.4    Shr

S1#
```

Output shows that MST0 is mapped with 1-9, 11-29,31-4094 VLANs. Priority is 0 and Root shows that this is the Root Bridge. Timer is set to the default values. As we use Ethernet 0/0 and Ethernet 0/1 Interface as Trunk, Both are in Designated Forwarding state.

The Output also shows the details of MST1030 that VLAN 10 and VLAN 30 are mapped on it. Root Bridge is the MAC address AABB.CC00.2100 with Priority 1030. MAC Address of this switch is AABB.CC00.1100 and the Priority of this switch is 33798 for MST 1030. Interface Ethernet 0/0 is the Root port in forwarding state whereas Ethernet 0/1 is in Alternate Blocking Port status.

S2#show spanning-tree mst

```
S2#show spanning-tree ms
S2#show spanning-tree mst

##### MST0     vlans mapped:    1-9,11-29,31-4094
Bridge         address aabb.cc00.2100  priority     32768 (32768 sysid 0)
Root           address aabb.cc00.1100  priority     0     (0 sysid 0)
               port    Et0/0           path cost    0
Regional Root  address aabb.cc00.1100  priority     0     (0 sysid 0)
                                       internal cost 2000000   rem hops 19
Operational    hello time 2 , forward delay 15, max age 20, txholdcount 6
Configured     hello time 2 , forward delay 15, max age 20, max hops    20

Interface        Role Sts Cost      Prio.Nbr Type
---------------- ---- --- --------- -------- --------------------------------
Et0/0            Root FWD 2000000   128.1    Shr
Et0/1            Altn BLK 2000000   128.2    Shr
Et0/2            Desg FWD 2000000   128.3    Shr
Et0/3            Desg FWD 2000000   128.4    Shr

##### MST1030  vlans mapped:   10,30
Bridge         address aabb.cc00.2100  priority    1030  (0 sysid 1030)
Root           this switch for MST1030

Interface        Role Sts Cost      Prio.Nbr Type
---------------- ---- --- --------- -------- --------------------------------
Et0/0            Desg FWD 2000000   128.1    Shr
Et0/1            Desg FWD 2000000   128.2    Shr

S2#
```

Output shows that MST0 is mapped with 1-9, 11-29,31-4094 VLANs. Priority the 0 and Root MAC address shows that the Root Bridge is the Switch having MAC AABB.CC00.1100. MAC address of this Switch is AABB.CC00.2100 and the priority is 32768. Timers are set to the default values. As we use Ethernet 0/0 is the Root port in forwarding state and Ethernet 0/1 Interface Alternate port in blocking state.

The Output also shows the details of MST1030 that VLAN 10 and VLAN 30 are mapped on it. Root Bridge is the MAC address AABB.CC00.2100 with Priority 1030 which this switch. MAC Address of this switch is AABB.CC00.2100 and the Priority of this switch is 1030 for MST 1030. Interface Ethernet 0/0 is the Designated port in forwarding state similarly Ethernet 0/1 is also Designated Port in forwarding state as it is the Root bridge fro MST 1030.

S1#show spanning-tree mst configuration

```
S1# show spanning-tree mst configuration
Name       [IPS]
Revision   1     Instances configured 2

Instance   Vlans mapped
--------   ------------
0          1-9,11-29,31-4094
1030       10,30

S1#
S1#
```

MST configuration should be the same in all the switches participating in Election.

S2#show spanning-tree mst configuration

```
S2#show spanning-tree mst configuration
Name       [IPS]
Revision   1     Instances configured 2

Instance   Vlans mapped
--------   ------------
0          1-9,11-29,31-4094
1030       10,30

S2#
S2#
```

MST configuration should be the same in all the switches participating in Election.

Compare the Results of Both Switches

S1#show spanning-tree mst interface Ethernet 0/0

```
S1#show spanning-tree mst interface eth 0/0

Ethernet0/0 of MST0 is designated forwarding
Edge port: no              (default)       port guard : none       (default)
Link type: shared          (auto)          bpdu filter: disable    (default)
Boundary : internal                        bpdu guard : disable    (default)
Bpdus sent 251, received 250

Instance Role Sts Cost       Prio.Nbr Vlans mapped
-------- ---- --- ---------  -------- -------------
0        Desg FWD 2000000    128.1    1-9,11-29,31-4094
1030     Root FWD 2000000    128.1    10,30
S1#
```

From the output, we can see the status of the Interface Ethernet 0/0, which is the trunk port between Switch 1 and Switch 2. This Interface is not enabled with any Port guard Feature, any bpdu filter or any bpdu guard. Instance 0 is in designated Port Role and Status is forwarding. Instance 1030 is in Root port role and in forwarding State. Similarly, compare the Output of Switch 2. It should be the opposite and vice versa.

S2#show spanning-tree mst interface Ethernet 0/0

```
S2#show spanning-tree mst interface ethernet 0/0

Ethernet0/0 of MST0 is root forwarding
Edge port: no              (default)       port guard : none       (default)
Link type: shared          (auto)          bpdu filter: disable    (default)
Boundary : internal                        bpdu guard : disable    (default)
Bpdus sent 274, received 273

Instance Role Sts Cost       Prio.Nbr Vlans mapped
-------- ---- --- ---------  -------- -------------
0        Root FWD 2000000    128.1    1-9,11-29,31-4094
1030     Desg FWD 2000000    128.1    10,30
S2#
```

From the output, we can see the status of the Interface Ethernet 0/0 which is the trunk port between Switch 1 and Switch 2. This Interface is not enabled with any Port guard Feature, any bpdu filter or any bpdu guard. Instance 0 is in Root Port Role and Status is Forwarding. Instance 1030 is in Designated port role and in forwarding State. Where as from previous output of Switch 1 For instance 0 is Designated Port. That's all we need from MST.

S1#show spanning-tree

```
S1#sho spanning-tree

MST0
  Spanning tree enabled protocol mstp
  Root ID    Priority    0
             Address     aabb.cc00.1100
             This bridge is the root
             Hello Time  2 sec  Max Age 20 sec  Forward Delay 15 sec

  Bridge ID  Priority    0        (priority 0 sys-id-ext 0)
             Address     aabb.cc00.1100
             Hello Time  2 sec  Max Age 20 sec  Forward Delay 15 sec

Interface          Role Sts Cost       Prio.Nbr Type
------------------ ---- --- ---------- -------- --------------------------------
Et0/0              Desg FWD 2000000    128.1    Shr
Et0/1              Desg FWD 2000000    128.2    Shr
Et0/2              Desg FWD 2000000    128.3    Shr
Et0/3              Desg FWD 2000000    128.4    Shr


MST1030
  Spanning tree enabled protocol mstp
  Root ID    Priority    1030
             Address     aabb.cc00.2100
             Cost        2000000
             Port        1 (Ethernet0/0)
             Hello Time  2 sec  Max Age 20 sec  Forward Delay 15 sec

  Bridge ID  Priority    33798  (priority 32768 sys-id-ext 1030)
             Address     aabb.cc00.1100
             Hello Time  2 sec  Max Age 20 sec  Forward Delay 15 sec

Interface          Role Sts Cost       Prio.Nbr Type
------------------ ---- --- ---------- -------- --------------------------------
Et0/0              Root FWD 2000000    128.1    Shr
Et0/1              Altn BLK 2000000    128.2    Shr
Et0/2              Desg FWD 2000000    128.3    Shr
Et0/3              Desg FWD 2000000    128.4    Shr

S1#
```

The command Show spanning-tree also shows the Output of MST ports so we can also just use Show Spanning-tree command.

S2#show spanning-tree

```
S2#show spanning-tree

MST0
  Spanning tree enabled protocol mstp
  Root ID    Priority    0
             Address     aabb.cc00.1100
             Cost        0
             Port        1 (Ethernet0/0)
             Hello Time  2 sec  Max Age 20 sec  Forward Delay 15 sec

  Bridge ID  Priority    32768  (priority 32768 sys-id-ext 0)
             Address     aabb.cc00.2100
             Hello Time  2 sec  Max Age 20 sec  Forward Delay 15 sec

Interface           Role Sts Cost      Prio.Nbr Type
------------------- ---- --- --------- -------- ----
Et0/0               Root FWD 2000000   128.1    Shr
Et0/1               Altn BLK 2000000   128.2    Shr
Et0/2               Desg FWD 2000000   128.3    Shr
Et0/3               Desg FWD 2000000   128.4    Shr


MST1030
  Spanning tree enabled protocol mstp
  Root ID    Priority    1030
             Address     aabb.cc00.2100
             This bridge is the root
             Hello Time  2 sec  Max Age 20 sec  Forward Delay 15 sec

  Bridge ID  Priority    1030   (priority 0 sys-id-ext 1030)
             Address     aabb.cc00.2100
             Hello Time  2 sec  Max Age 20 sec  Forward Delay 15 sec

Interface           Role Sts Cost      Prio.Nbr Type
------------------- ---- --- --------- -------- ----
Et0/0               Desg FWD 2000000   128.1    Shr
Et0/1               Desg FWD 2000000   128.2    Shr

S2#
```

What are VLAN's?

In a traditional LAN, workstations are connected to each other by means of a hub or a repeater. These devices propagate any incoming data throughout the network. However, if two people attempt to send information at the same time, a collision will occur and all the transmitted data will be lost. Once the collision has occurred, it will continue to be propagated throughout the network by hubs and repeaters. The original information will therefore need to be resent after waiting for the collision to be resolved, thereby incurring a significant wastage of time and resources. To prevent collisions from traveling through all the workstations in the network, a bridge or a switch can be used. These devices will not forward collisions, but will allow broadcasts (to every user in the network) and multicasts (to a pre-specified group of users) to pass through. A router may be used to prevent broadcasts and multicasts from traveling through the network.

The workstations, hubs, and repeaters together form a LAN segment. A LAN segment is also known as a collision domain since collisions remain within the segment. The area within which broadcasts and multicasts are confined is called a broadcast domain or LAN. Thus, a LAN can consist of one or more than one LAN segments. Defining broadcast and collision domains in a LAN depends on how the workstations, hubs, switches, and routers are physically connected together. Since this is a logical segmentation and not a physical one, workstations do not have to be physically located together. Users on different floors of the same building, or even in different buildings can now belong to the same LAN.be located in the same area.

VLAN's also allow broadcast domains to be defined without using routers. Bridging software is used instead to define which workstations are to be included in the broadcast domain. Routers would only have to be used to communicate between two VLAN's.

The Need For Routing

Each network has its own needs, though whether it is a large or small network, internal routing, in most cases, is essential - if not critical. The ability to segment your network by creating VLANs, thus reducing network broadcasts and increasing your security, is a tactic used by most engineers. Popular setups include a separate broadcast domain for critical services such as File Servers, Print servers, Domain Controllers etc., serving your users non-stop.

The issue here is how users from one VLAN (broadcast domain) can use services offered by another VLAN.

Thankfully, there is an answer to every problem and in this case, its InterVLAN routing:

InterVLAN routing makes use of the latest in technology switches ensuring a super-fast, reliable, and acceptable cost routing solution.

As we have learned that each VLAN is a unique broadcast domain, so, computers on separate VLANs are, by default, not able to communicate. There is a way to permit these computers to communicate; it is called inter-VLAN routing.

One of the ways of the ways to carry out inter-VLAN routing is by connecting a router to the switch infrastructure. VLANs are associated with unique IP subnets on the network.

This subnet configuration enables the routing process in a multi-VLAN environment. When using a router to facilitate inter-VLAN routing, the router interfaces can be connected to separate VLANs. Devices on those VLANs communicate with each other via the router.

- Traffic from PC1 on VLAN10 is routed through router R1 to reach PC3 on VLAN 20.
- PC1 and PC3 are on different VLANs and have IP addresses on different subnets.
- Router R1 has a separate interface configured for each of the VLANs.

Summary of Routing Between VLANs

- Inter-VLAN routing using a router on a stick utilizes an external router to pass traffic between VLANs.
- A router on a stick is configured with a sub interface for each VLAN and 802.1Q trunk encapsulation.

VLAN Lab Configuration

This example demonstrates that how can create Ethernet VLAN 2, name it test2, and add it to the VLAN database:

Creating VLAN

```
Switch# configure terminal
Switch(config)# vlan 2
Switch(config-vlan)# name test2
Switch(config-vlan)# end
```

This example shows how to configure a port as an access port in VLAN 2:

Assigning Interface to a VLAN

```
Switch# configure terminal
Enter configuration commands, one per line. End with CNTL/Z.
Switch(config)# interface gigabitethernet1/0/1
Switch(config-if)# switchport mode access
Switch(config-if)# switchport access vlan 2
Switch(config-if)# end
```

Trunk Port Configuration:

```
switch1(config)#int fastEthernet 0/9
switch1(config-if)#switchport trunk encapsulation dot1q
switch1(config-if)#switchport mode trunk
switch1(config-if)#switchport trunk allowed vlan 1,2,3,4
switch1(config-if)#switchport trunk native vlan 1
```

VTP Lab Configuration

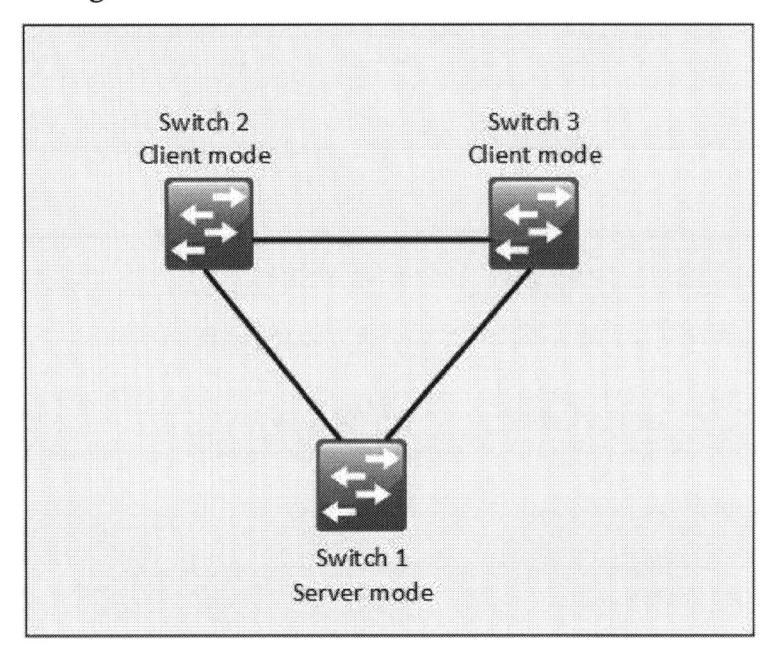

Figure 38

We configure Switch 1 as VTP server mode
switch1#conf t   Enter configuration commands, one per line. End with CNTL/Z.   switch1(config)#int fastEthernet 0/0   switch1(config-if)#switchport trunk encapsulation dot1q   switch1(config-if)#switchport mode trunk   switch1(config-if)#exit   switch1(config)#int fastEthernet 0/1   switch1(config-if)#switchport trunk encapsulation dot1q   switch1(config-if)#switchport mode trunk   switch1(config-if)#exit   switch1(config)#vtp domain lab.local   Changing VTP domain name from NULL to lab.local   switch1(config)#vtp password cisco   Setting device VLAN database password to cisco.   switch1(config)#end

Verifying Switch 1
switch1#sh vtp status   VTP Version : 2

```
Configuration Revision : 0
Maximum VLANs supported locally : 64
Number of existing VLANs : 6
VTP Operating Mode : Server
VTP Domain Name : lab.local
VTP Pruning Mode : Disabled
VTP V2 Mode : Disabled
VTP Traps Generation : Disabled
MD5 digest : 0x12 0xBF 0xAA 0x37 0xDC 0x26 0xF2 0x03
Configuration last modified by 10.0.1.210 at 3-1-93 03:11:00
Local updater ID is 10.0.1.210 on interface Vl1 (lowest numbered VLAN interface found)
```

Switch2 Configuration:

switch2#conf t
Enter configuration commands, one per line. End with CNTL/Z.
switch2(config)#interface fastEthernet 0/0
switch2(config-if)#switchport mode trunk
switch2(config-if)#exit

switch2(config)#vtp domain lab.local
```
Changing VTP domain name from NULL to lab.local
```
switch2(config)#vtp password cisco
```
Setting device VLAN database password to cisco
```
switch2(config)#vtp mode client
```
Setting device to VTP CLIENT mode.
```
switch2(config)#end

Verifying Switch 2

switch2#sh vtp status
```
VTP Version : 2
Configuration Revision : 0
Maximum VLANs supported locally : 64
Number of existing VLANs : 6
VTP Operating Mode : Client
VTP Domain Name : lab.local
VTP Pruning Mode : Disabled
VTP V2 Mode : Disabled
VTP Traps Generation : Disabled
MD5 digest : 0x12 0xBF 0xAA 0x37 0xDC 0x26 0xF2 0x03
Configuration last modified by 10.0.1.210 at 3-1-93 03:11:00
```

Switch3

Switch3#conf t

```
Enter configuration commands, one per line. End with CNTL/Z.
Switch3(config)#interface fastEthernet 0/0
Switch3(config-if)#switchport mode trunk
Switch3(config-if)#exit

Switch3(config)#vtp domain lab.local
Changing VTP domain name from NULL to lab.local
Switch3(config)#vtp password cisco
Setting device VLAN database password to cisco
Switch3(config)#vtp mode client
Setting device to VTP CLIENT mode.
Switch3(config)#end
```

Attempts to create a VLAN on switch2 fails as it is in Client mode

```
switch2#conf t
Enter configuration commands, one per line. End with CNTL/Z.
switch2(config)#vlan 4
VTP VLAN configuration not allowed when device is in CLIENT mode.
```

InterVLAN Routing

Lab 5-4 : Inter VLAN Configuration

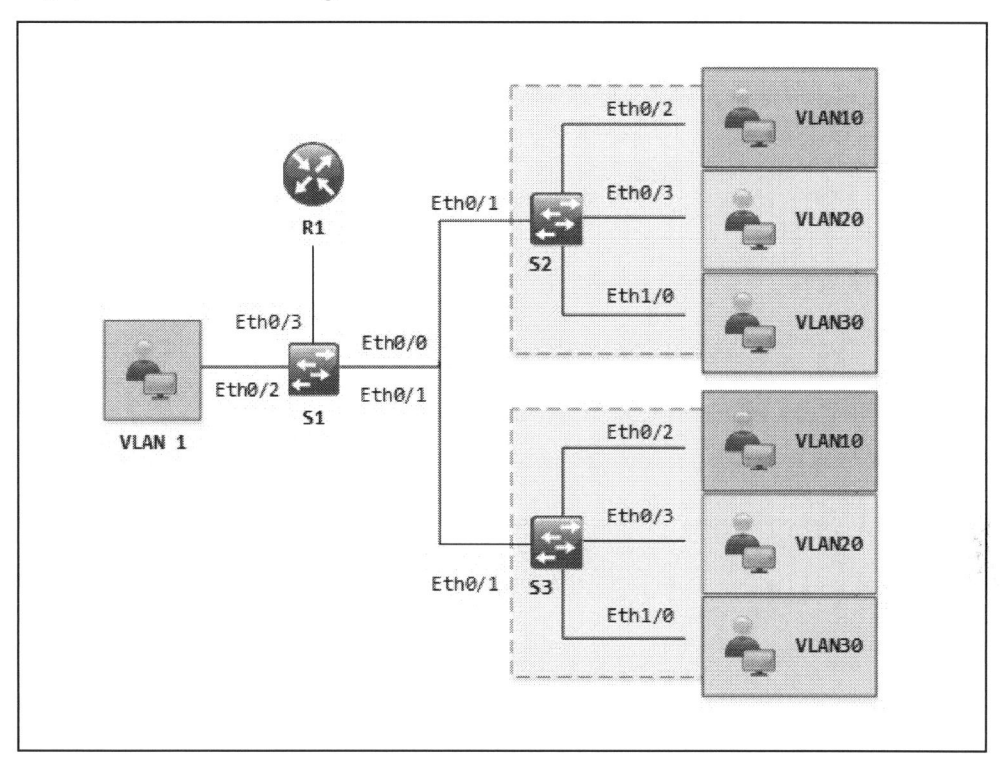

Figure 39

SW1 has two VLANs so we have two different subnets. If we want communication between these VLANs we'll have to use a device that can do routing. In this example we'll use a router for the job. R1 will need access to both VLANs so we'll create a 802.1Q trunk between SW1 and R1. Here's how to configure R1:

R1 Configuration:
R1(config)#int fa 0/0
R1(config-if)#no sh
R1(config-if)#ex
*Mar 1 00:01:17.347: %LINK-3-UPDOWN: Interface FastEthernet0/0, changed state to up
*Mar 1 00:01:18.347: %LINEPROTO-5-UPDOWN: Line protocol on Interface FastEthernet0/0, changed state to up
R1(config)#int fa 0/0.1
R1(config-subif)#encapsulation dot1Q 1
R1(config-subif)#ip add 1.0.0.254 255.0.0.0
R1(config-subif)#ex

```
R1(config)#int fa 0/0.10
R1(config-subif)#encapsulation dot1Q 10
R1(config-subif)#ip add 10.0.0.254 255.0.0.0
R1(config-subif)#ex

R1(config)#int fa 0/0.20
R1(config-subif)#encapsulation dot1Q 20
R1(config-subif)#ip add 20.0.0.254 255.0.0.0

R1(config)#int fa 0/0.30
R1(config-subif)#encapsulation dot1Q 30
R1(config-subif)#ip add 30.0.0.254 255.0.0.0
R1(config-subif)#ex
R1(config)#
```

Verification:

```
R1#show ip int brief
Interface              IP-Address      OK? Method Status                Protocol
FastEthernet0/0        unassigned      YES unset  up                    up
FastEthernet0/0.1      1.0.0.254       YES manual up                    up
FastEthernet0/0.10     10.0.0.254      YES manual up                    up
FastEthernet0/0.20     20.0.0.254      YES manual up                    up
FastEthernet0/0.30     30.0.0.254      YES manual up                    up
FastEthernet0/1        unassigned      YES unset  administratively down down
```

Sub Interfaces are configured with IP addresses and States of all sub interfaces are up.

This is how we configure SW1. Make interface Eth0/3 a trunk port and for security measures I made sure that only VLAN 1 and 10,20,and 30 are allowed.

Creating VLANs on Switch 1

```
Switch(config)#hostname S1
S1(config)#vlan 10
S1(config)#vlan 20
S1(config)#vlan 30
S1(config-vlan)#ex
```

Configuring Trunk Port on Switch 1

```
S1(config)#int range eth 0/3, eth 0/0, eth 0/1
S1(config-if-range)#switchport trunk encapsulation dot1q
S1(config-if-range)#switchport mode trunk
```

CCNA-SP Workbook

```
*Aug 16 20:53:36.556: %LINEPROTO-5-UPDOWN: Line protocol on Interface Ethernet0/3, changed state to down
*Aug 16 20:53:36.557: %LINEPROTO-5-UPDOWN: Line protocol on Interface Ethernet0/0, changed state to down
*Aug 16 20:53:36.557: %LINEPROTO-5-UPDOWN: Line protocol on Interface Ethernet0/1, changed state to down

*Aug 16 20:53:39.564: %LINEPROTO-5-UPDOWN: Line protocol on Interface Ethernet0/3, changed state to up
*Aug 16 20:53:39.566: %LINEPROTO-5-UPDOWN: Line protocol on Interface Ethernet0/0, changed state to up
*Aug 16 20:53:39.566: %LINEPROTO-5-UPDOWN: Line protocol on Interface Ethernet0/1, changed state to up

S1(config-if-range)#switchport trunk allowed vlan 1,10,20,30
S1(config-if-range)#ex
```

Assigning Interface to VLAN 1 on Switch 1

```
S1(config)#int eth 0/2
S1(config-if)#switchport mode access
S1(config-if)#switchport access vlan 1
S1(config-if)#ex
S1(config)#
```

To verify confoguraiton on Switch 1 issue the command

```
S1#show interface trunk
```

```
S1#show interfaces trunk

Port        Mode            Encapsulation   Status          Native vlan
Et0/0       on              802.1q          trunking        1
Et0/1       on              802.1q          trunking        1
Et0/3       on              802.1q          trunking        1

Port        Vlans allowed on trunk
Et0/0       1,10,20,30
Et0/1       1,10,20,30
Et0/3       1,10,20,30

Port        Vlans allowed and active in management domain
Et0/0       1,10,20,30
Et0/1       1,10,20,30
Et0/3       1,10,20,30

Port        Vlans in spanning tree forwarding state and not pruned
Et0/0       1,10,20,30
Et0/1       1,10,20,30
Et0/3       1,10,20,30
S1#
```

Now we configure VLANs, trunk and access ports on switch 2

Creating VLANs on Switch 2
Switch(config)#hostname S2
S2(config)#vlan 10
S2(config)#vlan 20
S2(config)#vlan 30
S2(config)#ex

Configuring Trunk Port on Switch 2
S2(config)#int range eth 0/0 , eth 0/1
S2(config-if-range)#switchport trunk encapsulation dot1q
S2(config-if-range)#switchport mode trunk
*Aug 16 21:06:17.165: %LINEPROTO-5-UPDOWN: Line protocol on Interface Ethernet0/0, changed state to down
*Aug 16 21:06:20.169: %LINEPROTO-5-UPDOWN: Line protocol on Interface Ethernet0/0, changed state to up
S2(config-if-range)#switchport trunk allowed vlan 1,10,20,30
S2(config-if-range)#ex

Assinging Interfaces to VLAN on Switch 2
S2(config)#int eth 0/2
S2(config-if)#switchport mode access

```
S2(config-if)#switchport access vlan 10
S2(config-if)#ex

S2(config)#int eth 0/3
S2(config-if)#switchport mode access
S2(config-if)#switchport access vlan 20
S2(config-if)#ex

S2(config)#int eth 1/0
S2(config-if)#switchport mode access
S2(config-if)#switchport access vlan 30
S2(config-if)#ex
```

Similarly configure Switch 3

Switch 3 Configuration

```
Switch(config)#hostname S3
S3(config)#vlan 10
S3(config)#vlan 20
S3(config)#vlan 30
S3(config)#ex

S3(config)#int range eth 0/0 , eth 0/1
S3(config-if-range)#switchport trunk encapsulation dot1q
S3(config-if-range)#switchport mode trunk
S3(config-if-range)#switchport trunk allowed vlan 1,10,20,30
S3(config-if-range)#ex

S3(config)#int eth 0/2
S3(config-if)#switchport mode access
S3(config-if)#switchport access vlan 10
S3(config-if)#ex


S3(config)#int eth 0/3
```

```
S3(config-if)#switchport mode access
S3(config-if)#switchport access vlan 20
S3(config-if)#ex

S3(config)#int eth 1/0
S3(config-if)#switchport mode access
S3(config-if)#switchport access vlan 30
S3(config-if)#ex
```

Verification: Go to VLAN 1 PC and Ping All other Users of Different VLANs

VPCS> ping 10.0.0.1
```
10.0.0.1 icmp_seq=1 timeout
84 bytes from 10.0.0.1 icmp_seq=2 ttl=63 time=14.076 ms
84 bytes from 10.0.0.1 icmp_seq=3 ttl=63 time=18.372 ms
84 bytes from 10.0.0.1 icmp_seq=4 ttl=63 time=18.142 ms
84 bytes from 10.0.0.1 icmp_seq=5 ttl=63 time=19.045 ms
```
VPCS> ping 10.0.0.2
```
10.0.0.2 icmp_seq=1 timeout
84 bytes from 10.0.0.2 icmp_seq=2 ttl=63 time=12.683 ms
84 bytes from 10.0.0.2 icmp_seq=3 ttl=63 time=17.925 ms
84 bytes from 10.0.0.2 icmp_seq=4 ttl=63 time=17.699 ms
84 bytes from 10.0.0.2 icmp_seq=5 ttl=63 time=18.714 ms
```

VPCS> ping 20.0.0.1
```
20.0.0.1 icmp_seq=1 timeout
84 bytes from 20.0.0.1 icmp_seq=2 ttl=63 time=13.029 ms
84 bytes from 20.0.0.1 icmp_seq=3 ttl=63 time=18.582 ms
84 bytes from 20.0.0.1 icmp_seq=4 ttl=63 time=17.523 ms
84 bytes from 20.0.0.1 icmp_seq=5 ttl=63 time=17.796 ms
```

VPCS> ping 20.0.0.2

```
20.0.0.2 icmp_seq=1 timeout
84 bytes from 20.0.0.2 icmp_seq=2 ttl=63 time=18.519 ms
84 bytes from 20.0.0.2 icmp_seq=3 ttl=63 time=16.475 ms
84 bytes from 20.0.0.2 icmp_seq=4 ttl=63 time=16.772 ms
84 bytes from 20.0.0.2 icmp_seq=5 ttl=63 time=16.910 ms


VPCS> ping 30.0.0.1
30.0.0.1 icmp_seq=1 timeout
84 bytes from 30.0.0.1 icmp_seq=2 ttl=63 time=16.638 ms
84 bytes from 30.0.0.1 icmp_seq=3 ttl=63 time=17.884 ms
84 bytes from 30.0.0.1 icmp_seq=4 ttl=63 time=16.725 ms
84 bytes from 30.0.0.1 icmp_seq=5 ttl=63 time=18.382 ms


VPCS> ping 30.0.0.2
30.0.0.2 icmp_seq=1 timeout
84 bytes from 30.0.0.2 icmp_seq=2 ttl=63 time=16.875 ms
84 bytes from 30.0.0.2 icmp_seq=3 ttl=63 time=18.470 ms
84 bytes from 30.0.0.2 icmp_seq=4 ttl=63 time=16.789 ms
84 bytes from 30.0.0.2 icmp_seq=5 ttl=63 time=17.762 ms
```

REP (Resilient Ethernet Protocol) Lab Configuration

Resilient Ethernet Protocol (REP) is a Cisco proprietary protocol, which allows you to build redundant Ethernet rings. It's an alternative to Spanning-Tree protocol and also avoids bridging loops or responds to link failures. Compared to STP, it offers a faster convergence time (< 300ms) and gives you a simple VLAN load-balancing method.

In our example, we interconnect three switches (Cisco ME3400 with me340x-metroaccess-mz.122-50.SE1.bin) to a ring topology. In REP terminology, this is called a segment.

A REP segment is a chain of ports connected to each other and configured with a segment ID. Each segment consists of standard (non-edge) segment ports and two user-configured edge ports. A switch can have only two ports belonging to the same segment, and each segment port can have only one external neighbor.

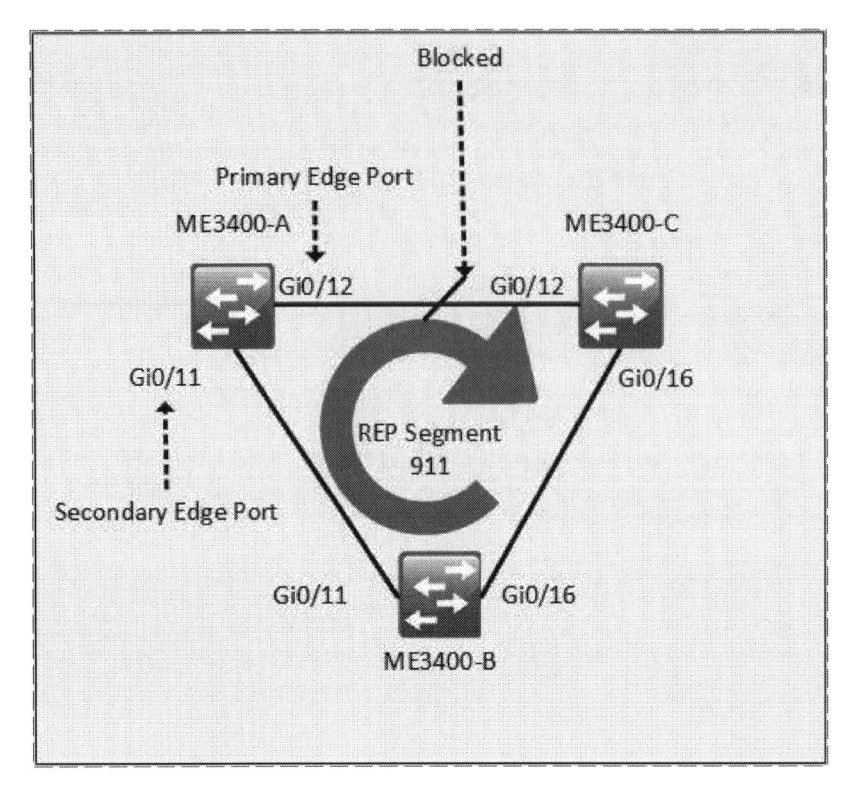

Figure 40

REP segments have the following characteristics:

- When all ports in a segment are operational, one port (referred to as the alternate port) is in the blocked state for each VLAN.

- If VLAN load balancing is configured, two ports in the segment control the blocked state of VLANs.

- If one or more ports in a segment is not operational, causing a link failure, all ports forward traffic on all VLANs to ensure connectivity.

- In case of a link failure, the alternate ports are unblocked as quickly as possible. When the failed link comes back up, a logically blocked port per VLAN is selected with minimal disruption to the network.

Valid port states in REP segments are *Failed, Open,* or *Alternate.*

- A port configured as a regular segment port starts as a failed port.

- After the neighbor adjacencies are determined, the port changes to alternate port state, blocking all VLANs on the interface. Blocked port negotiations occur and when the segment settles, one blocked port remains in the alternate role, and all other ports become open ports.

- When a failure occurs in a link, all ports move to the open state. When the alternate port receives the failure notification, it changes to the open state, forwarding all VLANs.

First, we configure all ring interfaces as REP ports with segment ID 911. All interface have to be Layer 2 trunk interfaces. To get REP working, we have to configure at least on edge port. For VLAN load-balancing, two edge ports are necessary.

We configure the two edge ports on switch ME_A. Ports on ME_B and ME_C are configured as standard segment ports.

```
ME_A:
interface GigabitEthernet0/11
 description Trunk to ME_B
 port-type nni
 switchport mode trunk
 rep segment 911 edge primary

interface GigabitEthernet0/12
 description Trunk to ME_C
 port-type nni
 switchport mode trunk
 rep segment 911 edge
```

```
ME_B:
interface GigabitEthernet0/11
 description Trunk to ME_A
 port-type nni
 switchport mode trunk
 rep segment 911

interface GigabitEthernet0/16
 description Trunk to ME_C
 port-type nni
 switchport mode trunk
 rep segment 911
```

```
ME_C:
interface GigabitEthernet0/12
 description Trunk to ME_A
 port-type nni
```

```
switchport mode trunk
rep segment 911

interface GigabitEthernet0/16
 description Trunk to ME_B
 port-type nni
 switchport mode trunk
 rep segment 911
```

Activating REP produces a log message and you can examine the topology with "show rep topology" on switch ME_C:

```
ME_C#sh rep topology
REP Segment 911
BridgeName      PortName  Edge Role
----------------  ---------- ---- ----
ME_A            Gi0/11     Pri  Open
ME_B            Gi0/11          Open
ME_B            Gi0/16          Open
ME_C            Gi0/16          Open
ME_C            Gi0/12          Open
ME_A            Gi0/12     Sec  Alt
```

As you can see, port Gi0/12 on ME_A is in "Alt-state" and does not forward traffic. (VLAN load balancing is disabled per default).

You can also examine the REP status of a particular interface with "show int <interface> rep [detail]"

```
ME_C#sh int g0/12 rep
Interface          Seg-id Type      LinkOp     Role
---------------------- ------ ---------------- ----------- ----
GigabitEthernet0/12   911              TWO_WAY    Open

ME_C#sh int g0/12 rep det
GigabitEthernet0/12   REP enabled
Segment-id: 911 (Segment)
PortID: 000C0024F7C1FE00
Preferred flag: No
Operational Link Status: TWO_WAY
Current Key: 00100024F7C1FE0070BB
```

```
Port Role: Open
Blocked VLAN: <empty>
Admin-vlan: 1
Preempt Delay Timer: disabled
LSL Ageout Timer: 5000 ms
Configured Load-balancing Block Port: none
Configured Load-balancing Block VLAN: none
STCN Propagate to: none
LSL PDU rx: 11400, tx: 7422
HFL PDU rx: 0, tx: 0
BPA TLV rx: 8680, tx: 860
BPA (STCN, LSL) TLV rx: 0, tx: 0
BPA (STCN, HFL) TLV rx: 0, tx: 0
EPA-ELECTION TLV rx: 148, tx: 19
EPA-COMMAND TLV rx: 0, tx: 0
EPA-INFO TLV rx: 2197, tx: 2202
```

I case of a link failure on Gi0/16 between ME_B and ME_C, you will see the following syslog message:

```
*Mar  1 07:03:17.617: %REP-4-LINKSTATUS: GigabitEthernet0/16 (segment 911) is non-operational due to port become non-trunk
```

REP converges immediately and unblocks the "Alt"-Link. Gi0/16 changes to "fail –state

```
ME_C#sh rep topology
REP Segment 911
Warning: REP detects a segment failure, topology may be incomplete

BridgeName      PortName    Edge Role
---------------  ----------  ---- ----
ME_C            Gi0/16      Fail
ME_C            Gi0/12      Open
ME_A            Gi0/12      Sec  Open
```

802.1Q Tunneling (Q-in-Q)

802.1Q tunneling (aka Q-in-Q) is a technique often used by Metro Ethernet providers as a layer 2 VPN for customers. 802.1Q (or dot1q) tunneling is simple as the service provider will put a 802.1Q tag on all the frames that it receives from a customer with a unique VLAN tag. By using a different VLAN tag for each customer, we can separate the traffic from different customers and transparently transfer it throughout the service provider network.

One of the advantages of this solution is that it is easy to implement, you don't need exotic hardware and don't need to run any routing protocols between the service provider and customer (unlike MPLS VPN). From the customer's perspective, it's just like their sites are directly connected on layer 2.

In the tutorial, we will configure 802.1Q tunneling. We are using the following topology for this:

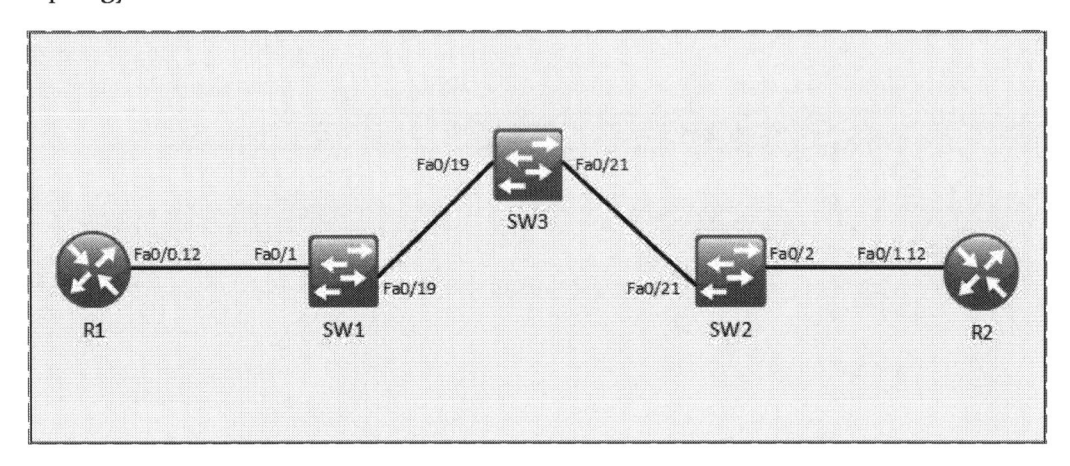

Figure 41

Above, you see two routers called R1 and R2, imagine these routers are the customer sites that we want to connect through the service provider network, which consists of SW1, SW2 and SW3. Our customer wants to use VLAN 12 between the two sites and expects our service provider to transport this from one site to another.

In example, our customer will be using VLAN 12 for traffic between their sites. The service provider has decided to use VLAN 123 to transport everything for this customer. This is what will happen when we send frames between R1 and R2:

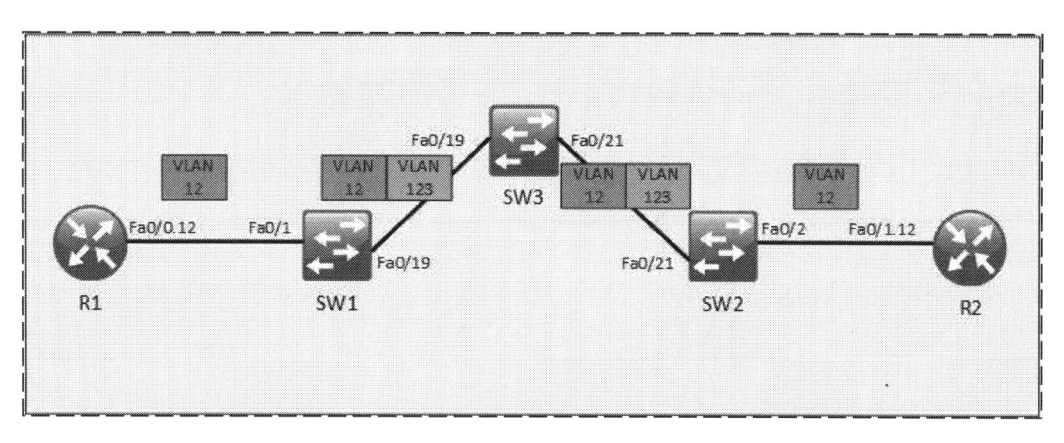

Figure 42

Whenever R1 sends traffic, it will tag its frames for VLAN 12. Once it arrives at the service provider, SW1 will add an additional VLAN tag (123). Once SW2 forwards the frame towards R2 it will remove the second VLAN tag and forwards the original tagged frame from R1.

Here's what the router config look like:

```
R1(config)#interface fastEthernet 0/0
R1(config-if)#no shutdown
R1(config-if)#interface fastEthernet 0/0.12
R1(config-subif)#encapsulation dot1Q 12
R1(config-subif)#ip address 192.168.12.1 255.255.255.0
```

```
R2(config)#interface fastEthernet 0/0
R2(config-if)#no shutdown
R2(config-if)#interface fastEthernet 0/0.12
R2(config-subif)#encapsulation dot1Q 12
R2(config-subif)#ip address 192.168.12.2 255.255.255.0
```

R1 and R2 are both configured with sub-interfaces and use subnet 192.168.12.0 /24. All their frames are tagged as VLAN 12.

On the service provider network we'll have to configure a number of items. First we will configure 802.1Q trunks between SW1 – SW3 and SW2 – SW3:

```
SW1(config)#interface fastEthernet 0/19
SW1(config-if)#switchport trunk encapsulation dot1q
SW1(config-if)#switchport mode trunk
```

```
SW2(config)#interface fastEthernet 0/21
```

```
SW2(config-if)#switchport trunk encapsulation dot1q
SW2(config-if)#switchport mode trunk
```

```
SW3(config)#interface fastEthernet 0/19
SW3(config-if)#switchport trunk encapsulation dot1q
SW3(config-if)#switchport mode trunk
SW3(config)#interface fastEthernet 0/21
SW3(config-if)#switchport trunk encapsulation dot1q
SW3(config-if)#switchport mode trunk
```

The next part is where we configure the actual "Q-in-Q" tunneling. The service provider will use VLAN 123 to transfer everything from our customer. We will configure the interfaces towards the customer routers to tag everything for VLAN 123:

```
SW1(config)#interface fastEthernet 0/1
SW1(config-if)#switchport access vlan 123
SW1(config-if)#switchport mode dot1q-tunnel
SW2(config)#interface fastEthernet 0/2
SW2(config-if)#switchport access vlan 123
SW2(config-if)#switchport mode dot1q-tunnel
```

The switchport mode dot1q-tunnel command tells the switch to tag the traffic and switchport access vlan command is required to specify the Q-in-Q VLAN of 123. Make sure that VLAN 123 is available on SW1, SW2 and SW3. By assigning the interfaces above to this VLAN, it was automatically created on SW1 and SW2 but I also have to make sure that SW3 has VLAN 123 in its database:

```
SW3(config)#vlan 123
```

Everything is now in place. Let us do a quick test to see if R1 and R2 can reach each other:

```
R1#ping 192.168.12.2

Type escape sequence to abort.
Sending 5, 100-byte ICMP Echos to 192.168.12.2, timeout is 2 seconds:
!!!!!
Success rate is 100 percent (5/5), round-trip min/avg/max = 1/2/4 ms
```

Our ping is working! Let us look at some commands to verify our work:

```
SW1#show dot1q-tunnel

dot1q-tunnel mode LAN Port(s)
-----------------------------
Fa0/1
```

```
SW2#show dot1q-tunnel

dot1q-tunnel mode LAN Port(s)
-----------------------------
Fa0/2
```

The show dot1q-tunnel command does not give me a lot of information. The only thing we see are the interfaces that are configured for dot1q tunneling. A good way to prove that the service provider switches are really tunneling the frames from the customer is by looking at the trunks between SW1, SW2 and SW3:

```
SW1#show interfaces fa0/19 trunk

Port      Mode       Encapsulation  Status     Native vlan
Fa0/19    on         802.1q         trunking   1

Port      Vlans allowed on trunk
Fa0/19    1-4094

Port      Vlans allowed and active in management domain
Fa0/19    1,123

Port      Vlans in spanning tree forwarding state and not pruned
Fa0/19    1,123
```

```
SW2#show interfaces trunk

Port      Mode       Encapsulation  Status     Native vlan
Fa0/21    on         802.1q         trunking   1

Port      Vlans allowed on trunk
Fa0/21    1-4094

Port      Vlans allowed and active in management domain
Fa0/21    1,123
```

Port	Vlans in spanning tree forwarding state and not pruned
Fa0/21	1,123

```
SW3#show interfaces trunk

Port      Mode      Encapsulation   Status      Native vlan
Fa1/0/19  on        802.1q          trunking    1
Fa1/0/21  auto      n-802.1q        trunking    1

Port      Vlans allowed on trunk
Fa0/19    1-4094
Fa0/21    1-4094

Port      Vlans allowed and active in management domain
Fa0/19    1,123
Fa0/21    1,123

Port      Vlans in spanning tree forwarding state and not pruned
Fa0/19    1,123
Fa0/21    1,123
```

As you can see above, the only VLAN that is active (besides VLAN 1) on these trunk links is VLAN 123. You will not see VLAN 12 here because that is the customer traffic and it is encapsulated with VLAN 123.

Chapter 6: Routed Network Technology- I

Technology Brief

Routing is the process of moving packets across a network from one host to another host. Dedicated devices, usually "routers" perform it. Packets are the fundamental unit of information transport in all modern computer networks, and increasingly in other communications networks as well. They are sent over packet switched networks, which are networks on which each message (i.e., data that is transmitted) is cut up into a set of small segments prior to transmission. Each packet is then sent individually and can follow the same path or a different path to the common destination. Once all of the packets have arrived at the destination, they are automatically reassembled to recreate the original message. Routing performed at layer 3/ Network Layer.

Classful Versus Classless Routing Protocols

Classful routing protocols do not carry subnet masks information. Classless routing protocols do. Older routing protocols, including RIP and IGRP, are Classful. Newer protocols, including RIP-2, EIGRP, and OSPF, are classless. What are the implications of using classful versus classless routing protocols in your networks?

Let us say that a router R received a RIP-1 update with the IP address 172.0.0.0. R would assume that the route being advertised was for the Class B network 172.0.0.0/16. In other words, since the subnet mask is lacking in the routing update, R assumes natural mask of /8, /16, and/24 for Class A, B, and C addresses, respectively. The only time a classful routing protocol can associate a mask other than the natural mask with an update is if R has a directly connected network with an IP address belonging to the same class as the IP address received in the update.

RIP-2 updates carry a subnet mask in each route entry. A routing protocol that carries subnet masks information in its updates earns the label "classless routing protocol." The term "classless" implies that routing decisions are not tied to the class of the IP address -- A, B, or C -- but may be based on any portion of the 32-bit IP address as specified by the mask. Router R could receive an update with the address and mask 192.168.0.0 and 255.255.0.0. This would imply that traffic for all IP addresses with "192.168" in the first two octets should be routed as per the routing advertisement. RIP-2 is thus a classless routing protocol.

Types of Routes

A router can learn a route using one of two methods: static and dynamic. The following two sections discuss the two types.

Static Route

A router can learn a static route in two ways. First, a router will look at its active interfaces, examine the addresses configured on the interfaces and determine the corresponding network numbers, and populate the routing table with this information. This is called a connected or directly connected route. The second way that a router can learn a static route is for you to configure the route manually. For example, you may configure a static route for the destination network of 192.168.2.0/24 with a next-hop address of 192.168.1.2 (the neighbor to forward the traffic to). One special type of static route is called a default route, commonly called the gateway of last resort. If the specified destination is not mentioned in the routing table, the default route can be used to route the packet. A default route has an IP address of 0.0.0.0 and a subnet mask of 0.0.0.0, often represented as 0.0.0.0/0. Default routes are commonly used in small networks on a perimeter router pointing to the directly connected ISP router.

Dynamic Routes

A router learns dynamic routes by running a routing protocol. Routing protocols will learn about routes from other neighboring routers running the same routing protocol. Dynamic routing protocols share reachability information concerning these networks. Through this sharing process, a router will learn about all of the reachable network and subnet numbers in the network. You should know that the terms routing protocol and routed protocol have two different meanings. A routing protocol learns about routes for a routed protocol. A routed protocol is a layer 3 protocol, such as Transmission Control Protocol/Internet Protocol (TCP/IP) or Internetwork Packet Exchange (IPX). A routed protocol carries user traffic such as e-mail, file transfers, and web downloads.

Autonomous Systems

Some routing protocols understand the concept of an autonomous system, and some do not. An autonomous system (AS) is a group of networks under a single administrative control, which could be your company, a division within your company, or a group of companies. An Interior Gateway Protocol (IGP) refers to a routing protocol that manages routing within a single autonomous system. IGPs include RIP, EIGRP, OSPF, and Intermediate System-Intermediate System (IS-IS). An Exterior Gateway Protocol (EGP) handles routing between various autonomous systems. Today, only one EGP is active: Border Gateway Protocol (BGP). BGP is used to route traffic across the Internet backbone between different autonomous systems. Not every routing protocol understands the concept of an AS. An AS can provide distinct boundaries for a routing protocol, and thus provides some advantages. For instance, you can control how far routers propagate a network number. In addition, you can control what routes you will advertise to other autonomous systems and what routes you'll accept from these systems. To differentiate one autonomous system from another, an AS can be assigned a unique number from 1 to 65,535. The Internet Assigned Numbers Authority (IANA) is responsible for assigning these numbers.

Administrative Distance

Each router needs to choose the best path to a destination. This process can become complicated if the router is receiving routing update information for a single network from multiple sources, such as connected, static, and IGP routing protocols, and must choose one of these sources as the best and place this choice in the router's routing table.

Router looks at two things when choosing a best path: administrative distance and routing metrics. The first item a router looks at is the administrative distance for a route source. Administrative distance is a Cisco-proprietary mechanism used to rank the IP routing protocols. As an example, if a router is running two IGPs, RIP and EIGRP, and is learning network 10.0.0.0/8 from both of these routing protocols, which one should the router pick and place in its routing table? Which one should the router believe more? Actually, the term administrative distance is somewhat misleading, since the term has nothing to do with measuring distance. The term believability better describes the process.

Administrative distance ranks the IP routing protocols, assigning a value, or you may call it weight, to each protocol. Distances can range from 0 to 255. A smaller distance is more believable or preferable by a router, with the best distance being 0 and the worst 255. Table displays some of the default administrative distances Cisco has assigned to its IP routing protocols. Going back to the previous example of a router learning network 10.0.0.0/8 from RIP and EIGRP, since RIP has a value of 120 and EIGRP has a value of 90, which is a better (lower) administrative distance value, the router will use the EIGRP route.

Administrative Distance	Route Type
0	Connected interface route
1	Static route
90	EIGRP
110	OSPF
120	RIPv1 and RIPv2 route
170	External EIGRP (Another AS)
255	Unknown route

Table 12 Value of Administrative distance for popular Routing protocols

Routing Metrics

As mentioned in the "Administrative Distance" section, if your router has learned two routes, such as RIP and EIGRP, for the same network number, the router uses the administrative distance to choose the best one. However, a situation might arise where two paths to the destination network exist, and the same routing protocol, RIP, for instance, discovers these multiple paths to the destination network. If this is the case, a routing protocol will use a measurement called a metric to determine which path is the best path to place in the routing table.

The table below lists some common metrics, the IP routing protocols that use them, and brief descriptions of the metrics. As you can see from this table, some routing protocols use only a single metric. For instance, RIP uses hop count as a metric, and

OSPF uses cost. Other routing protocols use multiple metric values to choose a best path to a destination. For instance, EIGRP can use bandwidth, delay, reliability, load, and maximum transmission unit (MTU) when choosing a best path to a destination.

Metric	Routing Protocols	Description
Bandwidth	EIGRP	The capacity of the link in Kbps (T1=1554)
Cost	OSPF	Measurement in the inverse of the bandwidth of the links
Delay	EIGRP	Time it takes to reach the destination
Hop count	RIP	How many layer 3 hops away from the destination
Load	EIGRP	The path with the least utilization
MTU	EIGRP	The path that support the largest frame sizes
Reliability	EIGRP	The path with the least amount of errors or downtime

Table 13 Table 12 Metric associated with routing protocol

RIP (Routing Information Protocol)

RIP is a distance vector protocol. RIP is an old protocol. Cisco does not do that much development on the protocol, unlike other, more advanced protocols. Therefore, you can feel safe that when you upgrade your IOS to a newer version, RIP will function the same way it did in the previous release.

RIPv1

RIPv1 uses local broadcasts to share routing information. These updates are periodic in nature, send by default, every 30 seconds, with a hold-down period of 180 seconds. Both versions of RIP use hop count as a metric, which is not always the best metric to use. For example, if you had two paths to reach a network, where one was a two-hop Ethernet connection and the other was a one-hop 64-Kbps WAN connection, RIP would use the slower 64-Kbps connection because it has a lesser-accumulated hop-count metric. You have to remember this little tidbit when looking at how RIP will populate your router's routing table.

To prevent packets from circling around a loop forever, both versions of RIP solve counting to infinity by placing a hop-count limit of 15 hops on packets. Any packet that reaches the 16th hop will be dropped. RIPv1 is a classful protocol. This is important for configuring RIP and subnetting your IP addressing scheme: you can use only one subnet mask value for a given Class A, B, or C network. For instance, if you have a Class B network such as 172.16.0.0, you can subnet it with only one mask. As an example, you could not use 255.255.255.0 and 255.255.255.128 on 172.16.0.0—you can choose only one.

Another interesting feature is that RIP supports up to six equal-cost paths to a single destination, where all six paths can be placed in the routing table and the router can load-balance across them. The default is actually four paths, but this can be increased up to a maximum of six. Remember that an equal-cost path is where the metric for the multiple paths to a destination is the same. RIP will not load-balance across unequal-cost paths.

RIPv2

One thing you should keep in the back of your mind when dealing with RIPv2 is that it is based on RIPv1 and is, at heart, a distance vector protocol with routing enhancements built into it. Therefore, it is called a hybrid protocol.

One major enhancement to RIPv2 pertains to how it deals with routing updates. Instead of using broadcasts, RIPv2 uses multicasts: updates are advertised to 224.0.0.9, which all RIPv2 routers will process. In addition, to speed up convergence, RIPv2 supports triggered updates—when a change occurs, a RIPv2 router will immediately send its routing information to its connected neighbors.

A second major enhancement in RIPv2 is that it is a classless protocol. RIPv2 supports variable-length subnet masking (VLSM), which allows you to use more than one subnet mask for a given class network number. VLSM allows you to maximize the efficiency of your addressing design as well as summarize routing information to create very large, scalable networks. As a third enhancement, RIPv2 supports authentication. You can restrict what routers you want to participate in RIPv2. This is accomplished using a clear-text or hashed password value.

RIPng (RIP Next Generation)

RIP (Routing Information Protocol) is the first routing protocol for IP. Because of the technical problems, new RIP, known as RIPv2 was developed. RIP for IPv6 (RIPng) is described in RFC 2080.

When IPv6 protocol came up, again a new version of RIP was required to support IPv6. This new version of RIP is now known as RIP New Generation (or RIPng). RIPng is the new routing protocol for IPv6 and it is based on RIPv2. RIPng is an entirely different protocol and does not support IPv4.

RIPng uses the same timers and message types as RIPv2. RIPng has a 30 second update timer and a 180 second hold down timer. The metric value of RIPng is also based on hop count.

RIPng sends and receives the Routing Protocol messages at UDP port 521.

Route Redistribution

Route redistribution is needed when you take a route from one routing protocol and inject it or distribute it into another protocol. By default, routers only advertise and share routes with other routers running the same protocol. Therefore, if you have 2 routers and one runs OSPF and the other runs EIGRP and you want them to know about each other's routes, by default, they won't share routing information because they are not running the same protocol. Therefore, you use route redistribution to 2 different protocols can still share and advertise routes to each other.

Redistribution is not just for between routing protocols, we have multiple options mentioned below:

- Between routing protocols (RIP, OSPF, EIGRP, BGP).
- Static routes can be redistributed into a dynamic routing protocol.
- Directly connected routes can be redistributed into a routing protocol.

Normally you use the network command to advertise directly connected routes into your routing protocol. You can also use the redistribute-connected command, which will redistribute it into the routing protocol.

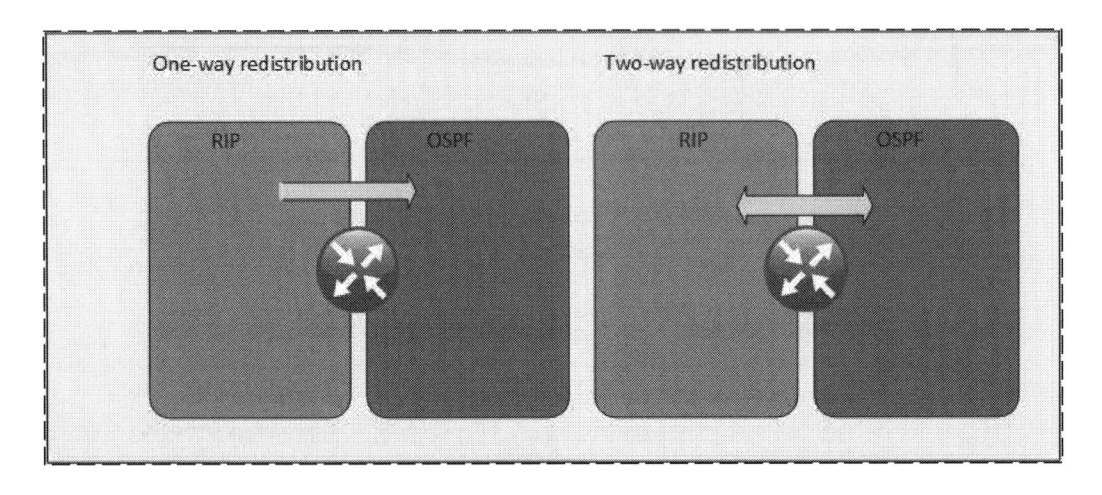

There are two types of redistribution

1) One-way redistribution
2) Two-way redistribution

Redistributing routes from one protocol to another is called one-way redistribution and from one protocol to another and vice versa is called two-way redistribution as shown in the following figure

Figure 43 Types of redistribution

Redistributing into EIGRP

EIGRP is a Cisco-proprietary hybrid routing protocol that, by default, uses a Composite of bandwidth and delay as its distance metric. EIGRP can additionally consider Reliability, Load, and MTU for its metric.

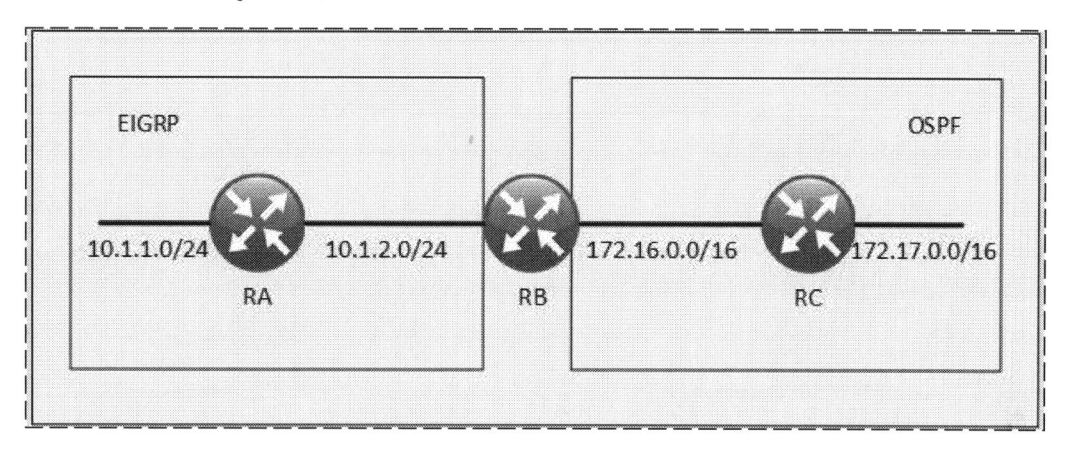

Figure 44 Redistribution into EIGRP

To redistribute all OSPF routes into EIGRP:

RouterB(config)# router eigrp 10
RouterB(config-router)# network 10.1.2.0 0.0.0.255
RouterB(config-router)#default-metric 1 1 1 1 1
RouterB(config-router)# redistribute ospf 20 metric 1 1 1 1 1

First, the router eigrp process was enabled for Autonomous System 15. Next, EIGRP was configured to advertise the network of 10.1.2.0/24. Finally, EIGRP was configured to redistribute all ospf routes from process ID 20, and apply a metric of 1 (bandwidth), 1 (delay), 1 (Reliability), 1 (load), and 1 (MTU) to the redistributed routes. Putting metric value to all 1s is not a good practice but to show you in simple steps we did this for lab purpose only

Redistributing into OSPF

OSPF is a standardized Link-State routing protocol that uses cost (based on Bandwidth) as its link-state metric. An OSPF router performing redistribution automatically becomes an ASBR.

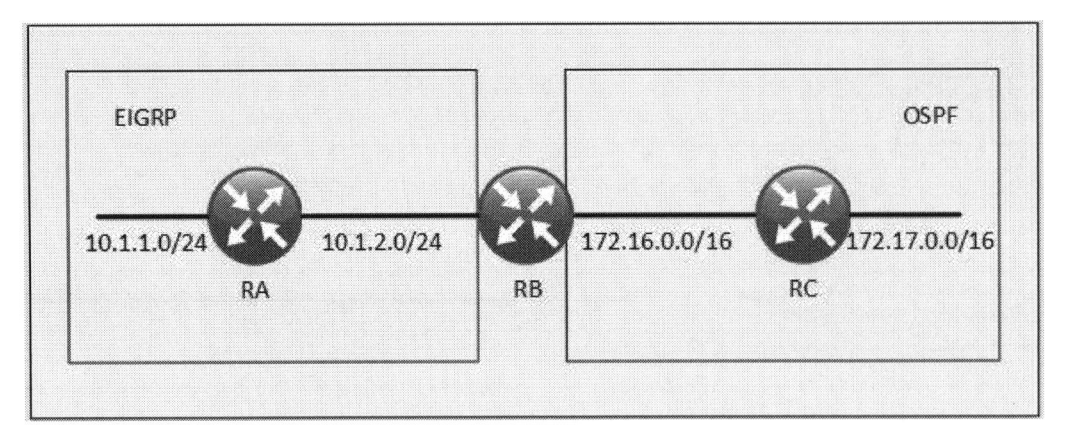

Figure 45 Redistribution into OSPF

To redistribute all EIGRP routes into OSPF:
RouterB(config)# router ospf 20
RouterB(config-router)# network 172.16.0.0 0.0.255.255 area 0
RouterB(config-router)# redistribute eigrp 15 subnets

First, the router ospf process was configured with a process-ID of 20. Next, OSPF was configured to place any interfaces in the network of 172.16.0.0/16 into area 0. Then, OSPF will redistribute all eigrp routes from AS 15.I apply subnets to ensure all eigrp subnetted routes should be redistributed. If the default-metric or a manual metric is not specified for the redistributed routes, a default metric of 20 will be applied to routes of all routing protocols except for BGP. Redistributed BGP routes will have a default metric of 1 applied by OSPF. By default, OSPF will only redistribute classful routes into the OSPF domain.

VRF (Virtual routing and forwarding)

Virtual routing and forwarding (VRF) is a technology that allows multiple logical instances of a routing table to co-exist within the same physical router at the same time. Because the routing instances are independent, Same IP addresses can be used without conflicting with each other. The multiple Routing instances can be made to traverse different path (i.e. take different outgoing interfaces).

VRFs are the same methods of network isolation/virtualization as VLANs. VLANs are used at the L2 and VRFs are L3 tools. VRFs are to routing table as VLANs are to LANs. Using VRFs, we are virtualizing routing table into multiple routing tables, similarly to VLANs used to virtualize LANs. One could say that VLANs performs L2 virtualization, VRFs performs L3 virtualization. VLANs make a single switch look like several switches; VRFs make a single router look like several routers.

This works well, but we need a way to keep track of which 192.168.1.0/24 route belongs to which customer. This is where route distinguishers come in. As its name implies, a route distinguisher (RD) distinguishes one set of routes (one VRF) from another. It is a unique number prepended to each route within a VRF to identify it as belonging to that particular VRF or customer. RD is 64 bits in length.

The scenario below will help us understand how VRF works and logically separates traffic for multiple customer by having multiple routing table for each customer VRF. In the diagram, PE is the Provider Router connected on Fast Ethernet 0/0 to C1 and C2 Routers where C1 is customer 1 Router (Allocation under RED) and C2 is customer 2 Router (Allocation under GREEN).

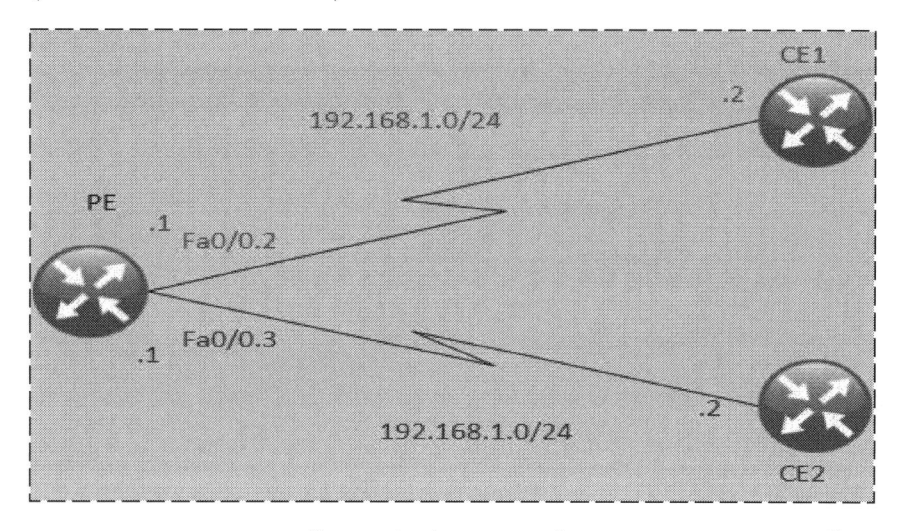

Figure 46 Implementation of VRF

Now let us configure RD's on the PE router.

PE(config)#ip vrf RED
PE(config-vrf)#rd 2:2
PE(config-vrf)#ip vrf BLUE
PE(config-vrf)#rd 3:3

We have created two VRFs and assign different RD values in order to distinguish the routes. Next, configure sub interface for both the customers. In this case, fa0/0.2 for RED vrf customer and fa0/0.3 for BLUE vrf customer. Please note the IP address at PE end for both the VRF will remain the same ie 192.168.1.1.

PE(config)#int fa0/0.2
PE(config-subif)#encapsulation dot1q 2
PE(config-subif)#ip vrf forwarding RED

```
PE(config-subif)#ip address 192.168.1.1 255.255.255.0
PE(config-subif)#int fa0/0.3
PE(config-subif)#encapsulation dot1q 3
PE(config-subif)#ip vrf forwarding  BLUE
PE(config-subif)#ip address 192.168.1.1 255.255.255.0
```

Now since configuration is complete, let us perform the connectivity test.

1st ping from Customer 1 Router towards PE IP address 192.168.1.1 (RED VRF)

2nd ping from customer 2 Router towards PE IP address 192.168.1.1 (GREEN VRF)

```
C1#ping 192.168.1.1
Type escape sequence to abort.
Sending 5, 100-byte ICMP Echos to 192.168.1.1, timeout is 2 seconds:
!!!!!
Success rate is 100 percent (5/5), round-trip min/avg/max = 10/35/70 ms


C2#ping 192.168.1.1
Type escape sequence to abort.
Sending 5, 100-byte ICMP Echos to 192.168.1.1, timeout is 2 seconds:
!!!!!
Success rate is 100 percent (5/5), round-trip min/avg/max = 10/35/70 ms
```

Ping test from PE towards customer Routers

```
PE#ping vrf RED 192.168.1.2
Type escape sequence to abort.
```

```
Sending 5, 100-byte ICMP Echos to 192.168.1.2, timeout is 2 seconds:
!!!!!
Success rate is 100 percent (5/5), round-trip min/avg/max = 10/35/70 ms
```

```
PE#ping vrf BLUE 192.168.1.2

Type escape sequence to abort.

Sending 5, 100-byte ICMP Echos to 192.168.1.2, timeout is 2 seconds:

!!!!!

Success rate is 100 percent (5/5), round-trip min/avg/max = 10/35/70 ms
```

GRE (Generic Routing Encapsulation)

Generic Routing Encapsulation (GRE) is a tunneling protocol developed by Cisco that allows the encapsulation of a wide variety of network layer protocols inside point-to-point links.

A GRE tunnel is needed when packets need to be sent from one network to another over the Internet or an insecure network. With GRE, a virtual tunnel is established between the two endpoints (Cisco routers) and packets are sent through the GRE tunnel.

It is important to note that packets travelling inside a GRE tunnel are not encrypted as GRE does not encrypt the tunnel but encapsulates it with a GRE header. If data protection is required, IPsec must be configured to provide data confidentiality – this is when a GRE tunnel is transformed into a secure VPN GRE tunnel.

Creating a Cisco GRE Tunnel

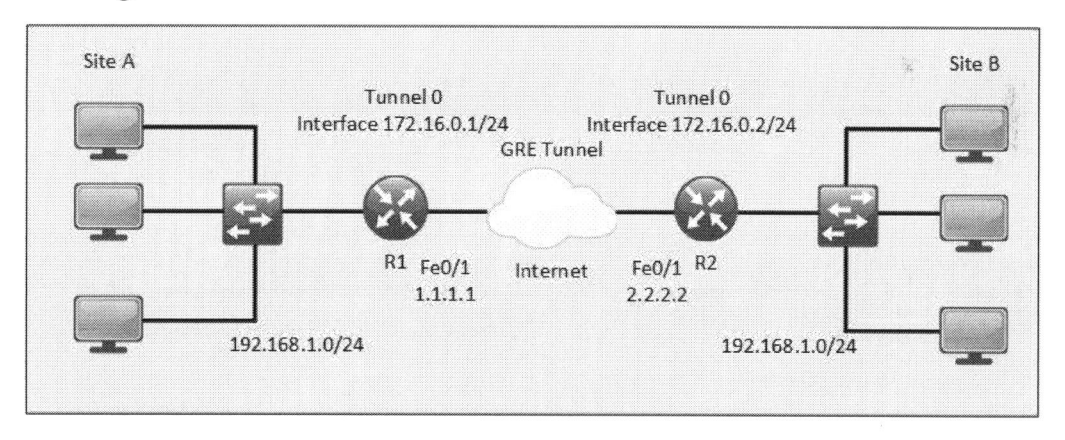

Figure 47 GRE tunneling

Configuration

GRE tunnel uses 'tunnel' interface – a logical interface configured on the router with an IP address where packets are encapsulated and DE capsulated as they enter or exit the GRE tunnel.

The first step is to create our tunnel interface on R1:

```
R1(config)# interface Tunnel0
R1(config-if)# ip address 172.16.0.1 255.255.255.0
R1(config-if)# ip mtu 1400
R1(config-if)# ip tcp adjust-mss 1360
R1(config-if)# tunnel source 1.1.1.10
R1(config-if)# tunnel destination 2.2.2.10
```

All Tunnel interfaces of participating routers must be configured with an IP address that is not used anywhere else in the network. Each Tunnel interface is assigned an IP address within the same network as the other Tunnel interfaces.

In our example, both Tunnel interfaces are part of the 172.16.0.0/24 network.

Since GRE is an encapsulating protocol, we adjust the maximum transfer unit (mtu) to 1400 bytes and maximum segment size (mss) to 1360 bytes. Because most transport MTUs are 1500 bytes and we have an added overhead because of GRE, we must reduce the MTU to account for the extra overhead. A setting of 1400 is a common practice and will ensure unnecessary packet fragmentation is kept to a minimum. Closing, we define the Tunnel source, which is R1's public IP address, and destination – R2's public IP address.

Since the Tunnel 0 interface is a logical interface it will never down even if there is, no GRE tunnel configured or connected at the other end.

Next, we must create the Tunnel 0 interface on R2:

```
R2(config)# interface Tunnel0
R2(config-if)# ip address 172.16.0.2 255.255.255.0
R2(config-if)# ip mtu 1400
R2(config-if)# ip tcp adjust-mss 1360
R2(config-if)# tunnel source 2.2.2.10
R2(config-if)# tunnel destination 1.1.1.10
```

R2's Tunnel interface is enabled with the appropriate tunnel source and destination IP address.

At this point, both tunnel end points are ready and can 'see' each other. An icmp echo from one end will confirm this:

```
R1# ping 172.16.0.2
```

```
Type escape sequence to abort.

Sending 5, 100-byte ICMP Echos to 172.16.0.2, timeout is 2 seconds:

!!!!!

Success rate is 100 percent (5/5), round-trip min/avg/max = 1/2/4 ms

R1#
```

Again, this result means that the two tunnel endpoints can see each other. Workstations on either network will still not be able to reach the other side unless a static route is placed on each endpoint:

```
R1(config)# ip route 192.168.2.0 255.255.255.0 172.16.0.2
```

On R1 we add a static route to the remote network 192.168.2.0/24 via 172.16.0.2, which is the other end of our GRE Tunnel. When R1 receives a packet for 192.168.2.0 network, it now knows the next hop is 172.16.0.2 and therefore will send it through the tunnel.

The same configuration must be repeated for R2:

```
R2(config)# ip route 192.168.1.0 255.255.255.0 172.16.0.1
```

EIGRP (Enhanced Interior Gateway Protocol)

Enhanced Interior Gateway Routing Protocol (EIGRP) is an advanced distance-vector routing protocol using Diffusing Update Algorithm (DUAL) to ensure loop-free route computation. Cisco Systems designed the protocol as a proprietary protocol, available only on Cisco devices.

EIGRP Features

Convergence

EIGRP uses the Diffusing Update Algorithm (DUAL) to achieve rapid convergence. EIGRP maintains a copy of its neighbor routes and calculates its own cost to each remote network. If the primary route is unreachable, EIGRP will look in to the topology table for an alternate route. If no appropriate route or backup route exists in the local routing table, EIGRP queries its neighbors to discover an alternative route. These queries are propagated until an alternative route is found, or it is determined that no alternative route exists.

VLSM

Unlike IGRP; EIGRP is a classless routing protocol supporting advertisement of the subnet mask with network advertisement. It enables EIGRP to support discontinuous sub networks and VLSM.

Partial Updates

EIGRP supports partial update instead of periodic updates. Updates are sent only when the path or the metric for a route changes and contains information about only the changed information. Propagation of these partial updates is automatically bounded so that only those routers that require the information are updated. As a result, EIGRP consumes significantly less bandwidth than IGRP.

Multiple Protocol Support

EIGRP supports IP, AppleTalk, and Novell NetWare Internetwork Packet Exchange (IPX) using protocol-dependent modules that are responsible for protocol requirements specific to the network layer.

EIGRP Terminology

Neighbor table

EIGRP routers use hello packets to discover neighbors. When a router discovers and forms an adjacency with a new neighbor, it includes the neighbor's address and the interface through which it can be reached in an entry in the neighbor table. This table is comparable to the neighborship (adjacency) database used by link-state routing protocols. It ensures bidirectional communication between each of the directly connected neighbors. EIGRP keeps a neighbor table for each network protocol supported for example an IP neighbor table, an IPX neighbor table, and an AppleTalk neighbor table.

Topology table

When the router dynamically discovers a new neighbor, it sends an update about the routes it knows to its new neighbor and receives the same from the new neighbor. These updates populate the topology table. The topology table contains all destinations advertised by neighbouring routers; in other words, each router stores its neighbours' routing tables in its EIGRP topology table. An EIGRP router maintains a topology table for each network protocol configured (IP, IPX, and AppleTalk).

Advertised distance (AD) and feasible distance (FD)

DUAL uses distance information, known as a metric or cost, to select efficient, loop-free paths. The lowest-cost route is calculated by adding the cost between the next-hop router and the destination—referred to as the advertised distance—to the cost between the local router and the next-hop router. The sum of these costs is referred to as the feasible distance.

Successor

A successor is a neighboring router that has a least-cost path to a destination (the lowest FD) that is guaranteed not to be part of a routing loop; successors are offered to the routing table to be used for forwarding packets. Multiple successors can exist if they have the same FD.

Routing table

The routing table holds the best routes to each destination and is used for forwarding packets. Successor routes are offered to the routing table.

Feasible successor (FS)

Along with keeping least-cost paths, DUAL keeps backup paths to each destination. The next-hop router for a backup path is called the feasible successor. To qualify as a feasible successor, a next-hop router must have an AD less than the FD of the current successor route; in other words, a feasible successor is a neighbor that is closer to the destination, but it is not the least-cost path and, thus, is not used to forward data. Feasible successors are selected at the same time as successors but are kept only in the topology table. The topology table can maintain multiple feasible successors for a destination.

If the route via the successor becomes invalid (because of a topology change) or if a neighbor changes the metric, DUAL checks for feasible successors to the destination. If a feasible successor is found, DUAL uses it, thereby avoiding re-computing the route. If no suitable feasible successor exists, a re-computation must occur to determine the new successor. Although re-computation is not processor-intensive, it does affect convergence time, so it is advantageous to avoid unnecessary re-computations.

Please refer to the diagram next page to understand EIGRP route computation.

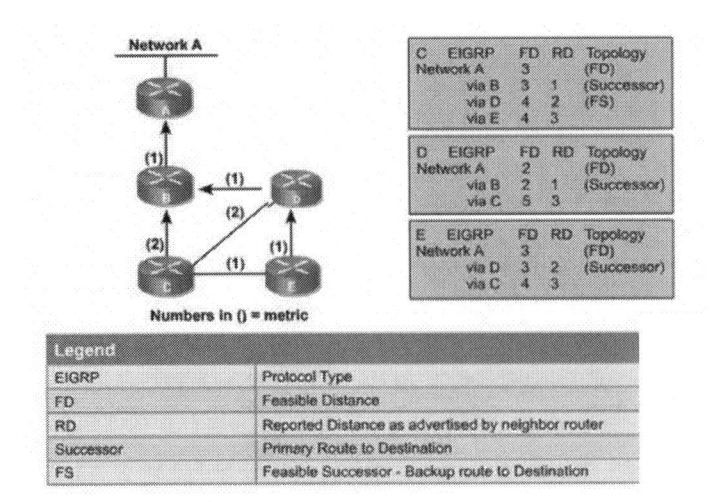

Figure 48 EIGRP route calculation

EIGRP Packet Types

Hello: Hello packets are used for neighbor discovery. They are sent as multicasts and do not require an acknowledgment. (They carry an acknowledgment number of 0.)

Update: Update packets contain route change information. An update is sent to communicate the routes that a particular router has used to converge; an update is sent only to affected routers. These updates are sent as multicasts when a new route is discovered, and when convergence is completed (when the route becomes passive). To synchronize topology tables, updates are sent as unicasts to neighbors during their EIGRP startup sequence. Updates are sent reliably.

Reply: A reply packet is sent in response to a query packet. Replies are unicast to the originator of the query and are sent reliably.

ACK: The ACK is used to acknowledge updates, queries, and replies. ACK packets are unicast hello packets and contain a nonzero acknowledgment number. (Note that hello and ACK packets do not require acknowledgment.)

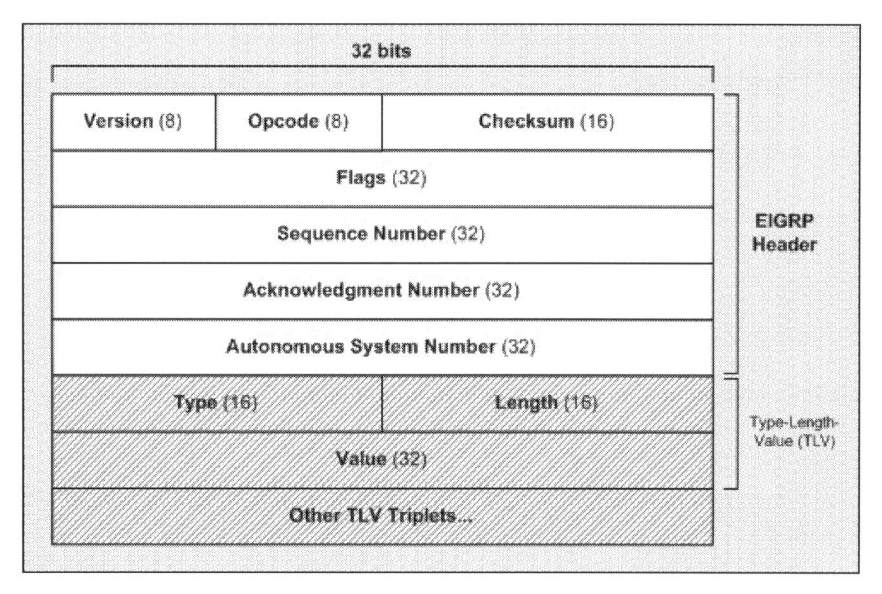

Figure 49 EIGRP Packet type

EIGRP Neighbors

A router discovers a neighbor when it receives its first hello packet on a directly connected network. The router requests DUAL to send a full route update to the new neighbor. In response, the neighbor sends its full route update. Thus, a new neighbor relationship is established in the following steps:

- When a router *A* receives a hello packet from a new neighbor *B*, *A* sends its topology table to router *B* in unicast updates with the *initialization bit* turned on.
- When router *B* receives a packet with the initialization bit on, it sends its topology table to router *A*.

The interval between hello packets from any EIGRP-speaking router on a network is five seconds (by default) on most media types. Each hello packet advertises *hold-time* -- the length of time the neighbor should consider the sender up. The default hold-time is 15 seconds. If no hellos are received for the duration of the hold-time, DUAL is informed that the neighbor is down. Thus, in addition to detecting a new neighbor, hello packets are also used to detect the loss of a neighbor.

A few points to note:

- If the EIGRP topology table has many entries that have an equal cost FD to a given destination network, all successors (up to four by default) for that destination network are installed in the routing table.

- To qualify as an FS, a next-hop router must have an AD less than the FD of the current successor route for the particular network. This is known as the feasibility condition.

- The cost to reach the next-time must be smaller than the cost of the successors to reach the desired network.

EIGRP Metric

Metric = [Bandwidth +Delay]x 256

Bandwidth is computed by taking the smallest bandwidth (expressed in kbits/s) from all outgoing interfaces to the destination (including the destination) and dividing 10,000,000 by this number (the smallest bandwidth). Delay is the sum of all the delay values to the destination network (expressed in tens of microseconds).

The following criteria, although available, are not commonly used, because they typically result in frequent recalculation of the topology table:

- Reliability— The worst reliability between the source and destination, based on keep alive.
- Loading— The worst load on a link between the source and destination based on the packet rate and the interface's configured bandwidth.
- Maximum transmission unit (MTU) — The smallest MTU in the path. (MTU is included in the EIGRP update but is actually not used in the metric calculation.)

Enhanced Interior Gateway Routing Protocol (EIGRP) considerd the following network performance related attributes to calculate the EIGRP metric value. 1) Bandwidth 2) Delay 3) Reliability and 4) Load

EIGRP Metric = 256*((K_1*Bandwidth) + (K_2*Bandwidth)/ (256-Load) + K_3*Delay) * (K_5/ (Reliability + K_4)))

By default, the values of K_1 and K_3 are set to 1, and K_2, K_4 and K_5 are set to 0.

Hence, the above equation is reduced to

EIGRP Metric = 256*(Bandwidth + Delay)

Where:
- Bandwidth = 10000000/bandwidth (i), where bandwidth (i) is the least bandwidth of all outgoing interfaces on the route to the destination network represented in kilobits.

- Delay = delay (i) where delay (i) is the sum of the delays configured on the interfaces, on the route to the destination network, in tens of microseconds.

Reliable Transport Protocol

The EIGRP transport mechanism uses a mix of multicast and unicast packets, using reliable delivery when necessary. All transmissions use IP with the protocol type field set to 88. The IP multicast address used is 224.0.0.10.

DUAL requires guaranteed and sequenced delivery for some transmissions. This is achieved using acknowledgments and sequence numbers. So, for example, update packets (containing routing table data) are delivered reliably (with sequence numbers) to all neighbors using multicast. Acknowledgment packets -- with the correct sequence number -- are expected from every neighbor. If the correct acknowledgment number is not received from a neighbor, the update is retransmitted as a unicast. Some transmissions do not require reliable delivery. For example, hello packets are multicast to all neighbors on an Ethernet segment, whereas acknowledgments are unicast. Neither hellos nor acknowledgments are sent reliably.

EIGRP also uses queries and replies as part of DUAL. Queries are multicast or unicast using reliable delivery, whereas replies are always reliably unicast. Query and reply packets are discussed in more detail in the next section.

Putting it All Together

Let us understand how the neighbor relationship works in EIGRP

- A new router (Router A) comes up on the link and sends out a hello packet through all of its EIGRP-configured interfaces.
- Routers receiving the hello packet on an interface (Router B) reply with update packets that contain all the routes they have in their routing table, except those learned through that interface (because of the split horizon rule). Router B sends an update packet to Router A, but a neighbor relationship is not established until Router B sends a hello packet to Router A. The update packet from Router B has the initial bit set, indicating that this is the initialization process. The update packet contains information about the routes that the neighbor (Router B) is aware of, including the metric that the neighbor is advertising for each destination.
- After both routers have exchanged hellos and the neighbor adjacency is established, Router A replies to Router B with an ACK packet, indicating that it received the update information.
- Router A inserts the update packet information in its topology table. The topology table includes all destinations advertised by neighboring (adjacent)

routers. It is organized so that each destination is listed, along with all the neighbors that can get to the destination and their associated metrics.
- Router A then sends an update packet to Router B.
- Upon receiving the update packet, Router B sends an ACK packet to Router A. After Router A and Router B successfully receive the update packets from each other, they are ready to choose the successor (best) and FS (backup) routes in the topology table, and offer the successor routes to the routing table.

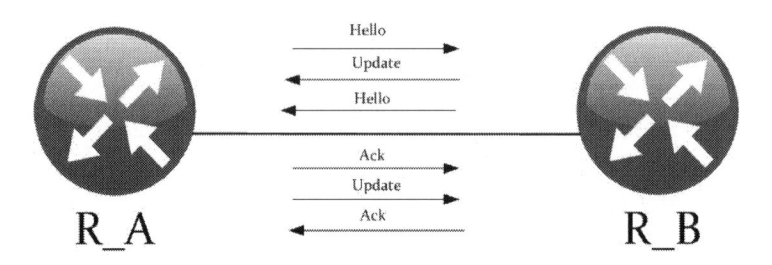

Figure 50 EIGRP Packet Exchange

EIGRP Mind map

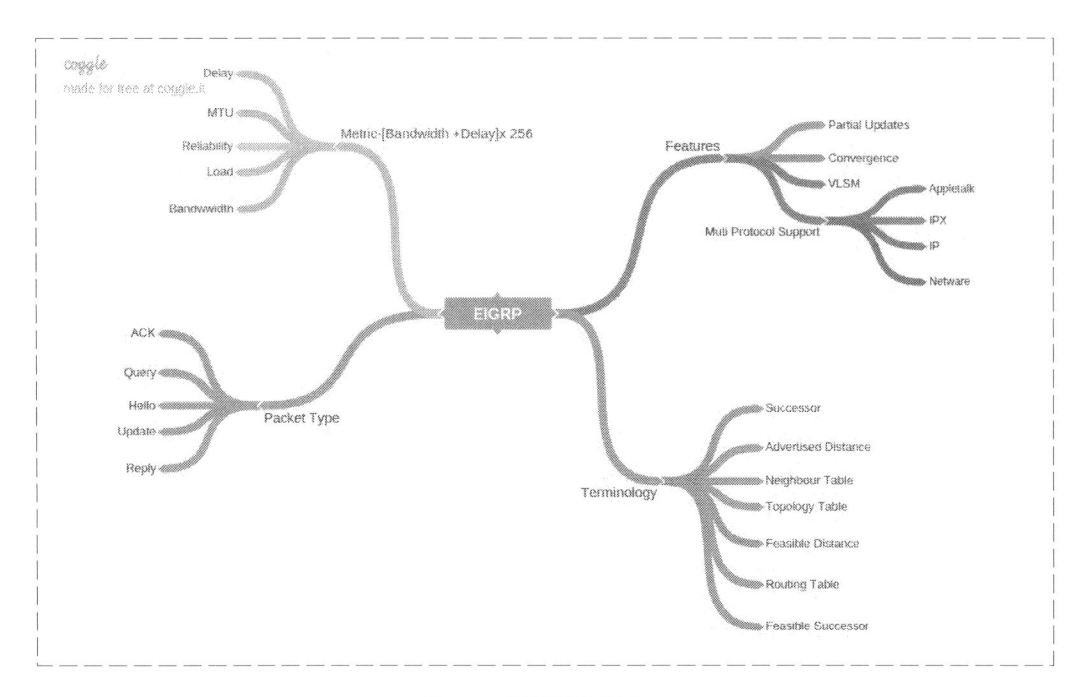

Figure 51 EIGRP Mind Map

Lab 6-1 : EIGRPv4

Case Study

IPS has a main campus in NY and branch campuses in South and North of Newyork. Sites are inter-connected by ISPs connection. The network team has decided to deploy EIGRP as routing protocol over the LAN and WAN network.

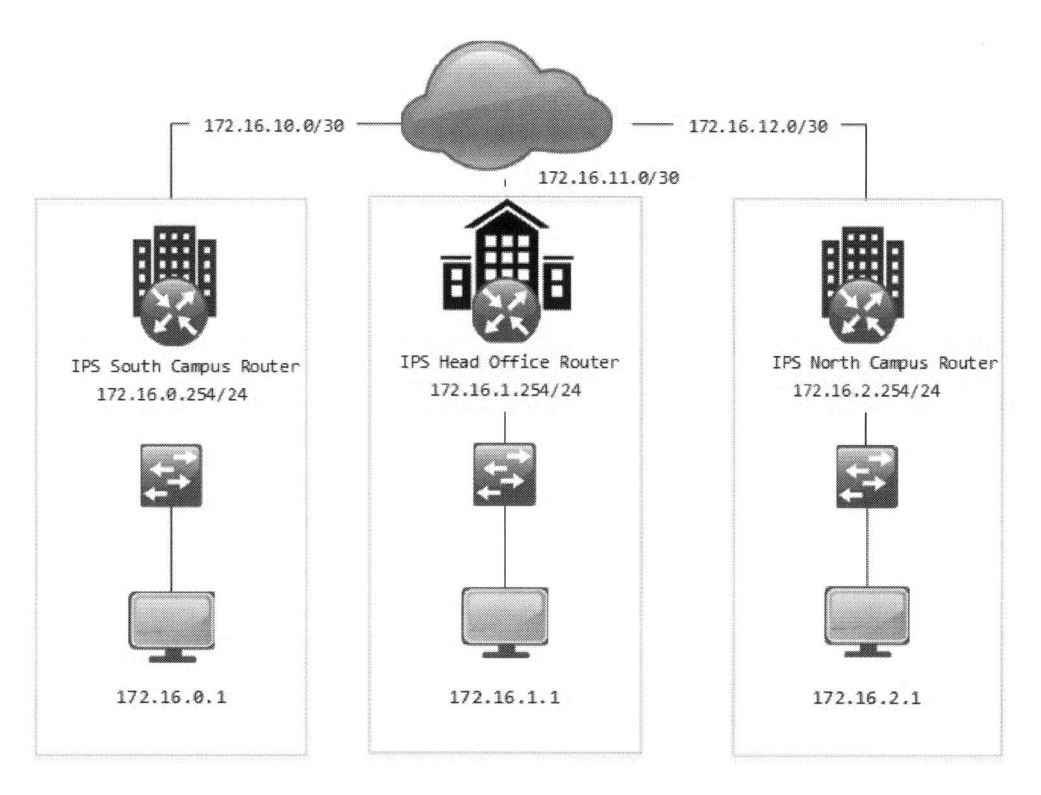

Figure 52 EIGRP Case Study

Lab 1: EIGRP Basic Configuration

The 'router eigrp' command enables EIGRP and puts the user in EIGRP configuration mode, in which one or more network commands are configured. For each interface matched by a network command, EIGRP tries to discover neighbors on that interface, and EIGRP advertises the subnet connected to the interface.

Let us configure EIGRP between R1/R2/R3 interfaces and R4/R5 WAN networks are preconfigured by ISPs.

R1 Configuration:
Router>
Router>en
Router#config t

```
Enter configuration commands, one per line.  End with CNTL/Z.
```
Router(config)#hostname R1

R1(config)#int eth 0/0
R1(config-if)#ip add 172.16.10.2 255.255.255.252
R1(config-if)#no sh
R1(config-if)#ex
```
*Aug 21 06:05:49.907: %LINK-3-UPDOWN: Interface Ethernet0/0, changed state to up
*Aug 21 06:05:50.907: %LINEPROTO-5-UPDOWN: Line protocol on Interface Ethernet0/0,
changed state to up
```

R1(config)#int eth 0/1
R1(config-if)#ip add 172.16.0.254 255.255.255.0
R1(config-if)#no sh
R1(config-if)#ex
```
*Aug 21 06:06:14.385: %LINK-3-UPDOWN: Interface Ethernet0/1, changed state to up
*Aug 21 06:06:15.389: %LINEPROTO-5-UPDOWN: Line protocol on Interface Ethernet0/1,
changed state to up
```

R1(config)#router eigrp 10
R1(config-router)#network 172.16.10.0 0.0.0.3
```
*Aug 21  06:06:31.108:  %DUAL-5-NBRCHANGE:  EIGRP-IPv4  10:  Neighbor  172.16.10.1
(Ethernet0/0) is up: new adjacency
```
R1(config-router)#network 172.16.0.0 0.0.0.255
R1(config-router)#no auto-summary
R1(config-router)#ex

R2 Configuration:

Router>en
Router#config t
```
Enter configuration commands, one per line.  End with CNTL/Z.
```

Router(config)#int eth 0/0
Router(config-if)#ip add 172.16.11.2 255.255.255.252
Router(config-if)#no sh
Router(config-if)#ex
```
*Aug 21 06:08:06.655: %LINK-3-UPDOWN: Interface Ethernet0/0, changed state to up
*Aug 21 06:08:07.659: %LINEPROTO-5-UPDOWN: Line protocol on Interface Ethernet0/0,
changed state to up
```

Router(config)#int eth 0/1
Router(config-if)#ip add 172.16.1.1 255.255.255.0
Router(config-if)#no sh

```
Router(config-if)#ex
*Aug 21 06:08:24.967: %LINK-3-UPDOWN: Interface Ethernet0/1, changed state to up
*Aug 21 06:08:25.975: %LINEPROTO-5-UPDOWN: Line protocol on Interface Ethernet0/1,
changed state to up

Router(config)#router eigrp 10
Router(config-router)#network 172.16.1.0 0.0.0.255
Router(config-router)#network 172.16.11.0 0.0.0.3
*Aug 21 06:08:58.082:  %DUAL-5-NBRCHANGE:  EIGRP-IPv4 10:  Neighbor  172.16.11.1
(Ethernet0/0) is up: new adjacency
Router(config-router)#no auto-summary
Router(config-router)#ex
```

R3 Configuration:

```
Router>
Router>en
Router#config t
Enter configuration commands, one per line.  End with CNTL/Z.
Router(config)#hostname R3
R3(config)#int eth 0/0
R3(config-if)#ip add 172.16.12.2 255.255.255.252
R3(config-if)#no sh
R3(config-if)#ex
*Aug 21 06:10:21.847: %LINK-3-UPDOWN: Interface Ethernet0/0, changed state to up
*Aug 21 06:10:22.852: %LINEPROTO-5-UPDOWN: Line protocol on Interface Ethernet0/0,
changed state to up

R3(config)#int eth 0/1
R3(config-if)#ip add 172.16.2.254 255.255.255.0
R3(config-if)#no sh
R3(config-if)#ex
*Aug 21 06:10:44.843: %LINK-3-UPDOWN: Interface Ethernet0/1, changed state to up
*Aug 21 06:10:45.846: %LINEPROTO-5-UPDOWN: Line protocol on Interface Ethernet0/1,
changed state to up

R3(config)#router eigrp 10
R3(config-router)#network 172.16.2.0 0.0.0.255
R3(config-router)#network 172.16.12.0 0.0.0.3
*Aug 21 06:11:16.597:  %DUAL-5-NBRCHANGE:  EIGRP-IPv4 10:  Neighbor  172.16.12.1
(Ethernet0/0) is up: new adjacency
R3(config-router)#no auto-summary
R3(config-router)#ex
```

Verification:

Ping from Network 1 LAN PC to Network 3 LAN PC

VPCS> ping 172.16.2.1

```
VPCS> ping 172.16.2.1

84 bytes from 172.16.2.1 icmp_seq=1 ttl=60 time=0.953 ms
84 bytes from 172.16.2.1 icmp_seq=2 ttl=60 time=1.038 ms
84 bytes from 172.16.2.1 icmp_seq=3 ttl=60 time=1.146 ms
84 bytes from 172.16.2.1 icmp_seq=4 ttl=60 time=0.804 ms
84 bytes from 172.16.2.1 icmp_seq=5 ttl=60 time=0.929 ms

VPCS>
```

Successful Ping Shows all route are learned to the destination Network LAN 3 for Network LAN 1,

R1# **show ip route**

```
R1#show ip route
Codes: L - local, C - connected, S - static, R - RIP, M - mobile, B - BGP
       D - EIGRP, EX - EIGRP external, O - OSPF, IA - OSPF inter area
       N1 - OSPF NSSA external type 1, N2 - OSPF NSSA external type 2
       E1 - OSPF external type 1, E2 - OSPF external type 2
       i - IS-IS, su - IS-IS summary, L1 - IS-IS level-1, L2 - IS-IS level-2
       ia - IS-IS inter area, * - candidate default, U - per-user static route
       o - ODR, P - periodic downloaded static route, H - NHRP, l - LISP
       a - application route
       + - replicated route, % - next hop override

Gateway of last resort is not set

      172.16.0.0/16 is variably subnetted, 8 subnets, 3 masks
C        172.16.0.0/24 is directly connected, Ethernet0/1
L        172.16.0.254/32 is directly connected, Ethernet0/1
D        172.16.1.0/24 [90/332800] via 172.16.10.1, 00:00:43, Ethernet0/0
D        172.16.2.0/24 [90/358400] via 172.16.10.1, 00:00:43, Ethernet0/0
C        172.16.10.0/30 is directly connected, Ethernet0/0
L        172.16.10.2/32 is directly connected, Ethernet0/0
D        172.16.11.0/30 [90/307200] via 172.16.10.1, 00:00:48, Ethernet0/0
D        172.16.12.0/30 [90/332800] via 172.16.10.1, 00:00:43, Ethernet0/0
      200.50.10.0/30 is subnetted, 1 subnets
D        200.50.10.0 [90/307200] via 172.16.10.1, 00:00:48, Ethernet0/0
R1#
```

Router 1 has learned all Routes by EIGRP denoted in the router table as "D".

R2# **show eigrp protocols**

```
R2#show eigrp protocols
EIGRP-IPv4 Protocol for AS(10)
  Metric weight K1=1, K2=0, K3=1, K4=0, K5=0
  NSF-aware route hold timer is 240
  Router-ID: 172.16.11.2
  Topology : 0 (base)
    Active Timer: 3 min
    Distance: internal 90 external 170
    Maximum path: 4
    Maximum hopcount 100
    Maximum metric variance 1
R2#
```

Showing EIGRP Protocol parameters.

Lab 6-2 : EIGRP IPv6 Configuration

In this example, two routers (R1 and R2) are configured with IPv6 address. Loopback addresses are assigned in both routers, and they are configured to be in EIGRP1. The EIGRPv6 is enabled per interface level with this command: **ipv6 eigrp as-number.**

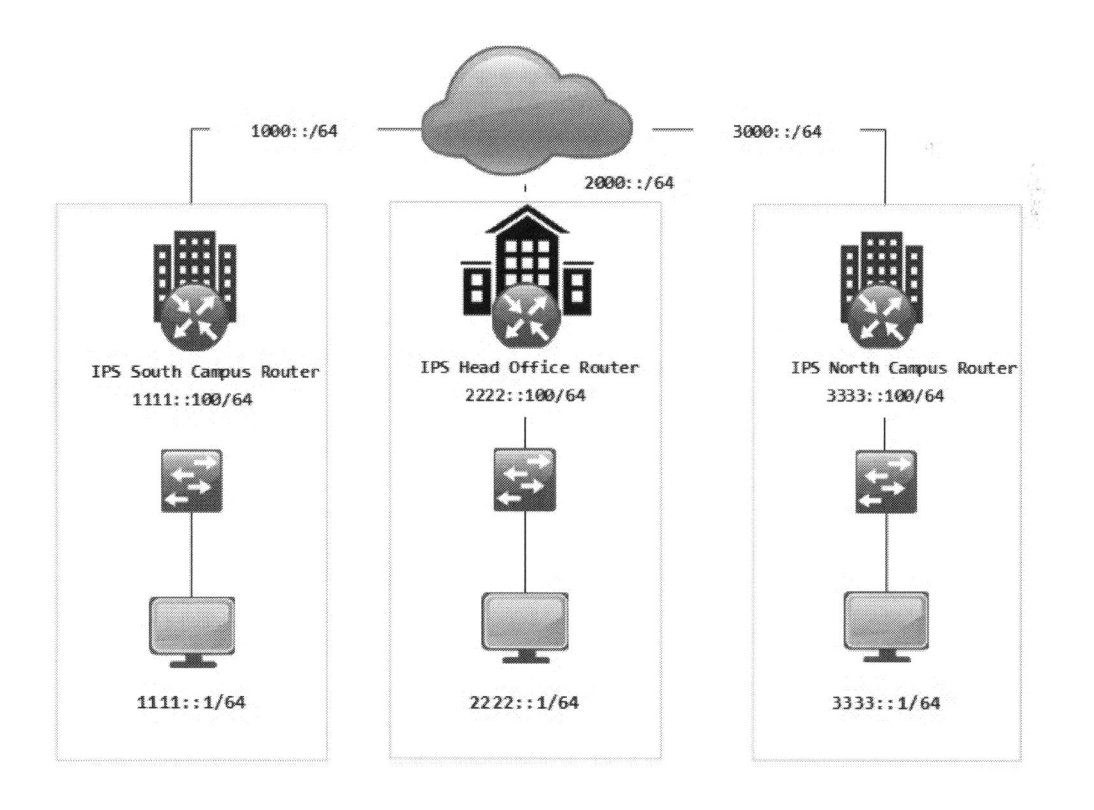

```
                        1000::/64 ─────── ┌────┐ ─────── 3000::/64
                                          │cloud│
                                          └────┘
                                       2000::/64

IPS South Campus Router    IPS Head Office Router    IPS North Campus Router
      1111::100/64              2222::100/64               3333::100/64

        1111::1/64                2222::1/64                 3333::1/64
```

Figure 53 IPv6 EIGRP Case Study

R1

Router>
Router>en
Router#config t
Enter configuration commands, one per line. End with CNTL/Z.
Router(config)#hostname R1
R1(config)#ipv6 unicast-routing
R1(config)#int eth 0/0
R1(config-if)#ipv6 add 1000::2/64
R1(config-if)#no sh
```
*Aug 21 07:08:09.635: %LINK-3-UPDOWN: Interface Ethernet0/0, changed state to up
*Aug 21 07:08:10.639: %LINEPROTO-5-UPDOWN: Line protocol on Interface Ethernet0/0, changed state to up
```
R1(config-if)#ipv6 eigrp 10
R1(config-if)#ex

R1(config)#int eth 0/1
R1(config-if)#ipv6 add 1111::100/64
R1(config-if)#no sh
```
*Aug 21 07:08:33.031: %LINK-3-UPDOWN: Interface Ethernet0/1, changed state to up
*Aug 21 07:08:34.031: %LINEPROTO-5-UPDOWN: Line protocol on Interface Ethernet0/1, changed state to up
```
R1(config-if)#ipv6 eigrp 10
R1(config-if)#ex

R1(config)#ipv6 router eigrp 10
R1(config-rtr)#no sh
R1(config-rtr)#eigrp router-id 1.1.1.3
```
*Aug 21 07:09:03.434: %DUAL-5-NBRCHANGE: EIGRP-IPv6 10: Neighbor FE80::A8BB:CCFF:FE00:4010 (Ethernet0/0) is up: new adjacency
```
R1(config-rtr)#ex

R2

Router(config)#hostname R2
R2(config)#ipv6 unicast-routing
R2(config)#int eth 0/0
R2(config-if)#ipv6 add 2000::2/64
R2(config-if)#no sh
```
*Aug 21 07:02:49.330: %LINK-3-UPDOWN: Interface Ethernet0/0, changed state to up
*Aug 21 07:02:50.334: %LINEPROTO-5-UPDOWN: Line protocol on Interface Ethernet0/0, changed state to up
```

R2(config-if)#ipv6 eigrp 10
R2(config-if)#ex

R2(config)#int eth 0/1
R2(config-if)#ipv6 add 2222::100/64
R2(config-if)#no sh
*Aug 21 07:03:33.018: %LINK-3-UPDOWN: Interface Ethernet0/1, changed state to up
*Aug 21 07:03:34.022: %LINEPROTO-5-UPDOWN: Line protocol on Interface Ethernet0/1, changed state to up
R2(config-if)#ipv6 eigrp 10
R2(config-if)#ex

R2(config)#ipv6 router eigrp 10
R2(config-rtr)#no sh
R2(config-rtr)#eigrp router-id 1.1.1.2
*Aug 21 07:04:07.595: %DUAL-5-NBRCHANGE: EIGRP-IPv6 10: Neighbor
FE80::A8BB:CCFF:FE00:4020 (Ethernet0/0) is up: new adjacency
R2(config-rtr)#ex

R3

R3(config)#ipv6 unicast-routing
R3(config)#int eth 0/0
R3(config-if)#ipv6 add 3000::2/64
R3(config-if)#no sh
R3(config-if)#ipv6 eigrp 10
*Aug 21 07:05:31.818: %LINK-3-UPDOWN: Interface Ethernet0/0, changed state to up
*Aug 21 07:05:32.822: %LINEPROTO-5-UPDOWN: Line protocol on Interface Ethernet0/0, changed state to up
R3(config-if)#ex

R3(config)#int eth 0/1
R3(config-if)#ipv6 add 3333::100/64
R3(config-if)#no sh
R3(config-if)#ipv6 eigrp 10
*Aug 21 07:05:52.738: %LINK-3-UPDOWN: Interface Ethernet0/1, changed state to up
*Aug 21 07:05:53.743: %LINEPROTO-5-UPDOWN: Line protocol on Interface Ethernet0/1, changed state to up
R3(config-if)#ex

R3(config)#ipv6 router eigrp 10
R3(config-rtr)#no sh
R3(config-rtr)#eigrp router-id 2.2.2.3
R3(config-rtr)#ex

```
*Aug 21 07:06:29.810: %DUAL-5-NBRCHANGE: EIGRP-IPv6 10: Neighbor
FE80::A8BB:CCFF:FE00:5010 (Ethernet0/0) is up: new adjacency
R3(config-rtr)#ex
```

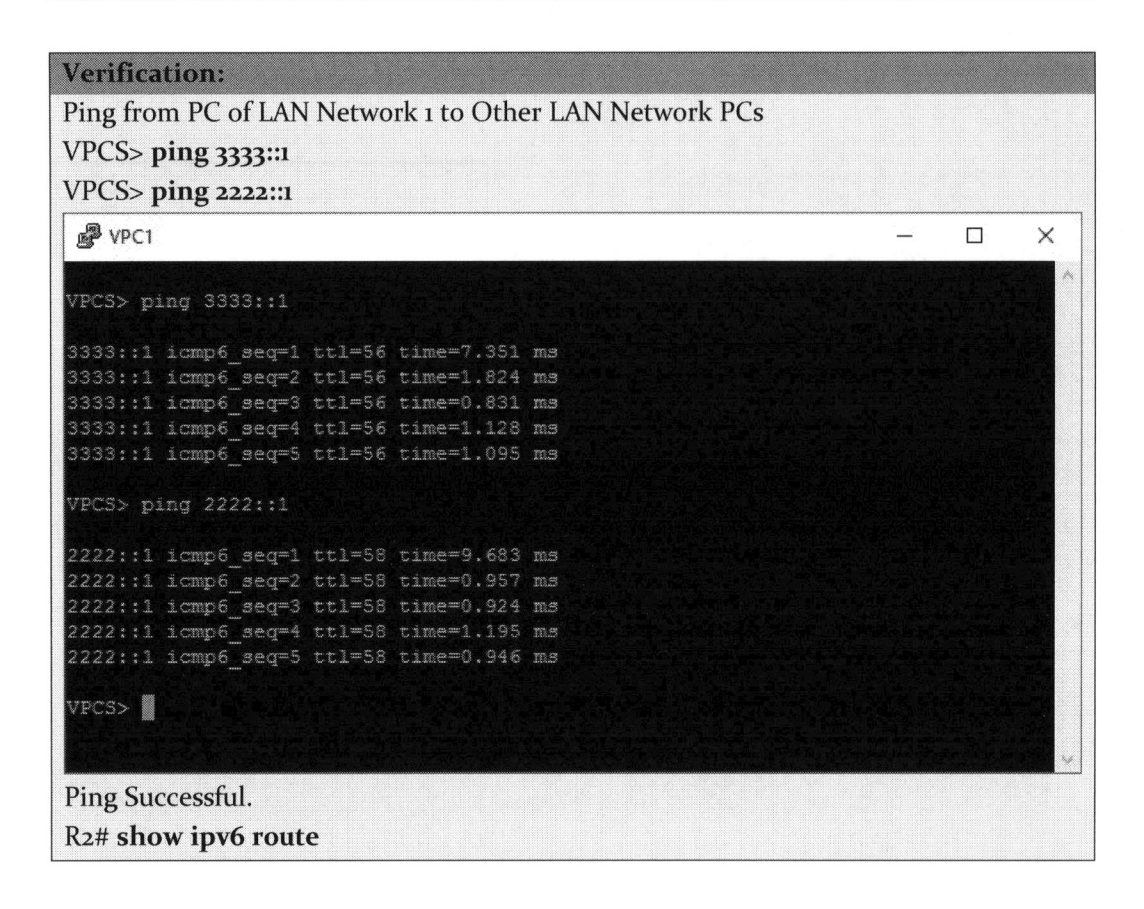

Verification:

Ping from PC of LAN Network 1 to Other LAN Network PCs
VPCS> **ping 3333::1**
VPCS> **ping 2222::1**

```
VPCS> ping 3333::1

3333::1 icmp6_seq=1 ttl=56 time=7.351 ms
3333::1 icmp6_seq=2 ttl=56 time=1.824 ms
3333::1 icmp6_seq=3 ttl=56 time=0.831 ms
3333::1 icmp6_seq=4 ttl=56 time=1.128 ms
3333::1 icmp6_seq=5 ttl=56 time=1.095 ms

VPCS> ping 2222::1

2222::1 icmp6_seq=1 ttl=58 time=9.683 ms
2222::1 icmp6_seq=2 ttl=58 time=0.957 ms
2222::1 icmp6_seq=3 ttl=58 time=0.924 ms
2222::1 icmp6_seq=4 ttl=58 time=1.195 ms
2222::1 icmp6_seq=5 ttl=58 time=0.946 ms

VPCS>
```

Ping Successful.
R2# **show ipv6 route**

```
R2>en
R2#show ipv6 route
IPv6 Routing Table - default - 11 entries
Codes: C - Connected, L - Local, S - Static, U - Per-user Static route
       B - BGP, HA - Home Agent, MR - Mobile Router, R - RIP
       H - NHRP, I1 - ISIS L1, I2 - ISIS L2, IA - ISIS interarea
       IS - ISIS summary, D - EIGRP, EX - EIGRP external, NM - NEMO
       ND - ND Default, NDp - ND Prefix, DCE - Destination, NDr - Redirect
       O - OSPF Intra, OI - OSPF Inter, OE1 - OSPF ext 1, OE2 - OSPF ext 2
       ON1 - OSPF NSSA ext 1, ON2 - OSPF NSSA ext 2, la - LISP alt
       lr - LISP site-registrations, ld - LISP dyn-eid, a - Application
D   200::/64 [90/307200]
     via FE80::A8BB:CCFF:FE00:4020, Ethernet0/0
D   1000::/64 [90/307200]
     via FE80::A8BB:CCFF:FE00:4020, Ethernet0/0
D   1111::/64 [90/332800]
     via FE80::A8BB:CCFF:FE00:4020, Ethernet0/0
C   2000::/64 [0/0]
     via Ethernet0/0, directly connected
L   2000::2/128 [0/0]
     via Ethernet0/0, receive
C   2222::/64 [0/0]
     via Ethernet0/1, directly connected
L   2222::100/128 [0/0]
     via Ethernet0/1, receive
D   3000::/64 [90/332800]
     via FE80::A8BB:CCFF:FE00:4020, Ethernet0/0
D   3333::/64 [90/358400]
     via FE80::A8BB:CCFF:FE00:4020, Ethernet0/0
D   ABCD::/64 [90/307200]
     via FE80::A8BB:CCFF:FE00:4020, Ethernet0/0
L   FF00::/8 [0/0]
     via Null0, receive
R2#
```

All routes are learned by Router 2.

R1# show ipv6 eigrp interfaces

```
R1#show ipv6 eigrp interfaces
EIGRP-IPv6 Interfaces for AS(10)
                    Xmit Queue    PeerQ         Mean    Pacing Time   Multicast    Pending
Interface    Peers  Un/Reliable   Un/Reliable   SRTT    Un/Reliable   Flow Timer   Routes
Et0/0        1      0/0           0/0           21      0/2           100          0
Et0/1        0      0/0           0/0           0       0/0           0            0
R1#
```

R1# show ipv6 eigrp topology

```
R1#show ipv6 eigrp topology
EIGRP-IPv6 Topology Table for AS(10)/ID(1.1.1.3)
Codes: P - Passive, A - Active, U - Update, Q - Query, R - Reply,
       r - reply Status, s - sia Status

P 1111::/64, 1 successors, FD is 281600
        via Connected, Ethernet0/1
P 200::/64, 1 successors, FD is 307200
        via FE80::A8BB:CCFF:FE00:4010 (307200/281600), Ethernet0/0
P 3333::/64, 1 successors, FD is 358400
        via FE80::A8BB:CCFF:FE00:4010 (358400/332800), Ethernet0/0
P 3000::/64, 1 successors, FD is 332800
        via FE80::A8BB:CCFF:FE00:4010 (332800/307200), Ethernet0/0
P 1000::/64, 1 successors, FD is 281600
        via Connected, Ethernet0/0
P ABCD::/64, 1 successors, FD is 307200
        via FE80::A8BB:CCFF:FE00:4010 (307200/281600), Ethernet0/0
P 2222::/64, 1 successors, FD is 332800
        via FE80::A8BB:CCFF:FE00:4010 (332800/307200), Ethernet0/0
P 2000::/64, 1 successors, FD is 332800
        via FE80::A8BB:CCFF:FE00:4010 (332800/307200), Ethernet0/0
R1#
```

Chapter 7: Routed Network Technologies II

Technology Brief

Large and complex network structure requires highly efficient and reliable routing protocols. OSPF (Open Shortest Path First) and IS-IS is a link state intra-AS routing protocol using Dijkstra's algorithm to calculate the best routes and adds those to the routing table. Dijkstra's algorithm finds a shortest path tree from a single source node, by building a set of nodes that have minimum distance from the source. BGP is a dynamic routing protocol used for inter-AS routing. Other advance strategies and technique used in routing includes ACL, MPLS, NAT, FHRP and LDP.

OSPF Features

Convergence: Routers running OSPF have to establish neighbor relationships before exchanging routes. Because OSPF is a link state routing protocol, neighbors don't exchange routing tables. Instead, they exchange information about network topology. Each OSFP router then runs SFP algorithm to calculate the best routes and adds those to the routing table. Because each router knows the entire topology of a network, a chance for a routing loop to occur is minimal.

VLSM: OSPF is a classless routing protocol supporting advertisement of the subnet mask with network advertisement.

Partial Updates: They send triggered updates when a network change occurs and send periodic updates, known as link-state refresh, at long time intervals, such as every 30 minutes. Each interface participating in OSPF uses the IP multicast address 224.0.0.5 to periodically send hello packets.

Independent transport: OSPF works on top of IP and uses protocol number 89. It does not rely on the functions of the transport layer protocols TCP or UDP.

Route summarization: OSPF, unlike EIGRP, doesn't support automatic summarization. Also, unlike EIGRP, where you can summarize routes on every router in an EIGRP network, OSFP can summarize routes only on ABRs and ASBRs. Route summarization helps reduce OSPF traffic and route computation.

Authentication: OSPF supports clear-text, MD5, and SHA authentication

OSPF Terminology
Neighbor

A connected (adjacent) router that is running a process with the adjacent interface assigned to the same area.

Adjacency

The logical connection between a router and the Designated Router (DR) and Backup Designated Router (BDR).

Link State Advertisement

The LSA is an OSPF data packet containing link-state and routing information, which is shared with the other routers.

Designated Router

The Designated Router (DR) is used only when the OSPF router is connected to a broadcast (Multi-Access) domain. It is used to minimize the number of adjacencies formed. The DR is chosen to push / receive routing information to / from the other routers.

Backup Designated Router

The Backup Designated Router (BDR) is used as a hot standby for the DR. The BDR still receives all of the routing updates but does not flood LSAs.

OSPF Areas

Similar to EIGRP Autonomous Systems, OSPF areas are used to establish a hierarchical network.

Area Border Router

An Area Border Router (ABR) is a router that has interfaces assigned to more than one area. An interface can only be assigned to one area but a router may have multiple interfaces. If the interfaces are assigned to different areas then the router is considered an ABR.

Autonomous System Boundary Router

An Autonomous System Boundary Router (ASBR) is a router with interface(s) connected to an external network or different AS. An example would be an interface connected to an EIGRP Autonomous Network. The ASBR is responsible for taking the routes learned from the EIGRP network and injecting them into the OSPF routing Protocol.

Router ID

The Router ID is the highest IP address of all configured Loopback interfaces. It is then used to represent the router. If there are no loopback interfaces configured the Router ID will use the highest IP address of any of its configured interfaces.

OSPF Tables

Neighbor table

Directly connected neighbors are present in neighbor table.

Topology table

Also called LSDB which maintain list of routers and their link information i.e. network destination, prefix length, link cost etc.

Routing table

The routing table holds the best routes to each destination and is used for forwarding packets. Successor routes are offered to the routing table.

OSPF Packet Types
Hello: Hello Builds adjacencies between neighbors.

DBD (Database Descriptor Packet): DBD for database synchronization between routers.

LSR (Link State Request Packet): Requests specific link-state records from router to router.

LSU (Link State Update Packet): Sends specifically requested link-state records.

LSAck (Link State Ack Packet): Acknowledges the above packet types.

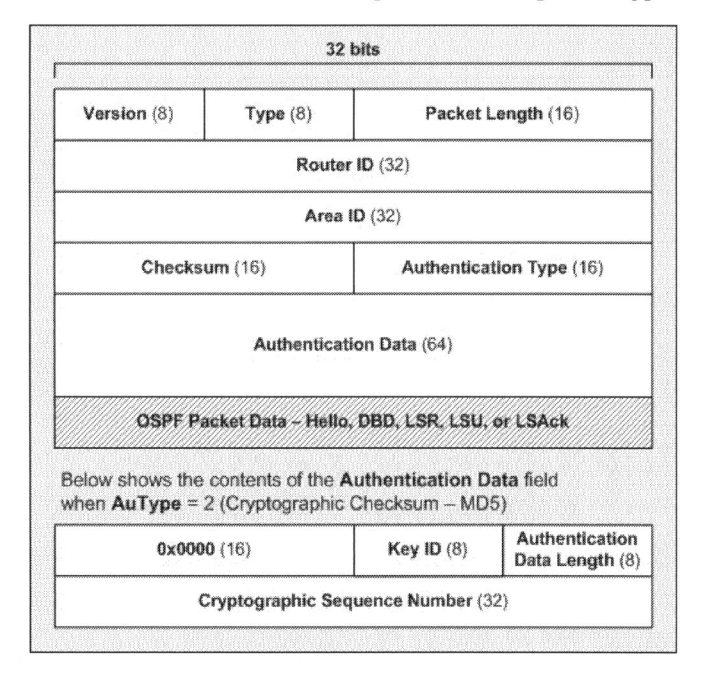

Figure 54 OSPF Packet

OSPF LSA (Link State Advertisement)

OSPF uses LSAs or Link state Advertisements to share information of each network and populate the LSDB (Link State Database). Cisco Router only supports LSA 1, 2, 3,4,5,7 and does not support other LSAs.

Type	LSA	Functionality
1	Router	Define the state and cost of the link to the neighbor and IP prefix associated with the point to point link
2	Network	Define the number of router attached to the segment. It gives the information of subnet mask on the segment
3	Summary Network	Describe the destination outside an area but within the OSPF domain. The summary for one area is flooded into other areas, and vice versa
4	Summary ASBR	Describe the information about the ASBR. In a single area, there will be no summary type 4 LSA
5	External	Define routes to destination external to OSPF domain. Every subnet is represented by a single external LSA
6	Group Membership	
7	NSSA	Define routes to external destination, but in separate LSA format known as type 7
8	Unused	
9-11	Opaque	

Table 14 OSPF Link State Advertisment (LSAs)

OSPF Area Types
Stub Area: Does not receive Type 5 LSAs. Uses default routes instead.

Totally Stubby Area: Does not receive Type 5 LSAs or Summary (Type 3 and 4 LSAs). This is a Cisco Specific feature

Not-so-Stubby area (NSSA): Does not receive type 5 LSAs but must utilize external routes on a limited basis. In this case, the NSSA imports type 7 LSAs and converts them to type 5 LSAs.

OSPF Neighbors

OSPF routers need to establish a neighbor relationship before exchanging routing updates. Sending Hello packets out each OSPF-enabled interface on a router dynamically discovers OSPF neighbors. Hello packets are sent to the multicast IP address of 224.0.0.5.

The process is explained in the following figure:

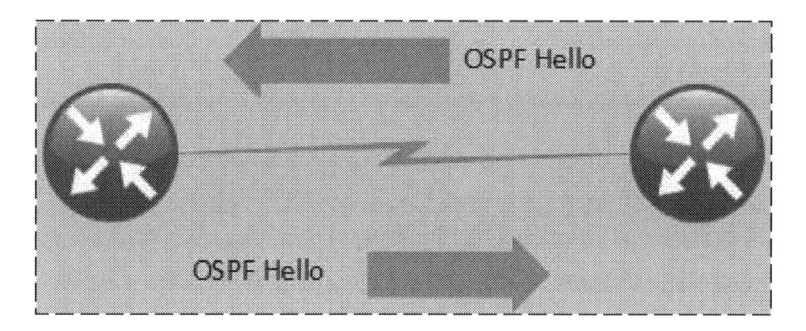

Figure 55 OSPF Hello

Routers R1 and R2 are directly connected. After OSFP is enabled both routers send Hellos to each other to establish a neighbor relationship. The following fields in the Hello packets must be the same on both routers in order for routers to become neighbors:

- subnet
- area id
- hello and dead interval timers
- authentication
- area stub flag
- MTU

By default, OSPF sends hello packets every 10 second on an Ethernet network (Hello interval). A dead timer is four times the value of the hello interval, so if a router on an Ethernet network doesn't receive at least one Hello packet from an OSFP neighbor for 40 seconds, the routers declares that neighbor "down". To select the best route in, OSPF election takes place, depending on the requirement we can choose the Designated Router (DR) through router id. Otherwise, the largest IP address wins. The key idea with a DR and backup DR (BDR) is that they are the ones to generate LSA, and they exchange database with other routers in the subnet. So, non-designated routers form adjacencies with the DR. The whole DR/BDR design is used to keep the protocol scalable. The only way to ensure that all routers have the same information is to make them synchronize their databases. The main reason behind electing DR/BDR is to reduce bandwidth and resource.

OSPF Neighbor States

Before establishing a neighbor relationship, OSPF routers need to go through several state changes. These states are explained below.

1. **Init state** – a router is received a Hello message from the other OSFP router
2. **2-way state** – the neighbor is received the Hello message and replied with a Hello message of his own
3. **Exstart state** – beginning of the LSDB exchange between both routers. Routers are starting to exchange link state information.
4. **Exchange state** – DBD (Database Descriptor) packets are exchanged. DBDs contain LSAs headers. Routers will use this information to see what LSAs need to be exchanged.
5. **Loading state** – one neighbor sends LSRs (Link State Requests) for every network it does not know about. The other neighbor replies with the LSUs (Link State Updates), which contain information regarding requested networks. After all the requested information have been received, other neighbor goes through the same process
6. **Full state** – both routers have the synchronized database and are adjacent with each other.

OSPF Metric

The cost (also called metric) of an interface in OSPF is an indication of the overhead required to send packets across a certain interface. The cost of an interface is inversely proportional to the bandwidth of that interface. A higher bandwidth indicates a lower cost. There is more overhead (higher cost) and time delays involved in crossing a 56k serial line than crossing a 10M Ethernet line.

The formula used to calculate the cost is:

$$\text{Cost} = 10000\,0000/\text{bandwidth in bps}$$

For example, it will cost 10 EXP8/10 EXP7 = 10 to cross a 10M Ethernet line and will cost 10 EXP8/1544000 = 64 to cross a T1 line.

By default, the cost of an interface is calculated based on the bandwidth as mentioned in the following table.

Interface Type	10^8/bps=cost
Fast Ethernet and Faster	108/100,000,000 bps=1
Ethernet	10^8/10,000,000 bps=10
E1	10^8/2,048,000 bps=48
T1	10^8/1,544000 bps=64
128 kbps	10^8/128,000 bps=781
64 kbps	10^8/64,000 bps=1562
56kbps	10^8/56,000 bps=1785

Table 15 OSPF cost calculation

Putting it All Together

Let us understand how the neighbor relationship works in OSPF

- OSPF-enabled routers must form adjacencies with their neighbor before they can share information with that neighbor. An OSPF-enabled router sends Hello packets out all OSPF-enabled interfaces to determine whether neighbors are present on those links. If a neighbor is present, the OSPF-enabled router attempts to establish a neighbor adjacency with that neighbor.

- After adjacencies are established, routers then exchange link-state advertisements (LSAs). LSAs contain the state and cost of each directly connected link. Routers flood their LSAs to adjacent neighbors. Adjacent neighbors receiving the LSA immediately flood the LSA to other directly connected neighbors, until all routers in the area have all LSAs

- After the LSAs are received, OSPF-enabled routers builds, the topology table (LSDB) based on the received LSAs. This database eventually holds all the information about the topology of the network. It is important that all routers in the area have the same information in their LSDBs.

- Routers then execute the SPF algorithm. The SPF algorithm creates the SPF tree.

- From the SPF tree, the best paths are inserted into the routing table. Routing decisions are based on the entries in the routing table.

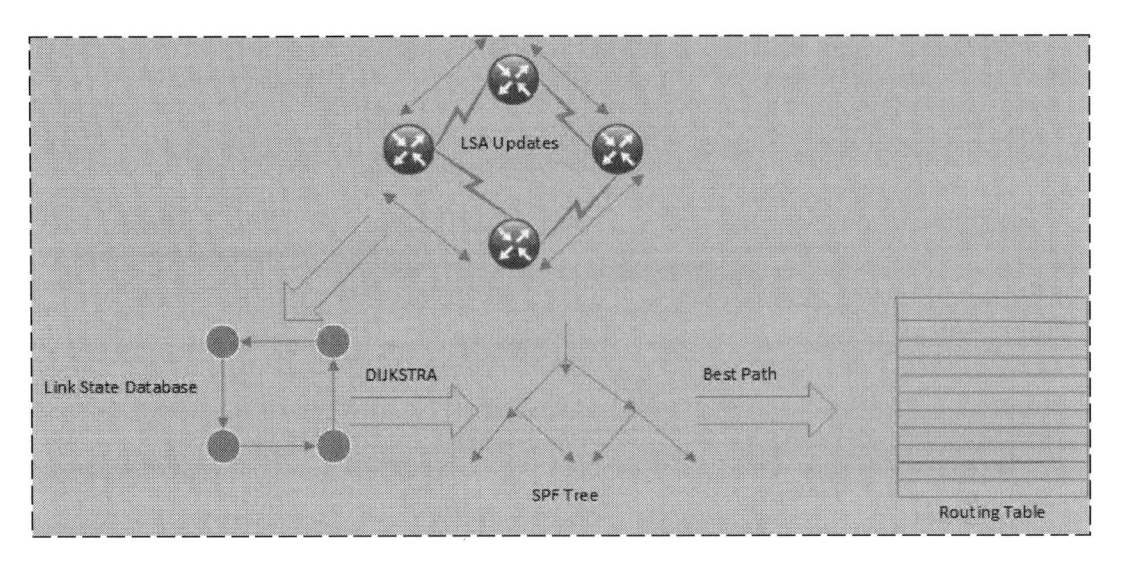

Figure 56 OSPF Operation

OSPF Mind Map

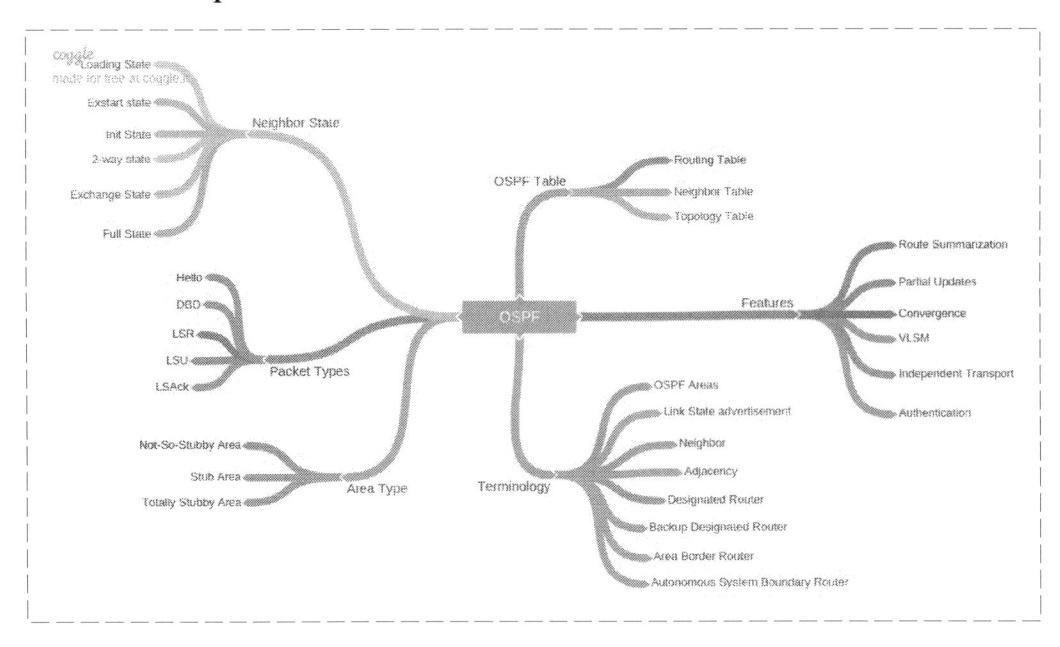

Figure 57 OSPF Mind Map

Lab 7-1 : OSPFv2 Single Area

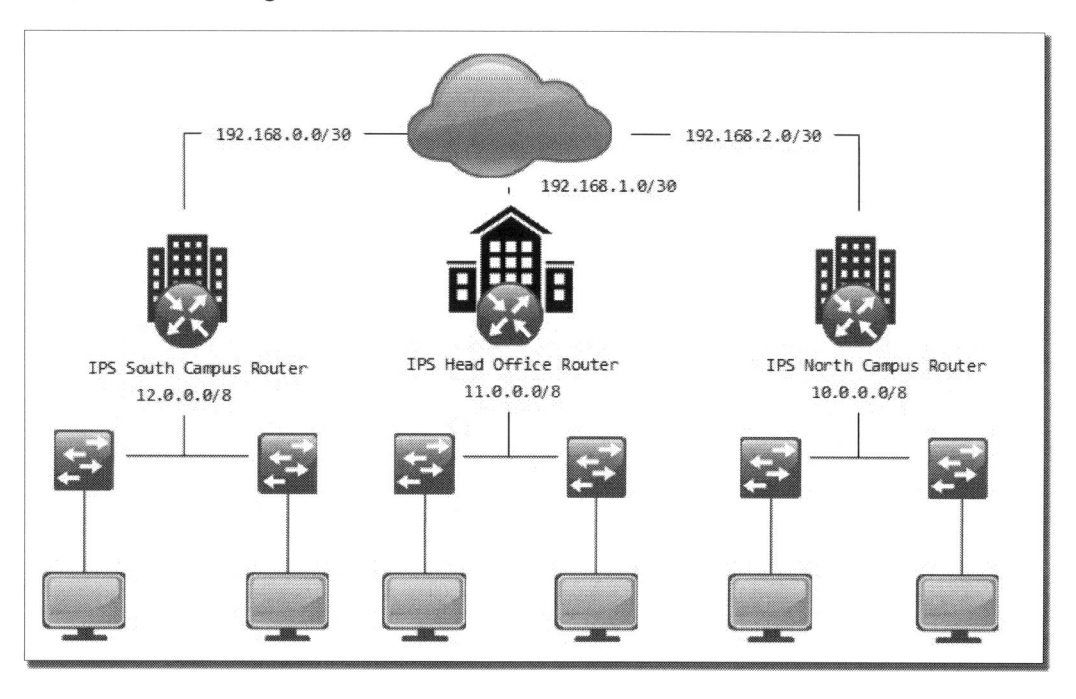

Figure 58 OSPF Diagram

OSPF Basic Configuration

Let us configure OSPF between R1/R2/R3 interfaces with above-mentioned IP scheme

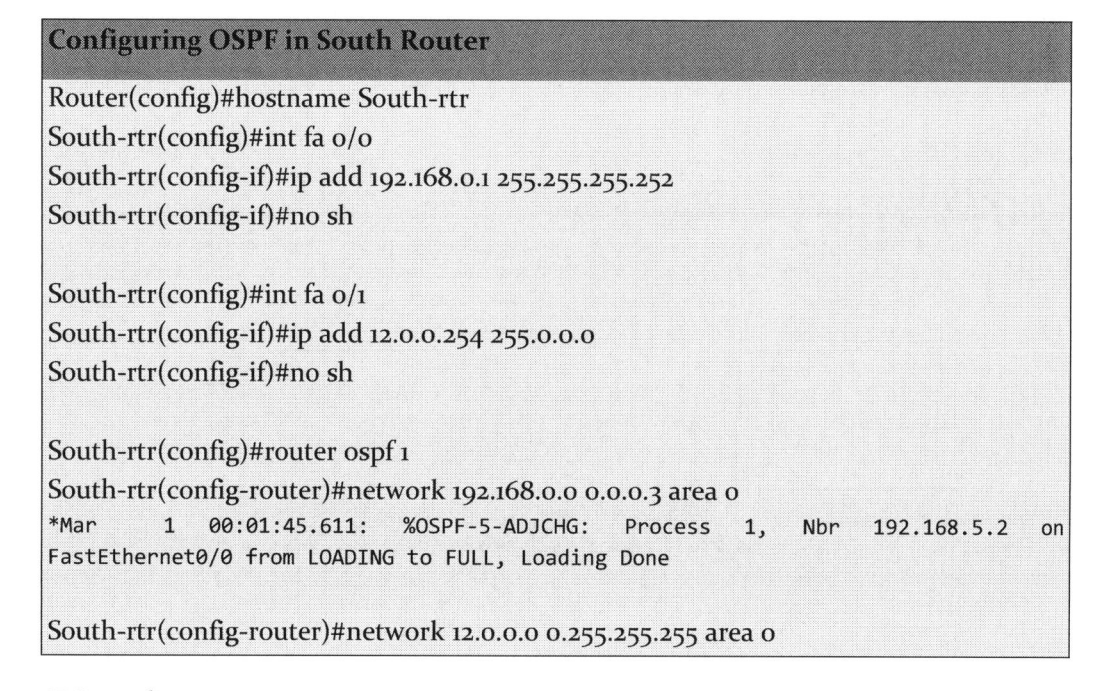

Configuring OSPF in South Router

Router(config)#hostname South-rtr
South-rtr(config)#int fa 0/0
South-rtr(config-if)#ip add 192.168.0.1 255.255.255.252
South-rtr(config-if)#no sh
 	
South-rtr(config)#int fa 0/1
South-rtr(config-if)#ip add 12.0.0.254 255.0.0.0
South-rtr(config-if)#no sh
 	
South-rtr(config)#router ospf 1
South-rtr(config-router)#network 192.168.0.0 0.0.0.3 area 0
`*Mar    1  00:01:45.611:  %OSPF-5-ADJCHG:  Process  1,  Nbr  192.168.5.2  on`
`FastEthernet0/0 from LOADING to FULL, Loading Done`
 	
South-rtr(config-router)#network 12.0.0.0 0.255.255.255 area 0

South-rtr(config-router)#ex

Configuring OSPF in North Router
| Router(config)#hostname North-rtr<br>North-rtr(config)#int fa 0/0<br>North-rtr(config-if)#ip add 192.168.2.1 255.255.255.252<br>North-rtr(config-if)#no sh<br><br>North-rtr(config)#int fa 0/1<br>North-rtr(config-if)#ip add 10.0.0.254 255.0.0.0<br>North-rtr(config-if)#no sh<br><br>North-rtr(config)#router ospf 1<br>North-rtr(config-router)#network 10.0.0.0 0.255.255.255 area 0<br>North-rtr(config-router)#network 192.168.2.0 0.0.0.3 area 0<br>```
*Mar  1 00:10:09.663: %OSPF-5-ADJCHG: Process 1, Nbr 192.168.4.1 on
FastEthernet0/0 from LOADING to FULL, Loading Done
``` |

Configuring OSPF in IPS-HO-rtr
Router(config)#hostname IPS-HO-rtr
IPS-HO-rtr(config)#int fa 0/0
IPS-HO-rtr(config-if)#ip add 192.168.1.1 255.255.255.252
IPS-HO-rtr(config-if)#no sh
IPS-HO-rtr(config)#int fa 0/1
IPS-HO-rtr(config-if)#ip add 11.0.0.254 255.0.0.0
IPS-HO-rtr(config-if)#no sh
IPS-HO-rtr(config)#router ospf 1
IPS-HO-rtr(config-router)#network 11.0.0.0 0.255.255.255 area 0
IPS-HO-rtr(config-router)#network 192.168.1.0 0.0.0.3 area 0
| ```
*Mar   1   00:15:48.483:   %OSPF-5-ADJCHG:   Process   1,   Nbr   192.168.5.1   on
FastEthernet0/0 from LOADING to FULL, Loading Done
``` |

Verification:

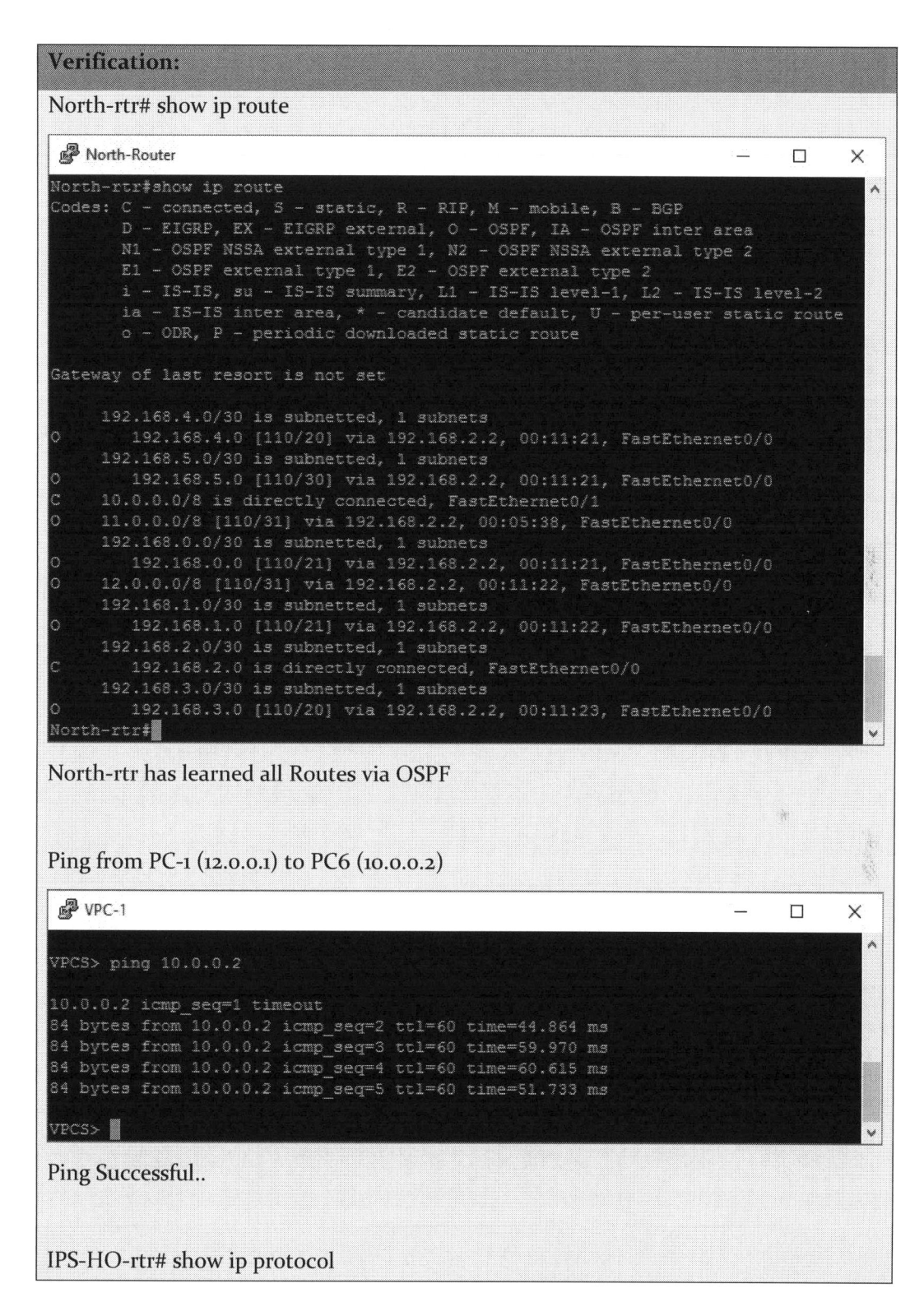

North-rtr# show ip route

```
North-rtr#show ip route
Codes: C - connected, S - static, R - RIP, M - mobile, B - BGP
       D - EIGRP, EX - EIGRP external, O - OSPF, IA - OSPF inter area
       N1 - OSPF NSSA external type 1, N2 - OSPF NSSA external type 2
       E1 - OSPF external type 1, E2 - OSPF external type 2
       i - IS-IS, su - IS-IS summary, L1 - IS-IS level-1, L2 - IS-IS level-2
       ia - IS-IS inter area, * - candidate default, U - per-user static route
       o - ODR, P - periodic downloaded static route

Gateway of last resort is not set

     192.168.4.0/30 is subnetted, 1 subnets
O       192.168.4.0 [110/20] via 192.168.2.2, 00:11:21, FastEthernet0/0
     192.168.5.0/30 is subnetted, 1 subnets
O       192.168.5.0 [110/30] via 192.168.2.2, 00:11:21, FastEthernet0/0
C    10.0.0.0/8 is directly connected, FastEthernet0/1
O    11.0.0.0/8 [110/31] via 192.168.2.2, 00:05:38, FastEthernet0/0
     192.168.0.0/30 is subnetted, 1 subnets
O       192.168.0.0 [110/21] via 192.168.2.2, 00:11:21, FastEthernet0/0
O    12.0.0.0/8 [110/31] via 192.168.2.2, 00:11:22, FastEthernet0/0
     192.168.1.0/30 is subnetted, 1 subnets
O       192.168.1.0 [110/21] via 192.168.2.2, 00:11:22, FastEthernet0/0
     192.168.2.0/30 is subnetted, 1 subnets
C       192.168.2.0 is directly connected, FastEthernet0/0
     192.168.3.0/30 is subnetted, 1 subnets
O       192.168.3.0 [110/20] via 192.168.2.2, 00:11:23, FastEthernet0/0
North-rtr#
```

North-rtr has learned all Routes via OSPF

Ping from PC-1 (12.0.0.1) to PC6 (10.0.0.2)

```
VPCS> ping 10.0.0.2

10.0.0.2 icmp_seq=1 timeout
84 bytes from 10.0.0.2 icmp_seq=2 ttl=60 time=44.864 ms
84 bytes from 10.0.0.2 icmp_seq=3 ttl=60 time=59.970 ms
84 bytes from 10.0.0.2 icmp_seq=4 ttl=60 time=60.615 ms
84 bytes from 10.0.0.2 icmp_seq=5 ttl=60 time=51.733 ms

VPCS>
```

Ping Successful..

IPS-HO-rtr# show ip protocol

```
IPS-HO-rtr#show ip protocol
Routing Protocol is "ospf 1"
  Outgoing update filter list for all interfaces is not set
  Incoming update filter list for all interfaces is not set
  Router ID 192.168.1.1
  Number of areas in this router is 1. 1 normal 0 stub 0 nssa
  Maximum path: 4
  Routing for Networks:
    11.0.0.0 0.255.255.255 area 0
    192.168.1.0 0.0.0.3 area 0
  Reference bandwidth unit is 100 mbps
  Routing Information Sources:
    Gateway         Distance      Last Update
    192.168.0.1       110         00:09:21
    192.168.2.1       110         00:09:21
    192.168.5.1       110         00:09:21
    192.168.4.1       110         00:09:21
    192.168.5.2       110         00:09:21
  Distance: (default is 110)

IPS-HO-rtr#
```

Lab 7-2 : OSPFv3 (OSPF for IPv6) Configuration

The following steps are involved in the OSPFv3 configuration on a Cisco router.

- Enable IPv6 routing using the ipv6 unicast-routing command from global configuration mode.

- Create an OSPFv3 routing process and enter OSPFv3 configuration mode using the ipv6 router ospf process-id from global configuration mode.

- Make sure that the router obtains an OSPFv3 router ID through one of available mechanisms for this.

- Enable OSPFv3 on interfaces using the ipv6 ospf process-id area area-number command in interface configuration mode, thus also setting the OSPFv3 area for the interface.

- In addition to the four steps, you may also configure one or more OSPFv3 interfaces as passive using the passive-interface interface-type interface-number command in router configuration mode.

- The OSPFv3 coverage in the new CCNA version 2 exams is mostly limited to single-area scenarios. However, you may also encounter multi-area scenarios occasionally. That is why we will also briefly cover multi-area concepts and configuration. If you understand single area concepts and configuration well, you will usually find it easy to understand multi-area details.

We will present complete IPv6 configuration, including addressing and OSPFv3, on three routers in a single-area OSPFv3 domain, as shown in Figure 35.

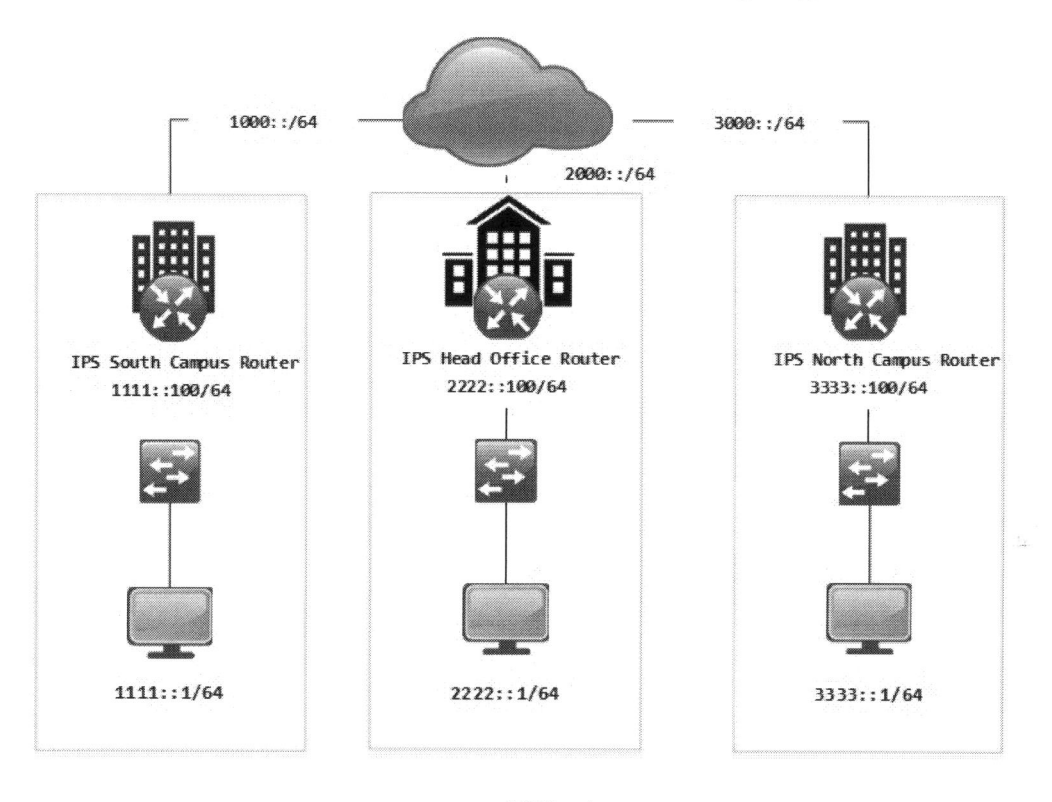

Figure 59 OSPFv3 Area 0

R1 Configuration:

```
Router#config t
Enter configuration commands, one per line.  End with CNTL/Z.
Router(config)#hostname R1
R1(config)#ipv6 unicast-routing
R1(config)#ipv6 router ospf 1
*Aug 21 08:56:59.531: %OSPFv3-4-NORTRID: Process OSPFv3-1-IPv6 could not pick a
router-id, please configure manually
R1(config-rtr)#router-id 1.1.1.1
R1(config-rtr)#ex

R1(config)#int eth 0/0
R1(config-if)#ipv6 address 1000::2/64
R1(config-if)#ipv6 ospf 1 area 0
R1(config-if)#no sh
R1(config-if)#ex
*Aug 21 08:57:36.009: %LINK-3-UPDOWN: Interface Ethernet0/0, changed state to up
*Aug 21 08:57:37.013: %LINEPROTO-5-UPDOWN: Line protocol on Interface Ethernet0/0,
changed state to up
```

```
*Aug 21 08:57:38.032: %OSPFv3-5-ADJCHG: Process 1, Nbr 1.1.1.0 on Ethernet0/0 from
LOADING to FULL, Loading Done
```

R1(config)#int eth 0/1
R1(config-if)#ipv6 add 1111::100/64
R1(config-if)#ipv6 ospf 1 area 0
R1(config-if)#no sh
R1(config-if)#ex
```
*Aug 21 08:58:00.450: %LINK-3-UPDOWN: Interface Ethernet0/1, changed state to up
*Aug 21 08:58:01.455: %LINEPROTO-5-UPDOWN: Line protocol on Interface Ethernet0/1,
changed state to up
```
R1(config)#end

R2 Configuration:

Router>en
Router#config t
```
Enter configuration commands, one per line.  End with CNTL/Z.
```
Router(config)#hostname R2
R2(config)#ipv6 unicast-routing
R2(config)#ipv6 router ospf 1
```
*Aug 21 08:59:35.288: %OSPFv3-4-NORTRID: Process OSPFv3-1-IPv6 could not pick a
router-id, please configure manually
```
R2(config-rtr)#router-id 1.1.1.2
R2(config-rtr)#ex

R2(config)#int eth 0/1
R2(config-if)#ipv6 address 2222::100/64
R2(config-if)#ipv6 ospf 1 area 0
R2(config-if)#no sh
R2(config-if)#ex
```
*Aug 21 09:00:18.655: %LINK-3-UPDOWN: Interface Ethernet0/1, changed state to up
*Aug 21 09:00:19.660: %LINEPROTO-5-UPDOWN: Line protocol on Interface Ethernet0/1,
changed state to up
```

R2(config)#int eth 0/0
R2(config-if)#ipv6 address 2000::2/64
R2(config-if)#ipv6 ospf 1 area 0
R2(config-if)#no sh
R2(config-if)#ex
```
*Aug 21 09:00:54.376: %LINK-3-UPDOWN: Interface Ethernet0/0, changed state to up
*Aug 21 09:00:55.380: %LINEPROTO-5-UPDOWN: Line protocol on Interface Ethernet0/0,
changed state to up
*Aug 21 09:00:56.394: %OSPFv3-5-ADJCHG: Process 1, Nbr 1.1.1.0 on Ethernet0/0 from
LOADING to FULL, Loading Done
```

R3 Configuration:

Router(config)#ipv6 unicast-routing

Router(config)#hostname R3

R3(config)#ipv6 router ospf 1

```
*Aug 21 09:02:04.381: %OSPFv3-4-NORTRID: Process OSPFv3-1-IPv6 could not pick a router-id, please configure manually
```

R3(config-rtr)#router-id 2.2.2.1

R3(config-rtr)#ex

R3(config)#int eth 0/0

R3(config-if)#ipv6 address 3000::2/64

R3(config-if)#ipv6 ospf 1 area 0

R3(config-if)#no sh

R3(config-if)#ex

```
*Aug 21 09:02:42.342: %LINK-3-UPDOWN: Interface Ethernet0/0, changed state to up
*Aug 21 09:02:43.346: %LINEPROTO-5-UPDOWN: Line protocol on Interface Ethernet0/0, changed state to up
*Aug 21 09:02:44.377: %OSPFv3-5-ADJCHG: Process 1, Nbr 2.2.2.0 on Ethernet0/0 from LOADING to FULL, Loading Done
```

R3(config)#int eth 0/1

R3(config-if)#ipv6 address 3333::100/64

R3(config-if)#ipv6 ospf 1 area 0

R3(config-if)#no sh

R3(config-if)#ex

```
*Aug 21 09:03:15.680: %LINK-3-UPDOWN: Interface Ethernet0/1, changed state to up
*Aug 21 09:03:16.684: %LINEPROTO-5-UPDOWN: Line protocol on Interface Ethernet0/1, changed state to up
```

Verification:

Ping from VPC of LAN Network 1 to LAN Networks

```
VPCS> ping 2222::1

2222::1 icmp6_seq=1 ttl=58 time=18.965 ms
2222::1 icmp6_seq=2 ttl=58 time=0.766 ms
2222::1 icmp6_seq=3 ttl=58 time=0.882 ms
2222::1 icmp6_seq=4 ttl=58 time=1.183 ms
2222::1 icmp6_seq=5 ttl=58 time=0.955 ms

VPCS> ping 3333::1

3333::1 icmp6_seq=1 ttl=56 time=9.402 ms
3333::1 icmp6_seq=2 ttl=56 time=0.894 ms
3333::1 icmp6_seq=3 ttl=56 time=1.075 ms
3333::1 icmp6_seq=4 ttl=56 time=1.083 ms
3333::1 icmp6_seq=5 ttl=56 time=0.611 ms
```

Ping Successful.

R2# show ip route

```
R2#show ipv6 route
IPv6 Routing Table - default - 10 entries
Codes: C - Connected, L - Local, S - Static, U - Per-user Static route
       B - BGP, HA - Home Agent, MR - Mobile Router, R - RIP
       H - NHRP, I1 - ISIS L1, I2 - ISIS L2, IA - ISIS interarea
       IS - ISIS summary, D - EIGRP, EX - EIGRP external, NM - NEMO
       ND - ND Default, NDp - ND Prefix, DCE - Destination, NDr - Redirect
       O - OSPF Intra, OI - OSPF Inter, OE1 - OSPF ext 1, OE2 - OSPF ext 2
       ON1 - OSPF NSSA ext 1, ON2 - OSPF NSSA ext 2, la - LISP alt
       lr - LISP site-registrations, ld - LISP dyn-eid, a - Application
O   1000::/64 [110/20]
     via FE80::A8BB:CCFF:FE00:4020, Ethernet0/0
O   1111::/64 [110/30]
     via FE80::A8BB:CCFF:FE00:4020, Ethernet0/0
C   2000::/64 [0/0]
     via Ethernet0/0, directly connected
L   2000::2/128 [0/0]
     via Ethernet0/0, receive
C   2222::/64 [0/0]
     via Ethernet0/1, directly connected
L   2222::100/128 [0/0]
     via Ethernet0/1, receive
O   3000::/64 [110/30]
     via FE80::A8BB:CCFF:FE00:4020, Ethernet0/0
O   3333::/64 [110/40]
     via FE80::A8BB:CCFF:FE00:4020, Ethernet0/0
O   ABCD::/64 [110/20]
     via FE80::A8BB:CCFF:FE00:4020, Ethernet0/0
L   FF00::/8 [0/0]
     via Null0, receive
R2#
```

IS-IS Network Protocol

IS-IS (Intermediate System -to- Intermediate System) is a standardized link-state protocol that is created to be the definitive routing protocol for the OSI (Open Systems Interconnect) Model, which was developed by ISO (International Standards Organization). IS-IS have many similarities to OSPF. However, it was designed as an interior gateway protocol (IGP), IS-IS is used by ISPs, due to its scalability. IS-IS adheres to the following Link State characteristics:

- IS-IS allows for a hierarchical network design using Areas.
- IS-IS form neighbor relationships with adjacent routers of the same IS-IS type.
- Instead of advertising the distance to connected networks, IS-IS advertises the status of directly connected "links" in the form of Link-State Packets. IS-IS only sends out update when there is a change to one of its links, and will only send the change in the update.
- IS-IS uses the Dijkstra Shortest Path First algorithm to determine the shortest path.
- IS-IS is a classless protocol, and supports VLSMs.

Other characteristics of IS-IS include:

- IS-IS was originally developed to route the ISO address space, and thus is not limited to IP routing.
- IS-IS routes have an administrative distance is 115.
- IS-IS uses an arbitrary cost for its metric. IS-IS additionally has three optional metrics: delay, expense, and error. Cisco does not support these optional metrics.
- IS-IS has no hop-count limit.

The IS-IS process builds and maintains three separate tables:

- **A neighbor table** – contains all neighboring routers.
- **A topology table** – contains all possible routes to all known networks within an area.
- **A routing table** – contains the best route for each known network.

IS-IS is only available on enterprise versions of the Cisco IOS.

IS-IS Protocols and Addressing

IS-IS consists of three sub-protocols that work in tandem to achieve end-to end routing which ISO defined as Connectionless Network Service (CLNS):

- **CLNP (Connectionless Network Protocol)** – serves as the Layer-3 protocol for IS-IS (and was developed by ISO).
- **ES-IS (End System -to- Intermediate System)** – used to route between hosts and routers.
- **IS-IS (Intermediate System -to- Intermediate System)** – used to route between routers.

IS-IS is originally developed to route ISO CLNP addresses (outlined in RFC 1142). However, CLNP addressing never became prominently used.

Thus, IS-IS was modified to additionally supports IP routing, and became Integrated (or Dual) IS-IS (outlined in RFC 1195). The IS-IS CLNP address is hexadecimal and of variable length, and can range from 64 to 160 bits in length. The CLNP addresses contain three "sections," including:

- **Area field** – (variable length)
- **ID field** – (from 8 to 64 bits, though usually 48 bits)
- **Selector (SEL) field** - (8 bits)

Thus, the CLNP addresses identify the "Area" in which a device is located, the actual host "ID," and the destination application on that host, in the form of the "SEL" field. The CNLP address is logically segmented even further, as demonstrated by the following table:

IDP		DSP		
AFI	IDI	HO-DSP	System ID	NSEL
Area Field			ID Field	SEL Field

The ISO CLNP address provides granular control by separating internal and external routing information:

- The IDP (Initial Domain Part) portion of the address identifies the Autonomous System of the device (and is used to route to or between Autonomous Systems)
- The DSP (Domain Specific Part) portion of the address is used to route within the autonomous system.

The IDP portion of the address is separated into two "sections," including:

- **AFI (Authority and Format Identifier)** – specifies the organization authorized to assign addresses, and the format and length of the rest of the CLNP address. The AFI is always 8 bits.
- **IDI (Initial Domain Identifier)** – identifies the "sub organization" under the parent AFI organization. The length of the IDI is dependent on the chosen AFI.

An AFI of 0x49 indicates a private CLNP address, which cannot be routed globally (the equivalent of an IPv4 private address). An AFI of 0x47 is commonly used for global IS-IS networks, with the IDI section identifying specific organizations.

The AFI plus the IDI essentially identifies the autonomous system of the address. However, this is not the equivalent of a BGP AS number, nor is it compatible with BGP as an exterior routing protocol.

The DSP portion of the address is separated into 3 "sections," including:

- **HO-DSP (High Order DSP)** – identifies the area within an autonomous system
- **System ID** – identifies the concerned host. Usually 48 bits (or 6 octets) in length, to accommodate MAC addresses
- **NSEL** – identifies the destination upper layer protocol of the host (always 8 bits)

Two "types" of CLNP addresses are mentioned:

- **NET address** – does not contain upper-layer information (in other words, the SEL field is always set to 0x00)
- **NSAP address** – the "full" CLNP address, with populated Area, ID, and SEL fields.

Please note: A NET address is simply an NSAP address with a zero value in the SEL field.

CLNS Address Example

The following is an example of a full ISO CLNS address:

47.1234.5678.9abc.def0.0001.1111.2222.3333.00

Correlating the above address to the appropriate fields:

IDP		DSP		
AFI	IDI	HO-DSP	System ID	NSEL
47.	1234.5678.9abc.def0.	0001.	1111.2222.3333.	00

Area Field	ID Field	SEL Field

The System-ID is usually populated by the device's MAC address or IP v4 address. Recall that CLNS addresses are of variable length. We can specify addresses without an IDI field:

$$47.0001.1111.2222.3333.00$$

Thus, the above address contains an AFI (Autonomous System), HO-DSP (Area), System-ID (in this example, a MAC Address), and the NSEL (SEL). Because the SEL field has a zero value (0x00), the above address is defined as a NET address, and not an NSAP address.

ISO CLNS addresses are not applied on an interface-by-interface basis.

Instead, a single CLNS address is applied to the entire device.

Even if Integrated IS-IS is being used (thus indicating that IPv4 is being routed instead of CLNS), a CLNS address is still required on the IS-IS router. This is configured under the IS-IS router process. Routers within the same area must share identical AFI, IDI, and HO-DSP values, but each must have a unique System-ID.

IS-IS Packet Types
IS-IS defines two categories of network devices:

- **ES (End System)** – identifies an end host.
- **IS (Intermediate System)** – identifies a Layer 3 router.

IS-IS additionally defines four categories of packet types:

- Hello
- LSP
- CSNP
- PSNP

Hello packets are exchanged for neighbor discovery. Three types of IS-IS Hello packets exist:

- IIH (IS-IS Hello) – exchanged between routers (or IS's) to form neighbor adjacencies.
- ESH (ES Hello) – sent from an ES for discovering a router.
- ISH (IS Hello) – sent from an IS to announce its presence to ES's

An **LSP (Link State Packet)** is used to share topology information between routers. There are separate LSPs for Level 1 and Level 2 routing. LSP's are covered in detail shortly.

A **CSNP (Complete Sequence Number PDU)** is an update containing the full link state database. IS-IS routers will refresh the full database every 15 minutes.

A **PSNP (Partial Sequence Number PDU)** is used by IS-IS routers to both request and acknowledge a link-state update.

IS-IS Neighbors

IS-IS routers create neighbor relationships, called adjacencies, by sending and receiving Hello packets (often referred to as IS-IS Hellos or IIH's). Hello packets are sent out every 10 seconds, regardless of media type. Only after an adjacency is formed can routers share routing information.

IS-IS supports three IIH packet formats; one for point-to-point links, and two for broadcast (or LAN) links (Level-1 and Level-2 broadcast Hellos).

Unlike OSPF, IS-IS neighbors do not have to share a common IP subnet to form an adjacency. Adjacencies are established across CLNP connections, not IP connections, even when using Integrated IS-IS. Thus, IS-IS actually requires no IP connectivity between its routers to route IP traffic!

There are two types of adjacencies:

- Level-1 adjacency – for routing within an area (intra-area routing)
- Level-2 adjacency – for routing between areas (inter-area routing)

IS-IS routers must share a common physical link to become neighbors, and the System-ID must be unique on each router. Additionally, the following parameters must be identical on each router:

- Hello packet format (point-to-point or broadcast)
- Hello timers
- Router "level" (explained shortly)
- Area (only for Level-1 adjacencies)
- Authentication parameters (Cisco devices currently support only clear-text authentication for IS-IS).
- MTU

Neighbors elect a DIS (Designated Intermediate System) on broadcast links. A DIS is the equivalent of an OSPF DR (Designated Router). Unlike OSPF, however, there is no

Backup DIS, and thus a new election will occur immediately if the DIS fails. Additionally, the DIS election is preemptive.

Whichever IS-IS router has the highest priority will be elected the DIS (default priority is 64). In the event of a tie, whichever IS-IS router has the highest SNPA (usually MAC) address will become the DIS. The DIS sends out hello packets every 3.3 seconds, instead of every 10 seconds.

The IS-IS Hierarchy
IS-IS defines 3 types of IS-IS routers:

- ❖ Level-1 Router – contain within a single area, with a topology table limited to only its local area (called the Level-1 Database)
- ❖ Level-2 Router - a backbone router that routes between areas, and builds a Level-2 Database
- ❖ Level-1-2 Router – similar to an area border router. Interfaces between a local area and the backbone area, and create both a Level-1 and a Level-2 database.

Each type of IS-IS router will form only specific adjacencies:

- ❖ Level-1 routers form Level-1 adjacencies with other Level-1 routers and Level-1-2 routers.
- ❖ Level-2 routers form Level-2 adjacencies with other Level-2 routers and Level-1-2 routers.
- ❖ Level-1-2 routers form both Level-1 and Level-2 adjacencies with other Level-1-2 routers.
- ❖ Level-1 routers will never form adjacencies with Level-2 routers.

The IS-IS backbone consists of multiple contiguous Level-2 routers, each of which can exist in a separate area.

Neighbors build their topology tables by sharing LSP's (Link-State Packets), which are roughly the equivalent of OSPF LSA's. Depending on the type of adjacency, a router will send out either a Level-1 or Level-2 LSP.

Level-1 routers share Level-1 LSP's, and will build a Level-1 topology table consisting of solely its own area (thus forming the equivalent of an OSPF Totally Stubby area). If a Level-1 router has a packet destined for the local area, it simply routes the packet to the System ID by using the local topology table (Level-1 database). If a Level-1 router has a packet destined for a remote area, it forwards it to the nearest Level-1-2 router.

Level-1-2 routers set an Attach (ATT) bit in their Level-1 LSP's, informing other Level-1 routers that they are attached to another area.

Level-2 routers share Level-2 LSP's, and will build a Level-2 topology table, which contains a list of reachable areas across the IS-IS domain.

Level-1-2 routers will share both Level-1 and Level-2 LSP's with its appropriate adjacencies. Level-1-2 routers maintain separate Level-1 and Level-2 topology tables.

Level-1 routes (locally originated) are always preferred over Level-2 routes(Originated from another area).

IS-IS routers will refresh the Link-State topology table every 15 minutes (as opposed to every 30 minutes for OSPF).

Basic IS-IS Configuration

To configure IS-IS, the IS-IS process must first be established:

Router(config)# router isis

The router must then be configured with a CLNP address:

Router(config)# router isis

Router(config-router)# net 49.0001.1921.6800.5005.00

To globally dictate the router-type of all interfaces (default is level-1-2):

Router(config)# router isis

Router(config-router)# is-type level-1

Router(config-router)# is-type level-1-2

Router(config-router)# is-type level-2

Finally, IS-IS must be explicitly enabled on the interface:

Router(config)# interface fa0/0

Router(config-if)# ip router isis

This not only allows IS-IS to form neighbor relationships out of this interface, it also adds the interface's network to the routing table. The globally configured router-type can be overridden on each individual interface:

Router(config)# interface fa0/0

Router(config-if)# isis circuit-type level-1
Router(config-if)# isis circuit-type level-1-2
Router(config-if)# isis circuit-type level-2

To adjust the priority (default is 64) of interface, increasing the likelihood that the router will be elected the DIS:
Router(config)# interface e0/0
Router(config-if)# isis priority 100

The IS-IS Metric

IS-IS utilizes an arbitrary cost for its metric (the optional metrics of delay, expense, and error are not supported by Cisco). By default, interfaces of all types (regardless of speed) are assigned a metric of 10.

To adjust the metric on an interface:

Router(config)# interface e0/0
Router(config-if)# isis metric 30

IS-IS Summarization

IS-IS supports both inter-area and external summarization, and uses the same command to accomplish both. If we wish to summarize the following networks into one summary route, the command below would be required.

- 172.16.0.0/16
- 172.17.0.0/16
- 172.18.0.0/16
- 172.19.0.0/16
- 172.20.0.0/16
- 172.21.0.0/16
- 172.22.0.0/16
- 172.23.0.0/16

RouterC(config)# router isis
RouterC(config-router)# summary-address 172.16.0.0 255.248.0.0

IS-IS Troubleshooting

To view any CLNS neighbors, including the type of adjacency:

Router# show clns neighbors

To view only IS neighbors:

Router# show clns is-neighbors

To view specific IS-IS information about an interface:

Router# show clns interface e0/0

To view the IS-IS link-state topology table:

Router# show isis database

To view a list of all known IS-IS routers in all areas:

Router# show isis topology

Lab 7-3 : ISIS Configuration

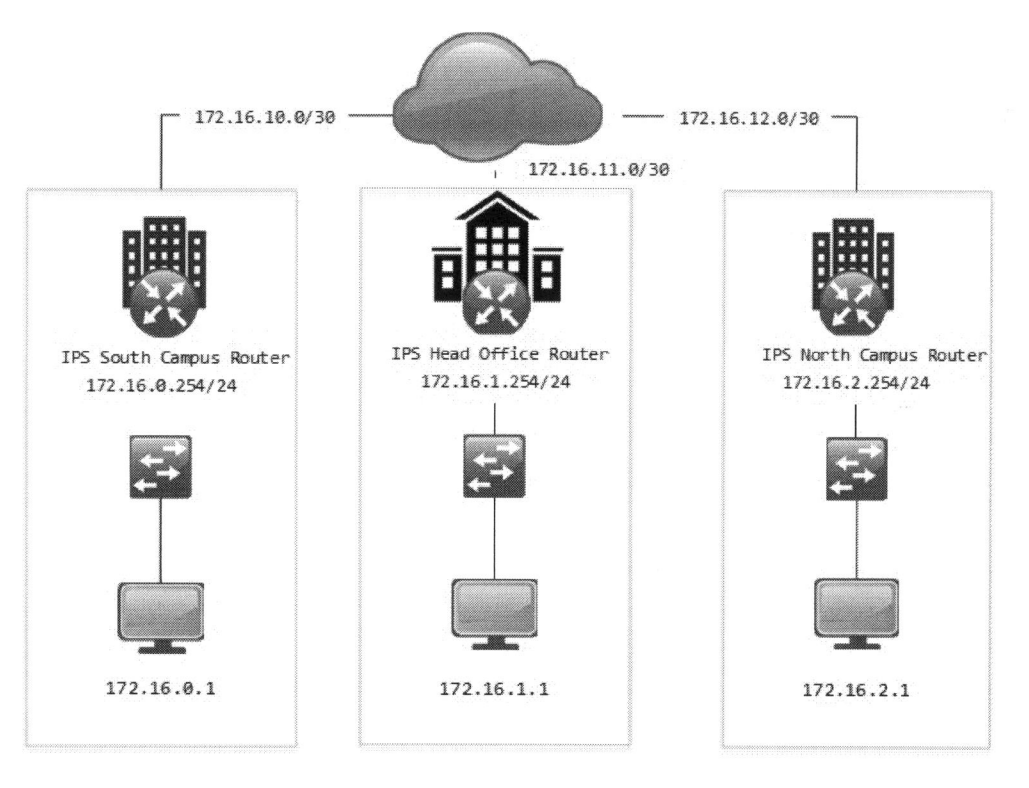

Figure 60 IS-IS Configuration

The sample configurations below configure all the routers in the above topology with these parameters:

Area 49.0001

Level 1 (L1) and Level 2 (L2) routers (this is the default unless otherwise specified)

No optional parameters

Running IS-IS for IP only

Loopback interfaces (loopbacks are advertised by IS-IS)

R1 Configuration:
```
Router>en
Router#config t
Enter configuration commands, one per line.  End with CNTL/Z.
Router(config)#hostname R1
R1(config)#int eth 0/0
R1(config-if)#ip add 172.16.10.2 255.255.255.252
R1(config-if)#ip router isis
R1(config-if)#no sh
R1(config-if)#ex
*Aug 21 10:29:07.265: %LINK-3-UPDOWN: Interface Ethernet0/0, changed state to up
*Aug 21 10:29:08.265: %LINEPROTO-5-UPDOWN: Line protocol on Interface Ethernet0/0, changed state to up

R1(config)#int eth 0/1
R1(config-if)#ip add 172.16.0.254 255.255.255.0
R1(config-if)#ip router isis
R1(config-if)#no sh
R1(config-if)#ex
*Aug 21 10:29:34.040: %LINK-3-UPDOWN: Interface Ethernet0/1, changed state to up
*Aug 21 10:29:35.045: %LINEPROTO-5-UPDOWN: Line protocol on Interface Ethernet0/1, changed state to up

R1(config)#router isis
R1(config-router)#net 49.0001.0000.0000.0003.00
R1(config-router)#ex
```

R2 Configuration:
```
Router>
Router>en
Router#config t
Enter configuration commands, one per line.  End with CNTL/Z.
Router(config)#hostname R2
R2(config)#int eth 0/0
R2(config-if)#ip add 172.16.11.2 255.255.255.252
R2(config-if)#ip router isis
R2(config-if)#no sh
R2(config-if)#ex
```

```
*Aug 21 10:31:42.758: %LINK-3-UPDOWN: Interface Ethernet0/0, changed state to up
*Aug 21 10:31:43.762: %LINEPROTO-5-UPDOWN: Line protocol on Interface Ethernet0/0,
changed state to up
```
R2(config)#int eth 0/1
R2(config-if)#ip add 172.16.1.254 255.255.255.0
R2(config-if)#ip router isis
R2(config-if)#no sh
R2(config-if)#ex
```
*Aug 21 10:32:11.338: %LINK-3-UPDOWN: Interface Ethernet0/1, changed state to up
*Aug 21 10:32:12.343: %LINEPROTO-5-UPDOWN: Line protocol on Interface Ethernet0/1,
changed state to up
```

R2(config)#router isis
R2(config-router)#net 49.0001.0000.0000.0004.00
R2(config-router)#ex

R3 Configuration:

Router>
Router>en
Router#config t
```
Enter configuration commands, one per line.  End with CNTL/Z.
```
Router(config)#hostname R3
R3(config)#int eth 0/0
R3(config-if)#ip add 172.16.12.1 255.255.255.252
R3(config-if)#ip router isis
R3(config-if)#no sh
R3(config-if)#ex
```
*Aug 21 10:35:25.222: %LINK-3-UPDOWN: Interface Ethernet0/0, changed state to up
*Aug 21 10:35:26.226: %LINEPROTO-5-UPDOWN: Line protocol on Interface Ethernet0/0,
changed state to up
```

R3(config)#int eth 0/1
R3(config-if)#ip add 172.16.2.254 255.255.255.0
R3(config-if)#ip router isis
R3(config-if)#no sh
R3(config-if)#ex
```
*Aug 21 10:35:51.115: %LINK-3-UPDOWN: Interface Ethernet0/1, changed state to up
*Aug 21 10:35:52.119: %LINEPROTO-5-UPDOWN: Line protocol on Interface Ethernet0/1,
changed state to up
```
R3(config)#router isis
R3(config-router)#net 49.0001.0000.0000.0005.00
R3(config-router)#ex

Verification:

Ping from vPC of LAN Network 1 to other LAN

```
VPC1                                                    —    □    ×

VPCS> ping 172.16.2.1

84 bytes from 172.16.2.1 icmp_seq=1 ttl=60 time=0.768 ms
84 bytes from 172.16.2.1 icmp_seq=2 ttl=60 time=1.274 ms
84 bytes from 172.16.2.1 icmp_seq=3 ttl=60 time=0.691 ms
84 bytes from 172.16.2.1 icmp_seq=4 ttl=60 time=1.008 ms
84 bytes from 172.16.2.1 icmp_seq=5 ttl=60 time=1.062 ms

VPCS> ping 172.16.1.1

84 bytes from 172.16.1.1 icmp_seq=1 ttl=61 time=1.437 ms
84 bytes from 172.16.1.1 icmp_seq=2 ttl=61 time=1.026 ms
84 bytes from 172.16.1.1 icmp_seq=3 ttl=61 time=1.025 ms
84 bytes from 172.16.1.1 icmp_seq=4 ttl=61 time=0.939 ms
84 bytes from 172.16.1.1 icmp_seq=5 ttl=61 time=1.082 ms

VPCS>
```

R1# show ip route

```
R1                                                      —    □    ×

R1>
R1>en
R1#show ip route
Codes: L - local, C - connected, S - static, R - RIP, M - mobile, B - BGP
       D - EIGRP, EX - EIGRP external, O - OSPF, IA - OSPF inter area
       N1 - OSPF NSSA external type 1, N2 - OSPF NSSA external type 2
       E1 - OSPF external type 1, E2 - OSPF external type 2
       i - IS-IS, su - IS-IS summary, L1 - IS-IS level-1, L2 - IS-IS level-2
       ia - IS-IS inter area, * - candidate default, U - per-user static route
       o - ODR, P - periodic downloaded static route, H - NHRP, l - LISP
       a - application route
       + - replicated route, % - next hop override

Gateway of last resort is not set

      172.16.0.0/16 is variably subnetted, 8 subnets, 3 masks
C        172.16.0.0/24 is directly connected, Ethernet0/1
L        172.16.0.254/32 is directly connected, Ethernet0/1
i L1     172.16.1.0/24 [115/30] via 172.16.10.1, 00:15:58, Ethernet0/0
i L1     172.16.2.0/24 [115/40] via 172.16.10.1, 00:12:01, Ethernet0/0
C        172.16.10.0/30 is directly connected, Ethernet0/0
L        172.16.10.2/32 is directly connected, Ethernet0/0
i L1     172.16.11.0/30 [115/20] via 172.16.10.1, 00:20:57, Ethernet0/0
i L1     172.16.12.0/30 [115/30] via 172.16.10.1, 00:20:47, Ethernet0/0
      200.50.10.0/30 is subnetted, 1 subnets
i L1     200.50.10.0 [115/20] via 172.16.10.1, 00:20:57, Ethernet0/0
R1#
```

All routes are learned by ISIS.

R1# **show isis neighbors**

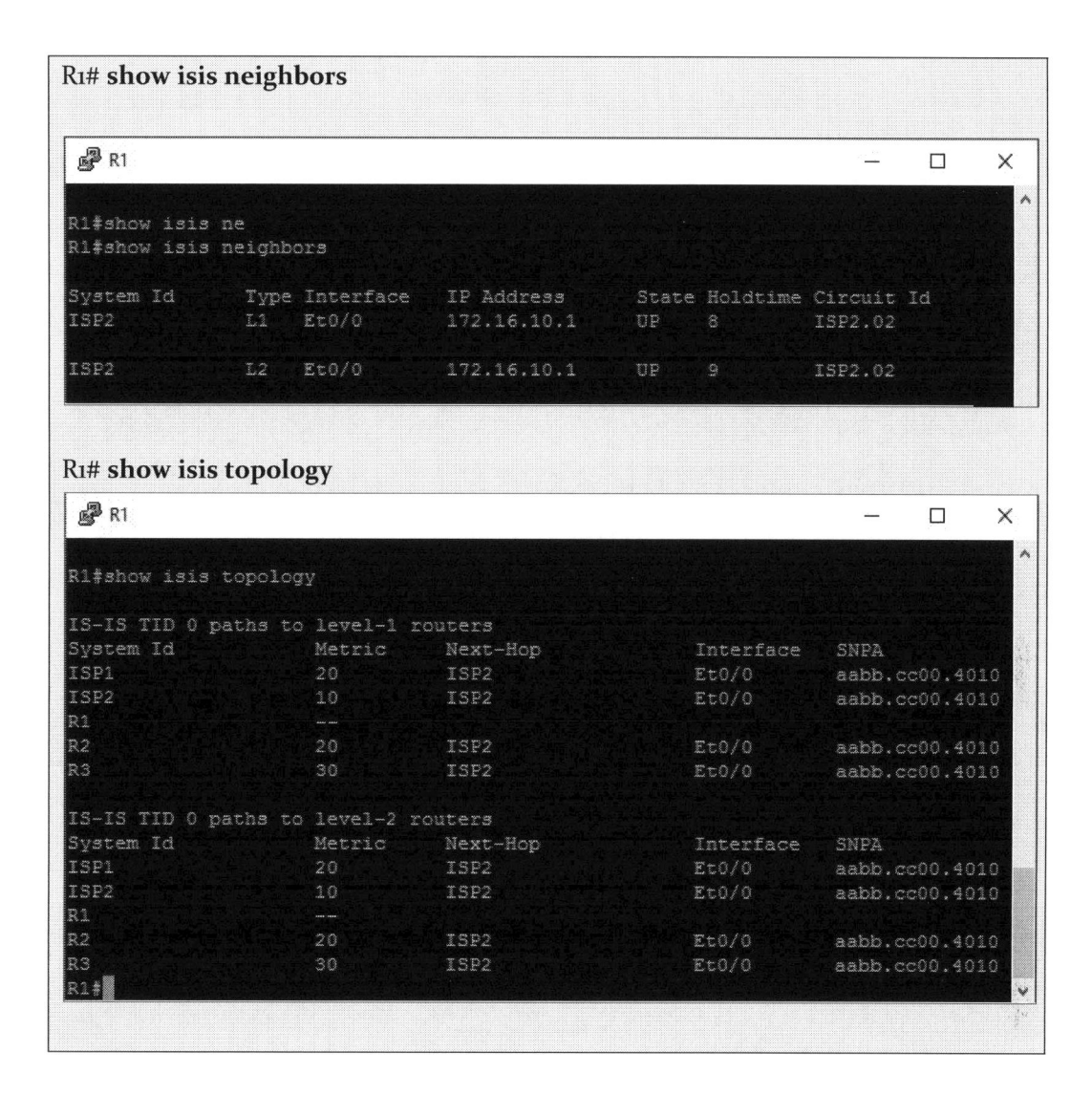

```
R1#show isis ne
R1#show isis neighbors

System Id        Type Interface    IP Address       State Holdtime Circuit Id
ISP2             L1   Et0/0         172.16.10.1      UP    8        ISP2.02

ISP2             L2   Et0/0         172.16.10.1      UP    9        ISP2.02
```

R1# **show isis topology**

```
R1#show isis topology

IS-IS TID 0 paths to level-1 routers
System Id           Metric      Next-Hop          Interface   SNPA
ISP1                20          ISP2              Et0/0       aabb.cc00.4010
ISP2                10          ISP2              Et0/0       aabb.cc00.4010
R1                  --
R2                  20          ISP2              Et0/0       aabb.cc00.4010
R3                  30          ISP2              Et0/0       aabb.cc00.4010

IS-IS TID 0 paths to level-2 routers
System Id           Metric      Next-Hop          Interface   SNPA
ISP1                20          ISP2              Et0/0       aabb.cc00.4010
ISP2                10          ISP2              Et0/0       aabb.cc00.4010
R1                  --
R2                  20          ISP2              Et0/0       aabb.cc00.4010
R3                  30          ISP2              Et0/0       aabb.cc00.4010
R1#
```

Static v/s Dynamic Routing

There are two basic methods of building a routing table:

- Static Routing
- Dynamic Routing

Static Routing

A static routing table is managed, and updated by a network administrator manually. A static route to every network must be configured on every router for full connectivity. This provides a granular level of control over routing, but quickly becomes impractical on large networks. Routers do not share static routes with each other, thus reducing CPU/RAM overhead and saving bandwidth. However, static routing is not fault-tolerant, as any change to the routing infrastructure (such as a link going down, or a new network added) requires manual intervention. Routers operating in a purely static environment cannot choose a best route if a link becomes unavailable.

Static routes have an Administrative Distance (AD) of 1, and therefore always preferred over dynamic routes, unless the default AD is changed. A static route with an adjusted AD is termed as floating static route, and is covered in detail in another guide. A dynamic routing table is created, maintained, and updated by a routing protocol running on the router. Examples of routing protocols include RIP (Routing Information Protocol), EIGRP (Enhanced Interior Gateway Routing Protocol), and OSPF (Open Shortest Path First).

Specific dynamic routing protocols are covered in detail in other guides. Routers do share dynamic routing information with each other, which increases CPU, RAM, and bandwidth usage. However, routing protocols are capable of dynamically choosing a different (or better) path when there is a change to the routing infrastructure.

Do not confuse routing protocols with routed protocols:

- A routed protocol is a Layer 3 protocol that applies logical addresses to devices and routes data between networks (such as IP)
- A routing protocol dynamically builds the network topology, and next hops reachability information in routing tables (such as RIP, EIGRP, etc.)

The following are the advantages and disadvantages of static routing:

Advantages of Static Routing

- Minimal CPU/Memory overhead
- No bandwidth overhead (updates are not shared between routers)
- Granular control on how traffic is routed

Disadvantages of Static Routing

- Infrastructure changes be manually adjusted
- No "dynamic" fault tolerance if a link goes down
- Impractical on large network

The following briefly outlines the advantages and disadvantages of dynamic routing:

Advantages of Dynamic Routing

- Simpler to configure on larger networks
- Will dynamically choose a different (or better) route if a link goes down
- Ability to load balance between multiple links

Disadvantages of Dynamic Routing

- Updates are shared between routers, thus consuming bandwidth
- Routing protocols put additional load on router CPU/RAM
- The choice of the "best route" is in the hands of the routing protocol, and not the network administrator

Dynamic Routing Categories

There are two different categories of dynamic routing protocols:

- **Distance-vector protocols**
- **Link-state protocols**

Examples of distance-vector protocols include RIP and IGRP. An example of link-state protocols includes OSPF and IS-IS. EIGRP exhibits both distance-vector and link-state characteristics, and is considered a hybrid protocol.

Distance-vector Routing Protocols

All distance-vector routing protocols share several key characteristics:

- Periodic updates of the full routing table are sent to routing neighbors.
- Distance-vector protocols have slow convergence, and are highly susceptible to loops.
- Some form of distance is used for calculating a route's metric.
- The Bellman-Ford algorithm is used to determine the shortest path.

A distance-vector routing protocol begins by advertising directly connected networks to its neighbors. These updates are sent regularly (RIP – every 30 seconds; IGRP – every 90 seconds).

Neighbors will add the routes from these updates to their own routing tables. Each neighbor trusts this information, and will forward their full routing table (connected and learned routes) to neighbors. Thus, routers fully (and blindly) rely on neighbors for route information, a concept known as routing by rumor.

There are several disadvantages of this behavior. Because routing information is propagated from neighbor to neighbor through periodic updates, distance-vector protocols suffer from slow convergence. This, in addition to blind faith of neighbor updates, results in distance-vector protocols being highly susceptible to routing loops.

Distance-vector protocols utilize some form of distance to calculate a route's metric. RIP uses hop count as its distance metric, and IGRP uses a composite of bandwidth and delay.

Link-State Routing Protocols

Link-state routing protocols were created to alleviate the convergence and loop issues of distance-vector protocols. Link-state protocols maintain 3 separate tables:

- Neighbor table – contains a list of all neighbors, and the interface each neighbor is connected of. Sending Hello packets forms neighbors.

- Topology table – otherwise known as the "link-state" table, contains a map of all links within an area, including each link's status.

- Shortest-Path table – contains all best routes to each particular destination (otherwise known as the "routing" table)

Link-state protocols do not "route by rumor." Instead, routers send updates advertising the state of their links (a link is a directly connected network). All routers know the state of all existing links within their area, and store this information in a topology table. All routers within an area have identical topology tables.

The best route to each link (network) is stored in the routing (or shortest path) table. If the state of a link changes, such as a router interface failing, an advertisement containing only this link-state change will be sent to all routers within that area. Each router will adjust its topology table accordingly, and will calculate a new best route if required.

By maintaining a topology table among all routers within an area, link-state protocols can converge very quickly and are immune to routing loops.

Additionally, because updates are sent only during a link-state change, and contain only the change (and not the full table), link-state protocols are less bandwidth intensive than distance-vector protocols. However, the three link-state tables utilize more RAM and CPU on the router itself.

Link-state protocols utilize some form of cost, usually based on bandwidth, to calculate a route's metric. The Dijkstra formula is used to determine the shortest path.

BGP (Border Gateway Protocol)

BGP is a standardized exterior gateway protocol (EGP), unlike RIP, OSPF, and EIGRP which are interior gateway protocols (IGP's). BGP Version 4 (BGPv4) is the current standard deployment. BGP is considered as "Path Vector" routing protocol. BGP was not built to route within an Autonomous System (AS), but rather to route between AS's. BGP maintains a separate routing table based on shortest AS Path and several other attributes, as opposed to IGP metrics like distance or cost. BGP is the routing protocol of choice on the Internet. Essentially, the Internet is a collection of interconnected Autonomous Systems. BGP Autonomous Systems are assigned an Autonomous System Number (ASN), which is a 16-bit number ranging from 1 – 65535. A specific subset of this range, 64512 – 65535, has been reserved for private (or internal) use. BGP utilizes TCP for reliable transfer of its packets, on port 179.

When to Use BGP

BGP is not necessary when multiple connections to the Internet are required. Fault tolerance or redundancy of outbound traffic can easily be handled by an IGP, such as OSPF or EIGRP. BGP is also unnecessary if there is only one connection to an external AS (such as the Internet). There are over 100,000 routes on the Internet, and interior routers should not be needlessly burdened.

BGP should be used under the following circumstances:

- Multiple connections exist to external AS's (such as the Internet) via different providers.
- Multiple connections exist to external AS's through the same provider, but connect via a separate CO or routing policy.
- The existing routing equipment can handle the additional demands.

BGP's true benefit is in controlling how traffic enters the local AS, rather than how traffic exits it.

BGP Peers (Neighbors)
For BGP to function, BGP routers (called speakers) must form neighbor relationships (called peers).

There are two types of BGP neighbor relationships:

- iBGP Peers – BGP neighbors within the same autonomous system.
- eBGP Peers – BGP neighbors connecting separate autonomous systems.

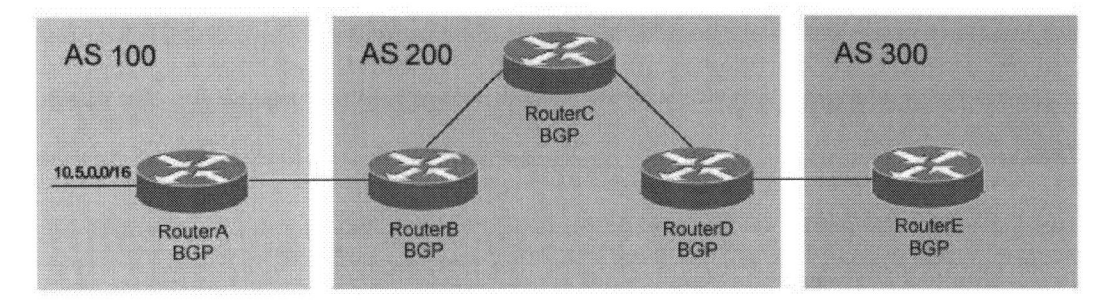

Figure 61 BGP Peering

In the figure above, Router B and Router C in AS 200 would form an iBGP peer relationship. Router A in AS 100 and Router B in AS 200 would form an eBGP peering.

Once BGP peers form a neighbor relationship, they share their full routing table. Afterwards, only changes to the routing table are forwarded to peers.

By default, BGP assumes that eBGP peers are a maximum of one hop away. This restriction can be ignored using the ebgp-multihop option with the neighbor command.

iBGP peers do not have a hop restrictions, and are dependent on the underlying IGP of the AS to connect peers together. By default, all iBGP peers must be fully meshed within the Autonomous System.

A Cisco router running BGP can belong to only one AS. The IOS will only allow one BGP process to run on a router. The Administrative Distance for routes learned outside the Autonomous System (eBGP routes) is 20, while the AD for iBGP and locally originated routes is 200.

BGP Peers Messages
BGP forms its peer relationships through a series of messages. First, an OPEN message is sent between peers to initiate the session.

The **OPEN** message contains several parameters:

- BGP Version, it must be the same between BGP peers
- Local AS Number
- BGP Router ID

KEEPALIVE messages are sent periodically after every 60 seconds by default to ensure that the remote peer is still available or alive. If a router does not receive a KEEPALIVE from a peer for a Hold-time period (by default, 180 seconds), the router declares that peer is dead.

UPDATE messages are used to exchange routes between peers.

Finally, NOTIFICATION messages are sent when there is a fatal error condition. If a NOTIFICATION message is sent, the BGP peer session is turn down and reset.

As a BGP peer session is forming, it will pass through several states. This process is called BGP Finite-State Machine (FSM):

1. Idle – the initial BGP state

2. Connect - BGP waits for a TCP connection with the remote peer. If successful, an OPEN message is sent. If unsuccessful, the session is placed in an Active state.

3. Active – BGP attempts to initiate a TCP connection with the remote peer. If successful, an OPEN message is sent. If unsuccessful, BGP will wait for a Connect Retry timer to expire, and place the session back in a Connect State.

4. OpenSent – BGP has both established the TCP connection and sent an OPEN Message, and is awaiting a reply OPEN Message. Once it receives a reply OPEN Message, the BGP peer will send a KEEPALIVE message.

5. OpenConfirm – BGP listens for a reply KEEPALIVE message.

6. Established – the BGP peer session is fully established. UPDATE messages containing routing information will now be sent.

If a peer session is stuck in an Active state, potential problems can include No IP connectivity (no route to host), an incorrect neighbor statement, or an access-list filtering TCP port 179.

BGP Attributes
BGP utilizes several attributes to determine the best path to a destination. Well-known attributes are supported by all implementations of BGP, while no BGP-speaking routers may support optional attributes.

Several subcategories of attributes exist:

- **Well-known Mandatory** – Standard attributes supported by all BGP implementations, and always included in every BGP update.

- **Well-known Discretionary** – Standard attributes supported by all BGP implementations, and are optionally included BGP updates.

- **Optional Transitive** – Optional attribute that may not be supported by all implementations of BGP. Transitive indicates that a noncompliant BGP router will forward the unsupported attribute unchanged, when sending updates to peers.

- **Optional Non-Transitive** - Optional attribute that may not be supported by all implementations of BGP. Non-Transitive indicates that a non-compliant BGP router will strip out the unsupported attribute, when sending updates to peers.

The following describes several specific BGP attributes:

- AS-Path (well-known mandatory) – Identifies the list (or path) of traversed AS's to reach a particular destination.
- Next-Hop (well-known mandatory) – Identifies the next hop IP address to reach a particular destination.
- Origin (well-known mandatory) – Identifies the originator of the route.
- Local Preference (well-known, discretionary) – Provides a preference to determine the best path for outbound traffic.
- Atomic Aggregate (well-known discretionary) – Identifies routes that have been summarized, or aggregated.
- Aggregator (optional transitive) – Identifies the BGP router that performed an address aggregation.
- Community (optional transitive) – Tags routes that share common characteristics into communities.
- Multi-Exit-Discriminator (MED) (optional non-transitive) – Provides a preference to eBGP peers to a specific inbound router.
- Weight (Cisco Proprietary) – Similar to Local Preference, provides a local weight to determine the best path for outbound traffic.

Each attribute is identified by a code:

- Origin (Code 1)
- AS-Path (Code 2)
- Next Hop (Code 3)
- MED (Code 4)
- Local Preference (Code 5)
- Automatic Aggregate (Code 6)
- Aggregator (Code 7)
- Community (Code 8)

BGP "Best Path" Determination

If BGP have multiple routes to the same destination, it compares the routes in pairs, starting with the newest entries (listed higher in the routing table), and working towards the oldest entries (listed lower in the table).

BGP determines the best path by successively comparing the attributes of each "route pair." The attributes are compared in a specific order:

- Weight – Which route has the highest weight?
- Local Preference – Which route has the highest local preference?
- Locally Originated – Did the local router originate this route? In other words, is the next hop to the destination 0.0.0.0?
- AS-Path – Which route has the shortest AS-Path?
- Origin Code – Where did the route originate? The following origin codes are listed in order of preference:

1. IGP (originated from an interior gateway protocol)
2. EGP (originated from an exterior gateway protocol)
3. ? (Unknown origin)

- MED – Which path has the lowest MED?
- BGP Route Type – Is this an eBGP or iBGP route? (eBGP routes are preferred)
- Age – Which route is the oldest? (oldest is preferred)
- Router ID – Which route originated from the router with the lowest BGP router ID?
- Peers IP Address – Which route originated from the router with the lowest IP?

When applying attributes, Weight and Local Preference are applied to inbound routes, dictating the best outbound path. AS-Path and MED are applied to outbound routes, dictating the best-inbound path.

The first step in configuring BGP is to enable the BGP process, and specify the router's Autonomous System (AS):

```
RouterB(config)# router bgp 100
```

Router B is now a member of AS 100. Next, neighbor relationships must be established. To configure a neighbor relationship with a router in the same AS (iBGP Peer):

```
RouterB(config)# router bgp 100
RouterB(config-router)# neighbor 10.1.1.1 remote-as 100
```

To configure a neighbor relationship with a router in a separate AS (eBGP Peer):

RouterB(config)# router bgp 100

RouterB(config-router)# neighbor 172.16.1.2 remote-as 900

Notice that the syntax is the same, and that the remote-as argument is always used, regardless if the peering is iBGP or eBGP.

For stability purposes, the source interface used to generate updates to a particular neighbor can be specified:

RouterB(config)# router bgp 100

RouterB(config-router)# neighbor 172.16.1.2 update-source loo

Router C must then point to RouterB's loopback (assume the address is 1.1.1.1/24) in its neighbor statement:

RouterC(config)# router bgp 900

RouterC(config-router)# neighbor 1.1.1.1 remote-as 100

Router C must have a route to Router B's loopback in its routing table.

Remember though: by default, BGP assumes that external peers are exactly one hop away. Using the loopback as a source interface puts Router B two hops away from Router C. Thus, the ebgp-multihop feature must be enabled:

RouterC(config)# router bgp 900

RouterC(config-router)# neighbor 1.1.1.1 ebgp-multihop 2

The 2 indicates the number of hops to the eBGP peer. If left blank, the default is 255. To authenticate updates between two BGP peers:

RouterB(config)# router bgp 100

RouterB(config-router)# neighbor 172.16.1.2 password CISCO

Lab 7-4 : BGP Configuration

Case Study:

Internal And External BGP are configure in this Lab with Autonomous System Number 65000 and 65001. External BGP link connected these routers. Internal Netowrk is operating on Internal BGPs.

Topology Diagram:

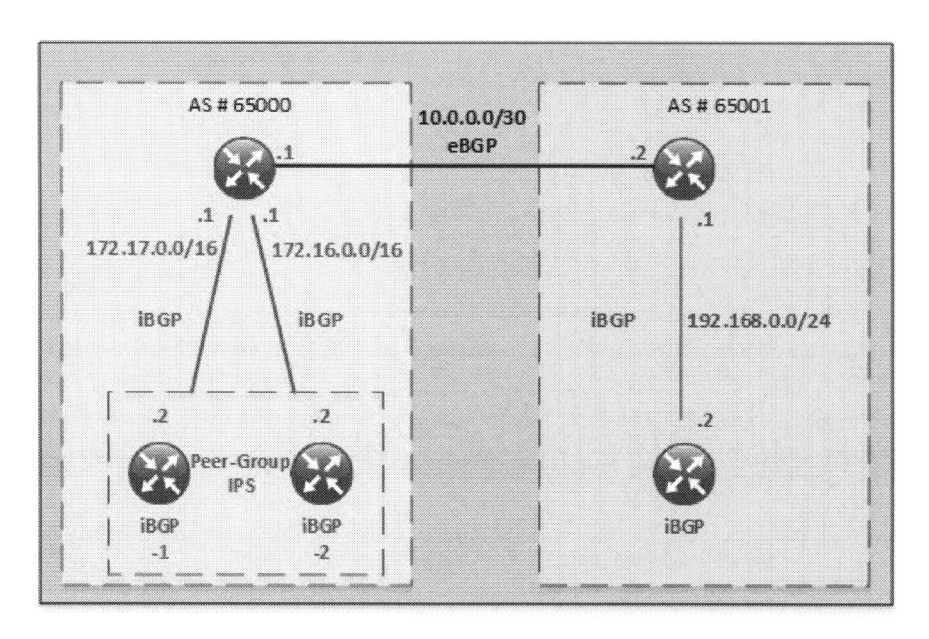

Figure 62 BGP Implementation

Configuration:

Border Router of Autonomous System 65000:

Router(config)#hostname Border-65000

Border-65000(config)#int eth 0/0

Border-65000(config-if)#ip add 10.0.0.1 255.255.255.252

Border-65000(config-if)#no sh

// In case of down interface, Or down line protocol, Adjacency will not formed

Border-65000(config-if)#ex

Border-65000(config)#

*May 18 06:29:36.524: %LINK-3-UPDOWN: Interface Ethernet0/0, changed state to up

*May 18 06:29:37.529: %LINEPROTO-5-UPDOWN: Line protocol on Interface Ethernet0/0, changed state to up

Border-65000(config)#int eth 0/1

Border-65000(config-if)#ip add 172.17.0.1 255.255.0.0

Border-65000(config-if)#no sh

// In case of down interface, Or down line protocol, Adjacency will not formed

Border-65000(config-if)#ex

Border-65000(config)#

*May 18 06:30:06.770: %LINK-3-UPDOWN: Interface Ethernet0/1, changed state to up

*May 18 06:30:07.774: %LINEPROTO-5-UPDOWN: Line protocol on Interface Ethernet0/1, changed state to up

Border-65000(config)#int eth 0/2

Border-65000(config-if)#ip add 172.16.0.1 255.255.0.0

Border-65000(config-if)#no sh

// In case of down interface, Or down line protocol, Adjacency will not formed

Border-65000(config-if)#ex

Border-65000(config)#

*May 18 06:30:26.953: %LINK-3-UPDOWN: Interface Ethernet0/2, changed state to up

*May 18 06:30:27.953: %LINEPROTO-5-UPDOWN: Line protocol on Interface Ethernet0/2, changed state to up

Border-65000(config)#

Border-65000(config)#router bgp 65000

// Autonomous system must be defined and same as in the neighbour details of remote router

Border-65000(config-router)#neighbor 10.0.0.2 remote-as 65001

// Autonomous system must be of same for iBGP and different for eBGP.

Border-65000(config-router)#neighbor IPS peer-group

Border-65000(config-router)#neighbor IPS remote-as 65000

// Make sure Autonomous system number having peer-group named as IPS

Border-65000(config-router)#neighbor 172.16.0.2 peer-group IPS

// Verify the peer-group name, In case of difference in spelling neighbour will be allocated in a new peer group.

Border-65000(config-router)#neighbor 172.17.0.2 peer-group IPS

Border-65000(config-router)#network 172.17.0.0 mask 255.255.0.0

Border-65000(config-router)#net 172.16.0.0 mask 255.255.0.0

Border-65000(config-router)#net 10.0.0.0 mask 255.255.255.252

// Make sure to advertise the correct IP addresses and Masks

Border-65000(config-router)#ex

Border-65000(config)#

Internal Router 1 of Autonomous System 65000:

Router(config)#hostname eBGP-1

iBGP-1(config)#int eth 0/0

```
iBGP-1(config-if)#ip add 172.17.0.2 255.255.0.0
iBGP-1(config-if)#no sh
iBGP-1(config-if)#ex
*May 18 06:37:03.582: %LINK-3-UPDOWN: Interface Ethernet0/0, changed state to up
*May 18 06:37:04.586: %LINEPROTO-5-UPDOWN: Line protocol on Interface Ethernet0/0, changed state to up
iBGP-1(config)#router bgp 65000
```
// Make sure Autonomous system number.
```
iBGP-1(config-router)#neighbor 172.17.0.1 remote-as 65000
```
// Make sure the advertisement of Neighbor with respect to its related Autonomous system number.
```
iBGP-1(config-router)#ex
iBGP-1(config)#
*May 18 06:37:41.303: %BGP-5-ADJCHANGE: neighbor 172.17.0.1 Up
iBGP-1(config)#
```

Internal Router 2 of Autonomous System 65000:

```
Router(config)#hostname eBGP-2
iBGP-2(config)#int eth 0/0
iBGP-2(config-if)#ip add 172.16.0.2 255.255.0.0
iBGP-2(config-if)#no sh
```
// In case of down interface, Or down line protocol, Adjacency will not formed
```
iBGP-2(config-if)#ex
*May 18 06:38:59.043: %LINK-3-UPDOWN: Interface Ethernet0/0, changed state to up
*May 18 06:39:00.043: %LINEPROTO-5-UPDOWN: Line protocol on Interface Ethernet0/0, changed state to up

iBGP-2(config)#router bgp 65000
```
// Make sure Autonomous system number.
```
iBGP-2(config-router)#neighbor 172.16.0.1 remote-as 65000
iBGP-2(config-router)#ex
```

Border Router of Autonomous System 65001:

```
Router(config)#hostname Border-65001
Border-65001(config)#int eth 0/0
Border-65001(config-if)#ip add 10.0.0.2 255.255.255.252
Border-65001(config-if)#no sh
```
// In case of down interface, Or down line protocol, Adjacency will not formed
```
Border-65001(config-if)#ex
Border-65001(config)#
*May 18 06:41:01.899: %LINK-3-UPDOWN: Interface Ethernet0/0, changed state to up
*May 18 06:41:02.903: %LINEPROTO-5-UPDOWN: Line protocol on Interface Ethernet0/0, changed state to up
Border-65001(config)#int eth 0/1
Border-65001(config-if)#ip add 192.168.0.1 255.255.255.0
Border-65001(config-if)#no sh
```
// In case of down interface, Or down line protocol, Adjacency will not formed
```
Border-65001(config-if)#ex
Border-65001(config)#
*May 18 06:41:24.960: %LINK-3-UPDOWN: Interface Ethernet0/1, changed state to up
*May 18 06:41:25.964: %LINEPROTO-5-UPDOWN: Line protocol on Interface Ethernet0/1, changed state to up
Border-65001(config)#
Border-65001(config)#router bgp 65001
```
// Make sure Autonomous system number.
```
Border-65001(config-router)#neighbor 10.0.0.1 remote-as 65000
```
// Make sure the advertisement of Neighbor with respect to its related Autonomous system number.
```
Border-65001(config-router)#
*May 18 06:41:51.143: %BGP-5-ADJCHANGE: neighbor 10.0.0.1 Up
Border-65001(config-router)#neighbor 192.168.0.2 remote-as 65001
```
// Make sure the advertisement of Neighbor with respect to its related Autonomous system number.
```
Border-65001(config-router)#network 192.168.0.0 mask 255.255.255.0
Border-65001(config-router)#network 10.0.0.0 mask 255.255.255.252
```
// Make sure to advertise the correct IP addresses and Masks
```
Border-65001(config-router)#ex
Border-65001(config)#
```

Internal Router 1 of Autonomous System 65001:

Router(config)#hostname eBGP

eBGP(config)#int eth 0/0

eBGP(config-if)#ip add 192.168.0.2 255.255.255.0

eBGP(config-if)#no sh

eBGP(config-if)#ex

eBGP(config)#

*May 18 06:50:01.078: %LINK-3-UPDOWN: Interface Ethernet0/0, changed state to up

*May 18 06:50:02.082: %LINEPROTO-5-UPDOWN: Line protocol on Interface Ethernet0/0, changed state to up

eBGP(config)#

eBGP(config)#

eBGP(config)#router bgp 65001

// Make sure Autonomous system number.

eBGP(config-router)#neighbor 192.168.0.1 remote-as 65001

// Make sure the advertisement of Neighbor with respect to its related Autonomous system number.

eBGP(config-router)#ex

eBGP(config)#

*May 18 06:50:34.601: %BGP-5-ADJCHANGE: neighbor 192.168.0.1 Up

Troubleshooting:

```
iBGP-1#
iBGP-1#ping 192.168.0.2
Type escape sequence to abort.
Sending 5, 100-byte ICMP Echos to 192.168.0.2, timeout is 2 seconds:
!!!!!
Success rate is 100 percent (5/5), round-trip min/avg/max = 1/1/2 ms
iBGP-1#
iBGP-1#
iBGP-1#
iBGP-1#
iBGP-1#
```

Successful ping shows the Layer 3 connectivity from internal BGP router to the remote BGP Autonomous System internal router.

Border-65000#show bgp ipv4 unicast neighbors

or

Border-65000#show bgp ipv4 unicast neighbors | section hold time

```
Border-65001#
Border-65001#
Border-65001#
Border-65001#show bgp ipv4 unicast neighbors | section hold time
  Last read 00:00:11, last write 00:00:08, hold time is 180, keepalive interval is 60 seconds
  Last read 00:00:49, last write 00:00:02, hold time is 180, keepalive interval is 60 seconds
Border-65001#
Border-65001#
Border-65001#
Border-65001#
```

```
nds
Border-65000#show bgp ipv4 unicast neighbors | section  hold time
  Last read 00:00:39, last write 00:00:39, hold time is 180, keepalive interval is 60 seconds
  Last read 00:00:28, last write 00:00:09, hold time is 180, keepalive interval is 60 seconds
  Last read 00:00:12, last write 00:00:14, hold time is 180, keepalive interval is 60 seconds
Border-65000#
```

The output shows the Hold timer and Keep Alive timer of all the neighbour. This command is issued on the Border Routers of the Autonomous System so that they show the output of all of its neighbour's timers. To troubleshoot the output in detail, issue the command without section

iBGP-1#show ip bgp neighbors

```
1BGP-1#show ip bgp neighbors
BGP neighbor is 172.17.0.1,  remote AS 65000, internal link
  BGP version 4, remote router ID 172.17.0.1
  BGP state = Established, up for 00:28:30
  Last read 00:00:45, last write 00:00:03, hold time is 180, keepalive interval is 60 seconds
  Neighbor sessions:
    1 active, is not multisession capable (disabled)
  Neighbor capabilities:
    Route refresh: advertised and received(new)
    Four-octets ASN Capability: advertised and received
    Address family IPv4 Unicast: advertised and received
    Enhanced Refresh Capability: advertised and received
    Multisession Capability:
    Stateful switchover support enabled: NO for session 1
  Message statistics:
    InQ depth is 0
    OutQ depth is 0

                         Sent       Rcvd
    Opens:                  1          1
    Notifications:          0          0
    Updates:                1          3
    Keepalives:            33         31
    Route Refresh:          0          0
    Total:                 35         37
  Default minimum time between advertisement runs is 0 seconds

 For address family: IPv4 Unicast
  Session: 172.17.0.1
  BGP table version 21, neighbor version 21/0
  Output queue size : 0
  Index 2, Advertise bit 0
  2 update-group member
  Slow-peer detection is disabled
  Slow-peer split-update-group dynamic is disabled
  Interface associated: (none)
                             Sent       Rcvd
  Prefix activity:           ----       ----
    Prefixes Current:           0          4 (Consumes 320 bytes)
    Prefixes Total:             0          4
    Implicit Withdraw:          0          0
    Explicit Withdraw:          0          0
    Used as bestpath:         n/a          4
    Used as multipath:        n/a          0
                          Outbound   Inbound
```

For neighbour Adjacency, BGP timers and states are very important. Hold time and keep alive timer must match at the both ends of a link to form adjacency. As shown in the Output, Hold time and Keep alive time are with their default values

Border-65000#show bgp ipv4 unicast summary

```
R3
172.16.0.2      4       65000   35      43      13      0       0 00:29:33
 0
172.17.0.2      4       65000   36      43      13      0       0 00:29:36
 0
Border-65000#show bgp ipv4 unicast summary
BGP router identifier 172.17.0.1, local AS number 65000
BGP table version is 13, main routing table version 13
4 network entries using 560 bytes of memory
5 path entries using 400 bytes of memory
2/2 BGP path/bestpath attribute entries using 288 bytes of memory
1 BGP AS-PATH entries using 24 bytes of memory
0 BGP route-map cache entries using 0 bytes of memory
0 BGP filter-list cache entries using 0 bytes of memory
BGP using 1272 total bytes of memory
BGP activity 6/2 prefixes, 10/5 paths, scan interval 60 secs

Neighbor        V       AS MsgRcvd MsgSent   TblVer  InQ OutQ Up/Down  State/PfxRcd
10.0.0.2        4       65001     7       8       13      0       0 00:03:19        2
172.16.0.2      4       65000    35      44       13      0       0 00:29:54        0
172.17.0.2      4       65000    36      44       13      0       0 00:29:58        0
Border-65000#
```

The output shows IPv4 neighbours of BGP router. Neighbour ID along with Autonomous System number and the states are also shown. If the state of any of the router is IDLE as shown in the figure below, it means the link is facing trouble. This may be of authentication, state difference or else.

Border-65000#show ip bgp summary

```
R3
        Refresh End-of-RIB              0       0

  Address tracking is enabled, the RIB does have a route to 172.16.0.2
  Connections established 2; dropped 1
  Last reset 00:01:02, due to User reset of session 1
  Transport(tcp) path-mtu-discovery is enabled
  Graceful-Restart is disabled

Border-65000#show ip bgp su
Border-65000#show ip bgp summary
BGP router identifier 172.17.0.1, local AS number 65000
BGP table version is 1, main routing table version 1
4 network entries using 560 bytes of memory
5 path entries using 400 bytes of memory
2/0 BGP path/bestpath attribute entries using 288 bytes of memory
1 BGP AS-PATH entries using 24 bytes of memory
0 BGP route-map cache entries using 0 bytes of memory
0 BGP filter-list cache entries using 0 bytes of memory
BGP using 1272 total bytes of memory
BGP activity 10/6 prefixes, 15/10 paths, scan interval 60 secs

Neighbor        V       AS MsgRcvd MsgSent   TblVer  InQ OutQ Up/Down  State/PfxRcd
10.0.0.2        4       65001     6       2       1       0       0 00:01:10        2
172.16.0.2      4       65000     5       3       1       0       0 00:01:02        0
172.17.0.2      4       65000     0       0       1       0       0 00:01:10 Idle
Border-65000#
```

In this figure, the output shows that 172.17.0.2 neighbour state is idle. In order to troubleshoot the fault, let us check the running configuration of both routers running the network 172.17.0.0 in Autonomous System 65000.

Border-65000#show run | section router bgp

```
Border-65000#show run | section router bgp
router bgp 65000
 bgp log-neighbor-changes
 network 10.0.0.0 mask 255.255.255.252
 network 172.16.0.0
 network 172.17.0.0
 neighbor IPS peer-group
 neighbor IPS remote-as 65000
 neighbor IPS transport connection-mode passive
 neighbor 10.0.0.2 remote-as 65001
 neighbor 172.16.0.2 peer-group IPS
 neighbor 172.17.0.2 peer-group IPS
Border-65000#
Border-65000#
Border-65000#
Border-65000#
```

The Border Router shows that the IPS peer group is set be in passive transport connection mode. Which means that IPS peer group members can not initiate the session. Now, if the other end is configured with Active state then it will be fine. In case if the other end is configured with Passive, no one will initiate the session.

iBGP-1#show run | section router bgp

```
iBGP-1#show run | section router bbgp
iBGP-1#show run | section router bgp
router bgp 65000
 bgp log-neighbor-changes
 neighbor 172.17.0.1 remote-as 65000
 neighbor 172.17.0.1 transport connection-mode passive
iBGP-1#
iBGP-1#
iBGP-1#
iBGP-1#
iBGP-1#
```

Neighbour 172.17.0.1 is also set with Passive mode of transport connection. Always make sure that one end of a link must be set in Active mode, another end may be in Active or Passive mode.

Address Family

Address-family is configured to exchange IP addresses between nodes (which can be used in the backbone of the ISP for infrastructure connectivity. Address-family ipv4" is configured to exchange IPv4 addresses and address-family ipv6" is configured to exchange IPv6 addresses.

IPv4 addresses is the usual IP address: NN.NN.NN.NN

VPNv4 is the IP address, but with the route-distinguisher appended: AS:RD:NN.NN.NN.NN

Address-family vpnv4 is used to exchange routing information in the specific VPN (i.e. the subnets reachable inside the particular VPN, most likely the service offered to your customer).

To put it another way: "address-family ipv4" exchange IPv4 routes in the Global Routing Table between BGP peers, while "address-family vpnv4 vrf <NAME>" exchange IPv4 routes in the specified VRF instance between peers.

The following example places the router in address family configuration mode for the IP Version 4 address family:

```
Router(config)# router bgp 100
Router(config-router)# address-family ipv4
Router(config-router-af)#
```

The following example places the router in address family configuration mode and specifies cisco as the name of the VRF instance to associate with subsequent IP Version 4 address family configuration mode commands:

```
Router(config)# router bgp 100
Router(config-router)# address-family ipv4 vrf cisco
Router(config-router-af)#
```

The following example places the router in address family configuration mode for the VPN Version 4 address family:

```
Router(config)# router bgp 100
(config-router)# address-family vpnv4
(config-router-af)#
```

IPv6 Transitioning Technologies

IPv6 is being deployed on more and more networks, but IPv4 is not going away any time soon. During this transition period, security is issue since you will be running both IPv4 and IPv6, along with various tunneling protocols (even if you did not configure them explicitly) that enable communication between IPv4 and IPv6 networks (such as Teredo, ISATAP, and 6to4).

To begin with, the designers of IPv6 realized that the transition from IPv4 to IPv6 would not happen overnight. There was a hope that there would be a large push and the transition would go rather rapidly, but as time moved on, that did not happen. The time for a fast transition has passed and we are in for a long and protracted transition. During this transition, nodes on your network will fit into one of the following buckets:

- IPv4-only node (only runs an IPv4 stack)
- IPv6-only node (only runs an IPv6 stack)
- IPv6/IPv4 node (runs both an IPv4 & IPv6 stack)

Given these types of nodes, the transition mechanisms fall into the following categories:

- Dual Stack (running IPv4 & IPv6 simultaneously)
- Tunneling (IPv6 over IPv4 & IPv4 over IPv6)
- Translation (IPv4 to IPv6 & IPv6 to IPv4)

Dual Stack

Running a dual stack environment is the simple way to support IPv4 and IPv6. In this configuration, devices run 2 different stacks (IPv4 and IPv6) simultaneously. Thus, devices can communicate through either IPv6 or IPv4. Although this appears to give you the best of both worlds, it also presents some interesting security concerns. First, since your devices are running two different stacks, existing ACLs for IPv4 do nothing to stop IPv6 traffic. You may think that this is not a problem since you have not configured IPv6 on your network yet. Many hosts have IPv6 enabled by default. Combine that with the ability of IPv6 to auto configure network addresses, and you have a situation in which an attacker can break your existing protections and potentially compromise devices on your network, even though you have not yet deployed IPv6.

Compatibility Addressing

To enable interoperability between IPv4 and IPv6 hosts, you need to encode the 32 bit, IPv4 address inside of the 128 bit, IPv6 address. This enables both the automatic tunneling of IPv6 traffic across an IPv4 network, as well as translation between IPv4 and IPv6 networks. Because of the size of the IPv6 address, numerous methods have been developed for encoding an IPv4 address inside of an IPv6 address. For instance, to maintain backward compatibility with IPv4, RFC 4291 defines both IPv4-compatible and IPv4-mapped addresses (both types begin with 80 0's) to provide a direct mapping for IPv4 addresses in IPv6.Various tunneling protocols such as ISATAP, 6to4, and Teredo also encode the IPv4 address in the IPv6 address.

ISATAP

Intra-Site Automatic Tunnel Addressing Protocol (ISATAP) is an automatic tunneling protocol that is enables dual-stack devices to transmit IPv6 traffic (encapsulated in IP protocol 41 packets) between each other across an IPv4 backbone. Protocol 41 is a communication protocol, which embeds internet protocol version 6 (IPv6) packets inside Internet protocol version 4 (IPv4) packets. Since ISATAP assumes that multicast is not available on the underlying IPv4 network, it has to have a mechanism for ISATAP hosts to identify potential ISATAP routers to communicate with. You can manually enable this list, but most implementations recommend using DNS to query the IPv4 network for isatap.company.com (where your local domain is company.com) to identify the location of the ISATAP router. Given an IPv4 address of 172.12.10.5, an ISATAP encodes the IPv4 address into the IPv6 address using the following format:

<64-bit network prefix>:0:5EFE:172.12.10.5 (private address)

<64-bit network prefix>:200:5EFE:172.12.10.5 (globally unique address)

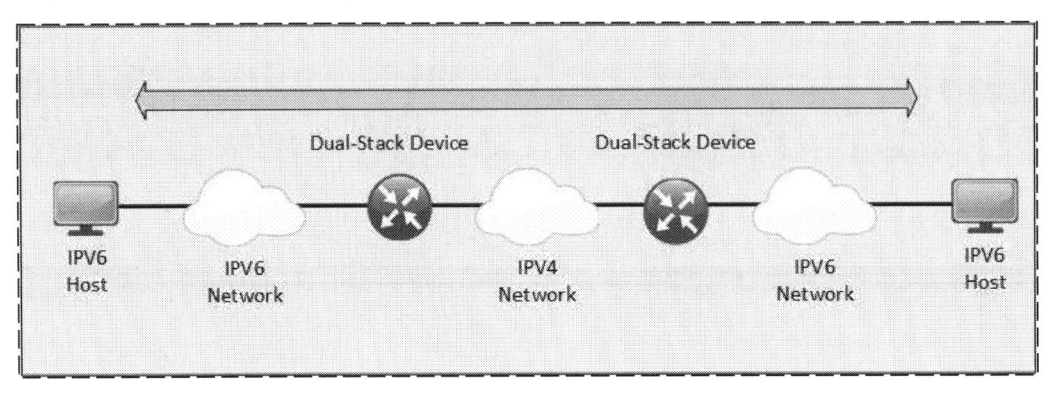

Figure 63 ISATAP

6to4

6to4 also enables dual-stack devices to transmit IPv6 traffic across an IPv4 backbone via 6to4 relay servers without the need to implement tunnels. Similar to ISATAP, the tunneled IPv6 traffic is encapsulated in IP protocol 41 packets on the IPv4 network. 6to4 can be used by an individual host, or by a local IPv6 network, but does require the use of a public IPv4 address. Given an IPv4 address of 172.12.10.5, 6to4 encodes the

IPv4 address into the IPv6 address by appending the IPv4 address to 2002::/16 in the following format:

2002 (16 Bits) + AABB:CCDD (32 Bits) + Subnet ID (16 Bits) + Interface ID (64 bits)

In the 6to4 address, AABB:CCDD represents the IPv6 colon representation of the a.b.c.d IPv4 address. Given our IPv4 address of 172.12.10.5, the 6to4 address would be 2002:ACC0:A005, followed by the Subnet ID and the Interface ID.

A 6to4 relay router connects both an IPv4 and an IPv6 network. When it receives encapsulated IPv6 traffic from the IPv4 network, it decapsulates the IPv6 traffic and sends it across the IPv6 network. For IPv6 traffic going to the IPv4 network, it encapsulates the IPv6 packet into an IP protocol 41 packet and uses the IPv4 address encoded in the IPv6 address as the destination address for that IPv4 packet. The 6to4 host must know how to reach the 6to4 relay. This is normally handled by defining a default gateway. To facilitate configuring this default gateway, the Anycast address of 192.88.99.1 has been allocated specifically for 6to4 relay routers. This enables you to define multiple 6to4 relays on your network without having to alter the configuration on your 6to4 hosts.

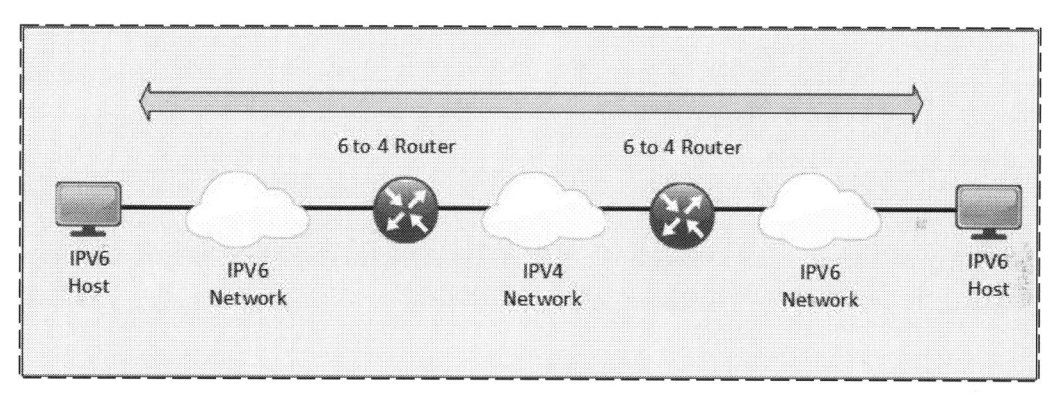

Figure 64 6to4 tunneling

Teredo

Teredo gives full IPv6 network reachability for dual-stack hosts that are connected to the Internet, but which have no direct native connection to an IPv6 network. Teredo encapsulates IPv6 data into IPv4 UDP packets and successfully operates through most NAT boundaries. A Teredo IPv6 address is constructed as follows:

Teredo Prefix (2001::/32) + Teredo Server IPv4 address + Flags + Obscured External Port + Obscured External Address

Unlike other tunneling protocols, Teredo actually obscures the IPv4 address and port to prevent "smart" NAT devices from translating the information. A Teredo environment is comprised of Teredo clients, Teredo Servers, and Teredo Relays. To communicate with another IPv6 device, a Teredo client encapsulates an ICMPv6 Echo Request to the other device in a UDP packet and sends this to the Teredo server. The server decapsulates the ICMPv6 Echo Request and sends it to the actual IPv6 node. The node will reply with an Echo Reply, but this reply is sent to the appropriate Teredo relays, which then contacts the Teredo client. Both the Teredo client and the native IPv6 node utilize the same Teredo relay, which is usually the relay closest to the IPv6 node. This design means that neither the Teredo server nor client needs to know the IPv4 address of any Teredo relays; a suitable one is automatically found by means of the global IPv6 routing table, since all Teredo relays advertise the network 2001:0::/32.

Besides using the Teredo Server to determine the NAT configuration between the Teredo server and the Teredo client, the client also regularly sends IPv4 UDP traffic to the server so that firewall pinholes remain open for the Teredo server and Teredo relay to communicate directly with the client. One of the large security concerns with Teredo tunnels is that it increases your attack surface by assigning globally routable IPv6 addresses to hosts behind NAT devices that are usually not directly accessible from the IPv4 network. This can expose IPv6 services on those hosts to direct attack.

Teredo Node Types

Teredo defines various kinds of node types. The below list specifies them:

- Teredo Client: Teredo client is host that has IPv4 connectivity to Internet behind a NAT device and uses Teredo tunneling to use an IPv6 segment.

- Teredo Server: Teredo Server is used for initial configuration of a Teredo tunnel. A node has IPv4 connectivity and can be used to provide IPv6 connectivity to Teredo clients.

- Teredo Relay: Teredo Relay is an IPv6 router, which is used to forward all of the data on behalf of Teredo client it serves.

- Teredo Service Port: Teredo service port determines the port from which a Teredo client sends Teredo packets. The port is attached to one or more client IPv4 addresses.

- Teredo Refresh Interval: This period states the time interval during which a Teredo IPv6 address is expected to remain valid in the absence of "refresh" traffic. For a client located behind a NAT, the interval depends on configuration parameters of the local NAT, or the combination of NATs in the path to the Teredo server.

- Teredo Node Identifier: It is a 64 bit identifier comprising of a port and IPv4 address at which a client can be reached through the Teredo service, as well as a flag indicating the type of NAT through which the client accesses the IPv4 Internet.

- Teredo Mapped Address and Mapped Port: A global IPv4 address and a UDP port that results from the translation of the IPv4 address and UDP port of a client's Teredo service port by one or more NATs.

How does Teredo Work?

- Teredo tunneling starts with Teredo clients communicating with a Teredo server. In this initial phase, client location is determined, i.e. whether it is behind a symmetric NAT, cone or a restricted cone.

- After the position of the client is determined, the Teredo IPv6 address embeds the address and port through which the client can receive IPv4/UDP packets encapsulating IPv6 packets.

- After this, Teredo clients can exchange the IPv6 packets with other compatible IPv6 nodes through Teredo relays. Teredo relays advertise reachability of the Teredo prefix to a certain subset of the IPv6 Internet.

- Then Teredo clients have to discover Teredo clients that are closed to the native IPv6 node. Here a spoofing attack is possible where a malicious node can act as a legitimate IPv6 compatible node. In order to prevent spoofing, the Teredo clients perform a relay discovery procedure by sending an ICMP echo request to the native host.

- Message is encapsulated in UDP and sent by the client to its Teredo serve, and then the server decapsulates the IPv6 message and forwards it to the intended IPv6 destination. The payload of the echo request contains a large random number. The echo reply is sent by the peer to the IPv6 address of the client, and is forwarded through standard IPv6 routing mechanisms.

- Thus, the packet will reach the relay that is closest to the TIPv6 node. For future requests, the Teredo client will discover the IPv4 address and UDP port used by the relay to send the echo reply, and will send further IPv6 packets to the peer by encapsulating them in a UDP packet sent to this IPv4 address and port. In order to prevent spoofing, the Teredo client verifies that the payload of the echo reply contains the proper random number. The Teredo server never carries actual data traffic

Securing Tunnels

Many tunneling protocols used to transition between IPv4 and IPv6 do not provide any security mechanisms. Thus, you need to secure these tunnels using ACLs and other network controls to prevent them from affecting the security of your overall network (such as preventing IP protocol 41 traffic from entering your network at the edge). This can be a challenging task for the automatic tunneling protocols (such as ISATAP and 6to4) because they can be built without any user interaction. Two main concerns with tunnels are the following:

IPv4 source address of the encapsulating "outer" packet can be spoofed IPv6 address of the encapsulated "inner" packet can be spoofed. Attackers injecting traffic into tunnels is as simple as sending the correctly formatted packets to the specific relay device. Therefore, defining the correct ACLs to limit which traffic can enter and leave tunnels, as well as preventing packets with "spoofed" source addresses from entering your network are crucial to manage the security of your network during this transition period.

Besides filtering traffic entering and leaving known tunnel endpoints, it is also vital to filter potential tunnel traffic at various locations within your network to make sure that attackers do not take advantage of these tunnels to transmit information out of your network without detection. These tunnels use UDP and IP Protocol 41 to encapsulate IPv6 traffic on the network. Therefore, you need to make sure that these 2 transports are adequately filtered with your regular network ACLs. Furthermore, if you are using these transition mechanisms to migrate your IPv4 network to an IPv6 network, you have to make sure that hosts are using an official relay device. An attacker impersonating a relay device can gain control of all of the traffic being relayed through it. With ISATAP, this should not be that difficult since the location of the relay is being learned from DNS. 6to4, however, utilizes an Anycast address so it is easier to impersonate a 6to4 relay unless controls have been implemented that restrict which hosts can generate the normal Router Advertisement messages.

PortProxy Interface

Besides tunneling, some Microsoft systems provide a proxy functionality that can be used to translate traffic between IPv4 and IPv6 network segments. Windows Server 2008 and Windows Vista provide a PortProxy interface that enables the following functionality:

    Proxy IPv4 TCP traffic to another IPv4 address

    Proxy IPv4 TCP traffic to an IPv6 address

    Proxy IPv6 TCP traffic to another IPv6 address

    Proxy IPv6 TCP traffic to an IPv4 address

These translation capabilities are managed by defining corresponding DNS entries that direct the initiating system to send traffic to the specific device that is configured with PortProxy. For instance, to proxy IPv4 TCP traffic to an IPv6 address, the DNS resolver is configured to return an IPv4 address for the IPv6-only host. Therefore, when the IPv4 host initiates the TCP conversation, it sends the packets to the IPv4 address provided by DNS. This causes the traffic to be sent to the host with the PortProxy interface, which converts the traffic to IPv6 and sends it to the specific IPv6-only host.

The main security concern with PortProxy is that an attacker may utilize it to bypass existing security controls that are in place on your network. For instance, you may have specific controls in place to limit who can connect between different segments of your network. The PortProxy interface may be used to bypass these restrictions. Note that this is not new to IPv6 since this applies to traffic between two IPv4 addresses as well and is more the result of an attacker taking advantage of a misconfiguration.

First Hop Router Redundancy Protocol

Cisco supports three protocols to provide transparent Layer-3 redundancy:

1. Hot Standby Router Protocol (HSRP)
2. Virtual Router Redundancy Protocol (VRRP)
3. Gateway Load Balancing Protocol (GLBP)

Hot Standby Router Protocol (HSRP)

Cisco developed the proprietary Hot Standby Router Protocol (HSRP) to allow multiple routers or multilayer switches to masquerade as a single gateway. This is achieved by assigning a virtual IP and MAC address to all routers participating in an HSRP group.

Routers within the same HSRP group must be assigned the same group number, which can range from 0 to 255. However, most of the Cisco platforms only support 16 configured HSRP groups.

HSRP routers are elected to specific roles:

- Active Router – router currently serving as the gateway
- Standby Router – backup router to the Active Router
- Listening Router – all other routers participating in HSRP

Only one active and one standby router are allowed per HSRP group. Thus, HSRP provides Layer-3 redundancy, but no inherent load balancing. Hello packets are used to elect HSRP roles and to ensure all routers are functional. If the current active router fails, the standby router will immediately take over as active, and a new standby is elected. By default, hello packets are sent every 3 seconds.

The role of an HSRP router is dictated by its priority. The priority can range from 0 – 255, with a default of 100. A higher priority is preferred.

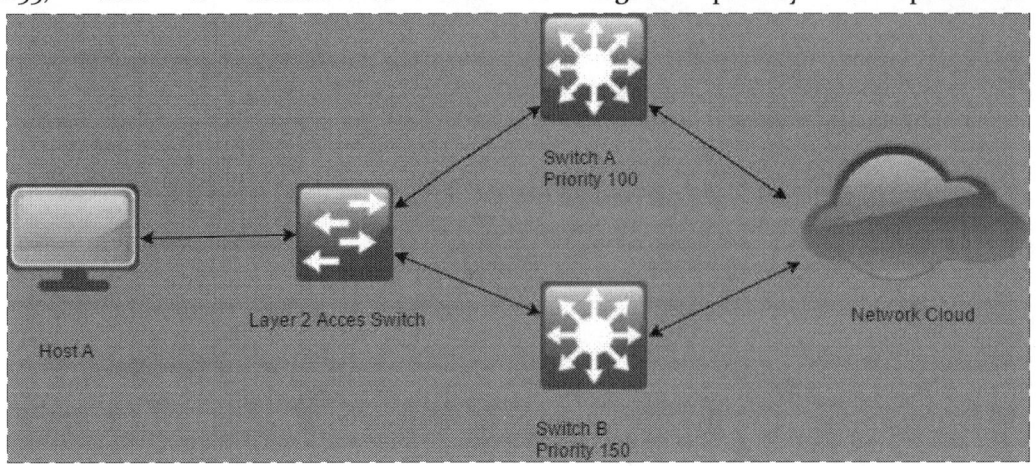

Figure 65 HSRP Diagram

Thus, the router with the highest priority is elected the active router – Switch B in the above example. The router with the second highest priority becomes the standby router – Switch A in the example. If all priorities are equal, whichever router has the highest IP Address on its HSRP interface is elected the active router.

HSRP States

A router interface participating in HSRP must progress through several states before settling into a role:

- Disabled
- Initial
- Learn
- Listen
- Speak
- Standby
- Active

A disabled state indicates that the interface is either not configured for HSRP, or is administratively shutdown. An interface begins in an initial state when first configured with HSRP, or taken out of an administratively shutdown state. An interface enters a learn state if it does not know the HSRP virtual IP address. Normally the virtual IP is configured manually on the interface – otherwise, it will be learned from the current Active router via hello packets. An interface in a listen state knows the virtual IP address, but was not elected as either the Active or Standby Router. Interfaces in a speak state are currently participating in the election of an active or standby router. Elections are performed using hello packets, which are sent out every

3 seconds by default. A standby state indicates that the interface is acting as a backup to the active router. The standby router continuously exchanges hello packets with the active router, and will take over if the active router fails.

An interface in an active state is the live gateway, and will forward traffic sent to the virtual IP address. Hosts will use the virtual IP address as their default gateway. The active router will respond to ARP requests for the virtual IP with the virtual MAC address.

Note that hello packets are only exchanged in three HSRP states:

- Speak
- Standby
- Active

Interfaces in a listen state will only listen for hello packets. If an active or standby router fails, a listen interface will transition to a speak state to participate in a new election.

Enabling HSRP

The standby ip interface configuration command is to activate the HSRP on the interface. If an IP address is given, that address is used as the designated address for the Hot Standby group. If no IP address is given, the address is learned via standby function. You must configure at least one Layer 3 port on the LAN with the designated address. Configuring an IP address always overrides another designated address currently in use.

When the standby ip command is enabled on an interface and proxy ARP is enabled, if the interface's Hot Standby state is active, proxy ARP requests are answered using the Hot Standby group MAC address. Proxy ARP responses are suppressed if the interface is in different state.

Type no standby [group-number] ip [ip-address] interface configuration command to disable HSRP.

This example demonstrates how to activate HSRP for group 1 on an interface. Using HSRP learns the IP address used by the hot standby group.

```
Switch# configure terminal
Switch(config)# interface gigabitethernet1/0/1
Switch(config-if)# no switchport
Switch(config-if)# standby 1 ip
Switch(config-if)# end
Switch# show standby
```

Configuring HSRP Priority

Type no standby [group-number] priority priority [preempt [delay delay]] and no standby [group-number] [priority priority] preempt [delay delay] interface configuration commands to restore default priority, preempt, and delay values.

Type no standby [group-number] track type number [interface-priority] interface configuration command to delete the tracking.

This example activates a port, sets an IP address and a priority of 120 (higher than the default value), and waits for 300 seconds (5 minutes) before attempting to become the active router:

```
Switch# configure terminal
Switch(config)# interface gigabitethernet1/0/1
Switch(config-if)# no switchport
Switch(config-if)# standby ip 172.20.128.3
Switch(config-if)# standby priority 120 preempt delay 300
Switch(config-if)# end
```

Lab 7-5 : Hot Standby Router Protocol (HSRP)

Case Study: In this case, Admin has to configure HSRP on the router for Backup. If HSRP1 router goes down, HSRP2 will become active and traffic keep sending to the gateway.

Topology Diagram:

CCNA-SP Workbook

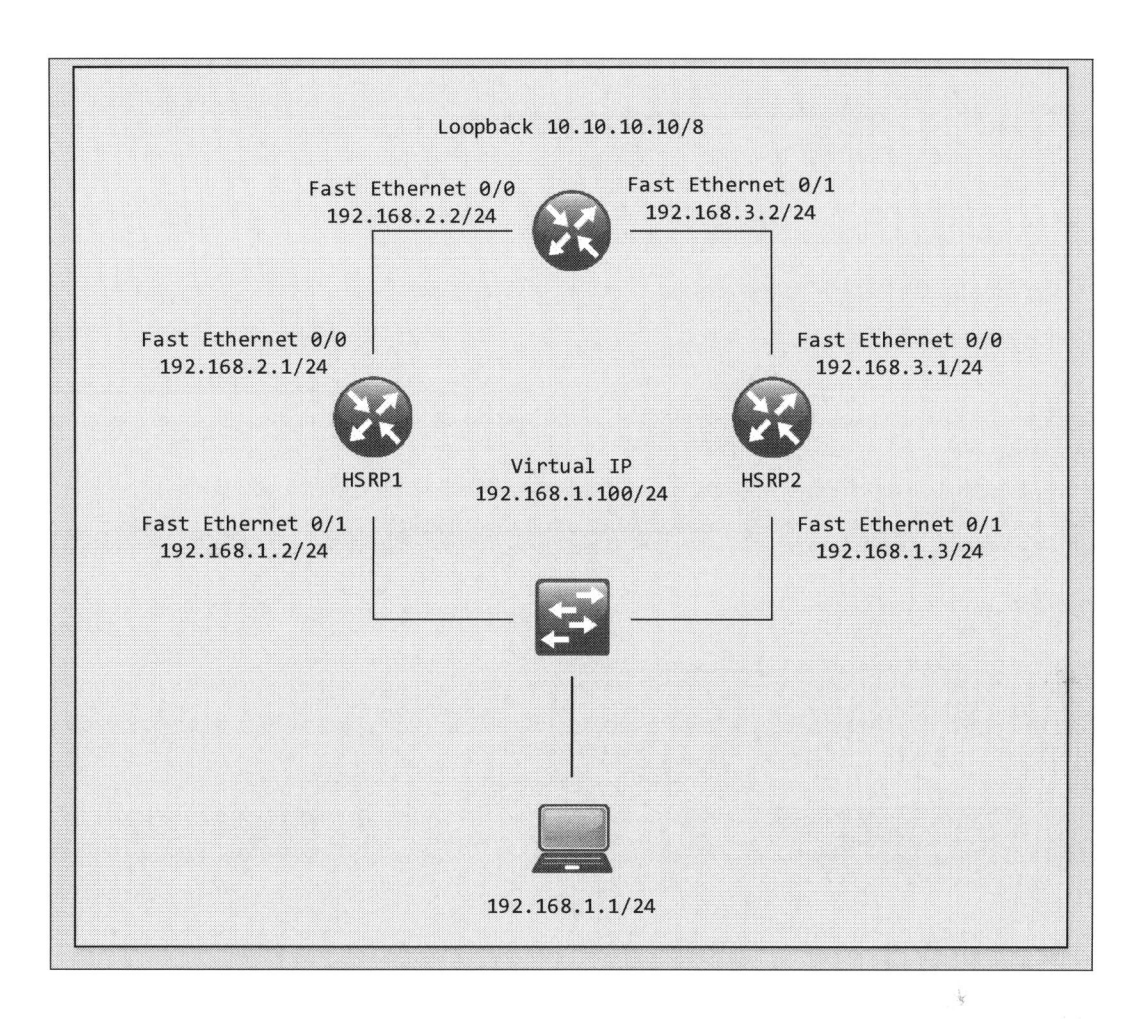

```
                    Loopback 10.10.10.10/8
         Fast Ethernet 0/0      Fast Ethernet 0/1
         192.168.2.2/24         192.168.3.2/24


 Fast Ethernet 0/0                              Fast Ethernet 0/0
 192.168.2.1/24                                 192.168.3.1/24




              HSRP1        Virtual IP      HSRP2
                        192.168.1.100/24
 Fast Ethernet 0/1                              Fast Ethernet 0/1
 192.168.1.2/24                                 192.168.1.3/24




                          192.168.1.1/24
```

Router Configuration:
Router(config)#interface Loopback0
Router(config-if)#ip address 10.10.10.10 255.0.0.0
Router(config)#interface FastEthernet0/0
Router(config-if)#ip address 192.168.2.2 255.255.255.0
Router(config)#interface FastEthernet0/1
Router(config-if)#ip address 192.168.3.2 255.255.255.0
Router(config)#router eigrp 10
Router(config-if)#network 10.0.0.0
Router(config-if)#network 192.168.2.0
Router(config-if)#network 192.168.3.0
Router(config-if)#no auto-summary

HSRP1 Configuration
HSRP1(config)#interface FastEthernet0/0
HSRP1(config-if)#ip address 192.168.2.1 255.255.255.0
HSRP1(config)#interface FastEthernet0/1
HSRP1(config-if)#ip address 192.168.1.2 255.255.255.0
HSRP1(config-if)#standby 1 ip 192.168.1.100
HSRP1(config-if)#standby 1 priority 200
HSRP1(config-if)#standby 1 preempt
HSRP1(config)#router eigrp 10
HSRP1(config-router)#network 192.168.1.0
HSRP1(config-router)#network 192.168.2.0
HSRP1(config-router)#no auto-summary

HSRP2 Configuration:
HSRP2(config)#interface FastEthernet0/0
HSRP2(config-if)#ip address 192.168.3.1 255.255.255.0
HSRP2(config)#interface FastEthernet0/1
HSRP2(config-if)#ip address 192.168.1.3 255.255.255.0
HSRP2(config-if)#standby 1 ip 192.168.1.100
HSRP2(config)#router eigrp 10
HSRP2(config-router)#network 192.168.1.0
HSRP2(config-router)#network 192.168.3.0
HSRP2(config-router)#no auto-summary

Verification:
HSRP1# show standby

```
HSRP1#show standby
FastEthernet0/1 - Group 1
  State is Active
    2 state changes, last state change 00:11:19
  Virtual IP address is 192.168.1.100
  Active virtual MAC address is 0000.0c07.ac01
    Local virtual MAC address is 0000.0c07.ac01 (v1 default)
  Hello time 3 sec, hold time 10 sec
    Next hello sent in 1.076 secs
  Preemption enabled
  Active router is local
  Standby router is 192.168.1.3, priority 100 (expires in 7.420 sec)
  Priority 200 (configured 200)
  Group name is "hsrp-Fa0/1-1" (default)
HSRP1#
```

Interface Fast Ehernet 0/1 is in Active State, Last changing time is also mentioned along with Virtual IP address and MAC address.

HSRP1# show standby

```
HSRP2#show standby
FastEthernet0/1 - Group 1
  State is Standby
    1 state change, last state change 00:12:01
  Virtual IP address is 192.168.1.100
  Active virtual MAC address is 0000.0c07.ac01
    Local virtual MAC address is 0000.0c07.ac01 (v1 default)
  Hello time 3 sec, hold time 10 sec
    Next hello sent in 1.620 secs
  Preemption disabled
  Active router is 192.168.1.2, priority 200 (expires in 9.204 sec)
  Standby router is local
  Priority 100 (default 100)
  Group name is "hsrp-Fa0/1-1" (default)
HSRP2#
```

Interface Fast Ehernet 0/1 is in Satndby. Priorities of Standby and Active Routers are shown as well

Ping 10.10.10.10

```
VPCS> ping 10.10.10.10

84 bytes from 10.10.10.10 icmp_seq=1 ttl=254 time=12.864 ms
84 bytes from 10.10.10.10 icmp_seq=2 ttl=254 time=8.490 ms
84 bytes from 10.10.10.10 icmp_seq=3 ttl=254 time=16.185 ms
84 bytes from 10.10.10.10 icmp_seq=4 ttl=254 time=8.493 ms
84 bytes from 10.10.10.10 icmp_seq=5 ttl=254 time=17.237 ms

VPCS>
```

Ping Successful..

Virtual Router Redundancy Protocol (VRRP)

The Virtual Router Redundancy Protocol (VRRP) is an industry-standard Layer-3 redundancy protocol, originally defined in RFC 2338. VRRP is nearly identical to HSRP, with some notable exceptions:

- The router with the highest priority becomes the master router.
- All other routers become backup routers.
- The virtual MAC address is the reserved 0000.5e00.01xx, with xx representing the hexadecimal group number.
- Hello packets are sent every 1 second, by default, and sent to multicast address 224.0.0.18.
- VRRP will preempt by default.
- VRRP cannot directly track interfaces – it can track an object, which is tied to an interface, though.

Configuration of VRRP is also very similar to HSRP:

```
SwitchB(config)# interface vlan 100
SwitchB(config-if)# ip address 10.1.1.3 255.255.255.0
SwitchB(config-if)# vrrp 1 priority 150
SwitchB(config-if)# vrrp 1 authentication STAYOUT
SwitchB(config-if)# vrrp 1 ip 10.1.1.1
```

As with HSRP, the default VRRP priority is 100, and a higher priority is preferred. Unlike HSRP, preemption is enabled by default.

To manually disable preempt:

```
Switch(config-if)# no vrrp 1 preempt
```

Lab 7-6 : Virtual Router Redundancy Protocol (VRRP)

Case Study: In this case, Admin has to configure VRRP on the router for Backup. If VRRP1 router goes down, VRRP2 will become active and traffic keep sending to the gateway.

Topology Diagram:

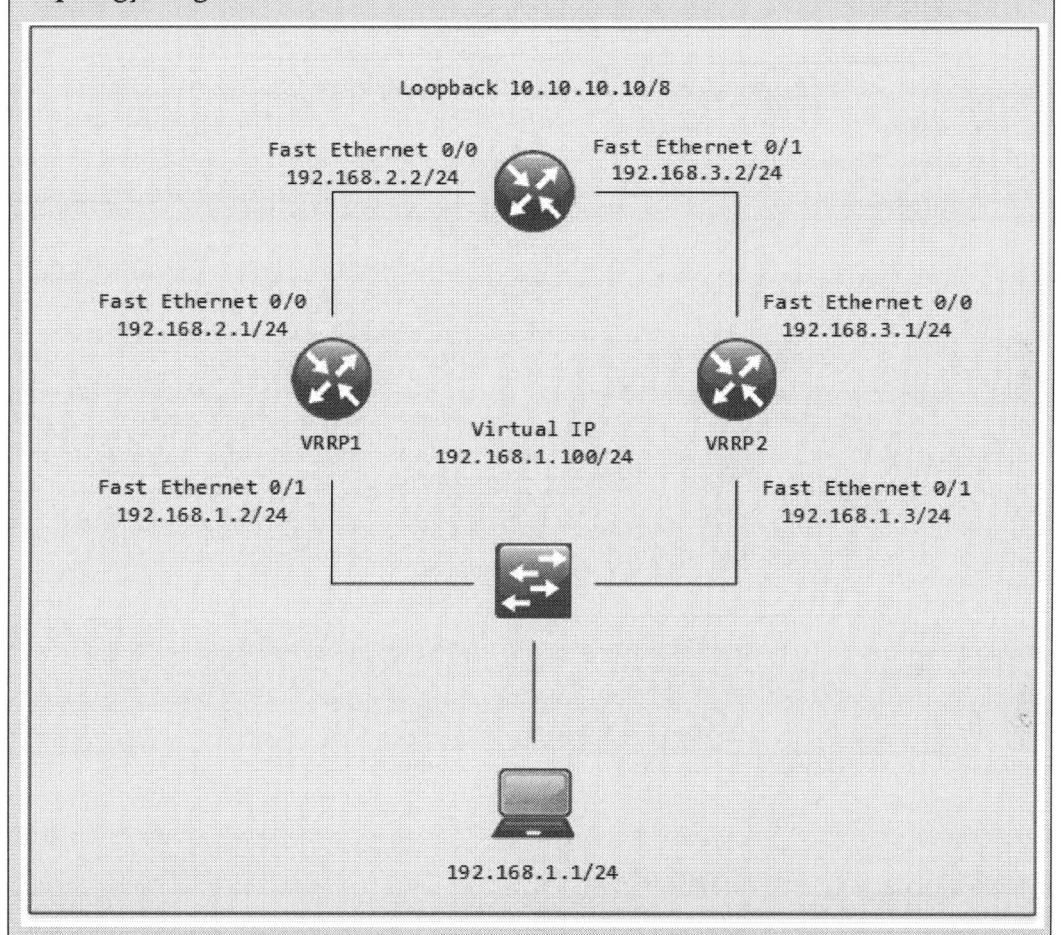

Loopback 10.10.10.10/8

Fast Ethernet 0/0 — 192.168.2.2/24
Fast Ethernet 0/1 — 192.168.3.2/24

Fast Ethernet 0/0 — 192.168.2.1/24
Fast Ethernet 0/0 — 192.168.3.1/24

VRRP1
Virtual IP 192.168.1.100/24
VRRP2

Fast Ethernet 0/1 — 192.168.1.2/24
Fast Ethernet 0/1 — 192.168.1.3/24

192.168.1.1/24

Router Configuration:

Router(config)#interface Loopback0

Router(config-if)#ip address 10.10.10.10 255.0.0.0

Router(config)#interface FastEthernet0/0

Router(config-if)#ip address 192.168.2.2 255.255.255.0

Router(config)#interface FastEthernet0/1

Router(config-if)#ip address 192.168.3.2 255.255.255.0

```
Router(config)#router eigrp 10
Router(config-if)#network 10.0.0.0
Router(config-if)#network 192.168.2.0
Router(config-if)#network 192.168.3.0
Router(config-if)#no auto-summary
```

VRRP 1 Configuration:

```
VRRP1(config)#interface FastEthernet0/0
VRRP1(config-if)#ip address 192.168.2.1 255.255.255.0
VRRP1(config)#interface FastEthernet0/1
VRRP1(config-if)#ip address 192.168.1.2 255.255.255.0
VRRP1(config-if)#vrrp 1 ip 192.168.1.100
VRRP1(config)#router eigrp 10
VRRP1(config-router)#network 192.168.1.0
VRRP1(config-router)#network 192.168.2.0
VRRP1(config-router)#no auto-summary
```

VRRP 2 Configuration:

```
VRRP2(config)#interface FastEthernet0/0
VRRP2(config-if)#ip address 192.168.3.1 255.255.255.0
VRRP2(config)#interface FastEthernet0/1
VRRP2(config-if)#ip address 192.168.1.3 255.255.255.0
VRRP2(config-if)#vrrp 1 ip 192.168.1.100
VRRP2(config-if)#vrrp 1 priority 90
VRRP2(config)#router eigrp 10
VRRP2(config-router)#network 192.168.1.0
VRRP2(config-router)#network 192.168.3.0
VRRP2(config-router)#no auto-summary
```

Verification:

VRRP1# show vrrp all

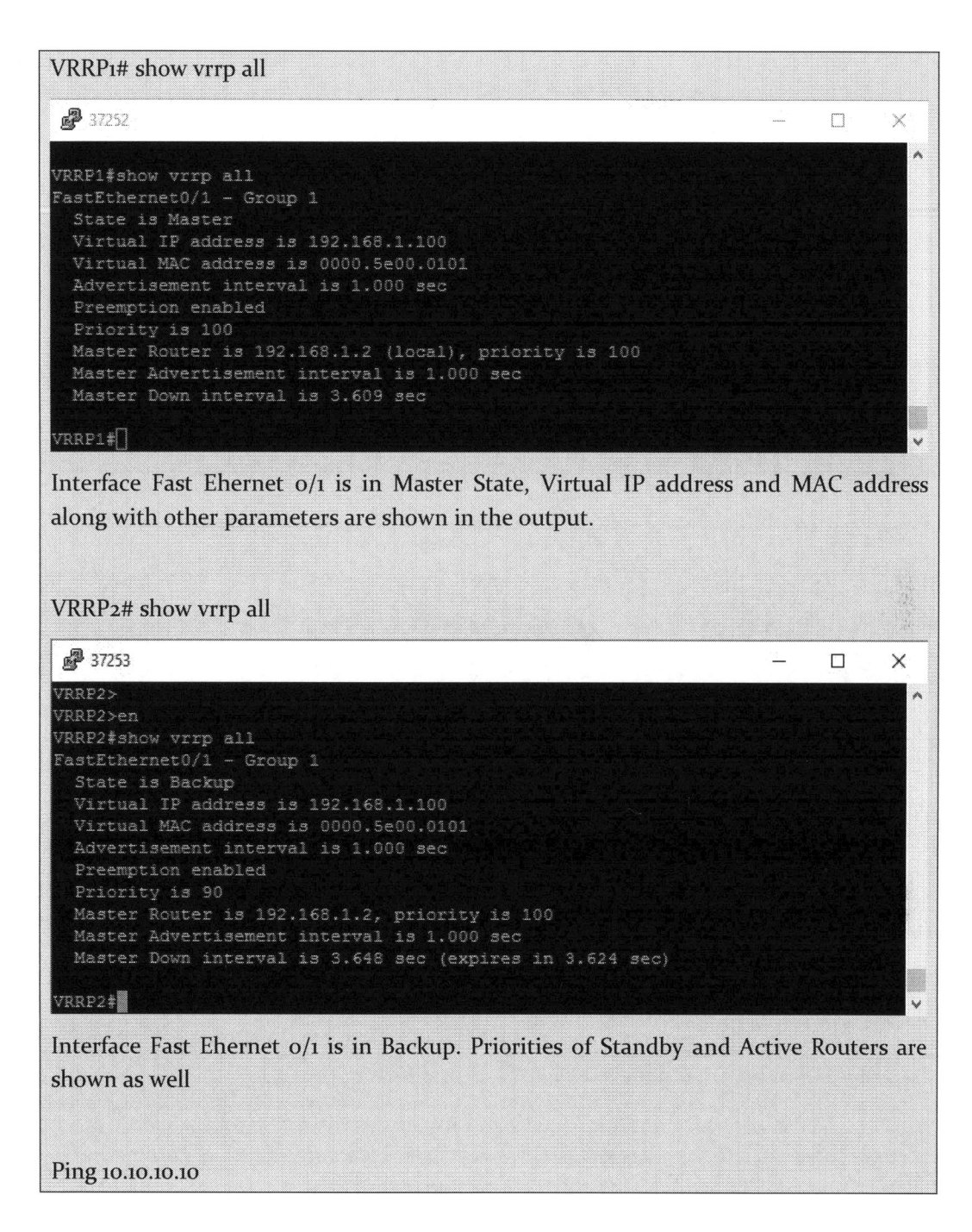

```
VRRP1#show vrrp all
FastEthernet0/1 - Group 1
  State is Master
  Virtual IP address is 192.168.1.100
  Virtual MAC address is 0000.5e00.0101
  Advertisement interval is 1.000 sec
  Preemption enabled
  Priority is 100
  Master Router is 192.168.1.2 (local), priority is 100
  Master Advertisement interval is 1.000 sec
  Master Down interval is 3.609 sec
VRRP1#
```

Interface Fast Ehernet 0/1 is in Master State, Virtual IP address and MAC address along with other parameters are shown in the output.

VRRP2# show vrrp all

```
VRRP2>
VRRP2>en
VRRP2#show vrrp all
FastEthernet0/1 - Group 1
  State is Backup
  Virtual IP address is 192.168.1.100
  Virtual MAC address is 0000.5e00.0101
  Advertisement interval is 1.000 sec
  Preemption enabled
  Priority is 90
  Master Router is 192.168.1.2, priority is 100
  Master Advertisement interval is 1.000 sec
  Master Down interval is 3.648 sec (expires in 3.624 sec)
VRRP2#
```

Interface Fast Ehernet 0/1 is in Backup. Priorities of Standby and Active Routers are shown as well

Ping 10.10.10.10

```
VPCS> ping 10.10.10.10

84 bytes from 10.10.10.10 icmp_seq=1 ttl=254 time=12.864 ms
84 bytes from 10.10.10.10 icmp_seq=2 ttl=254 time=8.490 ms
84 bytes from 10.10.10.10 icmp_seq=3 ttl=254 time=16.185 ms
84 bytes from 10.10.10.10 icmp_seq=4 ttl=254 time=8.493 ms
84 bytes from 10.10.10.10 icmp_seq=5 ttl=254 time=17.237 ms

VPCS>
```

Ping Successful..

VPCS> show ip

```
VPCS> show ip

NAME        : VPCS[1]
IP/MASK     : 192.168.1.1/24
GATEWAY     : 192.168.1.100
DNS         :
MAC         : 00:50:79:66:68:05
LPORT       : 20000
RHOST:PORT  : 127.0.0.1:30000
MTU         : 1500

VPCS>
```

Showing gateway configuration on Virtual PC.

Gateway Load Balancing Protocol (GLBP)

To overcome the shortcomings in HSRP and VRRP like utilization of both links and to achieve load balancing, Cisco developed the proprietary Gateway Load Balancing Protocol (GLBP). Routers are added to a GLBP group, numbered 0 to 1023. Unlike HSRP and VRRP, multiple GLBP routers can be active, achieving both redundancy and load balancing. A priority is assigned to each GLBP interface - 100 by default. The interface with the highest priority becomes the Active Virtual Gateway (AVG). If priorities are equal, the interface with the highest IP will become the AVG.

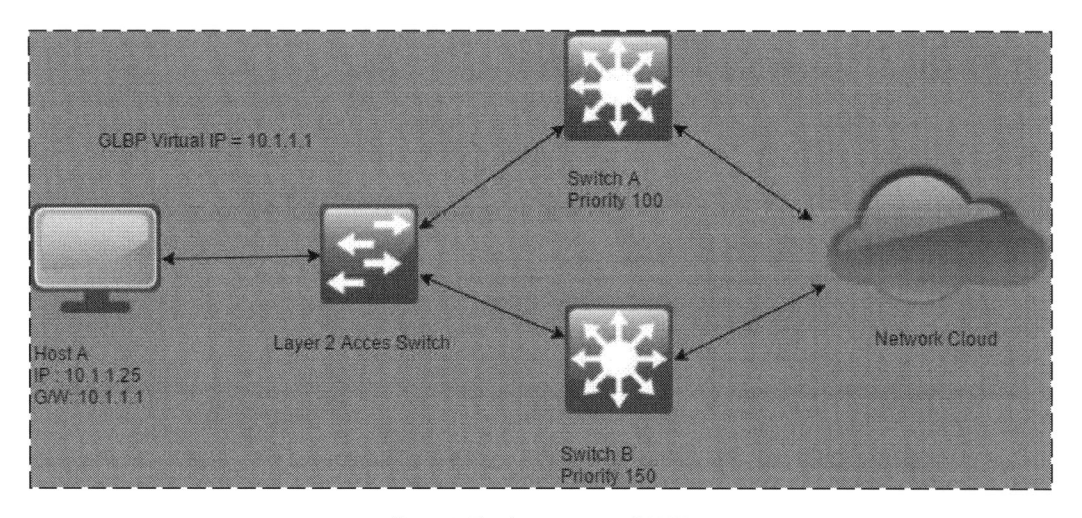

Figure 66 Implementation of GLBP

Routers in the GLBP group are assigned a single virtual IP address. Hosts will use this virtual address as their default gateway. The AVG will respond to ARP requests for the virtual IP with the virtual MAC address of an Active Virtual Forwarder (AVF).

Up to three routers can be elected as AVFs. The AVG assigns a virtual MAC address to each AVF, and to itself, for a maximum 4 virtual MAC addresses. Only the AVG and AVFs can forward traffic for hosts.

Any router not elected as an AVF or AVG will become a Secondary Virtual Forwarder (SVF), and will wait in standby until an AVF fails.

Basic GLBP configuration is nearly identical to HSRP:

SwitchB(config)# interface gi2/22
SwitchB(config-if)# glbp 1 priority 150
SwitchB(config-if)# glbp 1 preempt
SwitchB(config-if)# glbp 1 ip 10.1.1.1

Remember that the interface with the highest priority is elected as the AVG. Preemption is disabled by default with GLBP. What determines whether a router becomes an AVF or SVF? Each router is assigned a weight, and the default weight is 100. A higher weight is preferred.

Weight can be configured two ways:

- Statically
- Dynamically, by tracking an interface

To specify the weight of a router:

SwitchB(config)# interface gi2/22

SwitchB(config-if)# glbp 1 weighting 150

Lab 7-7 : Gateway Load balancing Protocol

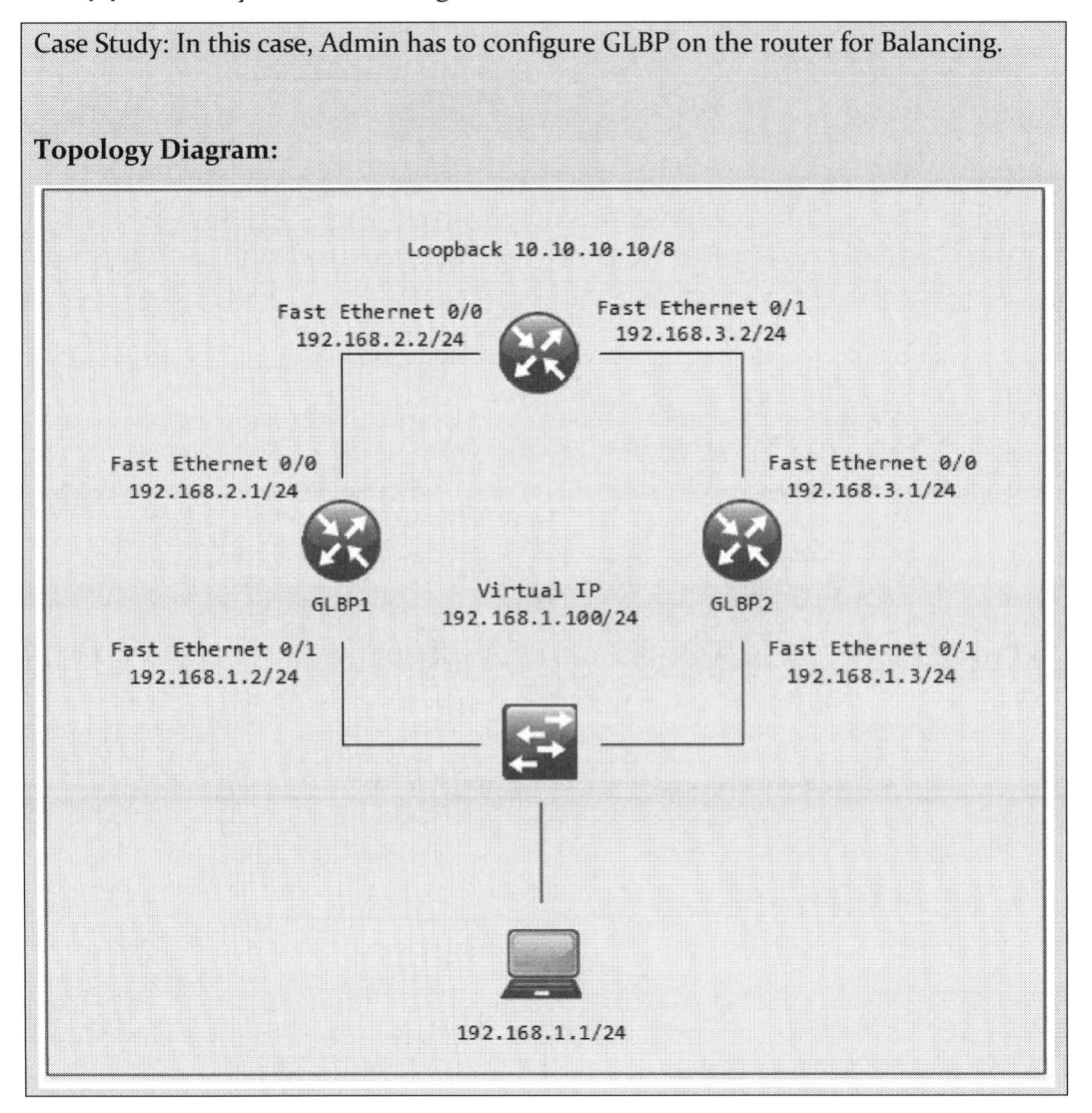

Case Study: In this case, Admin has to configure GLBP on the router for Balancing.

Topology Diagram:

Loopback 10.10.10.10/8

Fast Ethernet 0/0
192.168.2.2/24

Fast Ethernet 0/1
192.168.3.2/24

Fast Ethernet 0/0
192.168.2.1/24

Fast Ethernet 0/0
192.168.3.1/24

GLBP1

Virtual IP
192.168.1.100/24

GLBP2

Fast Ethernet 0/1
192.168.1.2/24

Fast Ethernet 0/1
192.168.1.3/24

192.168.1.1/24

Configuration:

```
Router(config)#interface Loopback0
Router(config-if)#ip address 10.10.10.10 255.0.0.0
Router(config)#interface FastEthernet0/0
Router(config-if)#ip address 192.168.2.2 255.255.255.0
Router(config)#interface FastEthernet0/1
Router(config-if)#ip address 192.168.3.2 255.255.255.0
Router(config)#router eigrp 10
Router(config-if)#network 10.0.0.0
Router(config-if)#network 192.168.2.0
Router(config-if)#network 192.168.3.0
Router(config-if)#no auto-summary


GLBP1(config)#interface FastEthernet0/0
GLBP1(config-if)#ip address 192.168.2.1 255.255.255.0
GLBP1(config)#interface FastEthernet0/1
GLBP1(config-if)#ip address 192.168.1.2 255.255.255.0
GLBP1(config-if)#glbp 1 ip 192.168.1.100
GLBP1(config-if)#glbp 1 priority 200
GLBP1(config-if)#glbp 1 preempt
GLBP1(config-if)#glbp 1 weighting 50
GLBP1(config-if)#glbp 1 load-balancing weighted
GLBP1(config)#router eigrp 10
GLBP1(config-router)#network 192.168.1.0
GLBP1(config-router)#network 192.168.2.0
GLBP1(config-router)#no auto-summary


GLBP2(config)#interface FastEthernet0/0
GLBP2(config-if)#ip address 192.168.3.1 255.255.255.0
GLBP2(config)#interface FastEthernet0/1
GLBP2(config-if)#ip address 192.168.1.3 255.255.255.0
```

GLBP2(config-if)#glbp 1 ip 192.168.1.100

GLBP2(config-if)#glbp 1 weighting 30

GLBP2(config-if)#glbp 1 load-balancing weighted

GLBP2(config)#router eigrp 10

GLBP2(config)#network 192.168.1.0

GLBP2(config)#network 192.168.3.0

GLBP2(config)#no auto-summary

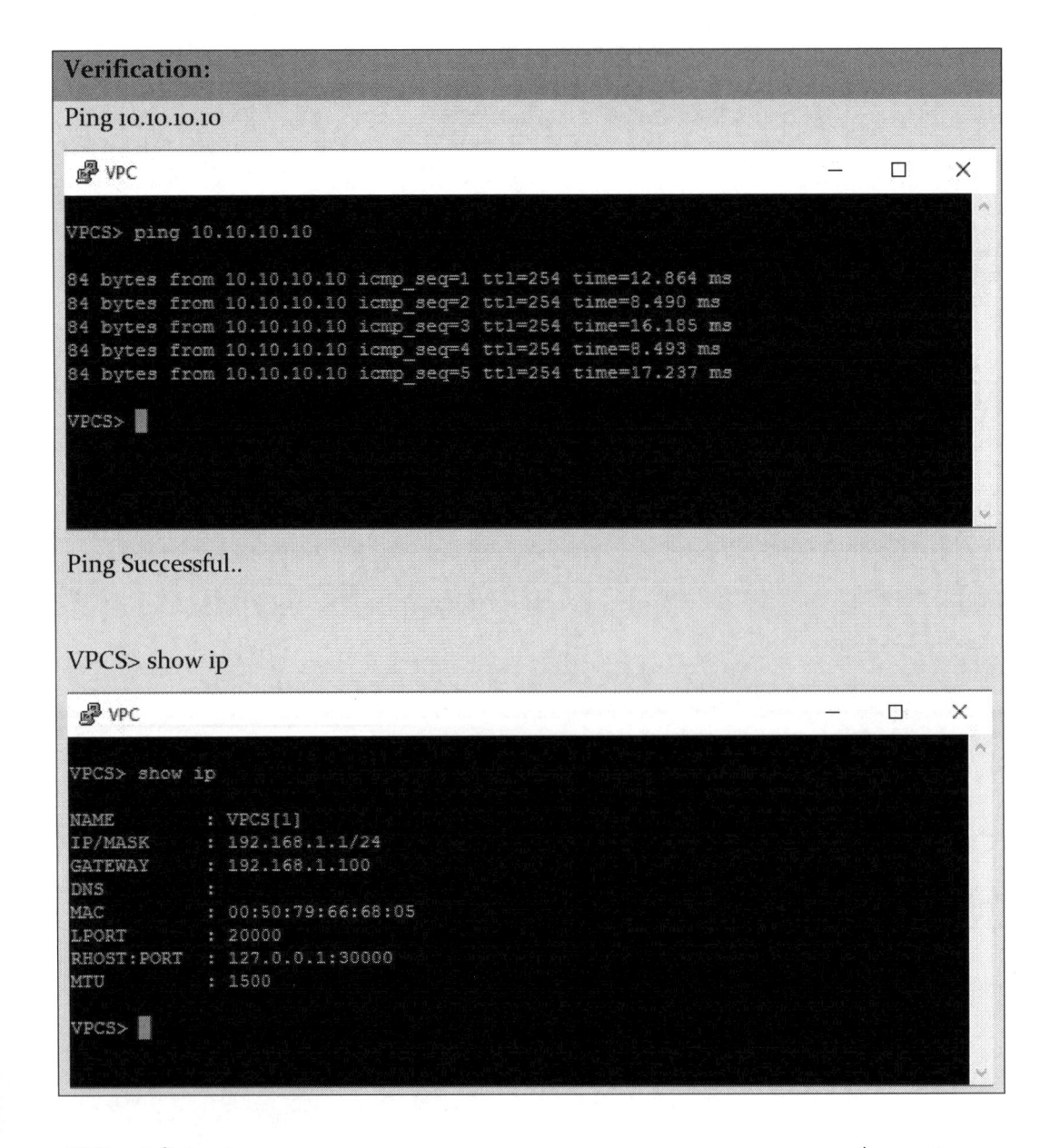

Verification:

Ping 10.10.10.10

```
VPCS> ping 10.10.10.10

84 bytes from 10.10.10.10 icmp_seq=1 ttl=254 time=12.864 ms
84 bytes from 10.10.10.10 icmp_seq=2 ttl=254 time=8.490 ms
84 bytes from 10.10.10.10 icmp_seq=3 ttl=254 time=16.185 ms
84 bytes from 10.10.10.10 icmp_seq=4 ttl=254 time=8.493 ms
84 bytes from 10.10.10.10 icmp_seq=5 ttl=254 time=17.237 ms

VPCS>
```

Ping Successful..

VPCS> show ip

```
VPCS> show ip

NAME        : VPCS[1]
IP/MASK     : 192.168.1.1/24
GATEWAY     : 192.168.1.100
DNS         :
MAC         : 00:50:79:66:68:05
LPORT       : 20000
RHOST:PORT  : 127.0.0.1:30000
MTU         : 1500

VPCS>
```

Showing gateway configuration on Virtual PC.

GLBP1# show glbp

```
GLBP1#
GLBP1#
GLBP1#show glbp
FastEthernet0/1 - Group 1
  State is Active
    2 state changes, last state change 00:10:55
  Virtual IP address is 192.168.1.100
  Hello time 3 sec, hold time 10 sec
    Next hello sent in 2.116 secs
  Redirect time 600 sec, forwarder timeout 14400 sec
  Preemption enabled, min delay 0 sec
  Active is local
  Standby is 192.168.1.3, priority 100 (expires in 6.696 sec)
  Priority 200 (configured)
  Weighting 50 (configured 50), thresholds: lower 1, upper 50
  Load balancing: weighted
  Group members:
    c202.6304.0001 (192.168.1.2) local
    c203.623a.0001 (192.168.1.3)
  There are 2 forwarders (1 active)
  Forwarder 1
    State is Active
      1 state change, last state change 00:10:44
    MAC address is 0007.b400.0101 (default)
    Owner ID is c202.6304.0001
    Redirection enabled
    Preemption enabled, min delay 30 sec
    Active is local, weighting 50
    Client selection count: 1
  Forwarder 2
    State is Listen
    MAC address is 0007.b400.0102 (learnt)
    Owner ID is c203.623a.0001
    Redirection enabled, 599.452 sec remaining (maximum 600 sec)
    Time to live: 14399.452 sec (maximum 14400 sec)
    Preemption enabled, min delay 30 sec
    Active is 192.168.1.3 (primary), weighting 30 (expires in 9.448 sec)
GLBP1#
```

Router is in Active state with weighting 50, priority 200

GLBP1# show glbp

```
GLBP2#show glbp
FastEthernet0/1 - Group 1
  State is Standby
    1 state change, last state change 00:06:31
  Virtual IP address is 192.168.1.100
  Hello time 3 sec, hold time 10 sec
    Next hello sent in 1.116 secs
  Redirect time 600 sec, forwarder timeout 14400 sec
  Preemption disabled
  Active is 192.168.1.2, priority 200 (expires in 9.204 sec)
  Standby is local
  Priority 100 (default)
  Weighting 30 (configured 30), thresholds: lower 1, upper 30
  Load balancing: weighted
  Group members:
    c202.6304.0001 (192.168.1.2)
    c203.623a.0001 (192.168.1.3) local
  There are 2 forwarders (1 active)
  Forwarder 1
    State is Listen
    MAC address is 0007.b400.0101 (learnt)
    Owner ID is c202.6304.0001
    Time to live: 14399.196 sec (maximum 14400 sec)
    Preemption enabled, min delay 30 sec
    Active is 192.168.1.2 (primary), weighting 50 (expires in 7.452 sec)
  Forwarder 2
    State is Active
      1 state change, last state change 00:06:43
    MAC address is 0007.b400.0102 (default)
    Owner ID is c203.623a.0001
    Preemption enabled, min delay 30 sec
    Active is local, weighting 30
GLBP2#
```

Router is in standby state with weighting 30, priority 100

Access Control Lists (ACLs)

Access control lists (ACLs) can be used for two purposes on Cisco devices:

- To filter traffic
- To identify traffic

Access lists are a set of rules, organized in a rule table. Each rule or line in an access list either provides a condition, permit or deny:

- When using an access-list to filter traffic, a permit statement is used to "allow" traffic, while a deny statement is used to "block" traffic.

- Similarly, when using an access list to identify traffic, a permit statement is used to "include" traffic, while a deny statement states that the traffic should "not" be included. It is thus interpreted as a true/false statement.

Filtering traffic is the primary use of access lists. However, there are several instances when it is necessary to identify traffic using ACLs, including:

- Identifying relevant traffic to bring up an ISDN link or VPN tunnel
- Identifying routes to filter or allow in routing updates
- Identifying traffic for QoS purposes

When filtering traffic, access lists are applied on interfaces. As a packet passes through a router, the top line of the rule list is checked first, and the router continues to go down the list until a match is made. Once a match is made, the packet is either permitted or denied.

There is an implicit 'deny all' at the end of all access lists. You do not create it, and you cannot delete it. Thus, access lists that contain only deny statements will prevent all traffic.

Access lists are applied either inbound (packets received on an interface, before routing), or outbound (packets leaving an interface, after routing). Only one access list per interface, per protocol, per direction is allowed. More specific and frequently used rules should be at the top of your access list, to optimize CPU usage. New entries to an access list are added to the bottom. You cannot remove individual lines from a numbered access list. You must delete and recreate the access to make changes. Best practice is to use a text editor to manage your access-lists.

Wild Card Masks

IP access-lists use wildcard masks to determine two things:

- Which part of an address must match exactly
- Which part of an address can match any number

This is as opposed to a subnet mask, which tells us what part of an address is the network (subnet), and what part of an address is the host. Wildcard masks look like inversed subnet masks.

Consider the following address and wildcard mask:

    Address: 172.16.0.0

    Wild Card Mask: 0.0.255.255

The above would match any address that begins "172.16." The last two octets could be anything. How do we know this?

Two Golden Rules of Access Lists:

- If a bit is set to 0 in a wild-card mask, the corresponding bit in the address must be matched exactly.
- If a bit is set to 1 in a wild-card mask, the corresponding bit in the address can match any number. In other words, we "don't care" what number it matches.

To see this more clearly, we'll convert both the address and the wildcard mask into binary:

Address: 10101100.00010000.00000000.00000000

Wild Card Mask: 00000000.00000000.11111111.11111111

Any 0 bits in the wildcard mask, indicates that the corresponding bits in the address must be matched exactly. Thus, looking at the above example, we must exactly match the following in the first two octets:

10101100.00010000 = 172.16

Any 1 bit in the wildcard mask indicates that the corresponding bits can be anything. Thus, the last two octets can be any number, and it will still match this access-list entry.

If we wanted to match a specific address with a wildcard mask (we'll use an example of 172.16.1.1), how would we do it?

Address: 172.16.1.1

Wild Card Mask: 0.0.0.0

Written out in binary, that looks like:

Address: 10101100.00010000.00000001.00000001

Wild Card Mask: 00000000.00000000.00000000.00000000

Remember what a wildcard mask is doing. A 0 indicates it must match exactly, a 1 indicates it can match anything. The above wildcard mask has all bits set to 0, which means we must match all four octets exactly.

There are actually two ways we can match a host:

- Using a wildcard mask with all bits set to 0 – 172.16.1.1 0.0.0.0
- Using the keyword "host" – host 172.16.1.1

How would we match all addresses with a wildcard mask?

Address: 0.0.0.0

Wild Card Mask: 255.255.255.255

Written out in binary, that looks like:

Address: 00000000.00000000.00000000.00000000

Wild Card Mask: 11111111.11111111.11111111.11111111

Notice that the wildcard mask above has all bits set to 1. Thus, each bit can match anything – resulting in the above address and wildcard mask matching all possible addresses. There are actually two ways we can match all addresses:

1. Using a wildcard mask with all bits set to 1 – 0.0.0.0 255.255.255.255
2. Using the keyword "any" – any

Types of Access Lists

Generally, there are 2 types of access list

- Standard Access List
- Extended Access List

Standard IP Access List

access-list [1-99] [permit | deny] [source address] [wildcard mask] [log]

Standard IP access-lists are based upon the source host or network IP address, and should be placed closest to the destination network.

Consider the following example:

Figure 67 Access List

In order to block network 172.18.0.0 from accessing the 172.16.0.0 network, we would create the following access-list on Router A:

Router(config)# access-list 10 deny 172.18.0.0 0.0.255.255

Router(config)# access-list 10 permit any

Notice the wildcard mask of 0.0.255.255 on the first line. This will match (deny) all hosts on the 172.18.x.x network.

The second line uses a keyword of any, which will match (permit) any other address. Remember that you must have at least one permit statement in your access list.

To apply this access list, we would configure the following on Router A:

```
Router(config)# int s0
Router(config-if)# ip access-group 10 in
```

To view all IP access lists configured on the router:

```
Router# show ip access-list
```

To view what interface an access-list is configured on:

```
Router# show ip interface
Router# show running-config
```

Extended IP Access List

> access-list [100-199] [permit | deny] [protocol] [source address] [wildcardmask] [destination address] [wildcard mask] [operator [port]] [log]

Extended IP access-lists block based upon the source IP address, destination IP address, and TCP or UDP port number. Extended access-lists should be placed closest to the source network.

Consider the following example:

Figure 68 Extended Access List Example

Assume there is a webserver on the 172.16.x.x network with an IP address of 172.16.10.10. In order to block network 172.18.0.0 from accessing anything on the 172.16.0.0 network, EXCEPT for the HTTP port on the web server, we would create the following access-list on Router B:

```
Router(config)# access-list 101 permit tcp 172.18.0.0 0.0.255.255 host 172.16.10.10 eq 80
Router(config)# access-list 101 deny ip 172.18.0.0 0.0.255.255 172.16.0.0 0.0.255.255
Router(config)# access-list 101 permit ip any any
```

The first line allows the 172.18.x.x network access only to port 80 on the web server. The second line blocks 172.18.x.x from accessing anything else on the 172.16.x.x network. The third line allows 172.18.x.x access to anything else.

We could have identified the web server in one of two ways:

```
Router(config)# access-list 101 permit tcp 172.18.0.0 0.0.255.255 host 172.16.10.10 eq80
```

```
Router(config)# access-list 101 permit tcp 172.18.0.0 0.0.255.255 172.16.10.10 0.0.0.0 eq80
```

To apply this access list, we would configure the following on Router B:

```
Router(config)# int e0
```

```
Router(config-if)# ip access-group 101 in
```

In the preceding example, we identified TCP port 80 on a specific host use the following syntax:

```
Router(config)# access-list 101 permit tcp 172.18.0.0 0.0.255.255 host 172.16.10.10 eq 80
```

We accomplished this using an operator of eq, which is short for equals. Thus, we are identifying host 172.16.10.10 with a port that equals 80. We can use several other operators for port numbers:

    eq : Matches a specific port

    gt : Matches all ports greater than the port specified

    lt : Matches all ports less than the port specified

    neq : Matches all ports except for the port specified range Match a specific inclusive range of ports

The following will match all ports greater than 100:

```
Router(config)# access-list 101 permit tcp any host 172.16.10.10 gt 100
```

The following will match all ports less than 1024:

```
Router(config)# access-list 101 permit tcp any host 172.16.10.10 lt 1024
```

The following will match all ports that do not equal 443:

```
Router(config)# access-list 101 permit tcp any host 172.16.10.10 neq 443
```

The following will match all ports between 80 and 88:

```
Router(config)# access-list 101 permit tcp any host 172.16.10.10 range 80 88
```

Multiprotocol Label Switching

Multiprotocol Label Switching (MPLS) is a Layer-2 switching technology. MPLS-enabled routers apply numerical labels to packets, and can make forwarding decisions based on these labels. The MPLS architecture is detailed in RFC 3031.

MPLS reduces CPU-usage on routers, by allowing routers to make forwarding decisions solely on the attached label, as opposed to parsing the full routing table.

Labels can based on a variety of parameters:

- Destination IP network
- Source IP address
- QoS parameters
- VPN destination
- Outgoing interface
- Layer-2 circuit

MPLS is not restricted to IP, or any specific Layer-2 technology, and thus is essentially protocol-independent. Labels are applied to and removed from packets on edge Label Switch Routers (edge LSRs). Only edge routers perform a route-table lookup on packets. All core routers (identified simply as LSRs) in the MPLS network forward solely based on the label. As a packet traverses the core MPLS network, core routers will swap the label on hop-by-hop basis. MPLS is completely dependent on Cisco Express Forwarding (CEF) to determine the next hop.

Cisco Express Forwarding (CEF)
Multilayer switches contain both a switching and routing engine. A packet must first be "routed," allowing the switching engine to cache the IP traffic flow. After this cache is created, subsequent packets destined for that flow can be "switched" as opposed to "routed," reducing latency. This concept is often referred to as route once, switch many. Cisco refers to this type of Multilayer switching as NetFlow switching or route cache switching.

As is their habit, Cisco replaced NetFlow multilayer switching with a more advanced method called Cisco Express Forwarding (CEF). CEF is enabled by default on all Catalyst multi-layer switches (at least, those that support CEF). CEF cannot even be disabled on the Catalyst 3550, 4500 and 6500.

CEF contains two basic components:

- Layer 3 Engine – Builds the routing table and then "routes" data
- Layer 3 Forwarding Engine – "Switches" data based on the FIB.

The Layer 3 Engine builds its routing table using either static routes, or routes dynamically learned through a routing protocol (such as RIP or OSPF).

The routing table is then reorganized into a more efficient table called the Forward Information Base (FIB). The most specific routes are placed at the top of the FIB. The Layer 3 Forwarding Engine utilizes the FIB to then "switch" data in hardware, as opposed to "routing" it through the Layer 3 Engine's routing table.

The FIB contains the following information:

- Destination networks
- Destination masks
- Next-hop addresses
- The MAC addresses of each next hop (called the Adjacency Table)

Following command is use to view the CEF FIB table:

```
Switch# show ip cef
```

Label Distribution Protocol

MPLS LDP provides the means for LSRs to request, distribute, and release label prefix binding information to peer routers in a network. LDP enables LSRs to discover potential peers and to establish LDP sessions with those peers for the purpose of exchanging label binding information.

MPLS LDP enables one LSR to inform another LSR of the label bindings it has made. Once a pair of routers communicates the LDP parameters, they establish a label-switched path (LSP). MPLS LDP enables LSRs to distribute labels along normally routed paths to support MPLS forwarding. This method of label distribution is also called hop-by-hop forwarding. With IP forwarding, when a packet arrives at a router the router looks at the destination address in the IP header, performs a route lookup, and forwards the packet to the next hop. With MPLS forwarding, when a packet arrives at a router the router looks at the incoming label, looks up the label in a table, and then forwards the packet to the next hop. MPLS LDP is useful for applications that require hop-by-hop forwarding, such as MPLS VPNs.

The MPLS Label

Two forms of MPLS exist:

- Frame Mode MPLS – utilizes a 32-bit label that is injected between the Layer-2 and Layer-3 headers.

- Cell Mode MPLS – used with ATM, and utilizes the VPI/VCI fields ATM header as the label.

This guide will concentrate on Frame Mode MPLS. The 32-bit label has the following format:

Label	Experimental	Bottom of Stack	TTL

| 20 | 3 | 1 | 8 |

- Label (20 bits) – Label Value
- Experimental (3 bits) – This field is officially undefined, but is used by Cisco as an IP precedence value.
- Bottom-of-Stack (1 bit) – This field indicates the last label, as multiple labels are supported in the same packet. A value of 1 identifies the last label in the stack.
- TTL (8 bits) – This field indicates the number of router this label can 'live' through.

An Ethernet header is modified to indicate the presence of an MPLS label.

- 0x8847 – indicates a labeled unicast IP packet
- 0x8848 – indicates a labeled multicast IP packet

The MPLS Components

MPLS router designations include:

- LSR (Label Switch Router) – responsible for forwarding packets through the provider core based on the packet's label. Cisco refers to this as a P (provider) router.
- Edge LSR (Label Edge Router) – responsible for adding or removing labels from packets. Cisco refers to this as a PE (provider edge) router.
- Non-Label Routers – Cisco refers to this as C (customer) routers

LSRs perform the following functions:

- Control Plane - exchanges routing and label information
- Data Plane - forwards actual packets based on label information

The Control Plane, in charge of information exchange, builds and maintains the following tables:

- Routing Table – routing information is exchanged between LSRs using a routing protocol, such as IGRP, EIGRP, IS-IS, OSPF, or BGP.
- Label Information Base (LIB) – label information is exchanged between LSRs using a label protocol, such as LDP (Label Distribution Protocol) or TDP (Tag Distribution Protocol).

LDP is now default on Cisco devices, and uses TCP port 646. TDP is a Cisco-proprietary label protocol, and uses TCP port 711. Label convergence will occur after routing convergence is completed. Label protocols require the underlying routing infrastructure in order to function.

The Data Plane, in charge of information forwarding, maintains the following tables:

- The CEF Forwarding Information Base (FIB) –for forwarding unlabeled packets. Contains destination IP networks, and the Layer-2 address of the next-hop router.

- Label Forwarding Information Base (LFIB) – for forwarding labeled packets.

The MPLS Process

There are four scenarios detailing how LSRs forward packets:

- An unlabeled IP packet is received, and is routed unlabeled to the next hop.

- An unlabeled IP packet is received; a label is inserted in the header, and is switched to the next hop.

- A labeled IP packet is received; the label is swapped, and is switched to the next hop.

- A labeled IP packet is received, the label is stripped off, and is routed to the next hop or destination.

Frame-mode MPLS performs as follows:

- An edge LSR receives a packet.

- The edge LSR performs a routing table lookup to determine the next hop (or exit interface).

- If destined for the MPLS network, the edge router inserts the label between the Layer-2 and Layer-3 headers.

- The edge LSR forwards the labeled packet to the core LSR.

- Core LSRs will route solely based on the label, and will not perform a routing table lookup.

Mind Map

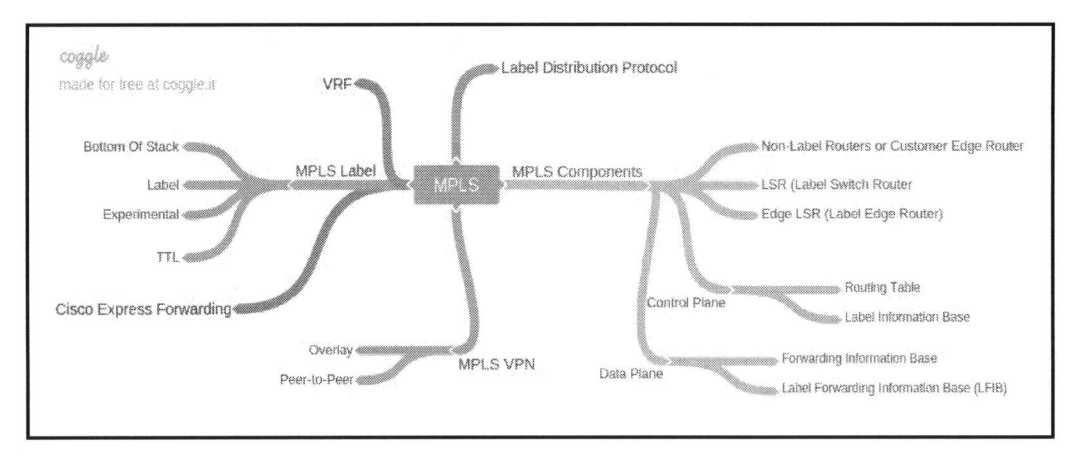

Figure 69 Mind Map of MPLS operation

Configuring Basic MPLS

The first step in configuring MPLS is enabling CEF switching, which can be accomplished globally (for all interfaces), or on a per interface basis:

Router(config)# ip cef
Router(config)# interface serial0/0
Router(config-if)# ip route-cache cef

To view CEF information:

Router(config)# show ip cef

Next, MPLS must be enabled on the interface:

Router(config)# interface serial0/0
Router(config-if)# mpls ip

The desired label protocol can then be specified (either ldp, tdp, or both):

Router(config)# interface serial0/0
Router(config-if)# mpls label protocol ldp
Router(config)# interface serial0/0
Router(config-if)# mpls label protocol tdp
Router(config)# interface serial0/0
Router(config-if)# mpls label protocol both

If a label protocol is not specified, Cisco devices will default to ldp (as of the IOS version 12.4). Because the MPLS label increases the size of the frame by 32 bits (4 bytes), the mtu for mpls packets should be adjusted to accommodate this:

Router(config)# interface serial0/0
Router(config-if)# mpls mtu 1504

MPLS VPNs require two labels, thus the mtu should be adjusted accordingly:

Router(config)# interface serial0/0
Router(config-if)# mpls mtu 1508

MPLS VPNs

Cisco identifies two key categories of VPNs:

- Overlay – connections are set up and maintained by the service provider. However, the provider has no knowledge of, and does not participate in, the customer's routing infrastructure.

- Peer-to-Peer – the provider directly participates in routing the customer's infrastructure. Routes from multiple customers are not kept separate. This may require customers to readdress their networks.

MPLS VPNs provide the best of both words. Advantages of MPLS VPNs include:

- The provider directly participates in routing the customer infrastructure.

- Peer-to-peer peering is not required, leading to a scalable infrastructure.

- Customer networks do not need to be readdressed

- Routes from multiple customers are kept separate.

MPLS VPNs use two labels. MPLS separates customer routes by assigning each a unique Virtual Routing Instance (VRI), stored in a Virtual Routing and Forwarding (VRF) table. If the addressing structure of multiple clients overlaps, each network is assigned a unique 64-bit route distinguisher (RD). The IP network and RD combination is called a VPNv4 address. Route targets are BGP attributes that designate MPLS VPN membership of routes.

MPLS functions in the SP IP NGN

MPLS is an acronym for Multiprotocol Label Switching. A NGN is a Next Generation Network.

MPLS was created to address the weaknesses in traditional IP networks. Please recall that IP was designed to support "best effort" services. In other words, routers contain no inherent perception of the existence of or proper functioning of connections or rings; they see the ports and addresses that are available to their discovery via priority cues and routing tables. Simply put, IP routing lacks intelligence. So-called "Least cost" routing was designed to conduct traffic along the network using the shortest possible number of hops, which means traffic on the network could potentially take shorter, congested paths rather than the potentially more efficient longer, uncongested paths, leading to network "hotspots" and degrading network performance.

The MPLS environment, which has been gaining increased attention, was born out of Cisco's tag switching. MPLS was originally proposed by the IETF (Internet Engineering Task Force) in 1997, with the core specifications being finalized in 2000. MPLS's ability to plot static paths through an IP network gives service providers the traffic-engineering ability they crave, and the capability for provisioning VPNs is greatly strengthened. In fact, MPLS provides a very solid base for VPNs – and with increased capability for traffic engineering, service providers are able to tightly control and maintain QoS as well as optimize network utilization.

Although technically not an IP network, despite the fact that it can run in routers and uses IP routing protocols like OSPF and IS-IS, MPLS is one of the most significant developments in IP. To truly understand why this is, you also need to know that although it can also use repurposed ATM switch hardware, MPLS is, again technically, not an ATM network.

MPLS is another type of network entirely: MPLS is a service-enabling technology. Think of MPLS like a general purpose, tunneling technology. As such, it is capable of carrying both IP and non-IP payloads. It uses what is called "label switching" to transport cells or packets over any data link layer throughout the network.

Much like the inband and out-of-band signaling on the PSTN, MPLS separates the forwarding, or transport, plane from the control plane. By so doing, it enables the capability to run the control plane on devices which cannot actually understand IP or recognize the boundaries of incoming packets. MPLS itself is an encapsulating protocol that has the ability to transport a number of other protocols. These protocols are encapsulated with a label that at each hop is swapped. The label is a number, or UID (Unique Identifier) that identifies a set of data flows along a particular logical link. They are only of local significance and they must change as a packets follow along a predetermined path – they literally switch.

MPLS's potential to untie IP and optical switching under one route-provisioning umbrella is of great benefit, but it was designed to address two problems inherent in IP networks: IP sends all traffic over the same route between two points, and it cannot absolutely guarantee network resources, because as you will recall, IP is a connectionless protocol. These two shortcomings, in times of heavy network traffic, lead to some routes becoming underutilized while others become congested. Lacking control over the routing assignments, the provider cannot steer traffic from congested to less busy routes. So one key differentiator between IP and MPLS is the simple fact the MPLS networks can steer packets between two points along different paths depending upon their switching MPLS labels.

Network Address Translation

The remapping of IP address space to another IP address space is termed as Network Address Translation (NAT). NAT can be implemented on both IPv4 and IPv6 addresses to efficiently utilize the limited resource of IP addresses in private network as used as a mechanism for avoiding IP address exhaustion.

Following are the two popular NAT techniques:

Carrier Grade NAT (CGN)

Carrier Grade NAT is a mechanism of translation of IPv4 address to IPv4 addresses. CGN is used in large network structure, often called as Large Scale NAT. It employs Network Address and Port Translation methods to aggregate multiple private IPv4 addresses into fewer public IPv4 addresses.

NAT64

NAT64 is utilized to provide a seamless Internet experience to users accessing IPv4 Internet services through IPv6-only networks. Mostly established network infrastructure is based on IPv4 address scheme. Transparent implementation of translation devices such as content providers and content enablers are used to provide network services to customers using IPV6 networks. These devices perform translation between IPv6 enabled users to IPV4 enable service network.

NAT64 allows adaptation and acceleration of IPv6 while using IPv4 enabled network simultaneously.

CDP (Cisco Discovery Protocol)

CDP is a device discovery protocol, which operates over Layer 2 (the data link layer) on all Cisco-manufactured devices and permits network management applications for discovering Cisco devices that are neighbours of already known devices. With CDP, network management applications can learn the device type and the Simple Network Management Protocol (SNMP) agent address of neighbouring devices running lower-layer, transparent protocols. This feature enables applications for sending SNMP queries to neighbouring devices.

CDP runs on all media that support Subnetwork Access Protocol (SNAP). Because CDP runs over the data-link layer only, two systems that support various network-layer protocols can learn about each other.

Every CDP-configured device sends periodic messages to a multicast address, advertising at least one address at which it can receive SNMP messages. The advertisements also contain time-to-live (TTL), or holdtime information, which is the length of time a receiving device, holds CDP information before discarding it. Every device listens to the messages forwarded by other devices to learn about neighbouring devices.

On the switch, CDP enables network administrator to display a graphical view of the network. The switch uses CDP to find cluster candidates and maintain information about cluster members and other devices up to three cluster-enabled devices away from the command switch by default.

For a switch & connected endpoint devices running Cisco Medianet:
- CDP identifies connected endpoints, which communicate directly with the switch.
- In order to avoid duplicate reports of neighbouring devices, only one wired switch reports the location information.
- The wired switch and the endpoints both forward and receive location information.

CDP is enabled by default.

This example shows how to enable CDP if it has been disabled.

| Switch# configure terminal |
| Switch(config)# cdp run |
| Switch(config)# end |

CDP is enabled by default on all supported interfaces to send and to receive CDP information.

This example shows how to enable CDP on a port when it has been disabled.

| Switch# configure terminal |
| Switch(config)# interface gigabitethernet1/0/2 |
| Switch(config-if)# cdp enable |
| Switch(config-if)# end |

Chapter 8: Cisco Operating Systems and Platforms I

Cisco has had many operating systems over the decades and several of them are listed here.

Basic Operation of Cisco Internetwork OS

IOS (Internetwork Operating System)
The classical IOS is a monolithic kernel that runs all of the necessary modules in the same memory space. This means that if something happens to the routing engine or the LED indicator, it can cause the whole IOS kernel to crash if it runs out of memory. That may have been okay years ago but today's mission critical networks cannot afford to have a rogue process bringing down an entire chassis switch.

To resolve mentioned issue Cisco's software engineers, rebuild the IOS CLI on a more robust platform known as IOS-XE

IOS-XE (Internetwork Operating System-XE)
IOS XE runs as a system daemon on a "modern Linux platform." Cisco also abstracted the system functions out of the main kernel and into separate processes. That means that if one of them goes bankrupt it will not take the core kernel with it. One of the other benefits of running the kernel as a system daemon is that you can now balance the workload of the processes across multiple processor cores. IOS XE utilizes key architectural components of IOS while improving upon the deficiencies of the IOS kernel. IOS XE's CLI and configuration is nearly identical to IOS. Network engineers familiar with IOS configuration will not notice a difference using the IOS XE operating system.

IOS-XR (Internetwork Operating System-XR)
IOS XR is what the Mirror Universe version of IOS would look like. Much like IOS XE, IOS XR does away with the monolithic kernel and shared memory space of IOS Classic. XR uses an OS from QNX to serve as the base for the IOS functions. XR also segments the ancillary process in IOS into separate memory spaces to prevent system crashes from an errant bug. XR is aimed at the larger service provider platforms like the ASR and CRS series of routers. You can see that in the way that XR can allow multiple routing protocol processes to be executed at the same time in different memory spaces. That is a big key to the service provider.

What makes IOS XR so different from IOS Classic? That lies in the configuration method. While the CLI may resemble the IOS that you are used to, Instead of making live config changes on a live system, the running configuration is forked into a separate memory space. Once you have created all the changes that you need to make, you have to perform a sanity check on the config before it can be moved into live production.

Following table demonstrate the comparision of different Cisco IOS:

	Kernel and OS Scheduling	Memory Management	Software Packaging
IOS	Monolithic kernel with priority run to completion scheduler	No virtual memory support and potential for corruption through memory aliasing	Compiled into single, unique files for each platform and features set
IOS XE	Distributed Linux kernel that allows process execution on multiple CPUs	64 bit virtual memory support	Newer version provide a universal image encompassing all features and allow the activating of the features by software license
IOS XR	Microkernel architecture that allows process execution on multiple CPUs with preemptive scheduling	Virtual memory support with dedicated MMU hardware controller to prevent memory corruption	Software is composed of DLLs that are packaged into a mini, PIEs, and SMUs. SMUs allows for patching of the IOS XR OS

Table 16 Comparision of Cisco IOS

CLI and Configuration

IOS

Router>
Router>enable
Router#
Router#configure terminal

```
Enter configuration commands, one per line. End with CNTL/Z.
```

```
! Global configuration prompt is shown below
Router(config)#
Router(config)#interface Gi0/0
! Interface configuration submode prompt is shown below
Router(config-if)#router eigrp 100
! Router configuration submode prompt is shown below
Router(config-router)#router bgp 100
! Router configuration submode prompt. Notice the prompt is the same even
! though the routing protocol is different
Router(config-router)#exit
Router(config)#
```

IOS devices store configuration files in two locations: startup configuration and running configuration. The running configuration refers to the router's active configuration and is stored in volatile memory. When the router reloads, the running configuration is lost. The startup configuration file is stored in nonvolatile memory, and the system references the startup configuration during boot to program the router's active (running) configuration.

The privileged command copy running-config startup-config saves system configurations across system reload, and the privileged command write erase deletes the startup configuration. A write erase followed by a system reload will restore the system to factory default.

IOS processes configuration changes as a single-stage commit. Upon entering a command, the command is parsed for syntax, and then the change is applied instantly into the running configuration.

IOS XR

EXEC mode is the default mode for users at login. The # after the router name indicates that the user is in EXEC mode, as shown in this example.

```
RP/0/RP0/CPU0:XR1#
```

IOS XR contains an admin mode that provides access to IOS XR's administrative plane. The administrative plane controls software versions, PIES, SMUs, and the power state for line cards. Admin mode is reachable with the command admin and indicated by state of admin, as shown in Example

---

RP/0/RP0/CPU0:XR1#admin

RP/0/RP0/CPU0:XR1(admin)#

The entire relevant configuration for routing will be done within the global configuration of an IOS XR node.

RP/0/RP0/CPU0:XR1#configure terminal

RP/0/RP0/CPU0:XR1(config)#

The command show running-config displays a copy of the running configuration.

RP/0/0/CPU0:ios#show running-config

Building configuration...

!! IOS XR Configuration

interface GigabitEthernet0/0/0/0

shutdown

!

interface GigabitEthernet0/0/0/1

shutdown

!

end

RP/0/0/CPU0:ios#

The command show configuration merge shows the target configuration merged with the running configuration.

RP/0/0/CPU0:ios(config-if)#show configuration merge

Building configuration...

!! IOS XR Configuration

!! Last configuration change at Fri Sep 20 15:42:00 2014 by xr

hostname XR1

```
cdp
interface GigabitEthernet0/0/0/0
cdp
shutdown
!
interface GigabitEthernet0/0/0/1
cdp
shutdown
!
End
```

IOS XR performs a final semantic check against the running configuration when the commit command is applied. Upon detecting configuration errors, the commit fails and the target configuration is not applied.

```
RP/0/0/CPU0: ios(config-if)#commit
RP/0/0/CPU0: Sep 21 00:26:25.360 : config[66391]: %MGBL-CONFIG-6-DB_COMMIT :
Configuration committed by user 'JCHAMBR'. Use 'show configuration commit changes1000000638' to view the changes.
RP/0/0/CPU0:XR1(config-if)#
```

The show configuration commit list is a helpful tool for reviewing configuration changes that have occurred on the router.

```
RP/0/0/CPU0:XR1#show configuration commit list
No  Label/ID    User     Line              Client  Time Stamp
~~  ~~~~~~~~   ~~~~      ~~~~              ~~~~~~  ~~~~~~~~~~
1   1000000038 JCHAMBR  vty3:node0_0_CPU0  CLI     Fri Sep 13 11:06:35 2014
2   1000000037 KJOHNS   vty3:node0_0_CPU0  CLI     Fri Sep 13 11:05:33 2014
3   1000000036 BEDGEW   vty3:node0_0_CPU0  CLI     Fri Sep 13 11:00:41 2014
4   1000000035 RAMIROG  vty3:node0_0_CPU0  CLI     Fri Sep 13 10:59:39 2014
5   1000000034 JCHAMBR  vty3:node0_0_CPU0  CLI     Tue Aug 27 15:08:04 2014
6   1000000033 KJOHNS   vty1:node0_0_CPU0  CLI     Tue Jul 16 15:32:27 2014
```

7	1000000032	RAMIROG	vty3:node0_0_CPU0	CLI	Mon Jul 15 16:22:54 2014
8	1000000031	BEDGEW	vty3:node0_0_CPU0	CLI	Mon Jul 15 16:21:14 2014
9	1000000030	JCHAMBR	vty3:node0_0_CPU0	CLI	Mon Jul 15 16:02:07 2014
10	1000000029	KJOHNS	vty4:node0_0_CPU0	CLI	Mon Jul 8 16:06:58 2014
11	1000000028	RAMIROG	vty4:node0_0_CPU0	CLI	Mon Jul 8 16:04:55 2014
12	1000000027	BEDGEW	vty4:node0_0_CPU0	CLI	Mon Jul 8 15:55:08 2014
13	1000000026	JCHAMBR	vty4:node0_0_CPU0	CLI	Mon Jul 8 15:54:03 2014
14	1000000025	KJOHNS	vty4:node0_0_CPU0	CLI	Mon Jul 8 15:49:53 2014
15	1000000024	FOSS	vty4:node0_0_CPU0	CLI	Mon Jul 8 15:48:49 2014

The command show configuration failed displays the reason for the failed semantic check during the commit.

```
RP/0/0/CPU0:XR1#conf terminal

RP/0/0/CPU0:XR1(config)#router bgp 100

RP/0/0/CPU0:XR1(config-bgp)#commit

RP/0/0/CPU0:XR1(config-bgp)#router bgp 200

RP/0/0/CPU0:XR1(config-bgp)#commit

% Failed to commit one or more configuration items during a pseudo-atomicoperation. All changes made have been reverted. Please issue 'show configuration     failed' from this session to view the errors

RP/0/0/CPU0:XR1(config-bgp)#show configuration failed

!! SEMANTIC ERRORS: This configuration was rejected by

!! the system due to semantic errors. The individual

!! errors with each failed configuration command can be

!! found below.

router bgp 200

!!% The process 'bpm' rejected the operation but returned no error

!

End
```

IOS XR allows one or more than one changes to be rolled back through the usage of the SysDB. Upon rolling back a configuration change, the operator can specify the number of committed changes to rollback with the command rollback configuration last number-of-changes.

```
RP/0/0/CPU0:XR1-COMMITREPLACE#rollback configuration last 3

Loading Rollback Changes.

Loaded Rollback Changes in 1 sec

Committing..

10 items committed in 2 sec (4) items/sec

Updating.

Updated Commit database in 1 sec

Configuration successfully rolled back 3 commits.

RP/0/0/CPU0:XR1#show configuration commit list

Fri Sep 20 16:37:20.748 UTCS

No.  Label/ID     User      Line         Client    Time Stamp
~~~  ~~~~~~~~     ~~~~      ~~~~         ~~~~~~    ~~~~~~~~~~
1    1000000021   JCHAMBR   con0_0_CPU0   Rollback  Fri Sep 20 16:37:10 2014
2    1000000020   JCHAMBR   con0_0_CPU0   CLI       Fri Sep 20 16:08:57 2014
3    1000000019   JCHAMBR   con0_0_CPU0   CLI       Fri Sep 20 16:07:55 2014
4    ROUTERNAME   JCHAMBR   con0_0_CPU0   CLI       Fri Sep 20 16:07:14 2014
```

IOS XR's two-stage commit allows for changes to be created in advance and stored as text files on the local storage. The configuration files can be loaded into the target configuration with the load filesystem:filename command.

```
RP/0/0/CPU0:XR1#conf terminal

RP/0/0/CPU0:XR1(config)#load bootflash:PRECONFIG-FILE.txt

Loading.

105 bytes parsed in 1 sec (104)bytes/sec
```

```
RP/0/0/CPU0:XR1(config)#show configuration
Building configuration...
!! IOS XR Configuration
hostname XR1-PRECONFIG
cdp
```

```
interface GigabitEthernet0/0/0/0
ipv4 address 10.12.1.1 255.255.255.0
!
!
route-policy PASS-ALL
pass
end-policy
!
End
```

IOS and IOS-XR configuration prompts change depending upon the sub mode while configuring the router. On IOS, the configuration prompt will mainly be under the interface IOS-R2(config-if)# or a router process IOS-R2(config-router)# sub modes. Rarely does the IOS configuration require three levels of submode configuration. IOS-XR configurations can be multiple submodes deep because of the hierarchical nature of the OS. To locate the submode of the configuration prompt, use the pwd command, which will display the context of the configuration prompt.

In the example, the configuration requires three submodes deep into the BGP configuration. The command pwd is issued to clarify the exact CLI configuration mode.

```
RP/0/0/CPU0:XR1#conf terminal
RP/0/0/CPU0:XR1(config)#router bgp 100
RP/0/0/CPU0:XR1(config-bgp)#neighbor 1.1.1.1
RP/0/0/CPU0:XR1(config-bgp-nbr)#address-family ipv4 unicast
RP/0/0/CPU0:XR1(config-bgp-nbr-af)#pwd
router bgp 100 \n neighbor 1.1.1.1 \n  address-family ipv4 unicast
```

Moving between sub configurations in IOS XR OS may require going back to the global configuration before changing configuration submodes. Instead of typing exit multiple times to take you to the global process, the command root may be used.

```
RP/0/0/CPU0:XR1(config-bgp-nbr-af)#root
RP/0/0/CPU0:XR1(config)#
```

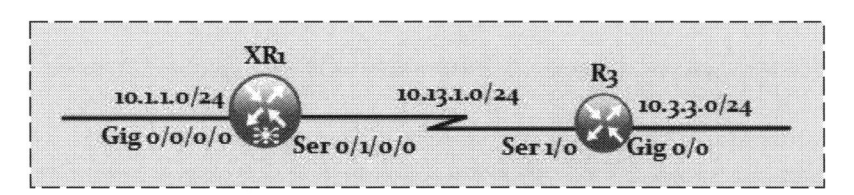

Figure 70

```
RP/0/0/CPU0:XR1#show route

Codes: C - connected, S - static, R - RIP, B - BGP
       D - EIGRP, EX - EIGRP external, O - OSPF, IA - OSPF inter area
       N1 - OSPF NSSA external type 1, N2 - OSPF NSSA external type 2
       E1 - OSPF external type 1, E2 - OSPF external type 2, E - EGP
       i - ISIS, L1 - IS-IS level-1, L2 - IS-IS level-2
       ia - IS-IS inter area, su - IS-IS summary null, * - candidate default
       U - per-user static route, o - ODR, L - local, G  - DAGR
       A - access/subscriber, (!) - FRR Backup path

Gateway of last resort is not set

C    10.1.1.0/24 is directly connected, 00:44:39, GigabitEthernet0/0/0/0
L    10.1.1.1/32 is directly connected, 00:44:39, GigabitEthernet0/0/0/0
C    10.13.1.0/24 is directly connected, 00:44:39, Serial 0/1/0/0
L    10.13.1.1/32 is directly connected, 00:44:39, Serial 0/1/0/0


RP/0/0/CPU0:XR1#show route 10.1.1.0
```

Routing entry for 10.1.1.0/24

Known via "connected", distance 0, metric 0 (connected)

Routing Descriptor Blocks

directly connected, via GigabitEthernet0/0/0/0

Route metric is 0

No advertising protos.

Static Routes Configuration

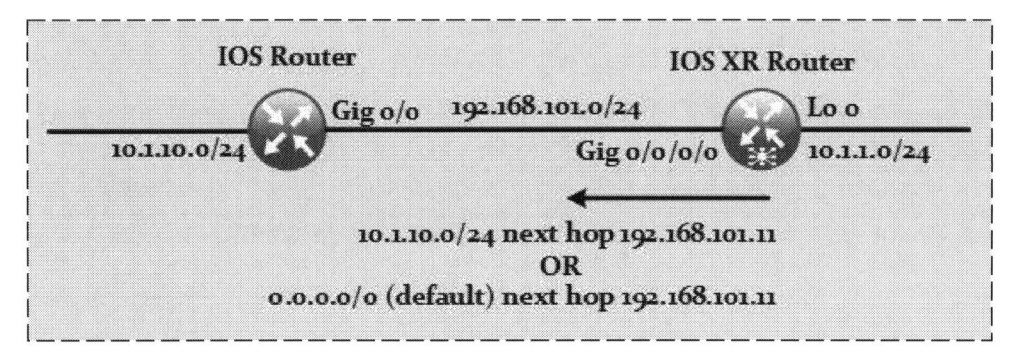

Figure 71 Configuration of static route

router static

  address-family ipv4 unicast

    10.1.10.0/24 192.168.101.11

This is for default route example, which is the same as static route using 0.0.0.0/0 as destination.

router static

  address-family ipv4 unicast

    0.0.0.0/0 192.168.101.11

As with any routing, you can have a look if your routes are working by looking at the routing table with show route.

RP/0/RSP0/CPU0:PE1#show route

< omitted >

Gateway of last resort is 192.168.101.10 to network 0.0.0.0

```
S*    0.0.0.0/0 [1/0] via 192.168.101.10
L     10.1.1.1/32 is directly connected, 19:09:10, Loopback0
S     10.1.10.0/24 [1/0] via 192.168.101.11, 00:03:08
C     192.168.101.0/24 is directly connected, 16:52:13, GigabitEthernet0/0/0
L     192.168.101.10/32 is directly connected, 16:52:13, GigabitEthernet0/0/0
```

RIPv2 (IPv4) configuration on IOS and IOS XR

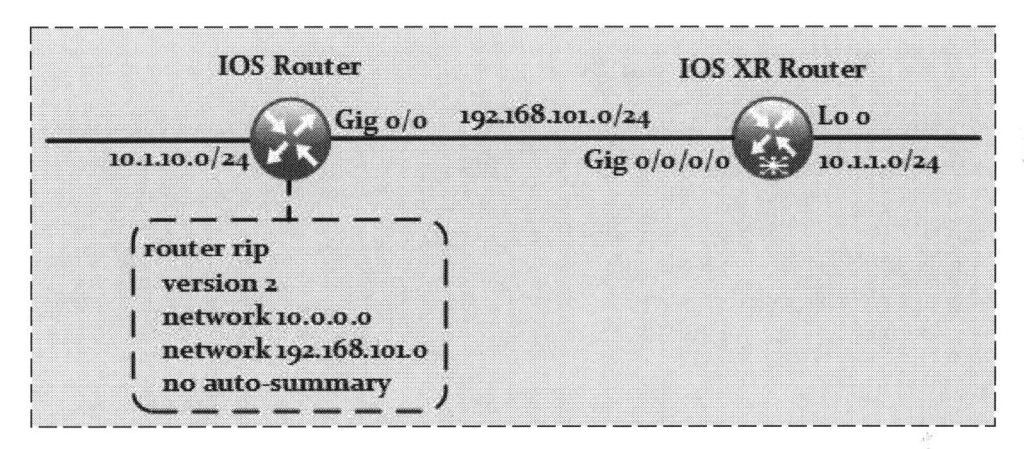

Figure 72 Configuration of RIP on IOS and IOS XR

The following configuration can be applied to the IOS-XR router to enable RIPv2 on the two interfaces and start receiving and announcing routes.

```
router rip
 interface loopback 0
 !
 interface GigabitEthernet 0/0/0/0
```

Verification of RIP working on IOS XR is simple and we just will look if we are getting the 10.1.10.0/24 network from the IOS Router neighbor.

```
RP/0/RSP0/CPU0:IOSXRRouter#show route rip
Fri Apr 14 23:22:08.242 UTC
```

```
R    10.1.10.0/24 [120/1] via 192.168.101.11, 00:05:50, GigabitEthernet0/0/0/0
```

```
IOSRouter#show ip route rip
< omitted >


10.0.0.0/8 is variably subnetted, 3 subnets, 2 masks
R    10.1.1.0/24 [120/1] via 192.168.101.10, 00:00:19, GigabitEthernet0/0
```

To also see interfaces associated with rip protocol, use the following command.

```
RP/0/RSP0/CPU0:PE1#show protocols rip default-context
Sat Apr 15 00:50:54.530 UTC
Routing Protocol RIP
  VRF default is Active
    2 interfaces configured, 2 active
    4 routes, 3 paths allocated
    Timers: Update 30s (next in 27s), Invalid 180s, Holddown 180s, Flush 240s
    OOM state is "Normal"
    Interface              Active     IP-Address        State   Send Recv Nbrs
    GigabitEthernet0_0_0_0 Active     192.168.101.10/24 Up      2    2    1
    Loopback0              Active     10.1.1.1/24       Up      2    2    0
```

To see the RIPv2 basic configuration including timers, you can enter the show rip command.

```
RP/0/RSP0/CPU0:PE1#show rip
Sat Apr 15 00:45:13.259 UTC


RIP config:
Active:              Yes
Added to socket:     Yes
```

Out-of-memory state:	Normal
Version:	2
Default metric:	Not set
Maximum paths:	4
Auto summarize:	No
Broadcast for V2:	No
Packet source validation:	Yes
NSF:	Disabled
Timers: Update:	30 seconds (26 seconds until next update)
Invalid:	180 seconds
Holddown:	180 seconds
Flush:	240 seconds

IOS-XE

Configuring the router eigrp autonomous-system-number command creates an EIGRP autonomous system configuration that creates an EIGRP routing instance, which can be used for tagging routing information.

STEPS

1. enable
2. configure terminal
3. router eigrp autonomous-system-number
4. network network-number
5. end

Configuring the router eigrp virtual-instance-name command creates an EIGRP named configuration. The EIGRP named configuration does not create an EIGRP routing instance by itself. The EIGRP named configuration is the base configuration, which is required to define address family configurations used for routing.

Steps

1. Enable
2. Configure terminal
3. Router eigrp virtual-instance-name
4. Enter one of the following:

Address-family ipv4 [multicast] [unicast] [vrf vrf-name] autonomous-system autonomous-system-number

Address-family ipv6 [unicast] [vrf vrf-name] autonomous-system autonomous-system-number

5. Network ip-address [wildcard-mask]
6. End

Configuring OSPF Interface Parameters

Steps

1.	Enable
2.	Configure terminal
3.	Interface type number
4.	ip ospf cost cost
5.	ip ospf retransmit-interval seconds
6.	ip ospf transmit-delay seconds
7.	ip ospf priority number-value
8.	ip ospf hello-interval seconds
9.	ip ospf dead-interval seconds
10.	ip ospf authentication-key key
11.	ip ospf message-digest-key key-id md5 key
12.	ip ospf authentication [message-digest	null]
13.	end

Chapter 9: Cisco Operating Systems and Platforms II

Technology Brief

Cisco continue offering advance and intelligent IOS platform for devices such as IOS XE, IOS XE etc with special consideration to service provider's network reqiuirments to provide optimized and efficient performance and smooth user experience.

IOS XR software packages

IOS XR packages utilize dynamic link libraries (DLLs). DLLs improve overall memory management on the system because DLLs allow memory sharing by all the applications that share the same library. In addition, if an application is no longer in use or not needed, the DLL is unloaded. For example, if BGP is not configured on the router, the libraries that support BGP do not need to be loaded into memory. IOS XR uses software packages instead of feature sets. The modularity of the software architecture allows package installation, removal, or modification without reloading the entire system.

Package installation envelopes (PIEs) are files that contain code for software features. The mini is the core composite file containing mandatory software components necessary for booting the router. The mini contains the kernel, memory management, and other core components. Additional functionality is optional and may be loaded with the appropriate PIE package. For example, multicast functionality resides in the optional multicast pie. Software maintenance upgrades (SMUs) are PIEs that provide software patches.

An SMU resolves a specific defect within a specific component of a package. SMUs provide software fixes for defects while allowing the router to stay on the same software release version. The table below demonstrates IOS XR's software modularity. The mini is a mandatory package consisting of the kernel, base image, admin plane, routing, and forwarding components. Optional packages include Multiprotocol Label Switching (MPLS), multicast, Broadcast Network Gateway (BNG), and other features.

Mandatory Package		Optional Packages	
Mini Composite File		Manageability	Adv. Video
OS-MBI	SNMP	MPLS	Optics
Admin	Alarm	Multicast	FPD
Base	Line Card	Security	Documentation

Forwarding	Routing	Services	Satellite
		BNG	

Table 17 Various available menadtory and optional packages of IOS XR

This example demonstrates how to determine the active software packages on the router with the command show install active summary.

```
XR1#show install active summary
Default Profile:
SDRs:
Owner Active
Packages:
disk0:asr9k-mini-px-4.3.2
disk0:asr9k-px-4.3.2.CSCuj99070-1.0.0
disk0:asr9k-px-4.3.2.CSCuj19861-1.0.0
disk0:asr9k-fpd-px-4.3.2
disk0:asr9k-mpls-px-4.3.2
disk0:asr9k-mgbl-px-4.3.2
disk0:asr9k-bng-px-4.3.2
disk0:asr9k-doc-px-4.3.2
disk0:asr9k-px-4.3.2.CSCuj22149-1.0.0
```

In addition to debug capability, IOS XR maintains detailed logs called traces that are enabled by default and do not affect the system stability or performance. Traces are a useful source of information when troubleshooting because they capture data before a problem occurs. Trace captures help support engineers identify the root cause of a problem. Traces are stored on the route processors (RPs) local storage and use circular logging, so time is of the essence when collecting trace files.

```
RP/0/0/CPU0:PE1#show ospf trace hello
```

Traces for OSPF 100 (Tue Jan 15 18:27:33)
Traces returned/requested/available: 2048/2048/2048
Trace buffer: hello
Jan 5 17:51:48.651 ospf_rcv_hello: intf Gio/1/0/0 area.0 from 100.1.1.11.10.10.254
Jan 5 17:51:48.651 ospf_check_hello_events: intf Gio/1/0/0 area.0 from1.10.10.1
Jan 5 17:51:49.066 ospf_send_hello: area.0 intf Gio/1/0/0 from 1.10.10.1
Jan 5 17:51:54.833 ospf_send_hello: area.0 intf Gio/1/0/3 from 14.1.1.1
Jan 5 17:51:54.932 ospf_rcv_hello: intf Gio/1/0/2 area.0 from 2.100.2.212.1.1.2

Cisco IOS XE Software Packaging

Cisco IOS XE Software distribution is in the form of a single binary file (.bin) for the respective RPs (ASR1000-RP1 and ASR1000-RP2 at this time). This single binary file is also referred as a consolidated package. This consolidated package can also be expanded, and the resulting files coming out of consolidated packages are known as sub packages (with the extension of .pkg). Besides ROMMON, which is common across all system boards, Cisco IOS XE Software consists of seven sub packages. Cisco IOS XE Software can also be booted in a monolithic fashion by way of running the single consolidated package or binary, much like booting an IOS binary on c7200 or c7300 routers.

This table describes the various Cisco IOS XE Software sub packages.

System Component	Sub package Name
RP	• IOSD • RP Control • RP Access • RP Base and Linux Software
ESP	• ESP Base: ESP Managers, QFP, and Linux software
SPA Interface Processor (SIP)	• SIP Base: SIP Managers and Linux software • SIP SPA: SPA Drivers

Table 18 Various packages of Cisco IOS XE

This example shows the file system structure on the RP's hard disk drive (HDD).

```
[ASR1006_RP_0:/]$ ls -la
total 40
drwxr-xr-x    19 18346    25           0 May 23 16:06 .
drwxr-xr-x    19 18346    25           0 May 23 16:06 ..
-rw-r--r--     1 root     root         0 May 23 16:05 .autofsck
-rw-r--r--     1 18346    25         486 Jan  1  1970 .pkgset
drwxr-xr-x     2 root     root         0 May 23 16:05 auto
drwxr-xr-x     2 18346    25           0 May 23 16:05 bin
drwxr-xr-x     7 root     root      4096 Jun  8 12:50 bootflash
-rwxrwxrwx     1 18346    25       21572 Jan  1  1970 common
lrwxrwxrwx     1 root     root        10 May 23 16:05 config -> /bootflash
drwxrwxrwt     6 root     root     14000 May 23 16:06 dev
lrwxrwxrwx     1 root     root        10 May 23 16:05 disk0 -> /vol/disk0
drwxr-xr-x    15 18346    25           0 May 23 16:05 etc
lrwxrwxrwx     1 root     root        13 May 23 16:05 harddisk -> /misc/scratch
lrwxrwxrwx     1 root     root        33 May 23 16:05 issu -> /tmp/sw/rp/0/0/rp_base/
   mount/issu
drwxr-xr-x     3 18346    25           0 May 23 16:05 lib
-rwxrwxrwx     1 18346    25        4071 Jan  1  1970 lkern_init
drwxr-xr-x     3 root     root         0 May 23 16:05 misc
drwxr-xr-x     3 root     root         0 May 23 16:05 mnt
dr-xr-xr-x   157 root     root         0 Jan  1  1970 proc
-rwxrwxrwx     1 18346    25        1077 Jan  1  1970 rommon_to_env
drwx------     2 root     root         0 Jun  5 15:43 root
drwxr-xr-x     2 18346    25           0 May 23 16:05 sbin
drwxr-xr-x    10 root     root         0 Jan  1  1970 sys
drwxr-xr-x     2 root     root         0 May 23 16:06 tftp
drwxr-xr-x    14 root     root         0 Jun  8 12:50 tmp
lrwxrwxrwx     1 root     root         9 May 23 16:05 usb0 -> /vol/usb0
lrwxrwxrwx     1 root     root         9 May 23 16:05 usb1 -> /vol/usb1
drwxr-xr-x     7 18346    25           0 May 23 16:05 usr
drwxr-xr-x    10 root     root         0 May 23 16:05 var
drwxr-xr-x     2 root     root         0 Jun  2 17:15 vol
[ASR1006_RP_0:/]$
```

Figure 73

Notice that boot flash and usb0/usb1 are all mounted volumes on the Linux file system. The file system used here is EXT2/EXT3. Recommended practice dictates shutting down the RP board before removal to avoid any possible file system corruption. Booting of IOS is recommended and supported via either bootflash or external USB slots. Booting the system in a modular fashion is done via booting off a file called pack-ages.conf, which essentially describes and dictates the provisioning of sub packages for the RP. This file and other sub packages are extracted using the consolidated package or binary file. The consolidated package or binary file is the only method of publishing the released image. This file must be in the same directory as the other sub packages file.

The following procedures will help solidify the concept. These are the steps involved in booting the system.

The non-modular boot procedure is as follows:

> **Step 1.** Download the Cisco IOS XE Software consolidated package file from Cisco.com (2.1.0 AdvEnterprise, asr1000rp1-adventerprisek9.02.01.00.122-33.XNA.bin).
>
> **Step 2.** Create a boot system command and point it to the preceding file.

The modular boot procedure is as follows:

> **Step 1.** Download the Cisco IOS XE Software consolidated package file from Cisco.com (2.1.0 AdvEnterprise, asr1000rp1-adventerprisek9.02.01.00.122-33.XNA.bin).
>
> **Step 2.** Expand the downloaded file using the platform CLI:

```
ASR1006# request platform software package expand file harddisk:
  asr1000rp1-adventerprisek9.02.01.00.122-33.XNA.bin to bootflash:/
  modular
ASR1006# dir bootflash:/modular
Directory of bootflash:/
   12  -rw-   52064460  asr1000rp1-espbase.02.01.00.122-33.XN.pkg
   13  -rw-   21833932  asr1000rp1-rpaccess-k9.02.01.00.122-
                        33.XN.pkg
   14  -rw-   21516492  asr1000rp1-rpbase.02.01.00
                        .122-33.XN.pkg
   15  -rw-   24965324  asr1000rp1-rpcontrol.02.01.00.122-33.XN.pkg
   16  -rw-   48451788  asr1000rp1-rpios-
                        advipservicesk9.02.01.00.122-33.XN.pkg
   17  -rw-   36954316  asr1000rp1-sipbase.02.01.00.122-33.XN.pkg
   18  -rw-   14782668  asr1000rp1-sipspa.02.01.00
                        .122-33.XN.pkg
   19  -rw-       6225  packages.conf
```

Figure 74

> **Step 3.** Create a boot system command and point it to the packages.conf file.

The next time ASR1000-RP boots, it will boot in a modular fashion, and you can perform an IOS ISSU (requires dual IOS) and ASR1000-SIP SPA drivers upgrade.

You can also take a snapshot of the running consolidated package on boot flash (as opposed to expanding it as shown before, where you actually need the file at the time of expanding it). Snapshotting can prove helpful if you did a network boot and want all your subsequent boots to be based on sub packages or modular.

Cisco SP router platforms, their operating system and placement in the SP IP NGN

Cisco SP router platforms

Following list shows the platform of routers offered by Cisco for service provider's environment:

- Cisco 4000 Series Integrated Services Routers
- Cisco 3900 Series Integrated Services Routers
- Cisco 3800 Series Integrated Services Routers
- Cisco 2900 Series Integrated Services Routers
- Cisco 2800 Series Integrated Services Routers
- Cisco 1900 Series Integrated Services Routers
- Cisco 1800 Series Integrated Services Routers
- Cisco 800 Series Routers

Operating system

Cisco has had many operating systems over the decades and several of them are mentioned here.

IOS – a monolithic operating system, which runs single, threaded on a wide range of CPUs. Designed and built in a different era. Obsolete at current time and on life support for recalcitrant customers. The software architecture was a product of its time and made it prone to memory leaks and packaging problems for different CPUs and motherboards. It was very much difficult to fix bugs and hard to add features. Bugs would often reappear in mainline because of internal problems with library management at compile time.

IOS-SX – a fork of IOS was developed in the mid-2000s, with Ethernet Switching features added to the code. It had all the limitations of IOS and took some years to stabilize into a reliable operating system. Many customers remain fearful to move on based on the pain experienced to date. Attempts to modularize this code and support modern features like process restart; ISSU, etc. have been abandoned due to poor results.

- It Supports Spanning Tree

- Instant Access is an 802.1BR implementation for Cat6800 family and acts like a virtual stacking function

- Backward compatibility remains vital for many customers and will be around for many years to come

IOS-XE – Addresses to IOS monolithic problem by abstracting some modules.

- The underlying operating system is based on a Linux distro but there is no access to it

- Runs on multi-core CPUs

- Isolates control plane and data plane in the software architecture

- Stabilizes the operational interfaces for SNMP, XML, HTTP for external operations

- Runs on multiple hardware platforms from different business units but mostly in the mid-to-low end market (perhaps reflecting, it has rumored skunk works development internally).

NX-OS – "Nexus Operating System" was built to overcome on IOS-SX and modernize Cisco's internal development process and tooling for software.

- It is very much-customized version of Linux.

- Provide Support for multiple CPUs (although most versions use only one CPU)

- Multithreaded preemptive multitasking capabilities

- Provide Support for Virtual Device Contexts and 802.1BR–called Fabric Extensions (FEX) by Cisco

- Implements memory protected process for process recovery and fault detection

- Offers Fault detection via process monitoring to detect internal errors

IOS-XR –High-end operating system developed internally by Cisco using a range of third party software.

- It Offers Preemptive, multitasking, memory protected, microkernel-based operating system.

- It Uses QNX as the operating system kernel on CRS and ASR families. Uses Linux kernel on NCS family where routing functions and the system administration functions are run on separate virtual machines (VMs).

- Provide high availability (largely through support for hardware redundancy and fault containment methods, as protected memory spaces for individual processes and process restart ability).

- Provide Better scalability for big hardware configurations.

- A package based software distribution model (allowing optional features such as multicast routing and MPLS to be installed and removed while the router is in service).

- Ability to install package upgrades and patches.

- A web-based GUI for system management (making use of a generic, XML management interface).

- Intended for service provider operations.

This software is found on the largest of Cisco routers and premium pricing applies. The Cisco CRS, NCS and ASR routers are the current product families.

CatOS/CatalystOS – acquired when Cisco bought Crescendo communications in the late 1990's. Used for the now obsolete Catalyst 5000 and 6000/6500 product families.

Although supported for many years because of customer reluctance to upgrade, it is now widely regarded as obsolete

The CLI was unlike any other Cisco IOS product

Placement in the SP IP NGN

- Cisco 12000 Series Routers
- Cisco 7300 Series Routers
- Cisco ASR 9000 Series Aggregation Services Routers
- Cisco ASR 1000 Series Aggregation Services Routers
- Cisco ASR 920 Series Aggregation Services Router
- Cisco ASR 901 Series Aggregation Services Routers
- Cisco ASR 901S Series Aggregation Services Routers
- Cisco ASR 900 Series Aggregation Services Routers
- Cisco XR 12000 Series Router

Chapter 10: Transport Technologies

SONET and SDH

- SONET, the Synchronous Optical Network.
- Initial standards built by Bellcore in 1985.
  - The CCITT (now ITU) joined with the SDH effort in 1987.
- SONET characteristics.
  - SONET-SDH is a global telecommunications standard.
  - It is a voice-oriented protocol.
  - It is an OSI layer 2-3 protocol set.
  - It defines point-to-point connections.
- Objectives:
  - Improve on current technology, particularly multiplexing.
  - Improve vender interoperability.
  - Prepare for high-speed, Gbits/sec networks and associated protocols (ATM).
  - Develop a survivable-ring standard.
  - Provide better network operations and administration management.
- SONET data rates.
  - SONET specifies two data rates: the optical rates (optical carrier or OC) and the electrical rates (synchronous transport signal or STS).
    - The OC and STS rates are identical.
  - The basic rate is OC-1 (STS-1) at 51.84 Mbits/sec.
  - The OC-n (STS-n) rate is a multiple of the OC-1 rate: $n*51.84$ Mbit/sec.
    - For example, the OC-24 rate is 24*51.84 = 1244.16 Mbits/sec.
- Sonet networks.
  - Sonet hardware consist of switches, (de-)multiplexers, and repeaters.
    - A section is a point-to-point connection between devices.
    - A line is a path between multiplexers.

- A path is an end-to-end connection.
- The multiplexers are referred as add-drop multiplexers.
  - They can add and remove data on the fly, without holding and regenerating.

- Sonnet frames.
  - The SONET frame is two-dimensional: 9 rows x 90 bytes per row.
    - (51.84 Mbits/sec)/(9*90 bytes/frame)*(8 bits/byte) = 8000 frames/sec.
    - (1 sec)/(8000 frames) = 0.000125 sec/frame = 125 msec/frame).
    - This corresponds to 28 DS-1 lines or one DS-3 line.
    - Transmission is from left to right and top to bottom.
  - The first three frame columns contain system management information.
    - The first three rows are section information; the remainder are line information.
  - The remaining 87 columns, known as the synchronous payload envelope (SPE), contain user data.

- Inter-frame multiplexing.
  - Higher data rates are formed by multiplexing (interleaving) lower rate frame streams.
    - OC-*n* contains *n* interleaved OC-1 streams.
  - The c data rates (e.g. OC-12c) are formed by straight frame catenation.
  - Lower-bit rate streams, called virtual tributaries, can also be multiplexed within a frame.

- Synchronous.
  - The "synchronous" means Sonet components share a common clock.
    - This is expensive and difficult, but useful.
  - Even so, frames drift, particularly in virtual tributaries.
    - This is called plestochrony.
  - Let components float in the payload portion of the frame.

- The overhead portion of the frame contains start pointers into the payload.
- Sonet network topologies.
  - Sonet networks for a ring, called the bidirectional line-switched ring (BLSR).
    - Bidirectional rings protect against ring breaks.
  - A BLSR/n network uses n fibers.
    - In addition, has a maximum of 16 nodes.
  - Propagation delay is capped at 6 msec (1200 km, 745 miles).
- Synchronous Digital Hierarchy.
  - Developed by the CCITT (now ITU), published in 1989.
  - It is a global standard; SONET (a North American standard) is a subset.
  - The T vs E rates.
    - DS-1 = 24*DS-0 = 24*(64 kbits/sec) = 1.45 Mbits/sec.
    - E-1 = 32*E-0 = 32*(64 Kbits/sec) = 2.048 Mbits/sec.
  - The SDH base rate, called synchronous transport module 1 or STM-1, is 155 Mbit/sec.
    - Moreover, lo, OC-3 = STM-1, almost.

Mind Map

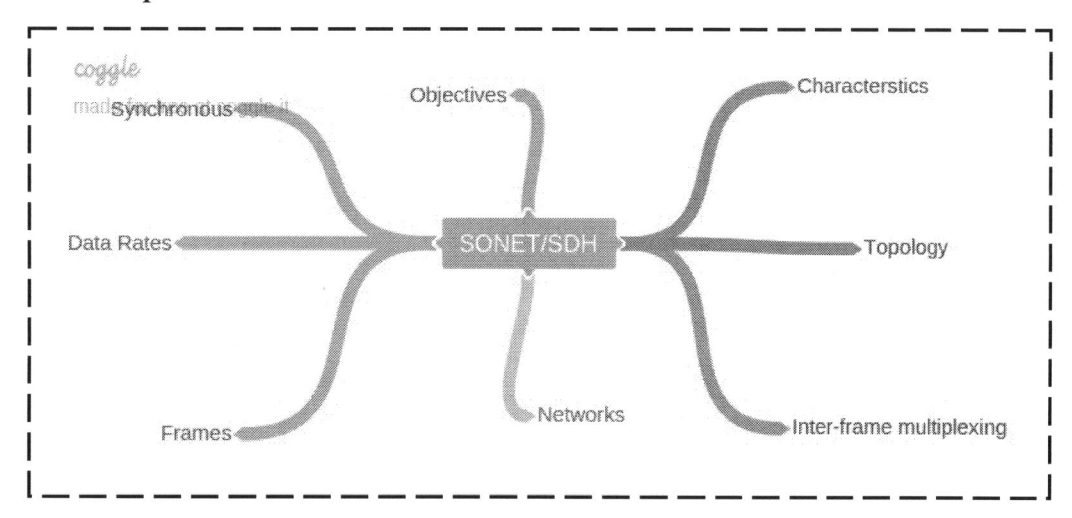

Figure 75 Mind Map of SONET/SDH

DWDM

DWDM is a technology, which is created to increase bandwidth over a single fiber by using different wavelengths. The spacing between the different wavelengths is 2nm.

IPoDWDM

To enable multiservice transport, OTN uses the concept of a wrapped overhead (OH). To illustrate this structure:

Optical channel payload unit (OPU) OH information is added to the information payload to form the OPU. The OPU OH includes information to support the adaptation of client signals. Optical channel data unit (ODU) OH is added to the OPU to create the ODU. The ODU OH includes information for maintenance and operational functions to support optical channels. Optical channel transport unit (OTU) OH together with the FEC is added to form the OTU. The OTU OH includes information for operational functions to support the transport by way of one or more optical channel connections. Optical channel (OCh) OH is added to form the OCh. The OCh provides the OTN management functionality and contains four subparts: the OPU, ODU, OTU, and frame alignment signal (FAS).

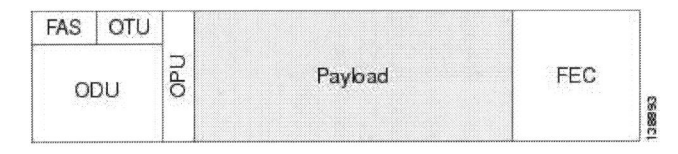

Figure 76 Structure of Optical Channel Transport Unit (OTU)

ROADM

Reconfigurable Optical Add-Drop Multiplexer (ROADM) is a way to drop certain lambda's within a DWDM ring at a specific POP. It is used on Cisco ONS equipment. The history of optical communications is often organized into generations, defined by technology innovations such as Wavelength-Division Multiplexing (WDM) and the Erbium-Doped-Fiber Amplifier (EDFA), which together enabled a rapid reduction in cost per bit and stimulated decades of explosive demand growth. Arguably the most epochal change was the commercial deployment of Reconfigurable Optical Add/Drop Multiplexers (ROADMs), which is gradually transforming an electronic network of optical "wires" into a highly interconnected, reconfigurable photonic mesh. Reconfigurable photonics have already contributed significantly to improved network efficiency, by enabling traffic to grow gracefully without a priori knowledge of future traffic demands, while minimizing the use of expensive optoelectronic regenerators.

To date, the widespread use of ROADMs has been driven by the cost savings and operational simplicity they provide to quasi-static networks (i.e. networks in which new connections are frequently set up, but rarely taken down). However, new applications exploiting the ROADMs' ability to dynamically reconfigure a photonic mesh network are now being investigated.

SRLG

The Shared Risk Link Group (SRLG) feature on the Cisco ONS 15454 allows the sharing of DWDM risk information between the optical layer and the IP layer. Typically, the IP part of a network is not aware of existing DWDM physical connectivity when performing routing decisions. The advent of multi-degree ROADM technology and IPoDWDM makes SRLG a valuable feature for planning routes that helps ensure survivability against all DWDM signal faults and for increasing utilization.

Implement 10/40/100 gigabit Ethernet interfaces on Cisco IOS-XR routers

The 10/40/100 gigabit based interfaces can be configured in a few different modes. Some can be configured in LAN/WAN mode. The idea behind WAN mode is to provide support for ATM/SDH/OTN. LAN mode is for basic Ethernet purposes. OTN mode can be used to

To configure WAN mode on IOS-XR:

To check the configuration of interface use,
RP/0/RSP0/CPU0:ios#sh running-config interface tenGigE 0/6/0/0
To configure WAN mode on,
interface TenGigE0/6/0/0
transport-mode wan
RP/0/RSP0/CPU0:IOS#sh running-config controller wanphy 0/6/0/0
controller wanphy0/6/0/0
wanmode on

Configuring LAN mode on IOS-XR:

```
RP/0/RSP0/CPU0:ios#conf t
RP/0/RSP0/CPU0:ios(config)#int tenGigE 0/6/0/0
RP/0/RSP0/CPU0:ios(config-if)#no transport-mode
RP/0/RSP0/CPU0:ios(config-if)#commit
```

Configuring OTN mode on IOS-XR:

```
RP/0/RSP0/CPU0:ios#sh running-config interface tenGigE 0/6/0/0
 interface TenGigE0/6/0/0
 transport-mode otn bit-transparent opu2e

RP/0/RSP0/CPU0:ios#sh running-config controller dwdm 0/6/0/0
 controller dwdm0/6/0/0
 admin-state in-service
```

The default mode on 10/40/100G is LAN mode.

The Unidirectional Link Routing (UDLR) feature is now supported only in 10GE LAN mode only. It allows a physical port to receive or transmit data with on a simplex fiber.

Frame relay

Frame relay is a data link layer, digital packet switching network protocol technology designed to connect Local Area Networks (LANs) and send data across Wide Area Networks (WANs). Frame Relay shares some of the same underlying technology as X.25 and achieved some popularity in the United States as the underlying infrastructure for Integrated Services Digital Network (ISDN) services sold to business customers.

How Frame Relay Works

Frame Relay supports multiplexing of traffic from multiple connections over a shared physical link using special-purpose hardware components including frame routers, bridges, and switches that package data into individual Frame Relay messages. Each connection utilizes a ten (10) bit Data Link Connection Identifier (DLCI) for unique channel addressing. Two connection types exist:

Permanent Virtual Circuits (PVC) - for persistent connections intended to be maintained for long periods even if no data is actively being transferred

Switched Virtual Circuits (SVC) - for temporary connections that last only for the duration of a single session

Frame Relay achieves better performance than X.25 at a lower cost primarily not performing any error correction (that is instead offloaded to other components of the network), greatly reducing network latency. It also supports variable-length packet sizes for more efficient utilization of network bandwidth.

Frame Relay operates over fiber optic or ISDN lines and can support different higher-level network protocols including Internet Protocol (IP).

Performance of Frame Relay

Frame Relay supports the data rates of standard T1 and T3 lines - 1.544 Mbps and 45 Mbps, respectively, with individual connections down to 56 Kbps.

It also supports fiber connections up to 2.4 Gbps.

Each connection can be configured with Committed Information Rate (CIR) that the protocol maintains by default. CIR refers to a minimum data rate that the connection should expect to receive under steady stage conditions (and can be exceeded when the underlying physical link has enough spare capacity to support it). Frame Relay does not restrict maximum performance to that of the CIR but also allows burst traffic, where the connection can temporarily (typically for up to 2 seconds) exceed its CIR.

Issues with Frame Relay

Frame Relay traditionally provided a cost-effective way for telecommunications companies to transmit data over long distances. This technology has decreased in popularity as companies are gradually migrating their deployments to other Internet Protocol (IP) based solutions.

Years ago, many viewed Asynchronous Transfer Mode (ATM) and Frame Relay as direct competitors. ATM technology differs substantially from Frame Relay, however - using fixed length rather than variable length packets and requires expensive hardware to operate.

Frame Relay ultimately faced much stronger competition from MPLS - Multi-Protocol Label Switching.

MPLS techniques have become widely used on Internet routers to configure Virtual Private Network (VPN) solutions that previously would have required Frame Relay or similar solutions.

ATM

ATM is a high-speed networking standard designed to support both voice and data communications. Internet service providers on their private long-distance networks normally utilize ATM. ATM operates at the data link layer (Layer 2 in the OSI model) over either fiber or twisted-pair cable.

ATM differs from more common data link technologies like Ethernet in several ways. For example, ATM utilizes no routing.

Hardware devices known as ATM switches establish point-to-point connections between endpoints and data flows directly from source to destination. Additionally, instead of using variable-length packets as Ethernet does, ATM utilizes fixed-sized cells. ATM cells are 53 bytes in length that includes 48 bytes of data and five (5) bytes of header information.

The performance of ATM is often expressed in the form of OC (Optical Carrier) levels, written as "OC-xxx." Performance levels as high as 10 Gbps (OC-192) are technically feasible with ATM. More common performance levels for ATM are 155 Mbps (OC-3) and 622 Mbps (OC-12).

ATM technology is built to improve utilization and quality of service (QoS) on high-traffic networks. Without routing and with fixed-size cells, networks can much more easily manage bandwidth under ATM than under Ethernet, for example. The high cost of ATM relative to Ethernet is one factor that has limited its adoption to backbone and other high-performance, specialized networks.

Metropolitan Ethernet (Metro Ethernet)

Metropolitan Ethernet (Metro Ethernet) uses carrier Ethernet technology in metropolitan networks. Corporations, academic institutions and government departments in large cities use Metro Ethernet to connect branch campuses and offices to the Internet. In other words, Metro Ethernet connects business local area networks (LAN) and end users to wide area networks (WAN) or the Internet.

Metro Ethernet is a service provider collection of layer 2 or layer 3 switches or routers connected through optical fiber. The topology may be a ring, hub and star or full or partial mesh.

Metro Ethernet can be used as pure Ethernet over synchronous digital hierarchy (SDH), Ethernet over multiprotocol label switching (MPLS) or Ethernet over dense wavelength division multiplexing (DWDM). Ethernet deployments are less expensive but also less scalable and reliable. Thus, they are also limited to small-scale and experimental deployment. SDH-based deployments are useful when there is an established SDH infrastructure that is used by large service providers.

Metro Ethernet feasibility grew in the late 1990s due to new technological developments that allowed transparent traffic tunneling through virtual LANs as point-to-point or multipoint-to-multipoint circuits.

Metro Ethernet is widely used for small-scale deployments with less than a few hundred customers.

DSL

Digital Subscriber Line (DSL) is a high-speed Internet service for homes and offices that competes with cable and other forms of broadband Internet. DSL provides high-speed networking over ordinary phone lines using broadband modem technology. The technology behind DSL enables Internet and telephone service to work over the same phone line without requiring customers to disconnect either their voice or Internet connections.

How fast is DSL?

Basic DSL supports maximum download data rates ranging between 1.544 Mbps and 8.448 Mbps. Actual speeds vary in practice depending on the quality of the copper phone line installation involved. The length of the phone line needed to reach the service provider's premise equipment (sometimes called the "central office") also can limit the maximum speed a DSL installation supports.

Symmetric vs. Asymmetric DSL

Most types of DSL service are asymmetric (also known as ADSL). ADSL offers higher download speeds than upload speeds, a tradeoff that most residential providers make to better match up with the needs of typical households who generally do much more downloading. Symmetric DSL (SDSL) maintains equal data rates for both uploads and downloads.

Residential DSL Service

Many smaller regional providers also offer DSL. Customers subscribe to a DSL service plan, pay a monthly or yearly subscription, and must agree to the provider's terms of service. Most providers supply compatible DSL modem hardware to their customers if needed, or they can purchased through various outlets.

Business DSL Service

Besides its popularity in homes, many businesses also rely on DSL for their Internet service. Business DSL differs from residential DSL in several key respects:

- Symmetric DSL (SDSL) is typically used, as businesses tend to generate much higher volumes of outgoing traffic than a typical home
- Providers often sell higher tiers of service to their customers including higher data rate plans, premier customer support options. And/or bundling of other products

Issues with DSL

DSL Internet service only works over a limited physical distance and remains unavailable in many areas where the local telephone infrastructure does not support DSL technology.

Although DSL has been a mainstream type of Internet service for many years, the experience of individual customers can vary greatly depending on their location, their provider, the quality of telephone wiring in their residence, and some other factors:

As with other forms of Internet service, the cost of DSL can vary dramatically from region to region. An area with few Internet connectivity options and few providers may be more costly simply due to the lack of business competition.

DSL does not perform nearly as fast as fiber Internet connections. Even some high-speed wireless Internet options can offer competitive speeds.

Leased lines (T1, T2, T3)

"Leased" lines enable transmission of data at medium and high speeds (64 Kbps to 140 Mbps) by point-to-point or multipoint connection (Transfix service).

In Europe, there are five types of lines distinguished according to their speed:

- E0 (64Kbps)
- E1 = 32 E0 lines (2Mbps)
- E1 = 128 E0 lines (8Mbps)
- E3 = 16 E1 lines (34Mbps)
- E4 = 64 E1 lines (140Mbps)

In the United States, the concept is as follows:

- T1 (1.544 Mbps)
- T2 = 4 T1 lines (6 Mbps)
- T3 = 28 T1 lines (45 Mbps)
- T4 = 168 T1 lines (275 Mbps)

Why do you need a leased line?

As a rule, to get an Internet connection, you must pay a subscription to an Internet Service Provider or online service. The cost of this connection depends on the data transfer speed.

Cable (DOCSIS)

Now known as Cable Labs Certified Cable Modems, DOCSIS (Data over Cable Service Interface Specifications) is a standard interface for cable modems, the devices that handle incoming and outgoing data signals between a cable TV operator and a personal or business computer or television set. The International Telecommunication

Union (ITU-TS) ratified DOCSIS 1.0 in March of 1998. Although "DOCSIS" continues to be used, the newer name emphasizes that the standard is now being used to certify the products of cable modem makers. Cable operators whose existing customers have non-standard cable modems can handle them by adding backwards compatible supports to the DOCSIS card at the cable operator's end. As DOCSIS continues to evolve to new versions, existing modems can be upgraded to the newer versions by changing the programming in the cable modem's EEPROM memory. DOCSIS-compliant cable modems are being integrated into set-top boxes for use with television sets. DOCSIS must also support or converge with the high definition television (HDTV) standard. The set-top box itself follows a standard known as OpenCable.

DOCSIS specifies modulation schemes and the protocol for exchanging bidirectional signals over cable. It supports downstream-to-the-user data rates up to 27 Mbps (megabits per second). Since this data rate is shared by a number of users and because many cable operators will be limited by a T1 connection to the Internet, the actual downstream data rate to an individual business or home will be more like 1.5 to 3 Mbps. Since the upstream data flow has to support much smaller amounts of data from the user, it is designed for an aggregate data rate of 10 Mbps with individual data rates between 500 Kbps and 2.5 Mbps.

BRAS and BNG routers

A broadband remote access server (BRAS, B-RAS or BBRAS) routes traffic to and from broadband remote access devices such as digital subscriber line access multiplexers (DSLAM) on an Internet service provider's (ISP) network. BRAS can also be referred to as a Broadband Network Gateway (BNG).

The BRAS sits at the edge of an ISP's core network, and aggregates user sessions from the access network. It is at the BRAS that an ISP can inject policy management and IP Quality of Service (QoS).

The specific tasks include:

- Aggregate the circuits from one or more link access devices such as DSLAMs
- Provides layer 2 connectivity through either transparent bridging or PPP sessions over Ethernet or ATM sessions
- Enforces quality of service (QoS) policies
- Provides layer 3 connectivity and routes IP traffic through an Internet service provider's backbone network to the Internet

A DSLAM collects data traffic from multiple subscribers into a centralized point so that it can be transported to a switch or router over a Frame Relay, ATM, or Ethernet connection.

The router provides the logical network termination. Common link access methods include PPP over Ethernet (PPPoE), PPP over ATM (PPPoA) encapsulated sessions, bridged Ethernet over ATM or Frame Relay (RFC 1483/RFC 1490), or just plain Ethernet. In the case of ATM or Frame Relay based access, Virtual Circuit IDs identify individual subscribers. Subscribers connected over Ethernet-based remote access devices are usually identified by VLAN IDs or MPLS tags. By acting as the network termination point, the BRAS is responsible for assigning network parameters such as IP addresses to the clients. The BRAS is also the first IP hop from the client to the Internet.

The BRAS is also the interface to authentication, authorization and accounting systems

Passive optical network (PON)

A passive optical network (PON) is a system that brings optical fiber cabling and signals all or most of the way to the end user. Depending on where the PON terminates, the system can be described as fiber-to-the-curb (FTTC), fiber-to-the-building (FTTB), or fiber-to-the-home (FTTH).

A PON consists of an Optical Line Termination (OLT) at the communication company's office and a number of Optical Network Units (ONUs) near end users. Typically, up to 32 ONUs can be connected to an OLT. The passive simply describes the fact that optical transmission has no power requirements or active electronic parts once the signal is going through the network.

All PON systems have essentially the same theoretical capacity at the optical level. The limits on upstream and downstream bandwidth are set by the electrical overlay, the protocol used to allocate the capacity and manage the connection. The first PON systems that achieved significant commercial deployment had an electrical layer built on Asynchronous Transfer Mode (ATM, or "cell switching") and were called "APON." These are still being used today, although the term "broadband PON" or BPON is now applied. APON/BPON systems typically have downstream capacity of 155 Mbps or 622 Mbps, with the latter now the most common. Upstream transmission is in the form of cell bursts at 155 Mbps.

Multiple users of a PON could be allocated portions of this bandwidth. A PON could also serve as a trunk between a larger system, such as a CATV system, and a neighborhood, building, or home Ethernet network on coaxial cable.

The successor to APON/BPON is GPON, which has a variety of speed options ranging from 622 Mbps symmetrical (the same upstream/downstream capacity) to 2.5 Gbps downstream and 1.25 Gbps upstream. GPON is also based on ATM transport. GPON is the type of PON most widely deployed in today's fiber-to-the-home (FTTH) networks in new installations and is generally considered suitable for consumer broadband services for the next five to 10 years. From GPON, the future could take two branches: 1) 10 GPON would increase the speed of a single electrical broadband feed to 10G; and 2) WDM-PON would use wavelength-division multiplexing (WDM) to split each signal into 32 branches.

Chapter 11: Security in a Network

Technology Brief

With the rapid growth of IP networks in the past years, high-end switching has played one of the most fundamental and essential roles in moving data reliably, efficiently, and securely across networks. Cisco Catalyst switches are the leader in the switching market and major players in today's networks.

The data-link layer (Layer 2 of the OSI model) provides the functional and procedural means to transfer data between network entities with interoperability and interconnectivity to other layers, but from a security perspective, the data-link layer presents its own challenges. Network security is only as strong as the weakest link, and Layer 2 is no exception. Applying first-class security measures to the upper layers (Layers 3 and higher) does not benefit your network if Layer 2 is compromised. Cisco switches offer a wide range of security features at Layer 2 to protect the network traffic flow and the devices themselves.

Understanding and preparing for network threats is important, and hardening Layer 2 is becoming imperative. Cisco is continuously raising the bar for security, and security feature availability at Layer 2 is no exception.

Layer 2 Security Best Practices

- Manage the switches in a secure manner. For example, use SSH, authentication mechanism, access list, and set privilege levels.
- Restrict management access to the switch so that untrusted networks are not able to exploit management interfaces and protocols such as SNMP.
- Always use a dedicated VLAN ID for all trunk ports.
- Be skeptical; avoid using VLAN 1 for anything.
- Disable DTP on all non- trunking access ports.

- Deploy the Port Security feature to prevent unauthorized access from switching ports.
- Use the Private VLAN feature where applicable to segregate network traffic at Layer 2.
- Use MD5 authentication where applicable.
- Disable CDP where possible.
- Prevent denial-of-service attacks and other exploitation by disabling unused services and protocols.
- Shut down or disable all unused ports on the switch, and put them in a VLAN that is not used for normal operations.
- Use port security mechanisms to provide protection against a MAC flooding attack.
- Use port-level security features such as DHCP Snooping, IP Source Guard, and ARP security where applicable.
- Enable Spanning Tree Protocol features (for example, BPDU Guard, Loopguard, and Root Guard).
- Use Switch IOS ACLs and Wire-speed ACLs to filter undesirable traffic (IP and non-IP).

Control Plane Protection in Cisco IOS

In the router, the most important traffic is control plain traffic in normal operation. Control plane traffic is the traffic originated on router itself by protocol services running on it, destined to other device on the network. In order to run properly, routers need to speak with each other. They speak with each other by rules defined in protocols and protocols are running in shape of router services.

Examples are BGP, EIGRP, OSPF or some other non-routing protocols like CDP.

When router is making BGP neighbor adjacency with the neighboring router, it means that both routers are running BGP protocol service on them. BGP service is generating control plane traffic, sending that traffic to BGP neighbor and receiving control plane traffic back from the neighbor.

Usage of Control Plane Protection is important on routers receiving heavy traffic of which too many packets are forwarded to Control Plane. In that case, we can filter traffic based on predefined priority classes that we are free to define based on our specific traffic pattern.

The control plane-policing (CoPP) feature increases security on the switch by protecting the RP from unnecessary or DoS traffic and giving priority to important control plane and management traffic. The PFC3 and DFC3 are forwarding engines used to provide hardware support for CoPP. CoPP works with the PFC3 rate limiters. By using CoPP, we can make a part of control plane traffic prioritized so that it can be efficiently processed by control plane in timely manner. Some other less important control traffic will be dropped on the entrance to control plane or slowed down by using buffering. We can use QoS techniques in the entrance to Router Processor enabling us to drop or even better, to throttle some less important control traffic flows.

Route Processor Virtual Interfaces

1. Control-Plane Host Sub-Interface
   This interface is receiving all control plane traffic that is destined for one of the router interfaces. This is usually management traffic and routing protocols traffic. Most control plane protection features operate on this sub-interface, so this sub-interface provides most features, like policing, port filtering, and per-protocol queue thresholds.

   Class-map type port-filter allows for automatically dropping of packets destined for the TCP/UDP ports not currently open in the router. The operating system automatically detects all open ports, and you can manually configure some exceptions. This can significantly reduce load on device CPU during flooding attacks.

   If traffic destined towards Route Processor is not TCP/UDP that kind of control traffic ends up on the CEF exception sub-interface.

   Per-protocol queue thresholds set selective queue limits for packets of different protocols, such as ICMP, BGP, OSPF, etc.

2. Control-Plane Transit Sub-Interface
   This sub-interface handles transit IP traffic that cannot be handled by faster hardware CEF mechanism. This usually happens when a packet must be routed out of Ethernet interface and there is no ARP mapping done already for that MAC. In this case, we will be switching in the processor by making ARP lookup to find the next-hop MAC address.

3. Control-Plane Cef Exception Sub-Interface
   Packet that causes an exception in CEF switching ends up at this interface. Example of this kind of traffic is non-IP traffic destined to router itself, CDP, OSPF updates, and ARP packets.

How Control Plane Protection Works And How Is Configured

There are 2 ways of doing this. We can apply separate rate-limiting policy to any of the sub-interfaces or apply one aggregate policy for all sub-interfaces, knows as classic control plane policing. Using both the sub-interface and aggregate policy is possible but can be unstable on some IOS versions thus is not recommended. In our configuration example below we will configure separate rate-limiting policy to each of the sub-interfaces.

Before packets reach one of specific control plane sub-interfaces, they are processed with more different ingress features. Packets are going through input access-list, URP checks and aggregate control-plane policy if one is enabled. After this, packets are forwarded to sub-interface-specific policy; the packets are then queued onto the respective interface input queue and handled via selective packet discard policy.

Configuration Example

Here is the example of Control Plane Protection. We will just put the example here and the explanation, bullet by bullet at the bottom.

The class-map type port-filter is cool. It allows matching some of the ports (like 2323 and 2424 in our example). The best part is that you are able to match all closed ports on the router dynamically and drop packets destined to non-listening ports before the router process them and responds with ICMP unreachable or TCP RST packet.

In the first part of the example above, we are blocking all closed ports except TCP 2323 and 2424.

```
class-map type port-filter match-all CLOSED_PORTS
  match closed-ports
  match not port tcp 2323
  match not port tcp 2424


policy-map type port-filter HOST_PORT_FILTER
  class CLOSED_PORTS
    drop
```

In the next part, we matching ICMP traffic and limiting that traffic going toward the host sub-interface, which means to the Route Processor.

```
ip access-list extended ICMP
  permit icmp any any
```

```
class-map ICMP
  match access-group name ICMP
policy-map ICMP_RATE_LIMIT
  class ICMP
    police rate 10 pps burst 5 packets
```

Next example is checking transit fragmented traffic matched with an access-list. Fragmented transit traffic will be limited to 1000000 packet per second rate on the transit sub-interface with some burst.

```
ip access-list extended FRAGMENTS
  permit ip any any fragment

class-map FRAGMENTS
  match access-group name FRAGMENTS

policy-map TRANSIT_RATE_LIMIT
  class FRAGMENTS
    police rate 1000000 pps burst 200000 packets
```

At the end of the example, all other packets resulting in CEF exceptions are limited to 400 packets per second.

```
policy-map CEF_EXCEPTION_RATE_LIMIT
  class class-default
    police rate 400 pps burst 20 packets
```

In the last few lines, we are applying service policies to all three sub-interfaces. With this step, we are actually applying the Control Plane Protection.

```
control-plane host
  service-policy input ICMP_RATE_LIMIT
  service-policy type port-filter input HOST_PORT_FILTER


control-plane transit
```

```
service-policy input TRANSIT_RATE_LIMIT

control-plane cef-exception

service-policy input CEF_EXCEPTION_RATE_LIMIT
```

What Is IPsec?

Internet Protocol security (IPsec) is a framework of open standards for helping to ensure private, secure communications over Internet Protocol (IP) networks with cryptographic security services. IPsec provide supports for network-level data integrity, data confidentiality, data origin authentication, and replay protection. Because IPsec is integrated at the Internet layer (layer 3), it provides security for almost all protocols in the TCP/IP suite, and because IPsec is applied transparently to applications, there is no need to configure separate security for each application that uses TCP/IP.

IPsec helps provide defense-in-depth against:

Network-based attacks from untrusted computers, attacks that can result in the denial-of-service of applications, services, or the network

- Data corruption
- Data theft
- User-credential theft
- Administrative control of servers, other computers, and the network.

You can use IPsec to defend against network-based attacks through a combination of host-based IPsec packet filtering and the enforcement of trusted communications.

IPsec is integrated with the Windows Server 2003 operating system and it can use the Active Directory directory service as a trust model. You can use Group Policy to configure Active Directory domains, sites, and organizational units (OUs), and then assign IPsec policies as required to Group Policy objects (GPOs). In this way, IPsec policies can be implemented to meet the security requirements of many several types of organizations.

RADIUS

RADIUS is an IETF standard for AAA. As with TACACS+, RADIUS follows a client/server model in which the client initiates the requests to the server. RADIUS is the protocol of choice for network access AAA, and it's time to get very familiar with RADIUS. If you connect to a secure wireless network regularly, RADIUS is most likely being used between the wireless device and the AAA server. Why? Because RADIUS is the transport protocol for EAP, along with many other authentication protocols.

Originally, RADIUS was used to extend the authentications from the Layer-2 Point-to-Point Protocol (PPP) used between the end user and the Network Access Server (NAS) and carry that authentication traffic from the NAS to the AAA server performing the authentication. This enabled a Layer-2 authentication protocol to be extended across Layer-3 boundaries to a centralized authentication server.

RADIUS has evolved far beyond just the dial-up networking use cases it was originally created for. Today it is still used in the same way, carrying the authentication traffic from the network device to the authentication server. With IEEE 802.1X, RADIUS is used to extend the Layer-2 EAP from the end user to the authentication server.

Basic AAA Configuration on IOS

Cisco IOS supports minimal password authentication at the console/VTY line and privilege exec boundaries, with static, locally defined passwords. For example:

```
enable secret 5 $1$J19J$Q2jB2AM64H0Uo01nHStLW1
!
no aaa new-model
!
line con 0
 password 7 0532091A0C595D1D3B00351D190900
 login
line vty 0 15
 password 7 152B0419293F38300A36172D010212
 login
```

While easily implemented, this approach is far from ideal for a production network. For much more robust and easily managed authentication schemes, IOS supports the Authentication, Authorization, and Accounting (AAA) model, using the RADIUS or TACACS+ protocols to centralize these functions on dedicated AAA servers.

This section will look at deploying a typical IOS router AAA configuration, which must meet 2 requirements:

- All users logging into the router must authenticate with a username and password to one of two redundant TACACS+ servers.

- Users must be able to log in using a backup local user account stored on the router only if neither TACACS+ server is reachable.

Configuring AAA on IOS for general administrative access entails four basic steps:

1. Enable the "new model" of AAA.
2. Configure the server(s) to be used for AAA (e.g. TACACS+ servers).
3. Define authentication and authorization method lists.
4. Enforce AAA authentication on the relevant lines (e.g. console and VTY lines).

Create a backup user account

```
Router(config)# username BackupAdmin privilege 15 secret MySecretPassword
```

Enabling AAA

```
Router(config)# aaa new-model
```

Configuring the TACACS+ servers

```
Router(config)# tacacs-server host 192.168.1.3 key MySecretKey1
Router(config)# tacacs-server host 192.168.2.3 key MySecretKey2
```

This approach is sufficient for many deployments, but is problematic if you want to reference only a subset of the defined servers for a certain AAA function. For example, suppose you want to use one TACACS+ server for control plane authentication on the router itself, and the second server for authenticating PPP connections. In this case, you would assign the servers to named AAA server groups:

```
Router(config)# aaa group server tacacs+ LoginAuth
Router(config-sg-tacacs+)# server 192.168.1.3
Router(config)# aaa group server tacacs+ PPPAuth
Router(config-sg-tacacs+)# server 192.168.2.3
```

Note that if using server groups, the servers are still defined with tacacs-server in global configuration mode. (Servers can optionally be defined only within a group by using the command private-server under group configuration.)

Define the AAA method lists

```
Router(config)# aaa authentication login default group tacacs+ local
```

This is a rather lengthy command, so let us work through it one bit at a time. aaa authentication login specifies that the following parameters are to be used for user login authentication. The word default is used in lieu of a custom name for the list (you can only define one default list for each AAA function).

The rest of the line specifies authentication methods. group tacacs+ means "use all configured TACACS+ servers." If you defined a named server group in step two, use the name of that group in place of the word tacacs+ here. Local defines a secondary authentication mechanism; it instructs the router to fail over to locally defined user accounts if none of the authentication servers in the first method is reachable. (Note that this only happens if the servers are unreachable, a response from a server-denying authentication will not trigger a fail-over to local authentication.)

The above method list handles only the authentication aspect of AAA. By itself, this list only allows us to authenticate as a user with privilege level 1 (user exec mode). To communicate a heightened privilege level (e.g. privilege level 15, or "enable mode") from the TACACS+ server, we also need to define an authorization method list for IOS shell creation.

```
Router(config)# aaa authorization exec default group tacacs+ local
```

This last step has actually been done for us already by enabling AAA in step one. However, if we were to create a custom authentication method list for these lines, we would use the command below, substituting the method list name for the word default.

```
Router(config)# line console 0
Router(config-line)# login authentication default
Router(config)# line vty 0 15
Router(config-line)# login authentication default
```

These commands will not appear in the running configuration if the default method list is specified.

At this point, we should have a fully functional AAA configuration for console authentication and authorization.

```
ipspeciaist@KHI ~ $ telnet 192.168.1.132
Trying 192.168.1.132...
Connected to 192.168.1.132.
Escape character is '^]'.
```

> Username: ipspecialist
>
> Password:

The completed AAA configuration is included below.

```
aaa new-model
!
aaa authentication login default group tacacs+ local
aaa authorization exec default group tacacs+ local
!
username BackupAdmin privilege 15 secret 5 $1$qLGb$VQ6BdqCEpzGZqPeC779Uh1
!
tacacs-server host 192.168.1.3 key 7 062B1612494D1B1C113C17125D
tacacs-server host 192.168.2.3 key 7 143A0B380907382E3003362C70
```

Lab 11.1: Configuring Administrative Access On A Cisco Router Using TACACS+ And ACS Server

In small office home office (SOHO) environments where a single or few network administrators have complete access of IT infrastructure, the local router database works well for implementing AAA. However, in large enterprises or service provider environments where a large number of network engineering team configure and provide support for overall network design, it becomes tedious to define a local database for Authentication, Authorization and Accounting purposes on every single device. In such scenarios, Cisco proprietary servers like ACS/ISE comes into play. By using centralized server for AAA, and every device being configured to verify any request by contacting ACS/ISE, the administration process becomes quite easy.

The following topology will be used in this lab.

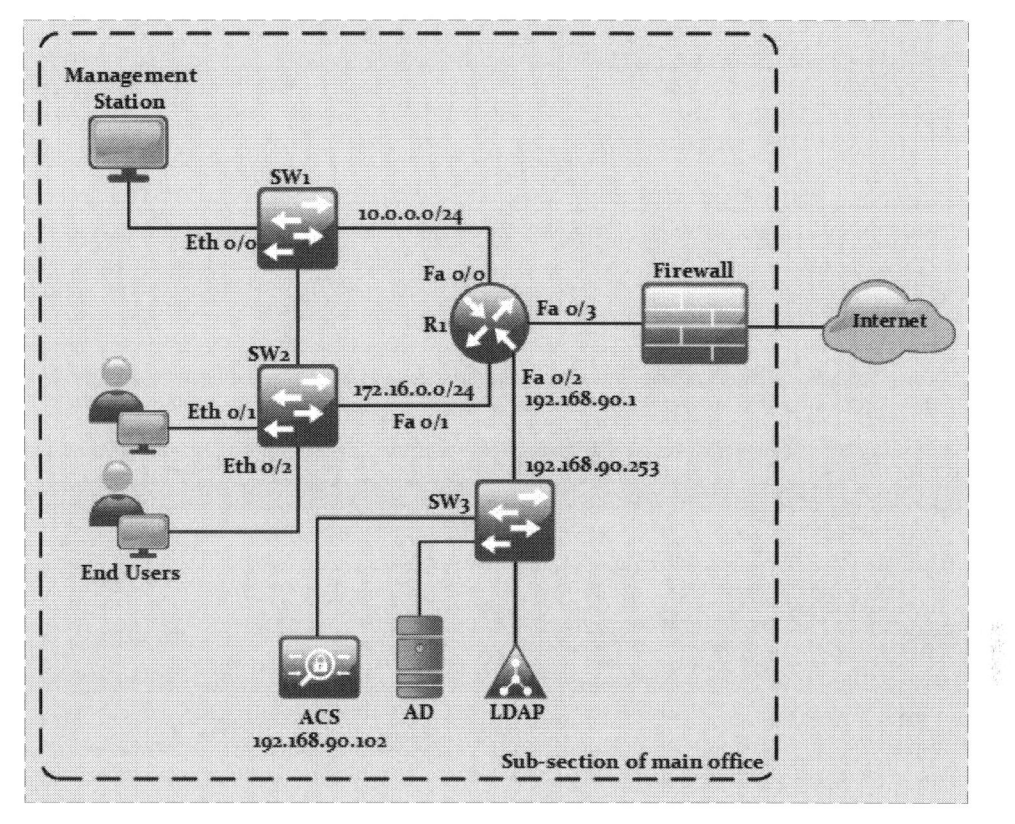

Figure 77 Topology Diagram

In the first part, different user accounts with different privilege levels will be defined on ACS server followed by their configuration and verification on R1 which can be further extended to Switches SW1, SW2 and SW3.

ACS:

! By accessing the management IP address of ACS which is 192.168.90.102, a certificate
! trust alert may appear which can be ignored, the following screen would appear.

https://192.168.90.102/acsadmin

! Use the following credentials for login

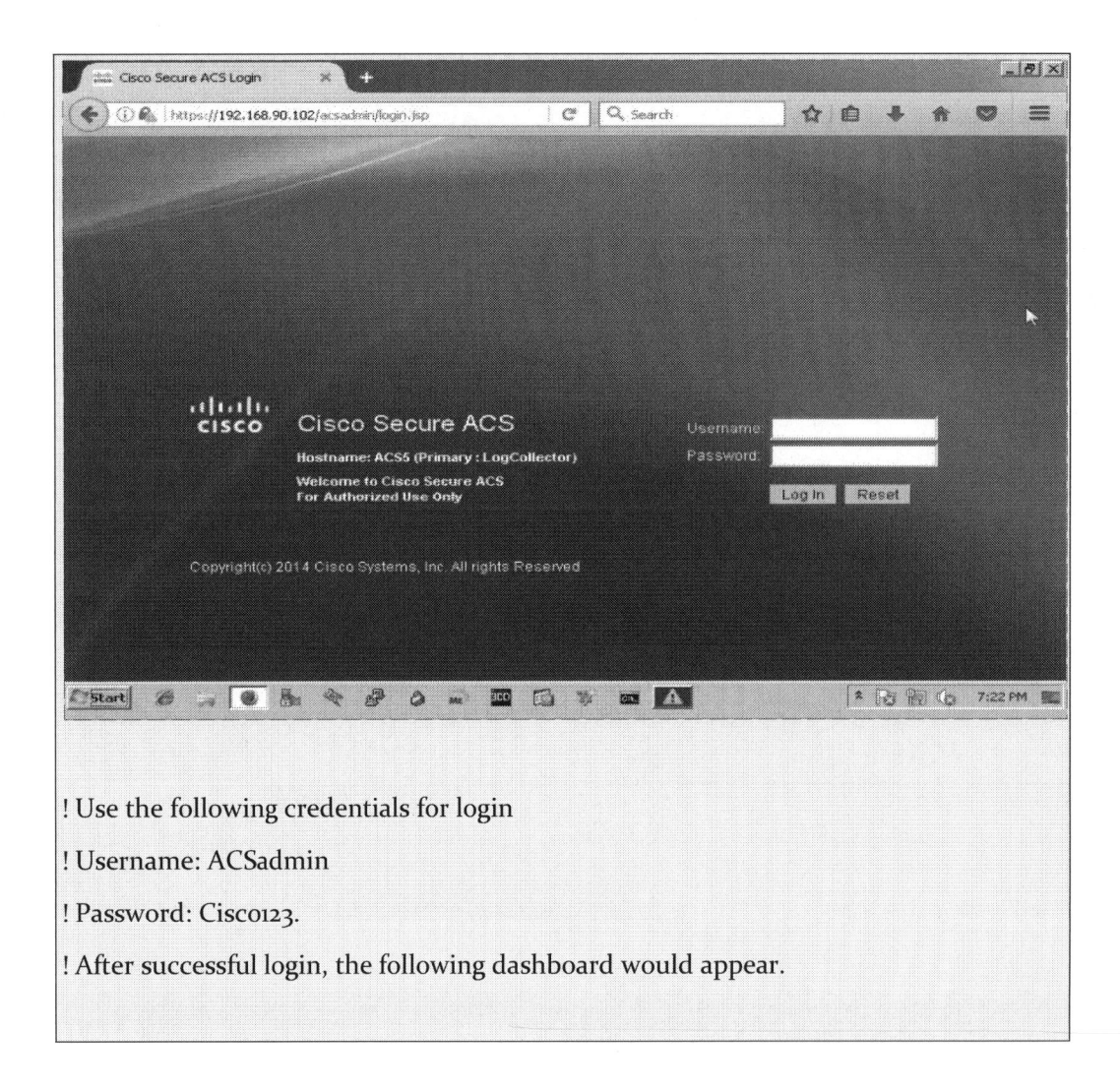

! Username: ACSadmin

! Password: Cisco123.

! After successful login, the following dashboard would appear.

Username1: IPSpecialist

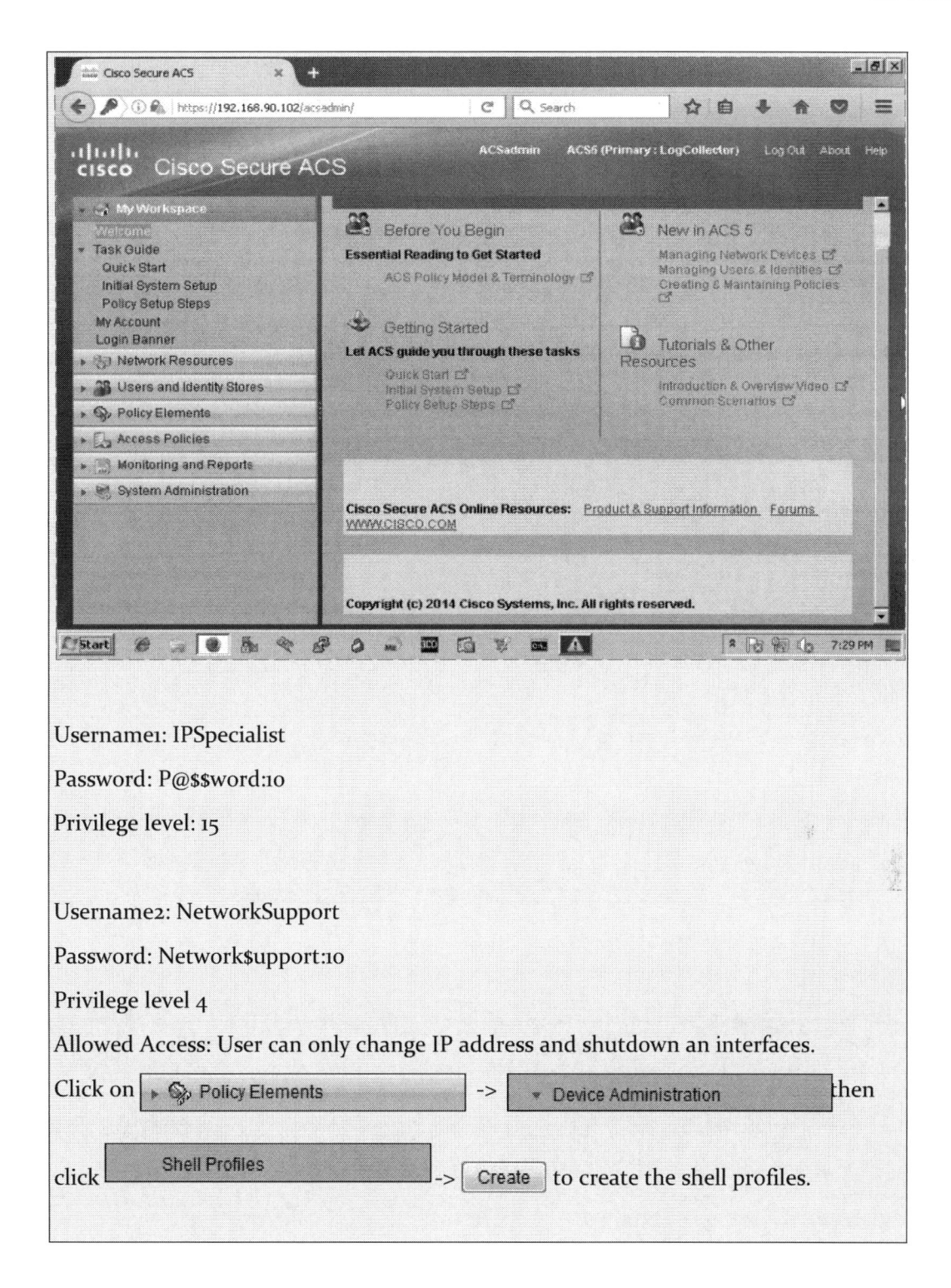

Password: P@$$word:10

Privilege level: 15

Username2: NetworkSupport

Password: Network$upport:10

Privilege level 4

Allowed Access: User can only change IP address and shutdown an interfaces.

Click on [Policy Elements] -> [Device Administration] then click [Shell Profiles] -> [Create] to create the shell profiles.

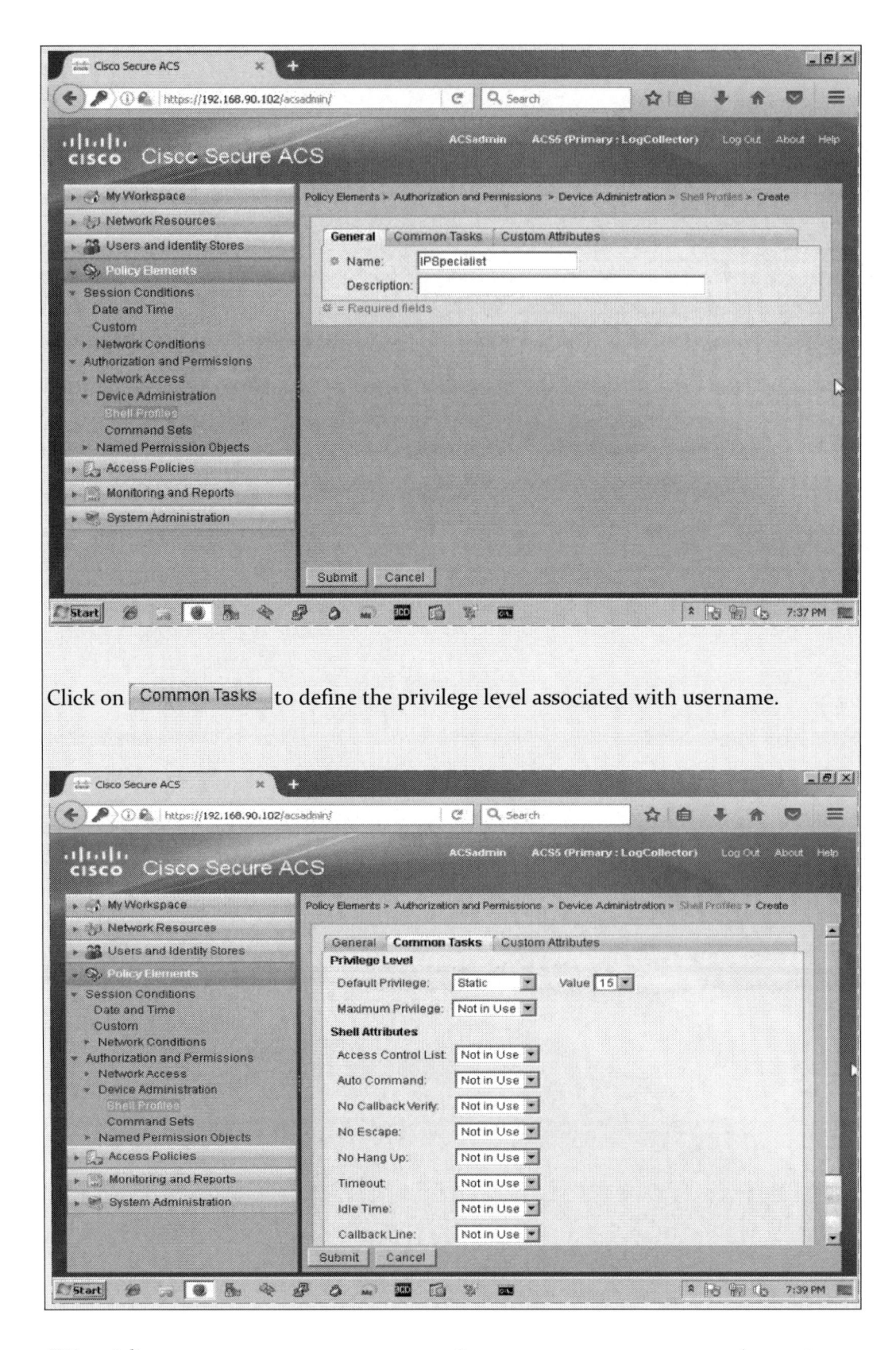

Click on **Common Tasks** to define the privilege level associated with username.

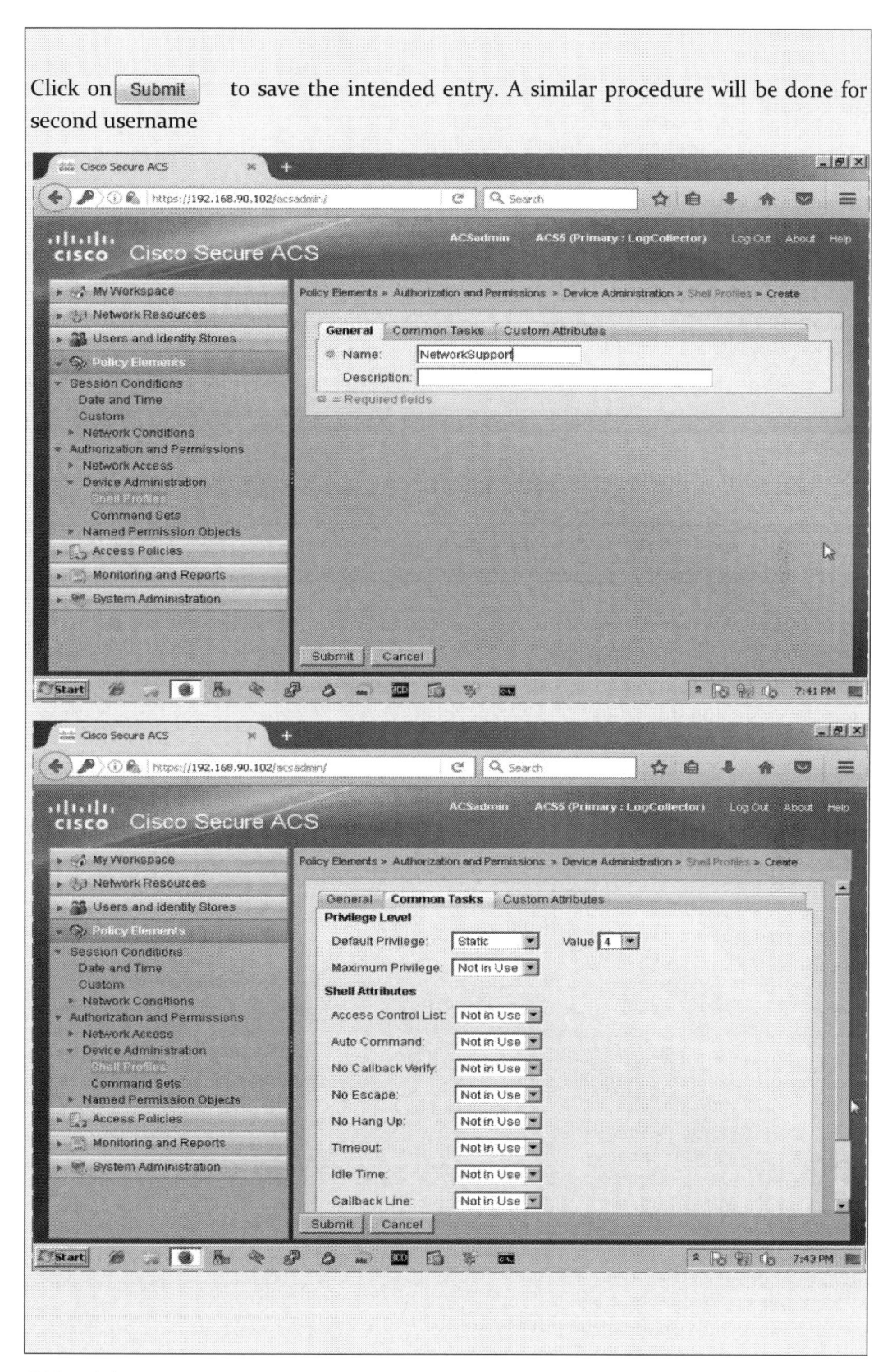

Click on [Submit] to save the intended entry. A similar procedure will be done for second username

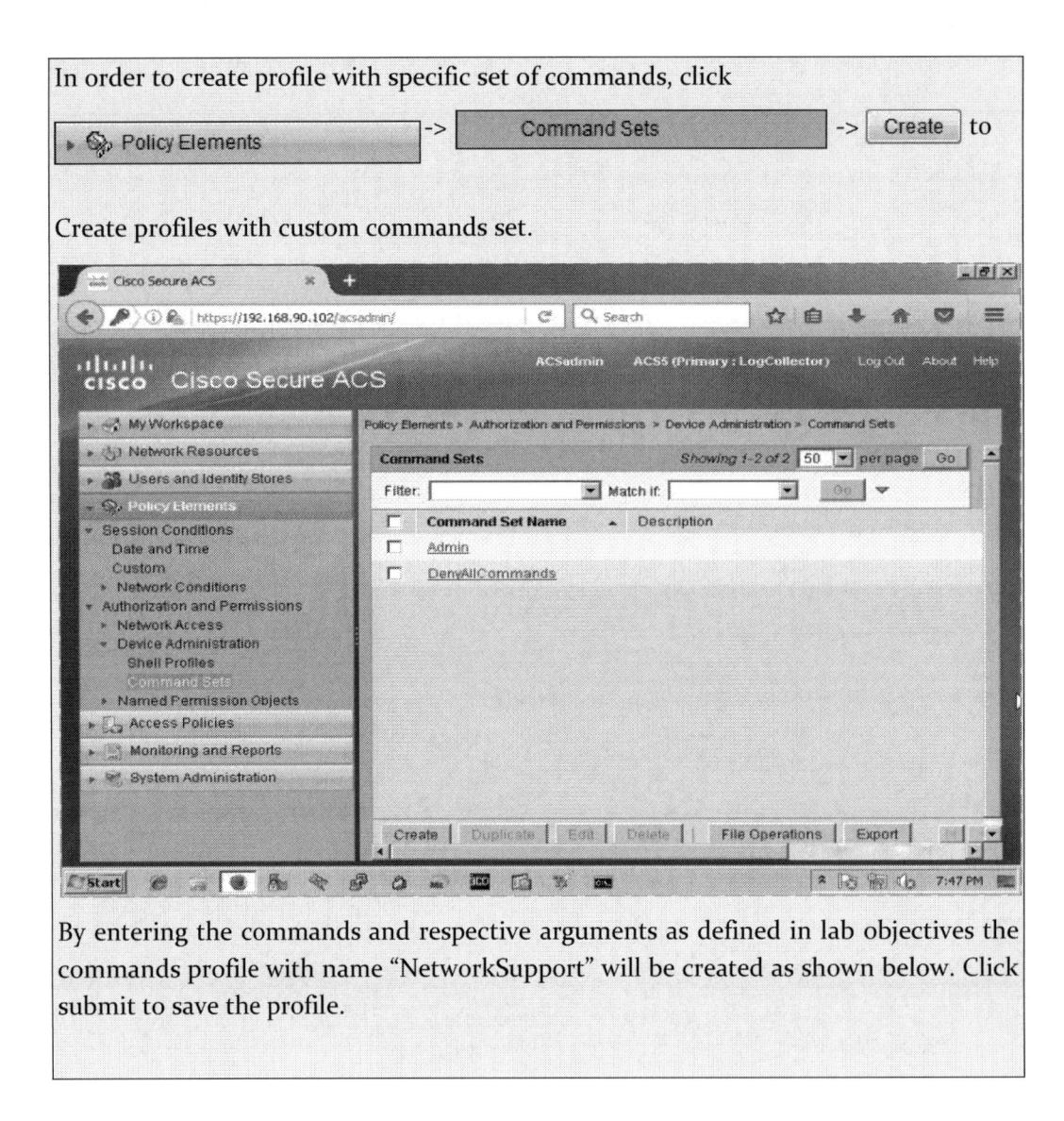

In order to create profile with specific set of commands, click **Policy Elements** -> **Command Sets** -> **Create** to Create profiles with custom commands set.

By entering the commands and respective arguments as defined in lab objectives the commands profile with name "NetworkSupport" will be created as shown below. Click submit to save the profile.

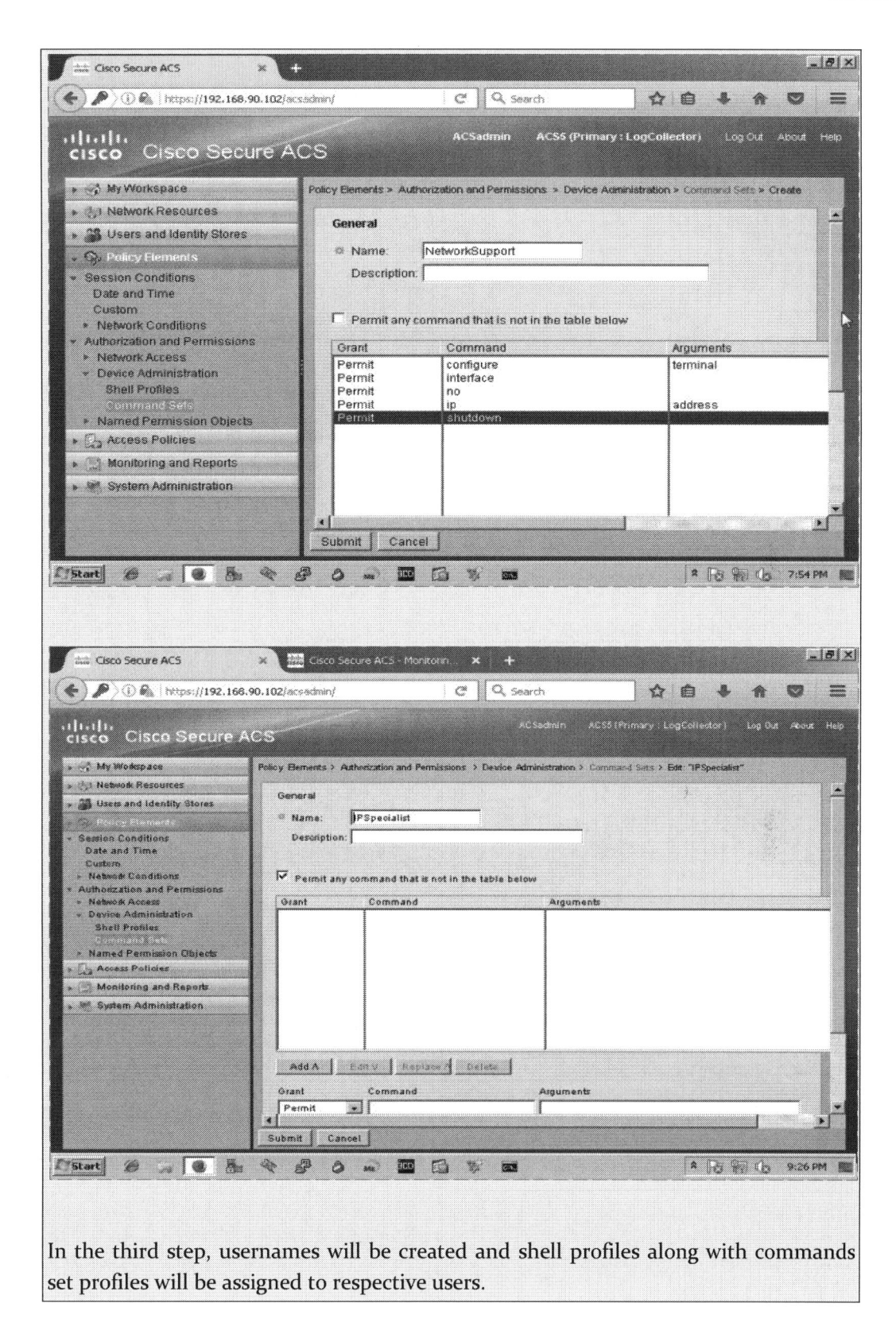

In the third step, usernames will be created and shell profiles along with commands set profiles will be assigned to respective users.

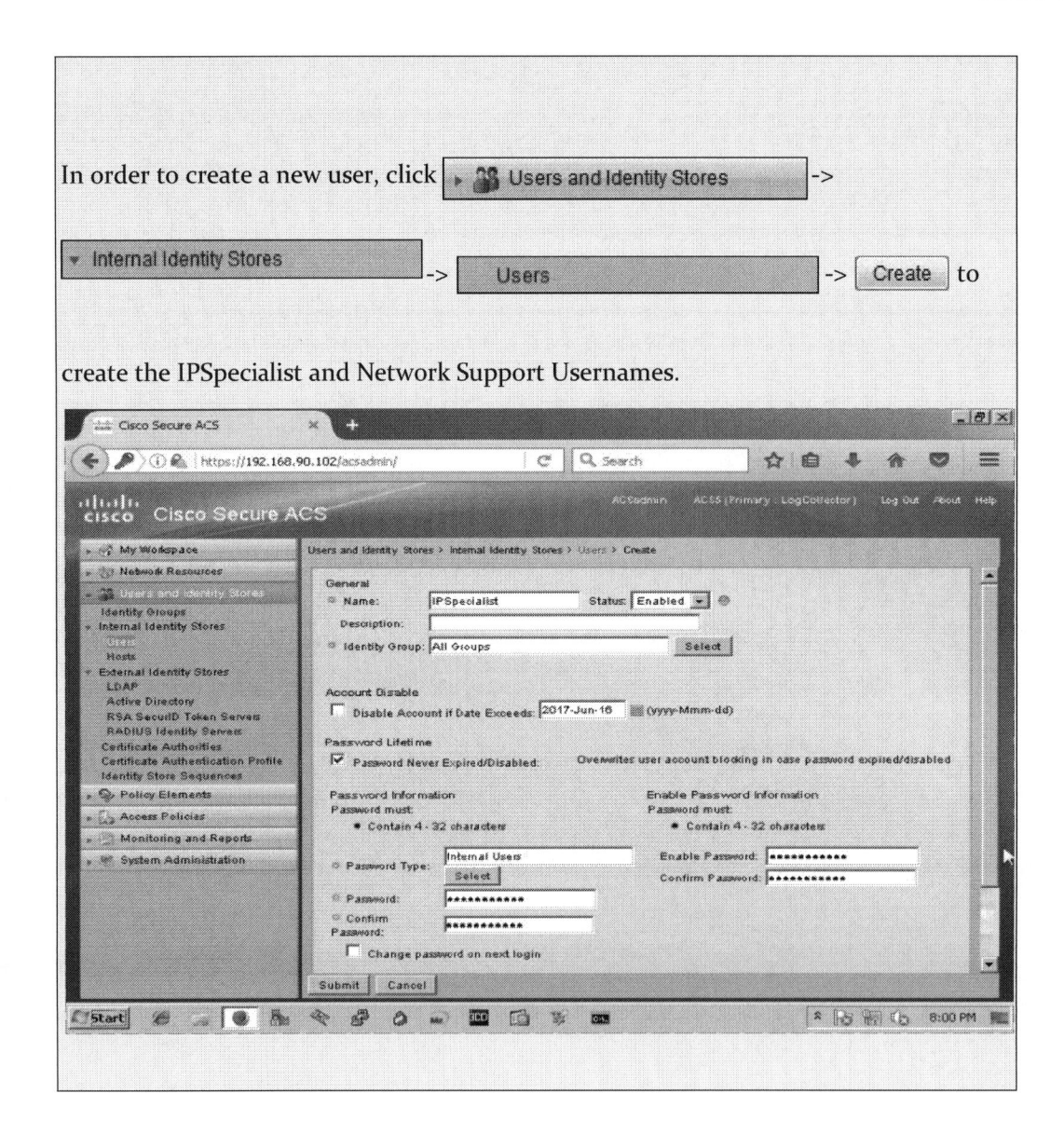

In order to create a new user, click **Users and Identity Stores** -> **Internal Identity Stores** -> **Users** -> **Create** to create the IPSpecialist and Network Support Usernames.

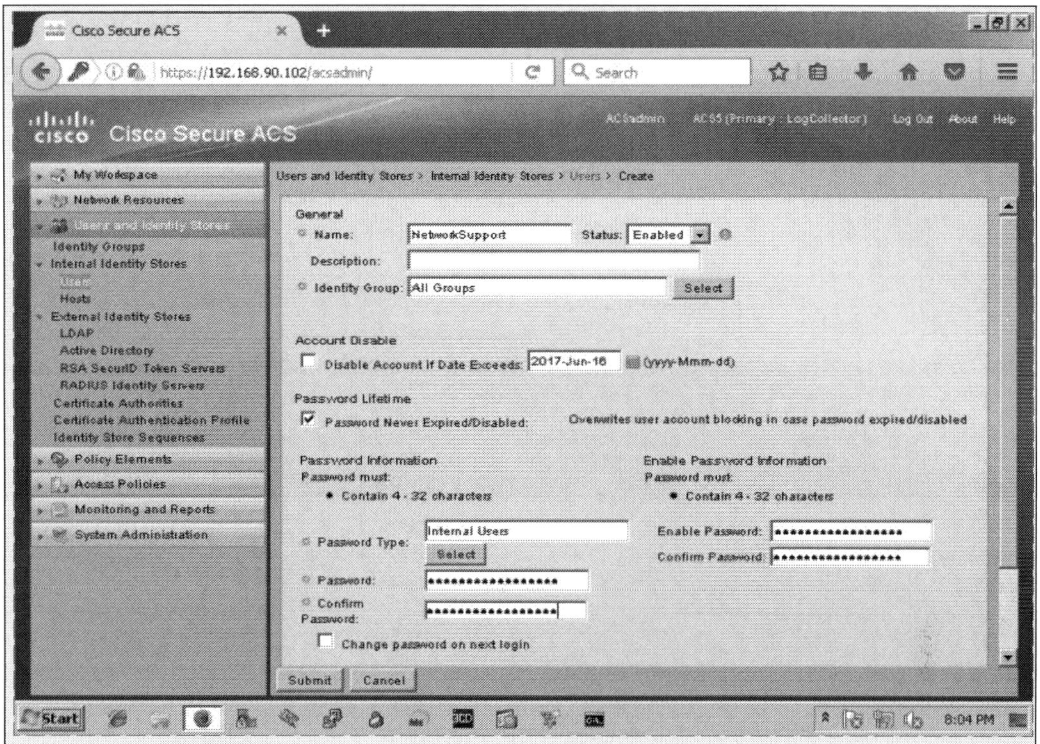

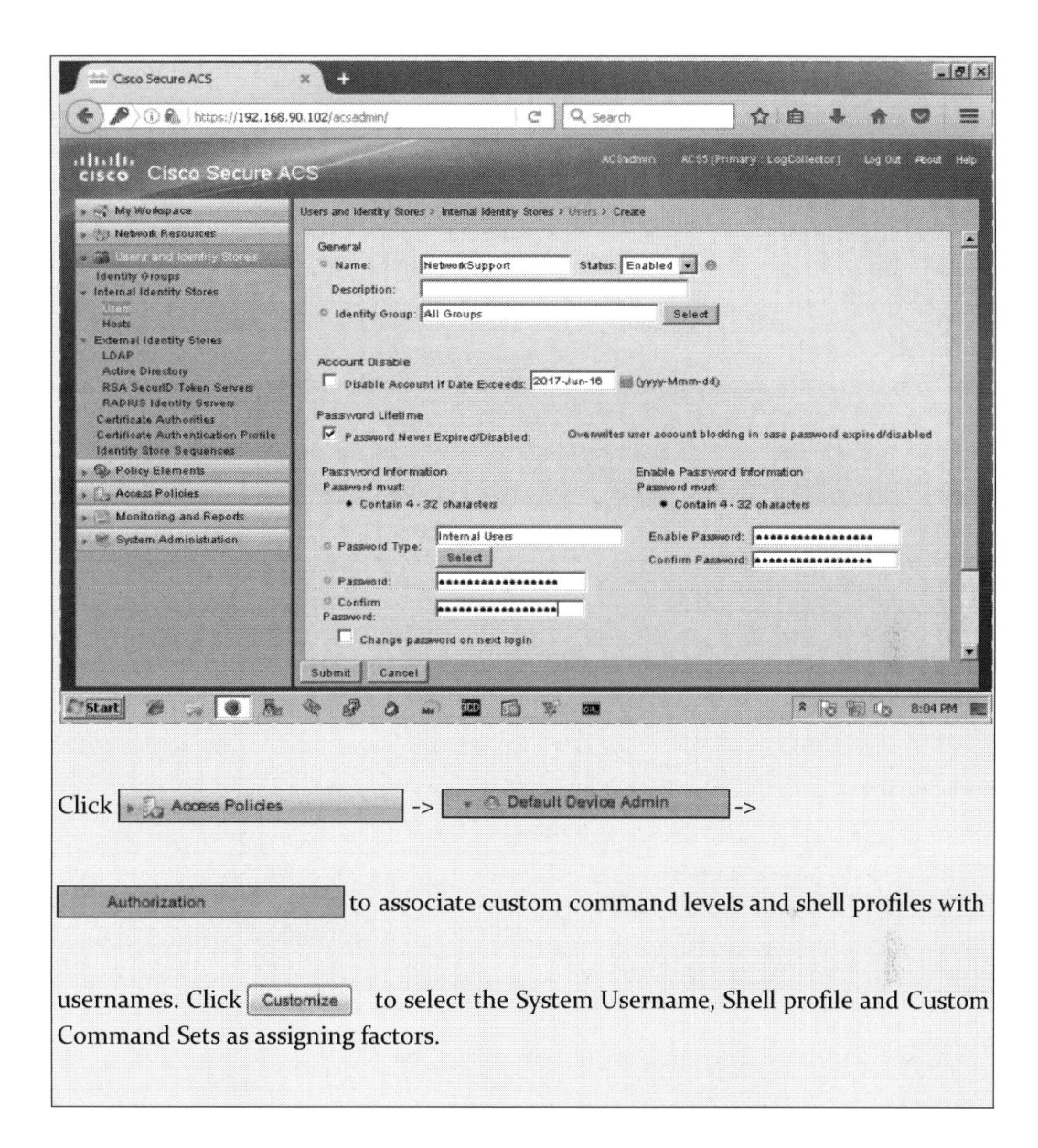

Click Access Policies -> Default Device Admin ->

Authorization to associate custom command levels and shell profiles with usernames. Click Customize to select the System Username, Shell profile and Custom Command Sets as assigning factors.

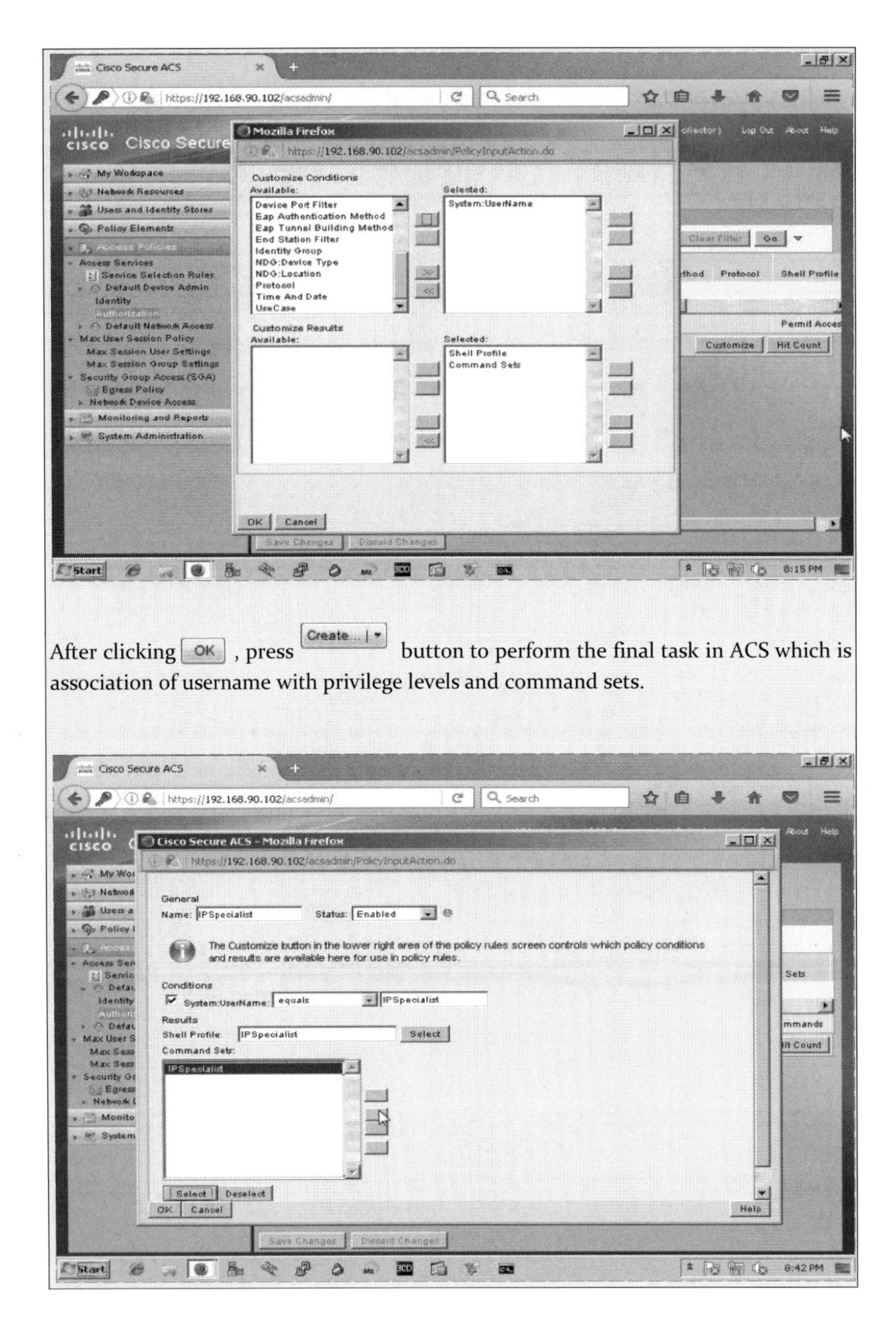

After clicking `OK`, press `Create..|▼` button to perform the final task in ACS which is association of username with privilege levels and command sets.

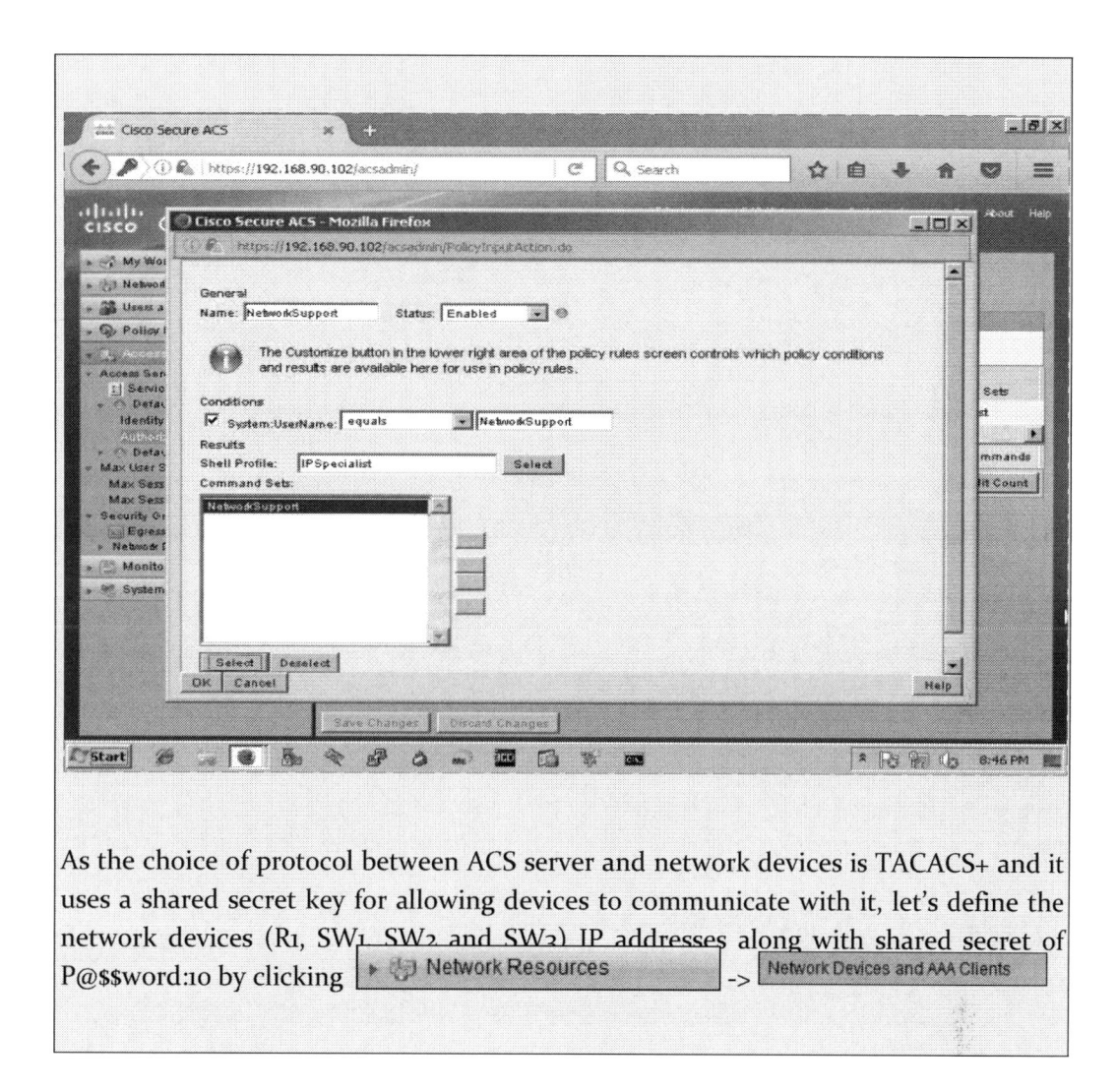

As the choice of protocol between ACS server and network devices is TACACS+ and it uses a shared secret key for allowing devices to communicate with it, let's define the network devices (R1, SW1, SW2 and SW3) IP addresses along with shared secret of P@$$word:10 by clicking Network Resources -> Network Devices and AAA Clients

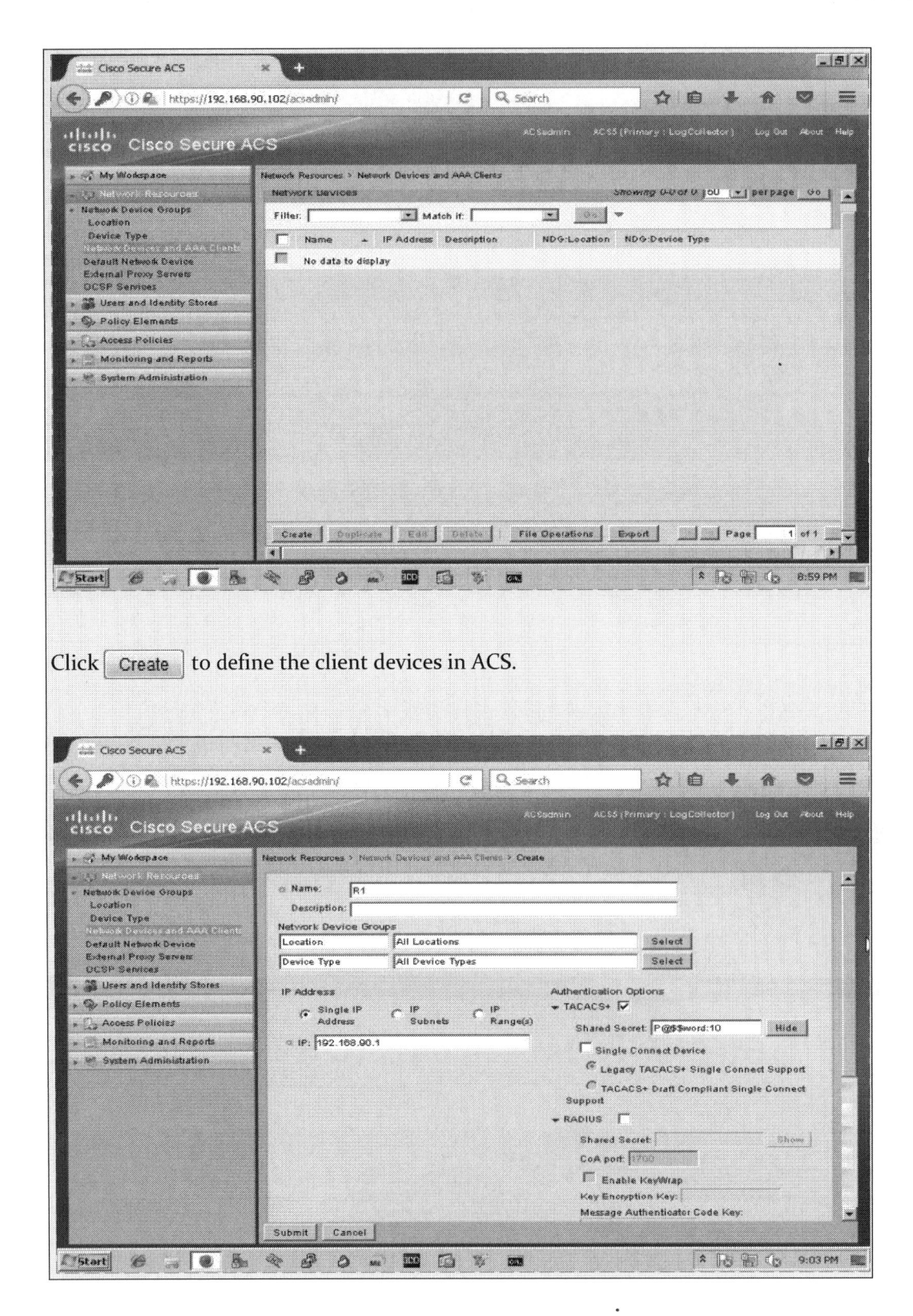

Click [Create] to define the client devices in ACS.

Similarly Switches SW1, SW2 and SW3 management IP address will be defined here.

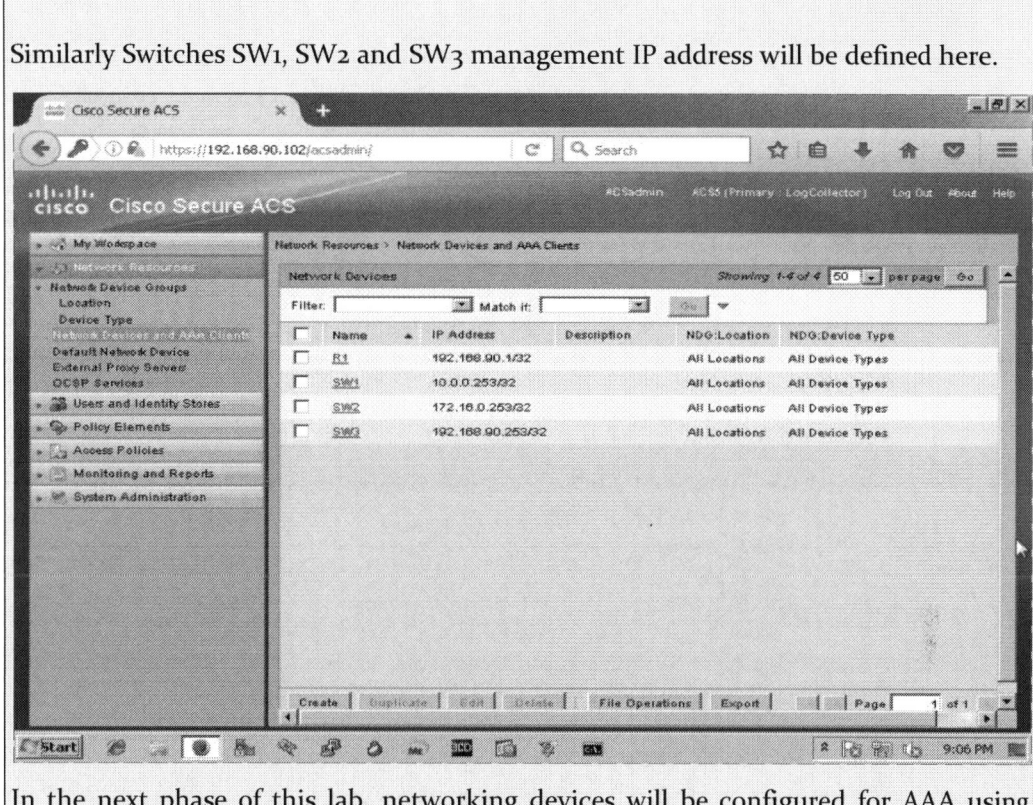

In the next phase of this lab, networking devices will be configured for AAA using TACACS+ protocol, followed by the verification section.

R1

R1(config)#aaa new-model

R1(config)#tacacs-server host 192.168.90.102

R1(config)#tacacs-server key P@$$word:10

R1(config)#aaa authentication login default group tacacs+ local

R1(config)#aaa authorization config-commands

R1(config)#aaa authorization exec default group tacacs+

R1(config)#aaa authorization commands 4 default group tacacs+

R1(config)#aaa accounting commands 4 default start-stop group tacacs+

Verification

The first thing to perform in verification is to ping the ACS server to make sure the L3 connectivity as show below:

R1#ping 192.168.90.102

Type escape sequence to abort.

Sending 5, 100-byte ICMP Echos to 192.168.90.102, timeout is 2 seconds:

!!!!!

Success rate is 80 percent (4/5), round-trip min/avg/max = 4/9/16 ms

Another important command is **test** command which can be used to verify the protocol level connectivity with ACS by providing the already defined credentials in ACS as shown below

R1# test aaa group tacacs+ IPSpecialist P@$$word:10 legacy

Attempting authentication test to server-group tacacs+ using tacacs+

User was successfully authenticated.

Similarly in ACS, by clicking [Monitoring and Reports] and then by launching the monitoring wizard, different tools can be used within ACS for troubleshooting.

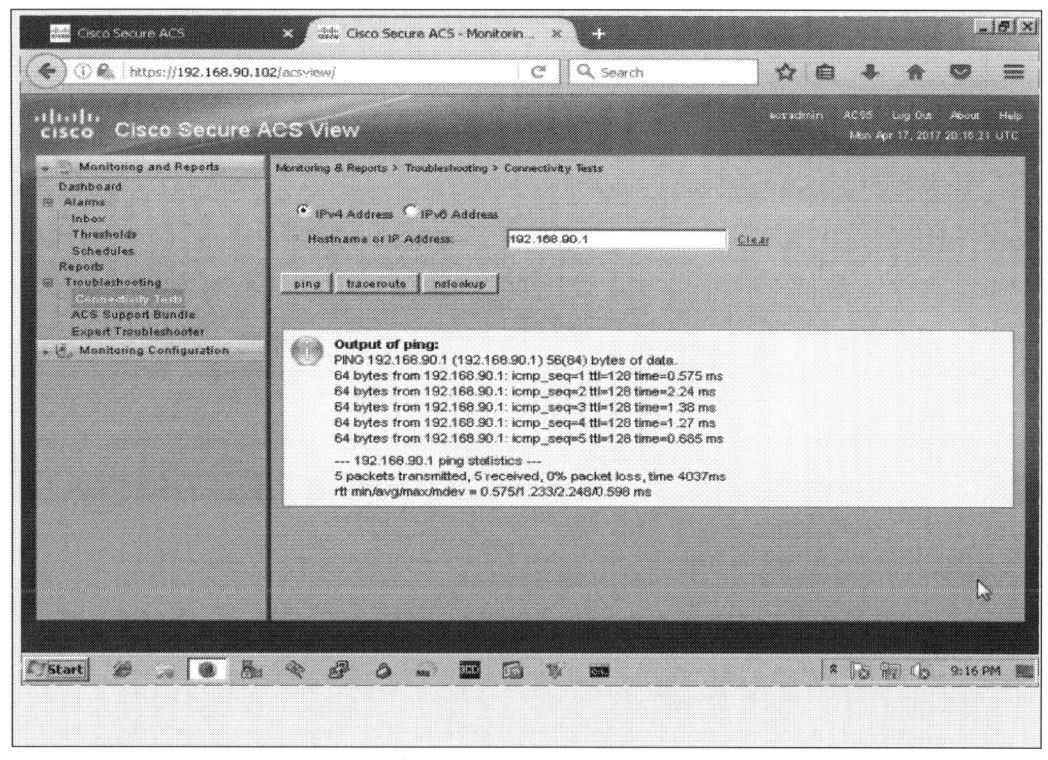

Lab 11.2: Configuring Administrative Access On A Cisco Router Using RADIUS And ISE Server

The main objective of this lab is same as the previous one but ISE will be used in this lab instead of Cisco's ACS server. The choice of protocol between client devices and ISE will be RADIUS.

Two users will be created with respective access limitations defined below:

> Username1: IPSpecialist
>
> Password: P@$$word:10
>
> Privilege level: 15
>
> Username2: ITHelpdesk
>
> Password: P@$$word:20
>
> Privilege level 4

The following topology will be used in this lab.

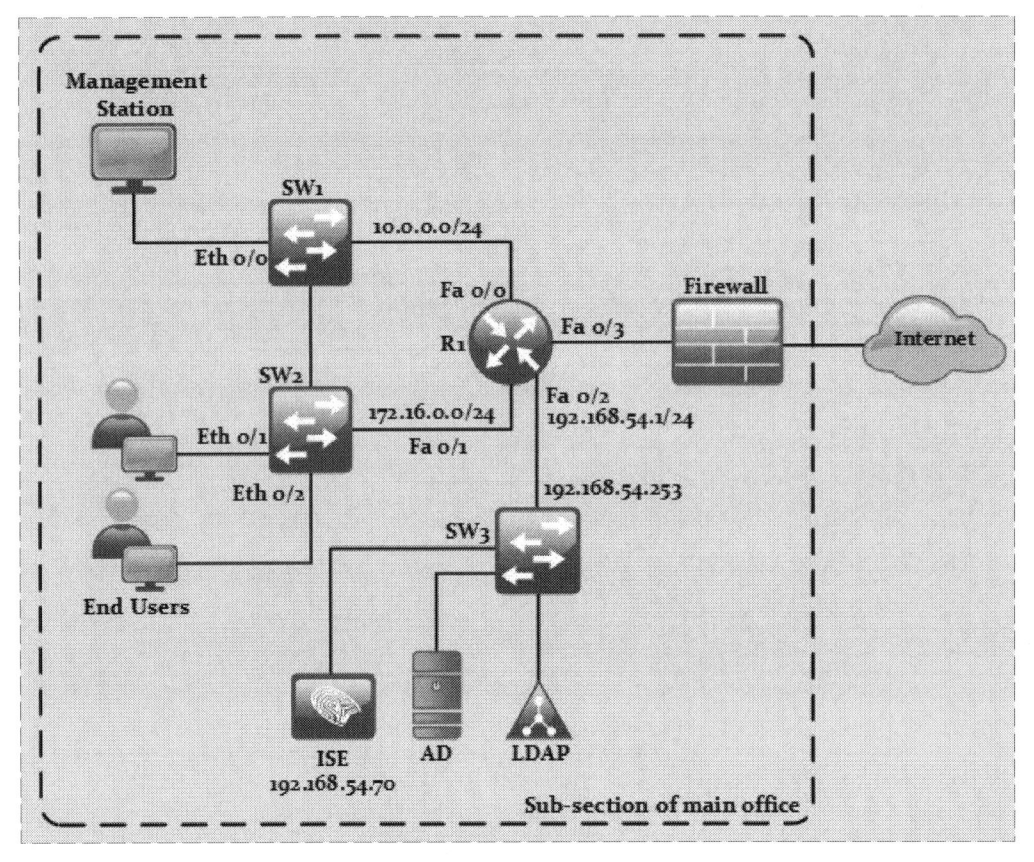

Figure 78 Topology Diagram

ISE
!By accessing the management IP address of ISE which is 192.168.54.70, a certificate trust !alert may appear which can be ignored, the following screen would appear.

! Use the following credentials for login

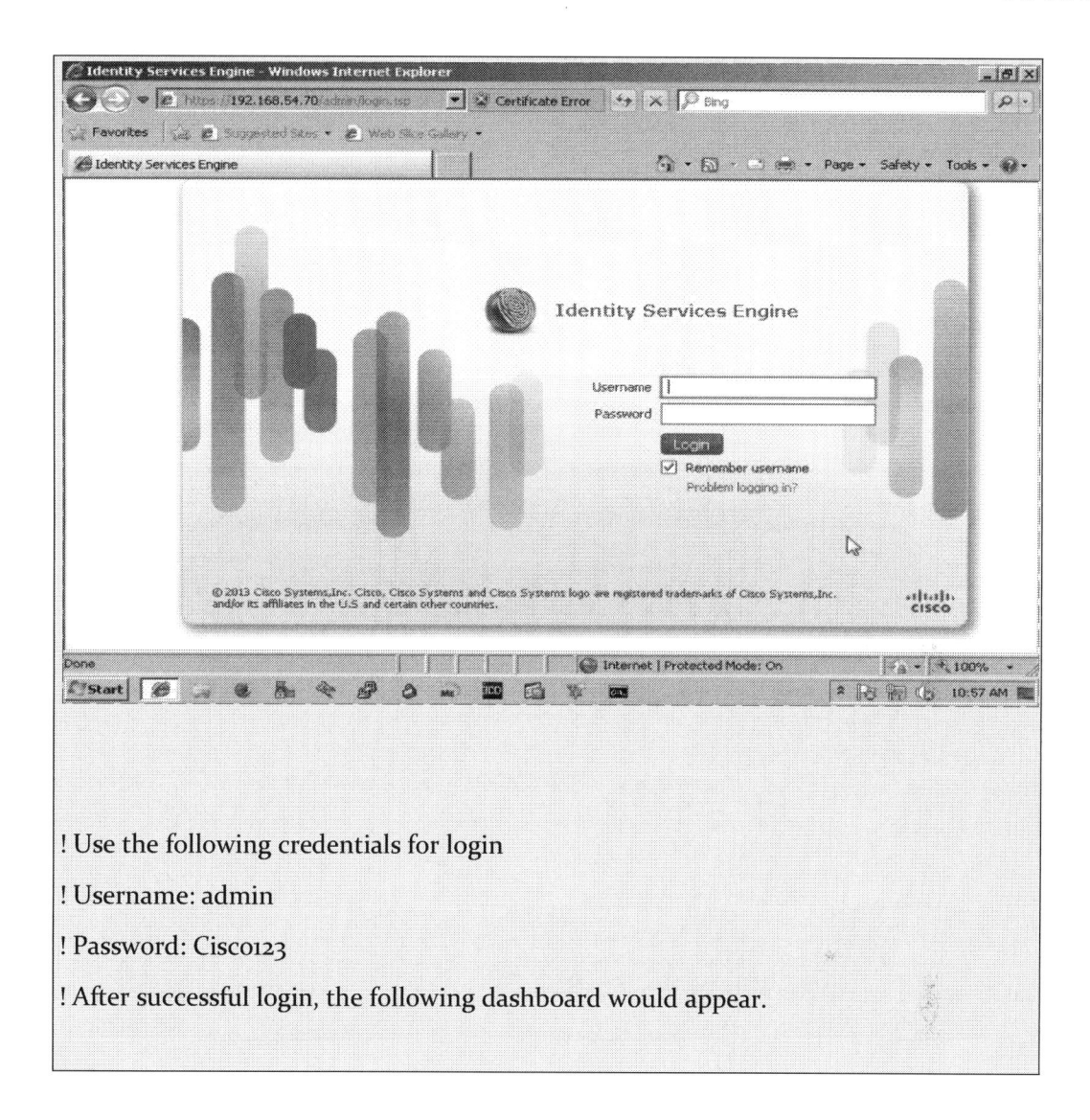

! Username: admin

! Password: Cisco123

! After successful login, the following dashboard would appear.

! In order to register RADIUS clients in ISE, click `Administration` -> `Network Resources`

! then click `Network Devices`. Click `+ Add` button to actually add new clients. The

! following screen would appear.

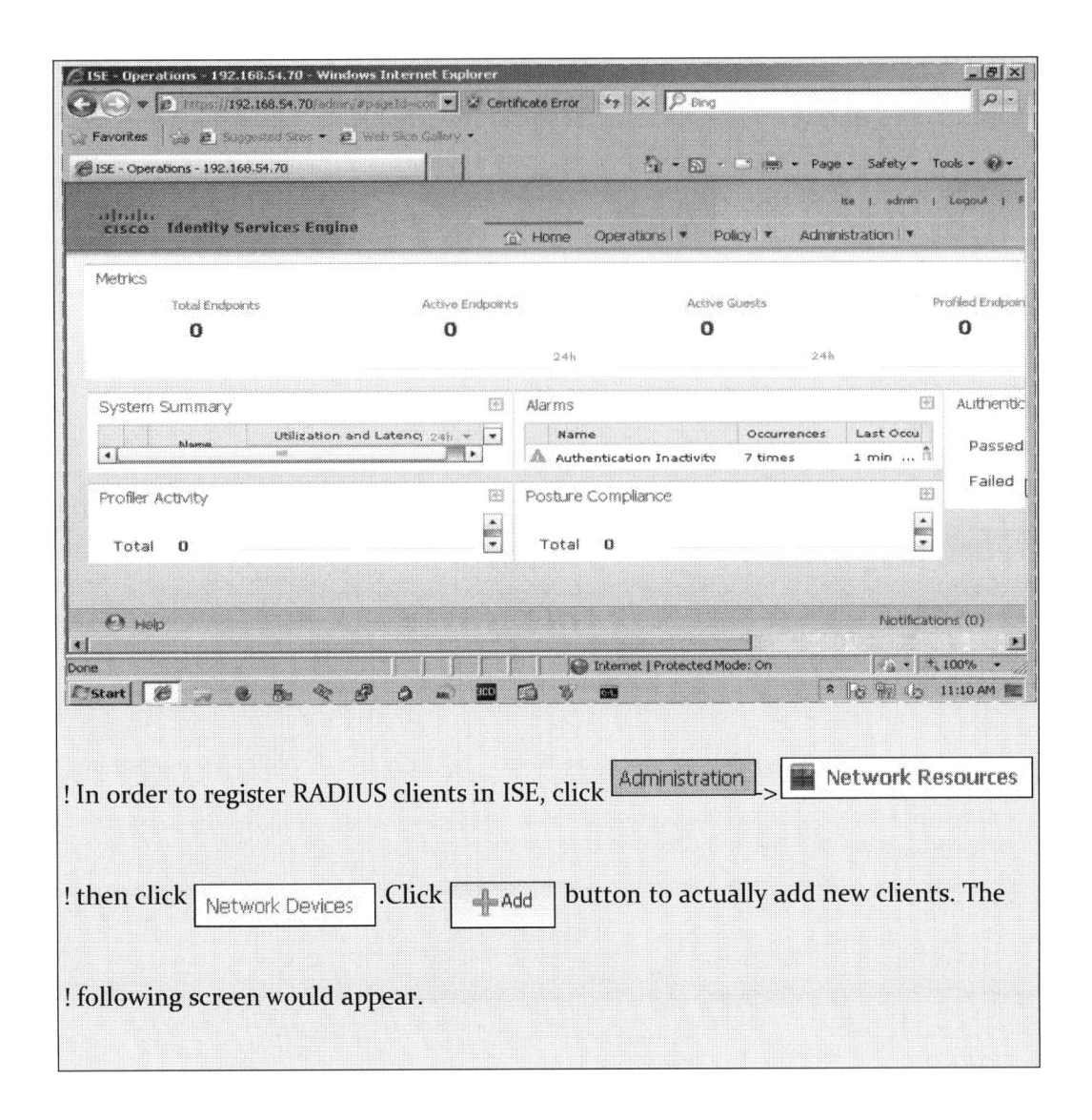

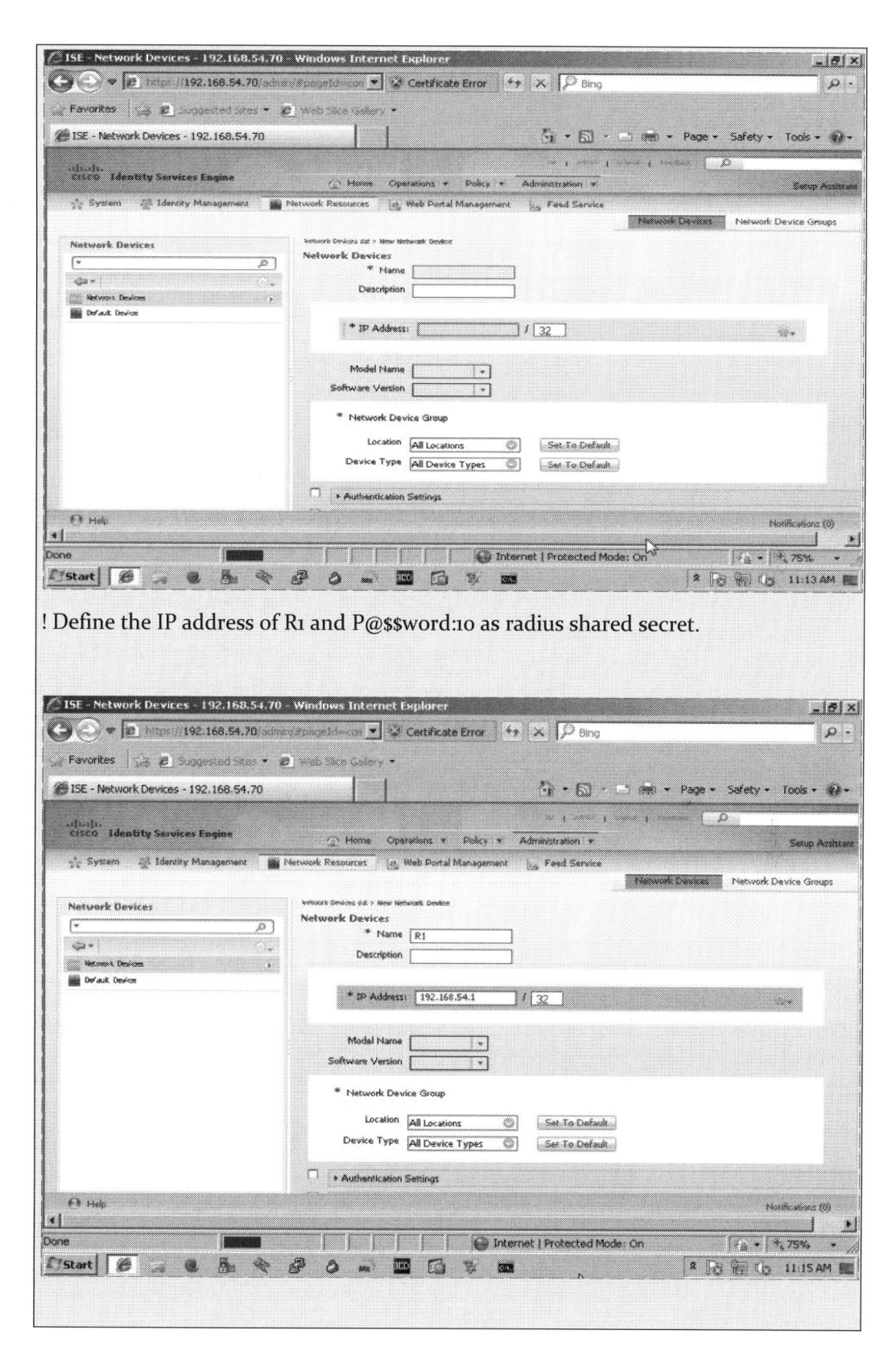

! Define the IP address of R1 and P@$$word:10 as radius shared secret.

! Click **Submit** to save the entry.

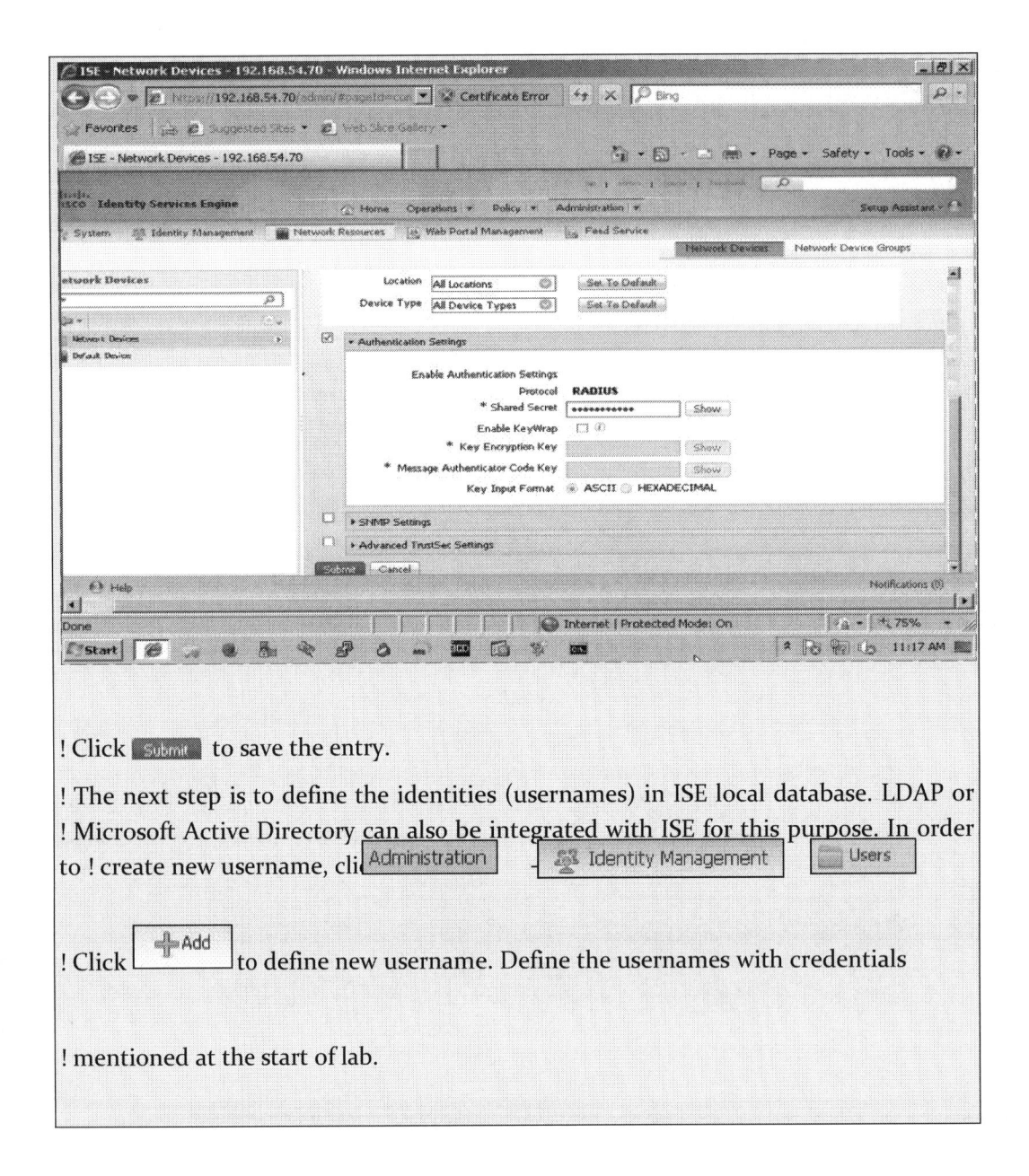

! The next step is to define the identities (usernames) in ISE local database. LDAP or
! Microsoft Active Directory can also be integrated with ISE for this purpose. In order
to ! create new username, click **Administration** » **Identity Management** » **Users**

! Click **Add** to define new username. Define the usernames with credentials

! mentioned at the start of lab.

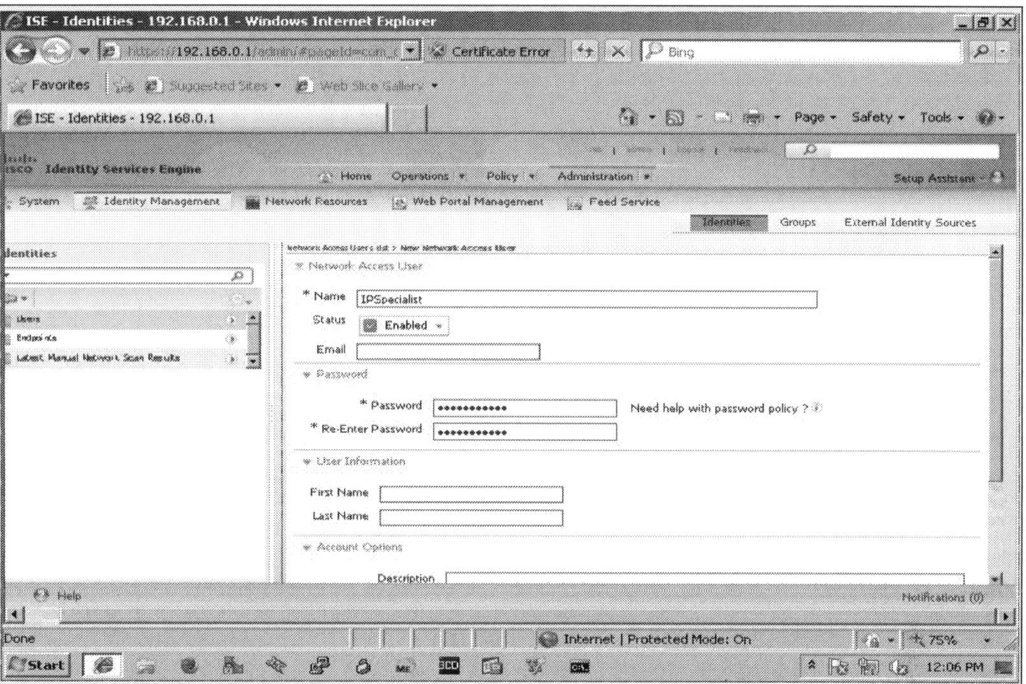
ISE - Identities - 192.168.0.1 - Windows Internet Explorer
https://192.168.0.1/admin/#pageId=com_
Certificate Error
Bing
Favorites
Suggested Sites
Web Slice Gallery
ISE - Identities - 192.168.0.1
Page
Safety
Tools
Identity Services Engine
Home
Operations
Policy
Administration
Setup Assistant
System
Identity Management
Network Resources
Web Portal Management
Feed Service
Identities
Groups
External Identity Sources
Identities
Users
Endpoints
Latest Manual Network Scan Results
Network Access User
* Name
IPSpecialist
Status
Enabled
Email
Password
* Password
Need help with password policy ?
* Re-Enter Password
User Information
First Name
Last Name
Account Options
Description
Help
Notifications (0)
Done
Internet | Protected Mode: On
75%
Start
12:06 PM

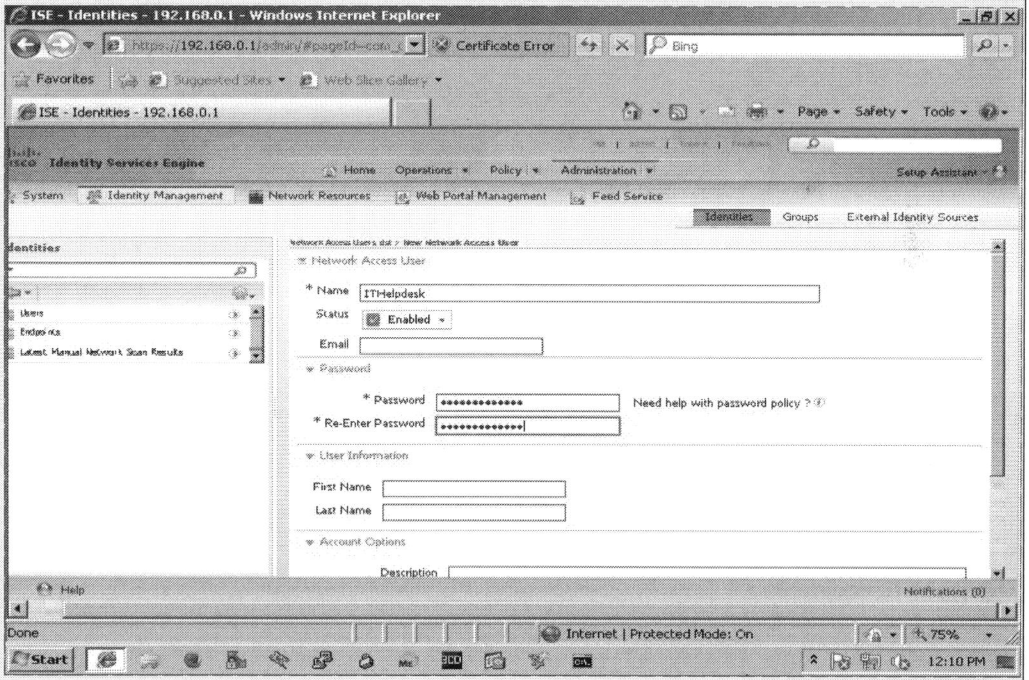
ISE - Identities - 192.168.0.1 - Windows Internet Explorer
https://192.168.0.1/admin/#pageId=com_
Certificate Error
Bing
Favorites
Suggested Sites
Web Slice Gallery
ISE - Identities - 192.168.0.1
Page
Safety
Tools
Identity Services Engine
Home
Operations
Policy
Administration
Setup Assistant
System
Identity Management
Network Resources
Web Portal Management
Feed Service
Identities
Groups
External Identity Sources
Identities
Users
Endpoints
Latest Manual Network Scan Results
Network Access User
* Name
ITHelpdesk
Status
Enabled
Email
Password
* Password
Need help with password policy ?
* Re-Enter Password
User Information
First Name
Last Name
Account Options
Description
Help
Notifications (0)
Done
Internet | Protected Mode: On
75%
Start
12:10 PM

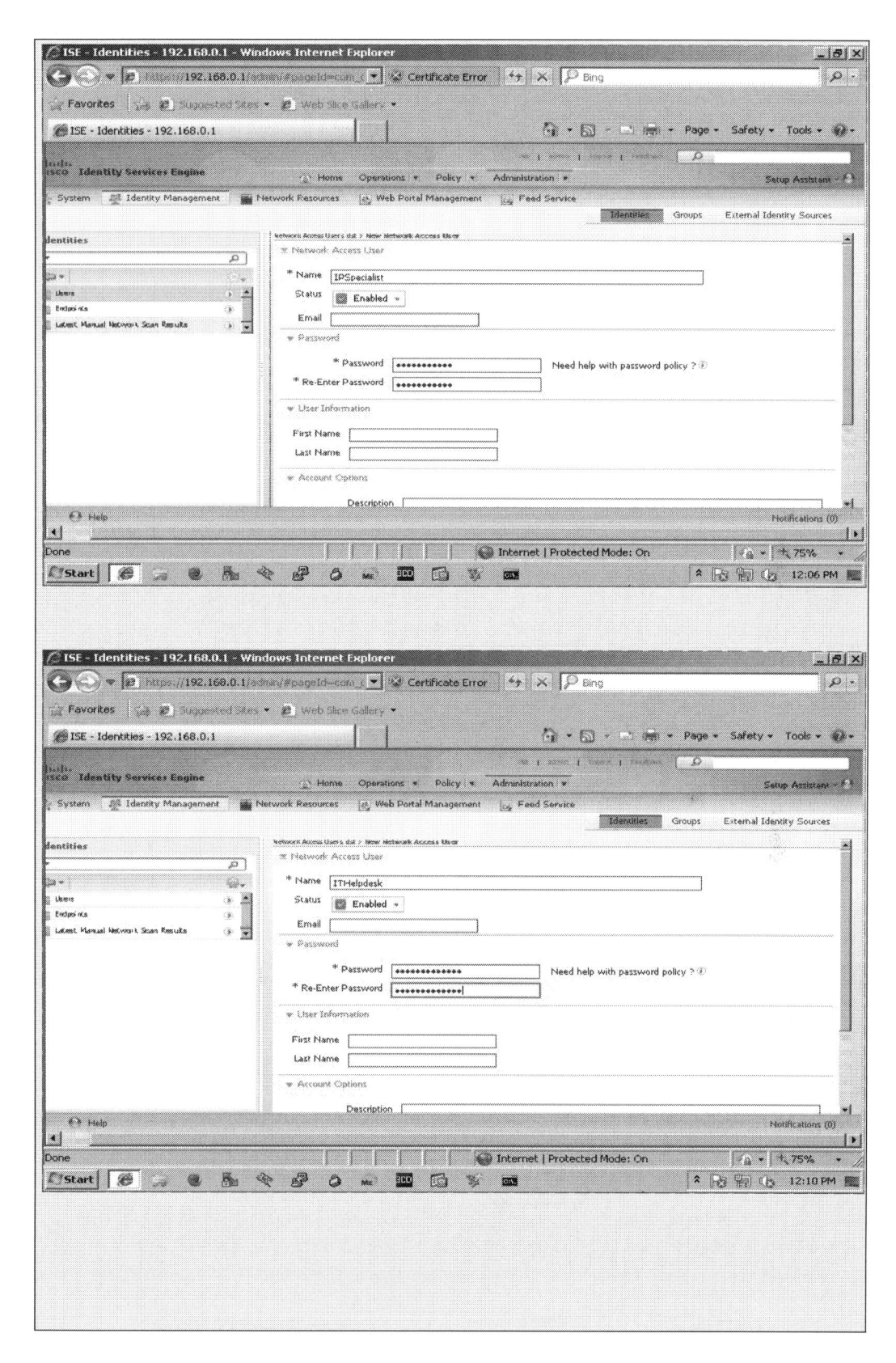

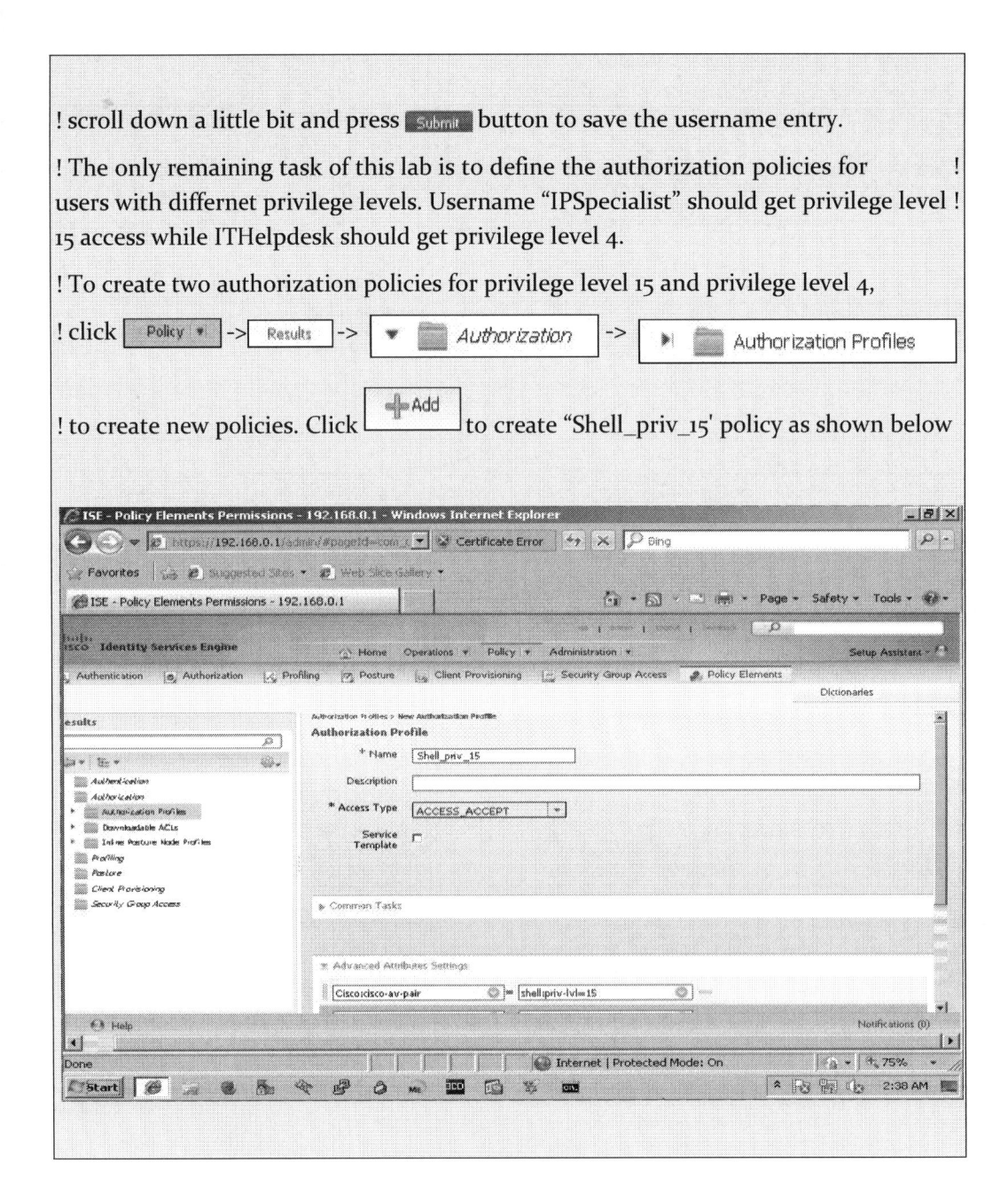

! scroll down a little bit and press [Submit] button to save the username entry.

! The only remaining task of this lab is to define the authorization policies for !
users with differnet privilege levels. Username "IPSpecialist" should get privilege level !
15 access while ITHelpdesk should get privilege level 4.

! To create two authorization policies for privilege level 15 and privilege level 4,

! click [Policy ▼] -> [Results] -> ▼ [Authorization] -> ▶ [Authorization Profiles]

! to create new policies. Click [Add] to create "Shell_priv_15" policy as shown below

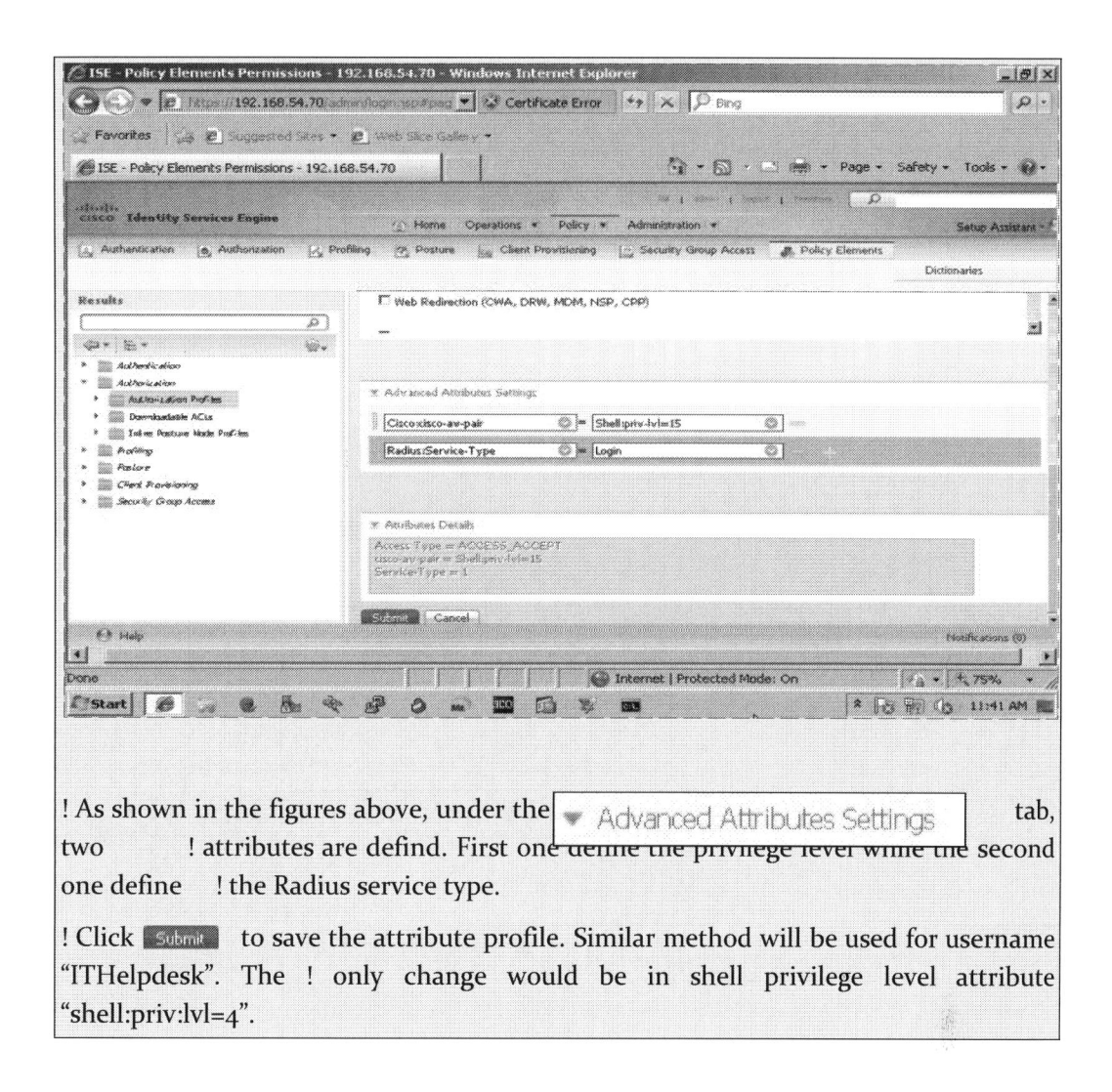

! As shown in the figures above, under the **Advanced Attributes Settings** tab, two ! attributes are defind. First one define the privilege level while the second one define ! the Radius service type.

! Click **Submit** to save the attribute profile. Similar method will be used for username "ITHelpdesk". The ! only change would be in shell privilege level attribute "shell:priv:lvl=4".

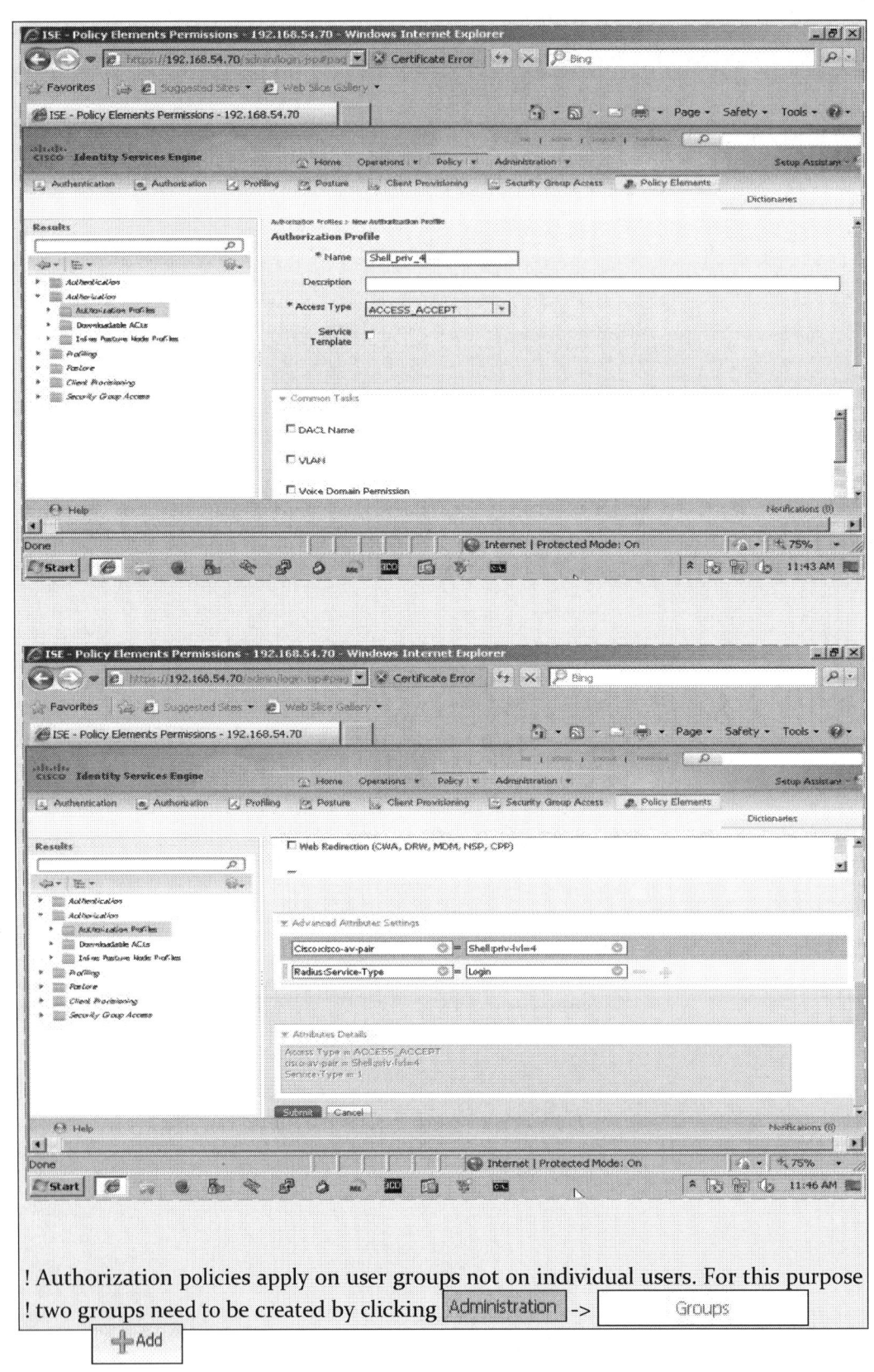

! Authorization policies apply on user groups not on individual users. For this purpose
! two groups need to be created by clicking Administration -> Groups
 Add

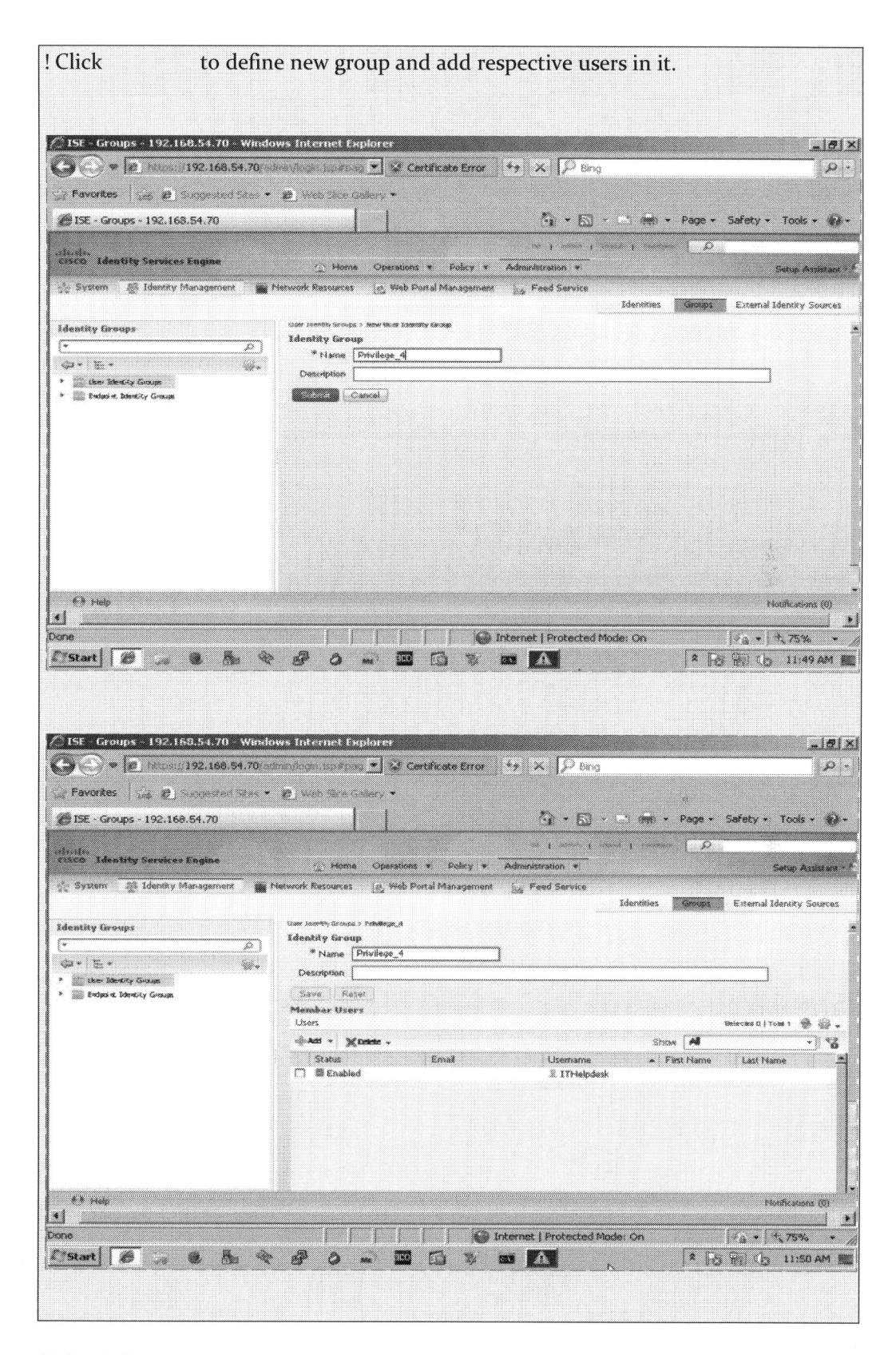

! Click to define new group and add respective users in it.

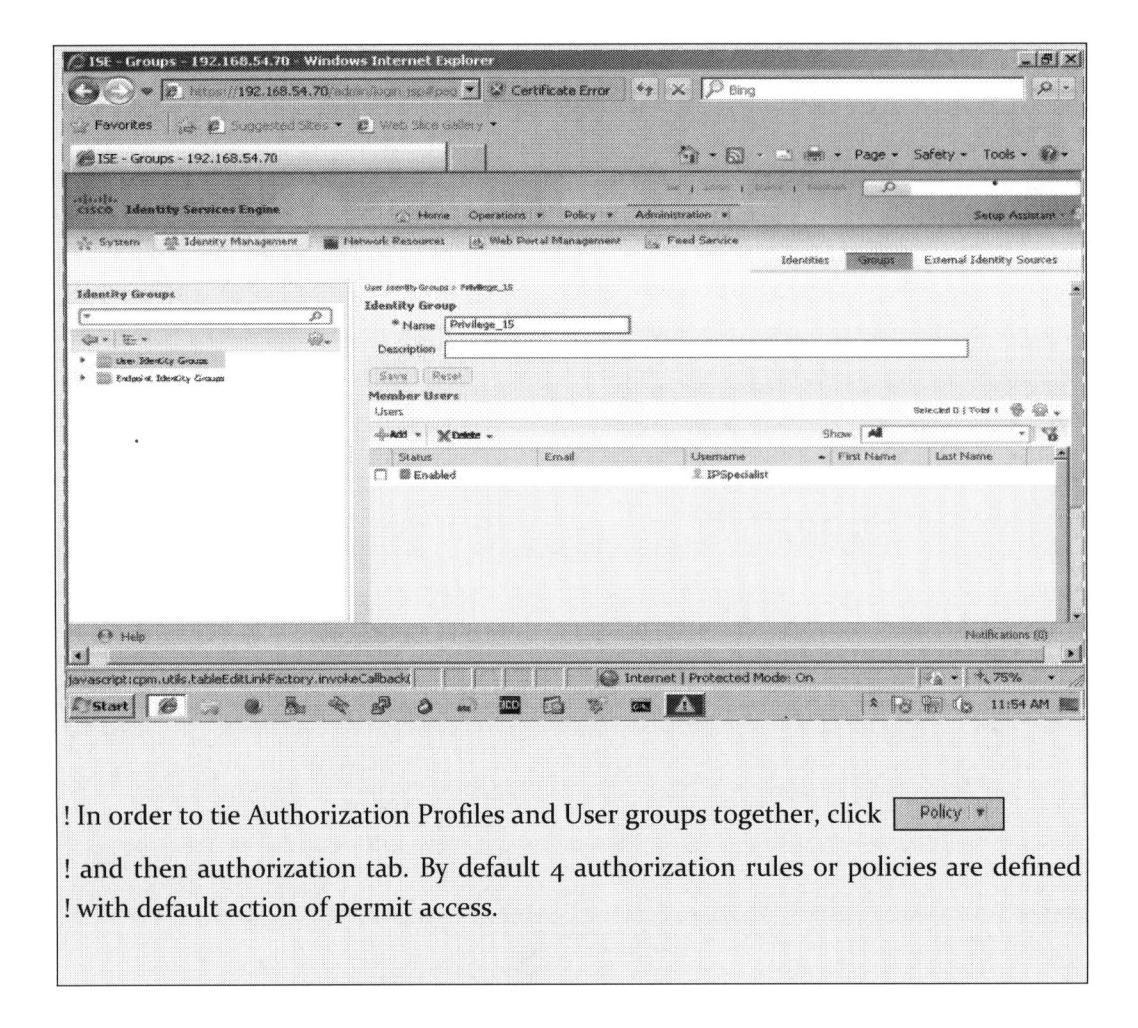

! In order to tie Authorization Profiles and User groups together, click `Policy ▼`
! and then authorization tab. By default 4 authorization rules or policies are defined
! with default action of permit access.

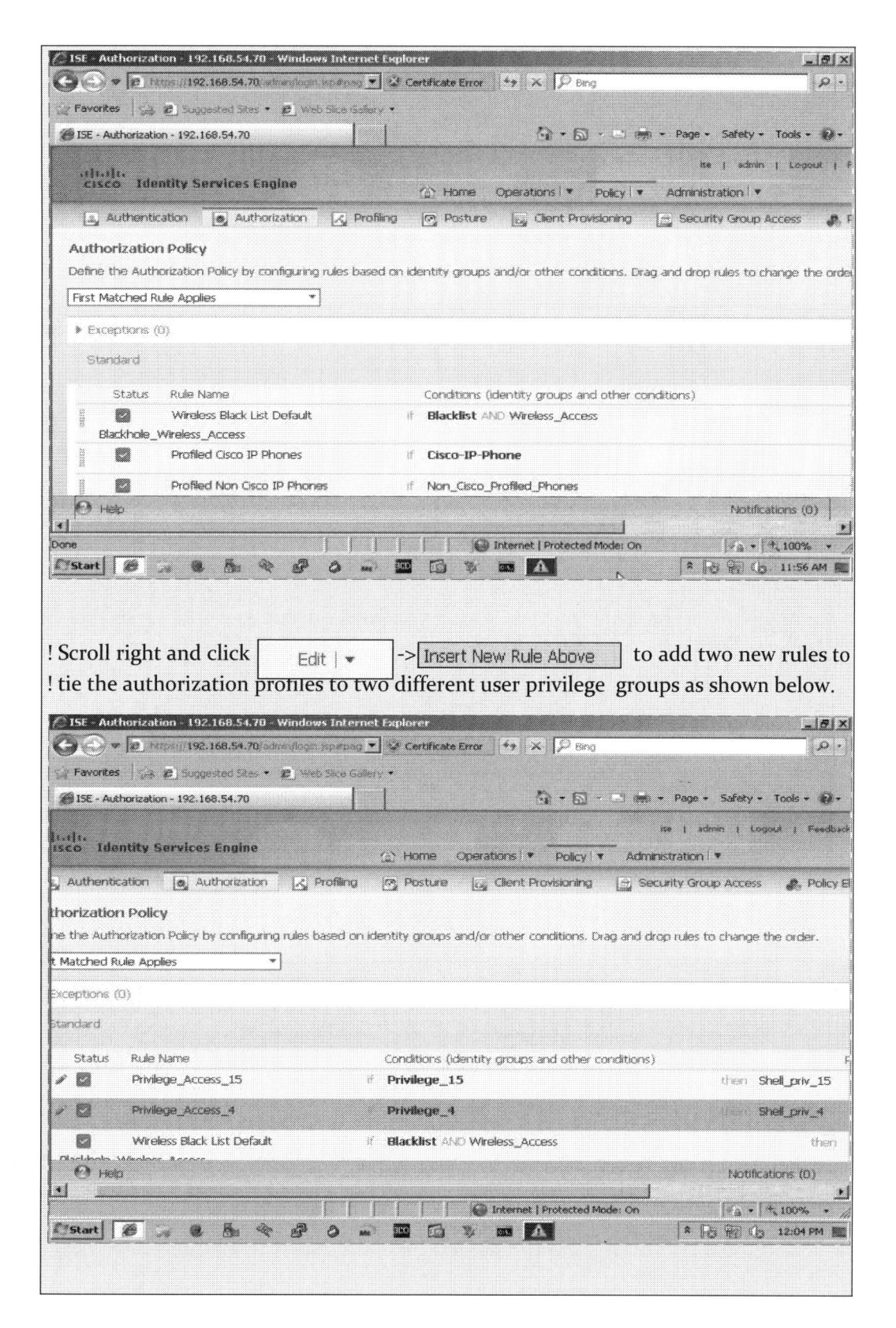

! Scroll right and click [Edit | ▼] -> [Insert New Rule Above] to add two new rules to
! tie the authorization profiles to two different user privilege groups as shown below.

R1

R1(config)#aaa new-model

R1(config)#aaa authentication login default group radius local

R1(config)#aaa authorization exec default group radius local

R1(config)#aaa accounting exec default start-stop group radius

R1(config)# radius-server host 192.168.54.70 auth-port 1812 acct-port 1813 key P@$$word:10

R1(config)#line vty 0 903

R1(config-line)#login authentication default

Verification

!

!

The first thing to perform in verification is to ping the ISE server to make sure the L3 connectivity as show below:

R1#ping 192.168.50.74

Type escape sequence to abort.

Sending 5, 100-byte ICMP Echos to 192.168.50.74, timeout is 2 seconds:

!!!!!

Success rate is 80 percent (4/5), round-trip min/avg/max = 4/9/16 ms

Another important command is **test** command which can be used to verify the protocol level connectivity with ACS by providing the already defined credentials in ACS as shown below

R1# test aaa group radius IPSpecialist P@$$word:10 new-code

User successfully authenticated.

R1# test aaa group radius ITHelpdesk P@$$word:20 new-code

User successfully authenticated.

Open the PuTTY on management station and access 10.0.0.254. Enter username "ITHelpdesk" and password "P@$$word:20"

In order to verify the connection request from ISE, click [Operations ▼] -> [Authentications] to see the results as shown below.

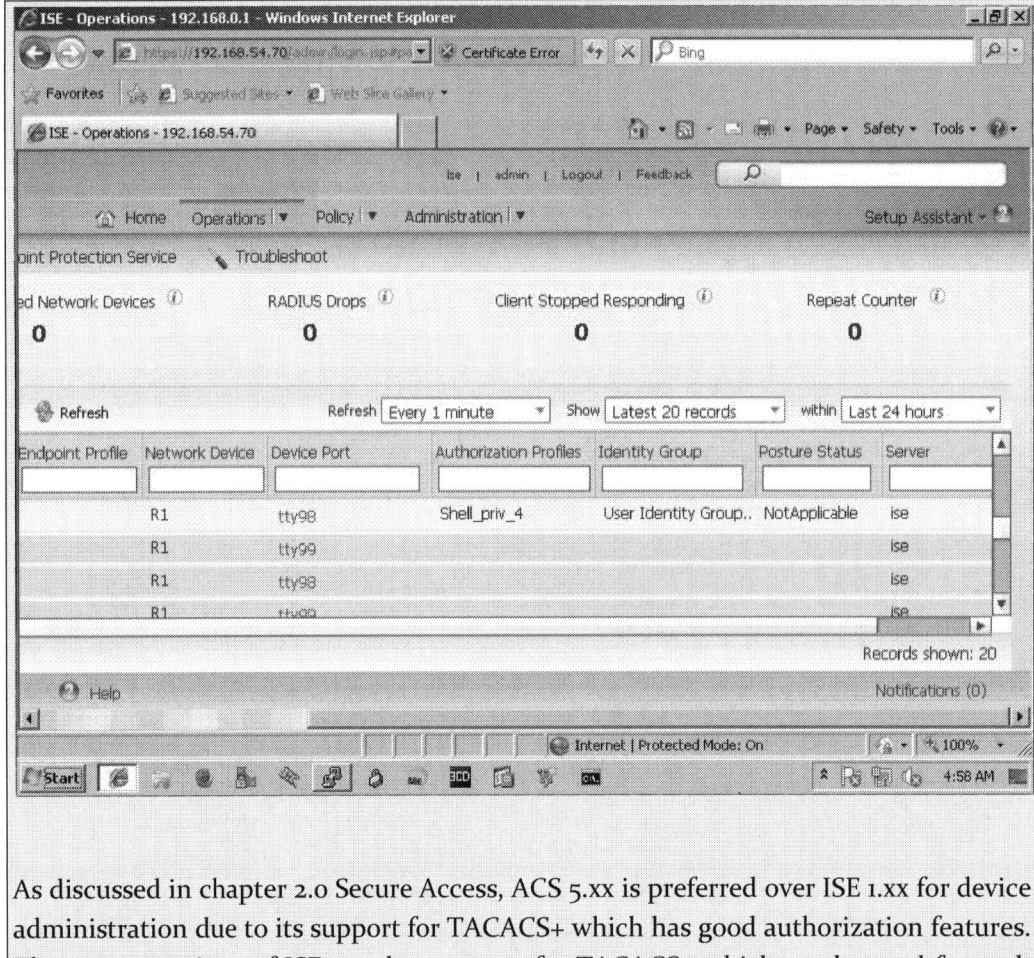

![ISE Operations screenshot]

As discussed in chapter 2.0 Secure Access, ACS 5.xx is preferred over ISE 1.xx for device administration due to its support for TACACS+ which has good authorization features. The newer versions of ISE 2.xx has support for TACACS+ which can be used for such purposes.

Routing Protocol Security

There are two general ways that authentication is implemented by most routing protocols: using a routing protocol centric solution that configures the passwords or keys to use within the routing protocol configuration, or by using a broader solution that utilizes separately configured keys that are able to be used by multiple routing protocols. Both OSPF and BGP use the prior of these methods and configure the specific authentication type and passwords/keys within their specific respective configurations. RIP and EIGRP utilize the former of these methods by utilizing a separate authentication key mechanism that is configured and then utilized for either RIP or EIGRP.

Keep in mind that these authentication solutions do not encrypt the information exchanged between the devices, but simply verifies that the identity of these devices.

Key Chains

The idea behind a key chain is rather simple as it simply replicates an electronic version of a key chain, a concept that most people are familiar with. The key chain functionality provides a mechanism for storing a number of different electronic keys, the key string value that is associated with a specific key and the lifetime that the key is valid. Any one of these configured keys can then be used by RIP or EIGRP for authentication.

Static Routing

The most secure routing configuration is static routing. With static routing, an administrator manually configures each router with all appropriate routes. Static routing gives an administrator much control over how packets are passed through a network, and since routers are configured manually, there are no routing protocols for an attacker to manipulate. However, static routing has one significant drawback—it scales horribly. When moving beyond two or three routers, manually configuring static routes on each router becomes a nightmare. Furthermore, adding a new router, or even a new network to an existing router, requires you to go back and change the configuration of every single router manually. Therefore, despite their security advantages, static routes lose their practicality when a network has frequent route changes or grows larger than three routers.

RIP v2

Router(config)# key chain RIPkey
Router(config-keychain)# key 0
Router(config-keychain)#　key-string cisco123
Router(config)# interface fa0/0
Router(config-if)# ip rip authentication key-string
Router(config-if)# ip rip authentication mode [md5	text]

OSPF

- Key chains are not used in OSPF authentication.
- Interface level configuration – you have more control as to which neighbor needs to be authenticated and by which type of authentication.
- Router level configuration – all the neighbors in an area will require to be authenticated by the specified type of authentication.
- Ip ospf authentication-key – truncates the key to 8 characters.

- If there are multiple neighbors in the same subnet being authenticated by MD5, you have to use different key IDs for each of the neighbor on the router that has adjacency to multiple neighbors.
- Interface-level authentication type is preferred over router-level authentication type, if both are specified.
- Following are the authentication types as seen in the debug output
  - aut0 – no authentication
  - aut1 – plain-text
  - aut2 – md5

Authentication:

Router(config)# router ospf 1

Router(config-router)# area 0 authentication message-digest

// Enables MD5 Authentication for Area 0

*Apr 27 09:05:34.325: %OSPF-4-NOVALIDKEY: No valid authentication send key is available on interface Ethernet0/0

Router(config)# int ethernet 0/0

Router(config-if)# ip ospf message-digest-key 1 md5 IPS

// Same password must be configured

*Apr 27 09:06:06.209: %OSPF-5-ADJCHG: Process 1, Nbr 192.168.1.1 on Ethernet0/0 from FULL to DOWN, Neighbor Down: Dead timer expired

---

EIGRP

- EIGRP uses key chains.
- Interface level configuration only.
- You can configure two key chains with different validity so that when one expires the other one takes over.
- Make sure the time is synchronized between the neighbors.

Router(config)# key chain KEY1
Router(config-keychain)# key 1
Router(config-keychain-key)# key-string cisco123key
Router(config-keychain-key)# accept-lifetime 18:00:00 Jan 1 2017 18:00:00 Jan 30 2017
Router(config-keychain-key)# send-lifetime 18:00:00 Jan 1 2017 18:00:00 Jan 30 2017

We have define the 1st key name, password and life of the key. Now we will configure 2nd key and set life for it.

```
Router(config)#key 2
Router(config-keychain)# key-string cisco321key
Router(config-keychain-key)#  accept-lifetime 17:00:00 Jan 30 2017 infinite
Router(config-keychain-key)#  send-lifetime 17:00:00 Jan 30 2017 infinite

Router(config)# interface FastEthernet0/0
Router(config-if)# ip address 136.1.13.3 255.255.255.0
Router(config-if)# ip authentication mode eigrp 10 md5
Router(config-if)# ip authentication key-chain eigrp 10 KEY1
```

We have Set the key on the interface with EIGRP process.

BGPv4

Only a password needs to be set for the 'neighbor'.

```
neighbor 150.1.1.1 password ciscoBGPpass
```

Common Types of Network Attacks

Without security measures and controls in place, your data could be subjected to an attack. Some attacks are passive, meaning information is monitored; others are active, meaning the information is altered with intent to corrupt or destroy the data or the network itself.

Your networks and data are vulnerable to any of the following types of attacks if you do not have a security plan in place.

Eavesdropping

In general, the majority of network communications occurs in an unsecured or "clear text" format, which allows an attacker who have access to data paths in your network to "listen in" or interpret (read) the traffic. When an attacker is eavesdropping on your communications, it is known as sniffing or snooping. The ability of an eavesdropper to monitor the network is generally the biggest security problem that administrators face in an enterprise. Without strong encryption services that are based on cryptography, your data can be read by others as it traverses the network.

Data Modification

After an attacker has read your data, the next logical step is to alter it. An attacker can modify the data in the packet without the knowledge of the sender or receiver. Even if you do not require confidentiality for all communications, you do not want any of your messages to be modified in transit. For example, if you are exchanging purchase requisitions, you do not want the items, amounts, or billing information to be modified.

Identity Spoofing (IP Address Spoofing)

Most networks and operating systems use the IP address of a computer to identify a valid entity. In certain cases, it is possible for an IP address to be falsely assumed—identity spoofing. An attacker might also use special programs to construct IP packets that appear to originate from valid addresses inside the corporate intranet.

After gaining access to the network with a valid IP address, the attacker can modify, reroute, or delete your data. The attacker can also conduct other types of attacks, as described in the following sections.

Password-Based Attacks

A common denominator of most operating system and network security plans is password-based access control. This means your access rights to a computer and network resources are determined by who you are, that is, your user name and your password.

Older applications do not always protect identity information as it is passed through the network for validation. This might allow an eavesdropper to gain access to the network by posing as a valid user.

When an attacker finds a valid user account, the attacker has the same rights as the real user. Therefore, if the user has administrator-level rights, the attacker also can create accounts for subsequent access later.

After gaining access to your network with a valid account, an attacker can do any of the following:

- Obtain lists of valid user and computer names and network information.
- Modify server and network configurations, including access controls and routing tables.
- Modify, reroute, or delete your data.

Denial-of-Service Attack

Unlike a password-based attack, the denial-of-service attack prevents normal use of your computer or network by valid users.

After gaining access to your network, the attacker can do any of the following:

- Randomize the attention of your internal Information Systems staff so that they do not see the intrusion immediately, which allows the attacker to make more attacks during the diversion.

- Transmit invalid data to applications or network services, which causes abnormal termination or behavior of the applications or services.
- Flood a computer or the entire network with traffic until a shutdown occurs because of the overload.
- Block traffic, which results in a loss of access to network resources by authorized users.

Man-in-the-Middle Attack

As the name indicates, a man-in-the-middle attack occurs when someone between you and the person with whom you are communicating is actively monitoring, capturing, and controlling your communication transparently. For example, the attacker can re-route a data exchange. When computers are communicating at low levels of the network layer, the computers might not be able to determine with whom they are exchanging data.

Man-in-the-middle attacks are like someone assuming your identity in order to read your message. The person on the other end might believe it is you because the attacker might be actively replying as you to keep the exchange going and gain more information. This attack is capable of the same damage as an application-layer attack.

Compromised-Key Attack

A key is a secret code or number necessary to interpret secured information. Although obtaining a key is a difficult and resource-intensive process for an attacker, it is possible. After an attacker obtains a key, that key is referred to as a compromised key.

An attacker uses the compromised key to gain access to a secured communication without the sender or receiver being aware of the attack. With the compromised key, the attacker can decrypt or modify data, and try to use the compromised key to compute additional keys, which might allow the attacker access to other secured communications.

Sniffer Attack

A sniffer is an application or device that can view/read, monitor, and capture network data exchanges and read network packets. If the packets are not encrypted, a sniffer provides a full view of the data inside the packet. Even encapsulated (tunneled) packets can be broken open and read unless they are encrypted and the attacker does not have access to the key.

Using a sniffer, an attacker can do any of the following:

- Analyze your network and gain information to eventually cause your network to crash or to become corrupted.
- Read your communications.

Application-Layer Attack

An application-layer attack targets application servers by deliberately causing a fault in a server's operating system or applications. This results in the attacker gaining the ability to bypass normal access controls. The attacker takes advantage of this situation, gaining control of your application, system, or network, and can do any of the following:

- Read, add, delete, or modify your data or operating system.
- Introduce a virus program that uses your computers and software applications to copy viruses in your entire network.
- Introduce a sniffer program to analyze your network and gain information that can eventually be used to crash or to corrupt your systems and network.
- Abnormally terminate your data applications or operating systems.
- Disable other security controls to enable future attacks.

Users, user groups, tasks groups and task IDs in IOS-XR

Cisco IOS XR software user attributes form the basis of the Cisco IOS XR software administrative model. Each router user is associated with the following attributes:

- User ID (ASCII string) that identifies the user uniquely across an administrative domain
- Length limitation of 253 characters for passwords and one-way encrypted secrets
- List of user groups (at least one) of which the user is a member (thereby enabling attributes such as task IDs)

User Categories

Router users are classified into the following categories:

- root system user (complete administrative authority)
- owner LR user (specific logical router administrative authority)
- logical router user (specific logical router user access)

Root System Users

The root system user is the entity authorized to "own" the entire router chassis. The root system user functions with the highest privileges over all router components and can monitor all logical routers in the system. At least one root system user account must be created during router setup. Multiple root system users can exist.

The root system user can perform any configuration or monitoring task, including the following:

- Configure logical routers.

- Create, delete, and modify owner LR users (after logging in to the logical router as the root system user).
- Create, delete, and modify logical router users and set user task permissions (after logging in to the logical router as the root system user).
- Access fabric racks or any router resource not allocated to a logical router, allowing the root system user to authenticate to any router node regardless of the logical router configurations.

Owner LR Users

An owner LR user controls the configuration and monitoring of a particular logical router (LR). The owner LR user can create users and configure their privileges within the LR. Multiple owner LR users can work independently on multiple LRs in the router system. A single LR may have more than one owner LR user.

An owner LR user can perform the following administrative tasks for a particular LR:

- Create, delete, and modify logical router users and their privileges for the LR.
- Create, delete, and modify user groups to allow access to the LR.
- Manage nearly all aspects of the LR.

An owner LR user cannot deny access to a root system user.

Logical Router Users

A logical router user has restricted access to an LR as determined by the root system user or owner LR user. The logical router user performs the day-to-day system and network management activities. The tasks that the logical router user is allowed to perform are determined by the task IDs associated with the user groups to which the logical router user belongs.

User Groups

The Cisco IOS XR software allows the system administrator to configure groups of users and the job characteristics that are common in groups of users. Groups must be explicitly assigned to users. Users are not assigned to groups by default. A user can be assigned to more than one group.

A user group defines a collection of users that share a set of attributes, such as access privileges. Each user may be associated with one or more user groups. User groups have the following attributes:

- List of task groups that define the authorization for the users. All tasks, except cisco-support, are allowed by default for root system users.
- Each user task can be assigned read, write, execute, or debug permission.

Predefined User Groups

The Cisco IOS XR software provides a collection of user groups whose attributes are already defined. The predefined groups are as follows:

- Cisco-support: the Cisco support team uses this group.
- netadmin: Has the ability to control and monitor all system and network parameters.
- operator: A demonstration group with basic privileges.
- root-lr: Has the ability to control and monitor the specific logical router.
- root-system: Has the ability to control and monitor the entire system.
- Sysadmin : Has the ability to control and monitor all system parameters but cannot configure network protocols.

The user group root-system has root system users as the only members. Root-system user group has predefined authorization that is; it has the complete responsibility for root-system user-managed resources and certain responsibilities in other LRs.

User-Defined User Groups

Administrators can configure their own user groups to meet particular needs.

User Group Inheritance

A user group can derive attributes from another user group. (Similarly, a task group can derive attributes from another task group). For example, when user group A inherits attributes from user group B, the new set of task attributes of the user group A is a union of A and B. The inheritance relationship among user groups is dynamic in the sense that if group A inherits attributes from group B, and change in group B affects group A, even if the group is not re-inherited explicitly.

Task Groups

A task group is defined by a collection of task IDs. Task groups contain task ID lists for each class of action.

Each user group is associated with a set of task groups applicable to the users in that group. A user's task permissions are derived from the task groups associated with the user groups to which that user belongs.

Predefined Task Groups

The following predefined task groups are available for administrators to use, typically for initial configuration:

- cisco-support: Cisco support personnel tasks
- netadmin: Network administrator tasks
- operator: Operator day-to-day tasks (for demonstration purposes)

- root-lr: Logical router administrator tasks
- root-system: System-wide administrator tasks
- sysadmin: System administrator tasks

User-Defined Task Groups

Users can configure their own task groups to meet particular needs.

Group Inheritance

Task groups support inheritance from other task groups. (Similarly, a user group can derive attributes from another user group.) For example, when task group A inherits task group B, the new set of attributes of task group A is the union of A and B.

Chapter 12: IP Services

Technology Brief

Internet Protocol is the most fundamental protocol in internetworking. It supports and facilitates efficient protocols to provide various IP services. These IP protocol includes, ICMP, DNS,DHCP, NET any many others. ICMP is IP protocol used to trace and track IP packets. DNS and DHCP are used to provide access to internet resources. Nat is implemented to efficiently utilize IP address block and access public network resources with guaranteed sururity.

Internet Control Message Protocol (ICMP)

ICMP is listed as a supporting protocol in Internet Protocol suite and used to send error and informational messages. Following are the major functions of ICMP protocol:

- Inform end-system or originator of IP packet about the status of transmitted packet (delivered or dropped)
- Calculate roundtrip time by calculating the path taken by the IP packet

ICMP messages are mostly used by attackers and hackers to obtain configuration and other information. Network administrator mostly blocked ICMP messages through firewall. However, this would cause other efficient network utilities such as ping, trace route to no not function properly.

Basic format of ICMP message is demonstrated in the following figure:

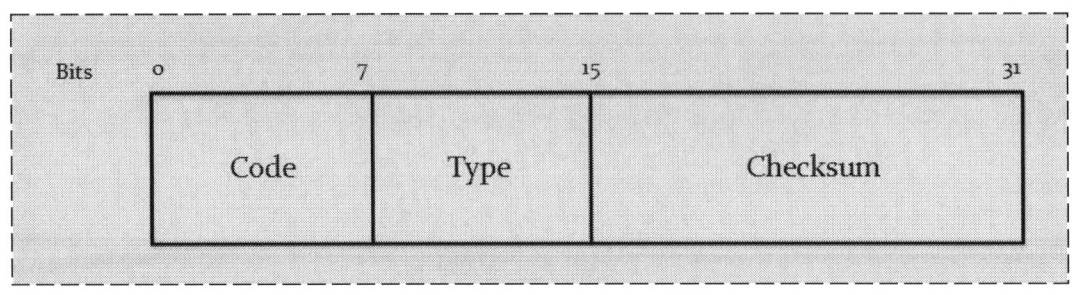

Bits 0	7	15	31
Code	Type	Checksum	

Figure 79 General ICMP Format

Code: 1 byte represents type of ICMP message

Type: 1 byte represents subtype of ICMP message

Checksum: 2 bytes calculated over entire ICMP message

Following table shows ICMP messages which are frequently seen and used:

Type	Code	Error
3	0-15	Destination Unreachable

5	0-3	Redirect
9	0-16	Route Information
11	0,1	Time Exceeded
12	0,1	Parameter Problem

Table 19 Frequent ICMP Messages

ICMP messages are used in both IPv4 (ICMP4) and IPv6 networks (ICMP6):

ICMP4

ICMPv4 message is encapsulated by IPv4 packet and transmitted over IP packet "data" field with protocol field set to 1 represents ICMPv4 message.

Following figure demonstrate the structure of ICMPv4 packet:

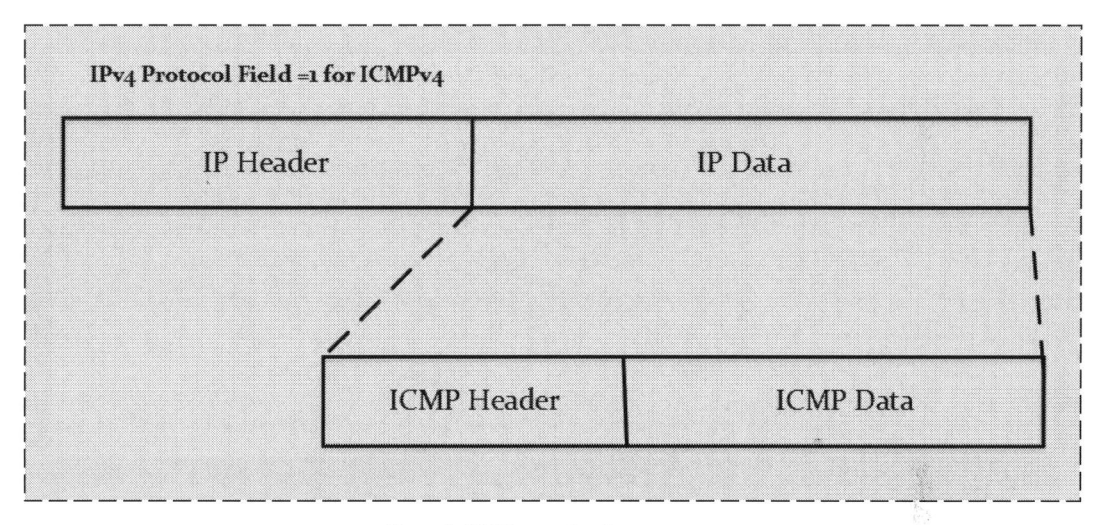

Figure 81 ICMPv4 packet Structure

ICMP6

ICMPv6 messages can be used for more than error reporting and providing information. Following are the features supported by ICMPv6:

- Neighbor Discovery
- Router Discovery
- Multicast Management
- Managing hand-offs in Mobile IPv6

ICMPv6 can be analyzed by next header value sets to 58.

Domain Name Servers (DNS)

Domain Name servers are use in Internetwork to maintain a directory of domain names with mapped IP addresses. Domain name server resolve domain names to IP address by translating from its database. DNS can be locate anywhere in the network and customer internet access significantly depends upon its location and speed. Following two domain name servers are configure on devices want to access public network:

- Primary DNS: Servers which resolve domain name addresses to IP address
- Secondary DNS: Act as a backup server in primary DNS failure

Following are two general record type of DNS:

A-record: Returns 32 bit IP address

AAAA-record: Returns 128 bit IP address

Network Address Translation

Lab 12-1 : Static Network Address Translation:

Topology Diagram:

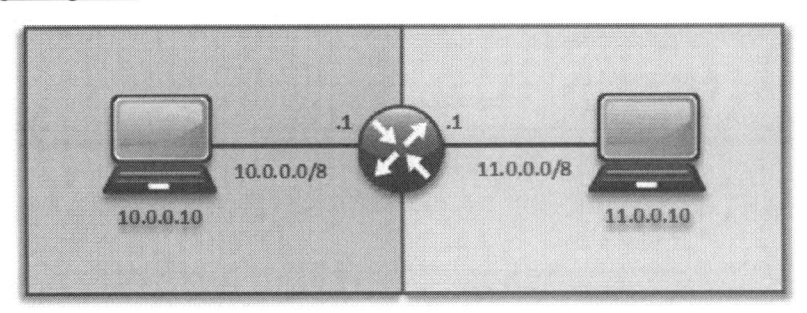

Case Study:

In this Case, Static (One to One mapping) is performed in the shown network topology. The Source IP address 10.0.0.10 is translated into 192.168.0.1 IP address.

Configuration:

Router(config)#int eth 0/0

Router(config-if)#ip add 10.0.0.1 255.0.0.0

//Configure correct IP address and Mask

Router(config-if)#no sh

//Must Turn Up the interface

Router(config-if)#ex

*May 23 05:32:38.546: %LINK-3-UPDOWN: Interface Ethernet0/0, changed state to up

//Interface is Up successfully

*May 23 05:32:39.550: %LINEPROTO-5-UPDOWN: Line protocol on Interface Ethernet0/0, changed state to up

//Interface Line Protocol is Up successfully

Router(config)#int eth 0/1

Router(config-if)#ip add 11.0.0.1 255.0.0.0

//Configure correct IP address and Mask

Router(config-if)#no sh

//Must Turn Up the interface

Router(config-if)#ex

Router(config)#

*May 23 05:32:52.626: %LINK-3-UPDOWN: Interface Ethernet0/1, changed state to up

//Interface is Up successfully

*May 23 05:32:53.630: %LINEPROTO-5-UPDOWN: Line protocol on Interface Ethernet0/1, changed state to up

//Interface Line Protocol is Up successfully

Router(config)#ip nat inside source static 10.0.0.10 192.168.0.1

//10.0.0.10 is Inside Local IP address nad 192.168.0.1 is Inside Global IP address. Make sure while configuring in addresses

*May 23 05:34:03.026: %LINEPROTO-5-UPDOWN: Line protocol on Interface NVI0, changed state to up

// Nating is enabled, Now apply it to the interfaces

Router(config)#int eth 0/0

Router(config-if)#ip nat inside

IP nat inside to the interface connected to the Inside Local Address

Router(config-if)#ex

Router(config)#int eth 0/1

Router(config-if)#ip nat outside

IP nat Outside to the interface connected translated address will send

Router(config-if)#ex

Router(config)#

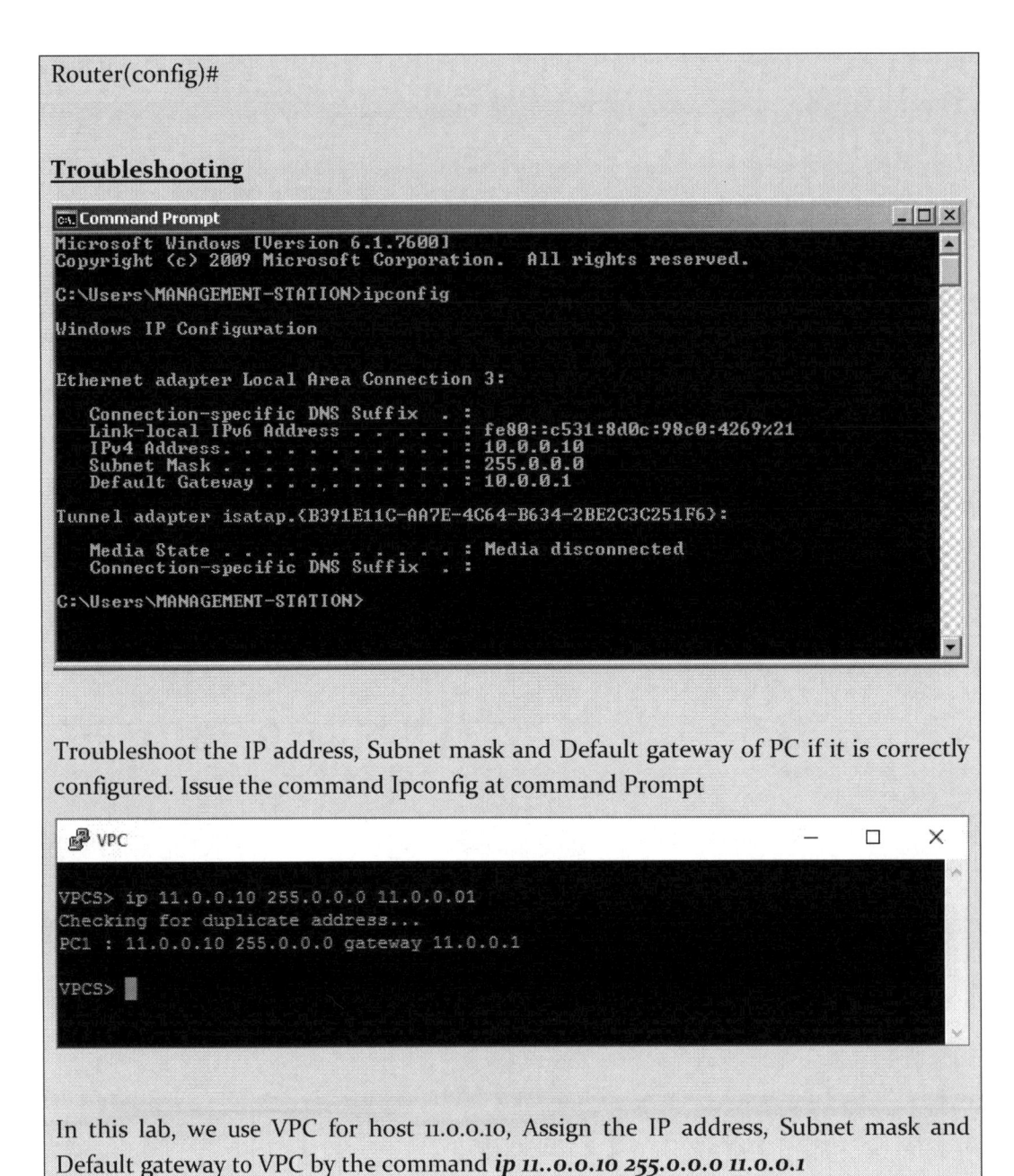

Troubleshooting

```
Command Prompt
Microsoft Windows [Version 6.1.7600]
Copyright (c) 2009 Microsoft Corporation.  All rights reserved.

C:\Users\MANAGEMENT-STATION>ipconfig

Windows IP Configuration

Ethernet adapter Local Area Connection 3:

   Connection-specific DNS Suffix  . :
   Link-local IPv6 Address . . . . . : fe80::c531:8d0c:98c0:4269%21
   IPv4 Address. . . . . . . . . . . : 10.0.0.10
   Subnet Mask . . . . . . . . . . . : 255.0.0.0
   Default Gateway . . . . . . . . . : 10.0.0.1

Tunnel adapter isatap.{B391E11C-AA7E-4C64-B634-2BE2C3C251F6}:

   Media State . . . . . . . . . . . : Media disconnected
   Connection-specific DNS Suffix  . :

C:\Users\MANAGEMENT-STATION>
```

Troubleshoot the IP address, Subnet mask and Default gateway of PC if it is correctly configured. Issue the command Ipconfig at command Prompt

```
VPC
VPCS> ip 11.0.0.10 255.0.0.0 11.0.0.01
Checking for duplicate address...
PC1 : 11.0.0.10 255.0.0.0 gateway 11.0.0.1

VPCS>
```

In this lab, we use VPC for host 11.0.0.10, Assign the IP address, Subnet mask and Default gateway to VPC by the command *ip 11..0.0.10 255.0.0.0 11.0.0.1*

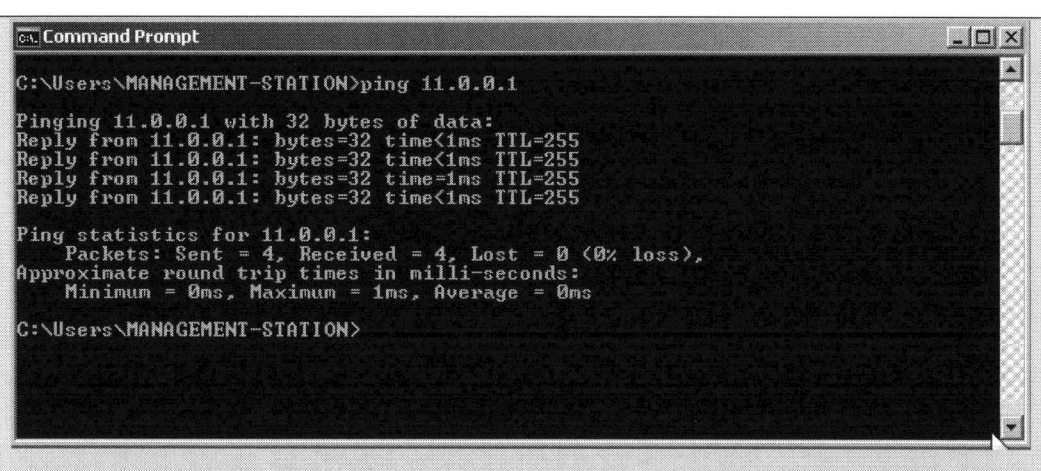

```
Command Prompt

C:\Users\MANAGEMENT-STATION>ping 11.0.0.1

Pinging 11.0.0.1 with 32 bytes of data:
Reply from 11.0.0.1: bytes=32 time<1ms TTL=255
Reply from 11.0.0.1: bytes=32 time<1ms TTL=255
Reply from 11.0.0.1: bytes=32 time=1ms TTL=255
Reply from 11.0.0.1: bytes=32 time<1ms TTL=255

Ping statistics for 11.0.0.1:
    Packets: Sent = 4, Received = 4, Lost = 0 (0% loss),
Approximate round trip times in milli-seconds:
    Minimum = 0ms, Maximum = 1ms, Average = 0ms

C:\Users\MANAGEMENT-STATION>
```

Ping the destination address 11.0.0.10 from the Windows PC 10.0.0.10 to troubleshoot the Network Address Translation

Router#Show ip nat translation

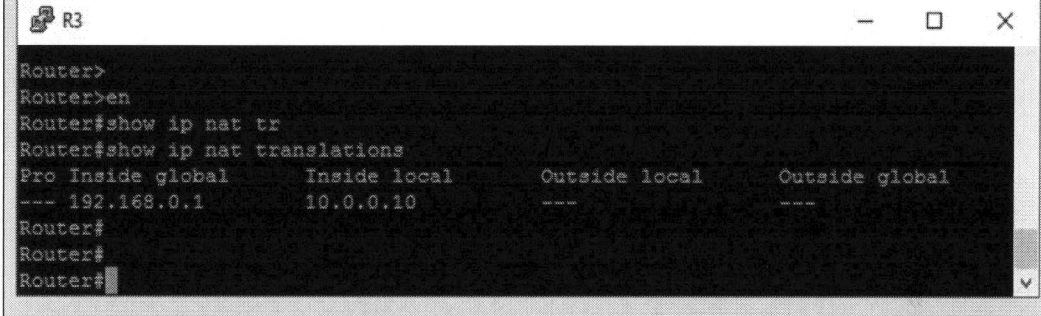

```
R3

Router>
Router>en
Router#show ip nat tr
Router#show ip nat translations
Pro  Inside global      Inside local       Outside local      Outside global
---  192.168.0.1        10.0.0.10          ---                ---
Router#
Router#
Router#
```

Issue the command **Router# show ip nat translation** to check if translated successfully

Router#Show ip nat statistics

```
Router#show ip nat s
Router#show ip nat statistics
Total active translations: 1 (1 static, 0 dynamic; 0 extended)
Peak translations: 1, occurred 00:07:28 ago
Outside interfaces:
  Ethernet0/1
Inside interfaces:
  Ethernet0/0
Hits: 0  Misses: 0
CEF Translated packets: 0, CEF Punted packets: 0
Expired translations: 0
Dynamic mappings:

Total doors: 0
Appl doors: 0
Normal doors: 0
Queued Packets: 0
Router#
```

Show ip nat statistics command defines Total Number of Active Translations, Number of Static, Dynamic and Port address Translation, Peak translation rate, Inside and Outside Interfaces and other details

Router#debug ip nat

```
Router#debug ip nat
IP NAT debugging is on
Router#clear ip nat translation *
Router#
*May 23 05:48:00.958: NAT: API parameters passed: src_addr:10.0.0.10, src_port:0
 dest_addr:224.0.0.252, dest_port:0, proto:17 if_input:Ethernet0/0 pak:C18EFE68
get_translated:1
*May 23 05:48:01.267: NAT: API parameters passed: src_addr:10.0.0.10, src_port:0
 dest_addr:10.255.255.255, dest_port:0, proto:17 if_input:Ethernet0/0 pak:C2297E
A0 get_translated:1
Router#
*May 23 05:48:03.570: NAT: API parameters passed: src_addr:10.0.0.10, src_port:0
 dest_addr:224.0.0.252, dest_port:0, proto:17 if_input:Ethernet0/0 pak:C3CE7258
get_translated:1
Router#
*May 23 05:48:06.177: NAT: API parameters passed: src_addr:10.0.0.10, src_port:0
 dest_addr:224.0.0.252, dest_port:0, proto:17 if_input:Ethernet0/0 pak:C3CE7740
get_translated:1
Router#
*May 23 05:48:08.755: NAT: API parameters passed: src_addr:10.0.0.10, src_port:0
```

Debug ip nat shows run time debugging data of Nat translation. As shows source address is 10.0.0.10 input interface is Ethernet 0/0 is translated.

Lab 12-2 : Dynamic Network Address Translation:

Case Study:

In this Lab, the network 10.0.0.0/8 is dynamically translated into the pool of network 192.168.1.100 to 192.168.1.110. The complete process of Dynamic Network Address Translation till verification and troubleshooting is defined below:

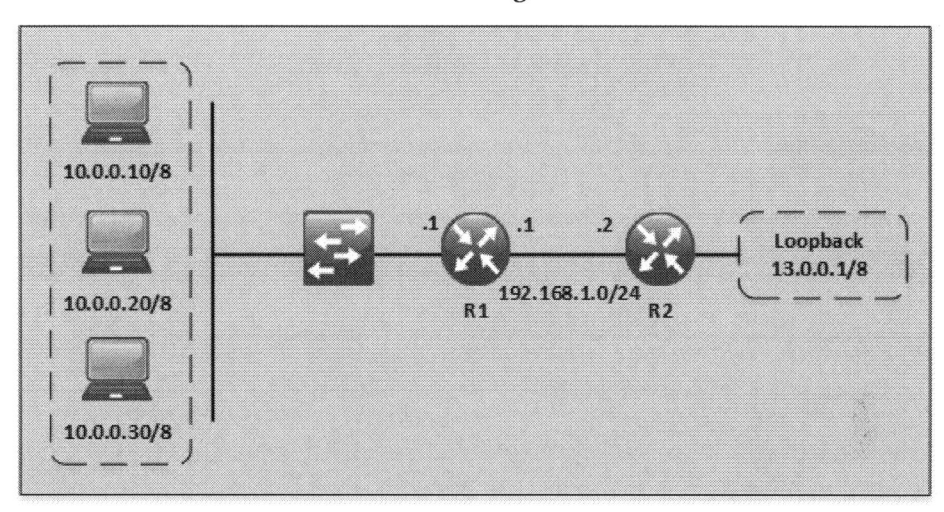

Router 1:

Router(config)#hostname R1

R1(config)#int eth 0/1

R1(config-if)#ip add 10.0.0.1 255.0.0.0

//Configure correct IP address and Mask

R1(config-if)#no sh

// Must Turn up the interface

R1(config-if)#ex

*Mar 1 00:00:47.987: %LINK-3-UPDOWN: Interface FastEthernet0/0, changed state to up

*Mar 1 00:00:48.987: %LINEPROTO-5-UPDOWN: Line protocol on Interface FastEthernet0/0, changed state to up

//Interface and Interface Line Protocol, Both are up

R1(config)#int eth 0/0

R1(config-if)#ip add 192.168.1.1 255.255.255.0

//Configure correct IP address and Mask

R1(config-if)#no sh

// Must Turn up the interface

R1(config-if)#ex

*Mar 1 00:01:20.571: %LINK-3-UPDOWN: Interface FastEthernet0/1, changed state to up

*Mar 1 00:01:21.571: %LINEPROTO-5-UPDOWN: Line protocol on Interface FastEthernet0/1, changed state to up

//Interface and Interface Line Protocol, Both are up

R1(config)#int eth 0/1

R1(config-if)#ip nat inside

IP nat inside to the interface connected to the Inside Local Address

R1(config)#int eth 0/0

R1(config-if)#ip nat outside

IP nat Outside to the interface connected translated address will send

R1(config)#access-list 10 permit 10.0.0.0 0.0.0.255

//Make sure Access-list number must be the same in NAT Command

R1(config)#ip nat pool IPS 192.168.1.100 192.168.1.110 netmask 255.255.255.0

R1(config)#ip nat inside source list 10 pool IPS

// Access list number and Pool Name must be the same

R1(config)#ip route 13.0.0.0 255.0.0.0 192.168.1.2

//Define a static route

Router 2

R2(config)#int eth 0/0

R2(config-if)#ip add 192.168.1.2 255.255.255.0

//Configure correct IP address and Mask

R2(config-if)#no sh

// Must Turn up the interface

R2(config-if)#ex

*Mar 1 00:06:27.403: %LINK-3-UPDOWN: Interface FastEthernet0/0, changed state to up

*Mar 1 00:06:28.403: %LINEPROTO-5-UPDOWN: Line protocol on Interface FastEthernet0/0, changed state to up

//Interface and Interface Line Protocol, Both are up

R2(config)#int lo 0

*Mar 1 00:06:34.319: %LINEPROTO-5-UPDOWN: Line protocol on Interface Loopback0, changed state to up

R2(config-if)#ip add 13.0.0.01 255.255.255.0

//Configure correct IP address and Mask

R2(config-if)#no sh

R2(config-if)#ex

Troubleshooting

Ping from PC 1 to Lo interface 13.0.0.1

```
VPCS> ip 10.0.0.10 255.0.0.0 10.0.0.1
Checking for duplicate address...
PC1 : 10.0.0.10 255.0.0.0 gateway 10.0.0.1

VPCS> ping 13.0.0.1

84 bytes from 13.0.0.1 icmp_seq=1 ttl=254 time=1.204 ms
84 bytes from 13.0.0.1 icmp_seq=2 ttl=254 time=1.364 ms
84 bytes from 13.0.0.1 icmp_seq=3 ttl=254 time=1.349 ms
84 bytes from 13.0.0.1 icmp_seq=4 ttl=254 time=1.193 ms
84 bytes from 13.0.0.1 icmp_seq=5 ttl=254 time=1.385 ms

VPCS>
VPCS>
```

Ping from PC 2 to Lo interface 13.0.0.1

```
VPCS> ip 10.0.0.20 255.0.0.0 10.0.0.1
Checking for duplicate address...
PC1 : 10.0.0.20 255.0.0.0 gateway 10.0.0.1

VPCS> ping 13.0.0.1

13.0.0.1 icmp_seq=1 timeout
84 bytes from 13.0.0.1 icmp_seq=2 ttl=254 time=1.616 ms
84 bytes from 13.0.0.1 icmp_seq=3 ttl=254 time=1.372 ms
84 bytes from 13.0.0.1 icmp_seq=4 ttl=254 time=1.361 ms
84 bytes from 13.0.0.1 icmp_seq=5 ttl=254 time=1.449 ms

VPCS>
VPCS>
```

Ping from PC 3 to Lo interface 13.0.0.1

```
VPCS> ip 10.0.0.30 255.0.0.0 10.0.0.1
Checking for duplicate address...
PC1 : 10.0.0.30 255.0.0.0 gateway 10.0.0.1

VPCS> ping 13.0.0.1

13.0.0.1 icmp_seq=1 timeout
84 bytes from 13.0.0.1 icmp_seq=2 ttl=254 time=1.260 ms
84 bytes from 13.0.0.1 icmp_seq=3 ttl=254 time=1.278 ms
84 bytes from 13.0.0.1 icmp_seq=4 ttl=254 time=1.395 ms
84 bytes from 13.0.0.1 icmp_seq=5 ttl=254 time=1.521 ms

VPCS>
VPCS>
```

Router#debug IP nat

```
Router#debug ip nat
IP NAT debugging is on
Router#
*May 23 06:56:52.343: NAT*: s=10.0.0.10->192.168.1.100, d=13.0.0.1 [56628]
Router#
*May 23 06:56:54.343: NAT*: s=10.0.0.10->192.168.1.100, d=13.0.0.1 [56629]
*May 23 06:56:54.344: NAT*: s=13.0.0.1, d=192.168.1.100->10.0.0.10 [56629]
*May 23 06:56:55.345: NAT*: s=10.0.0.10->192.168.1.100, d=13.0.0.1 [56630]
*May 23 06:56:55.346: NAT*: s=13.0.0.1, d=192.168.1.100->10.0.0.10 [56630]
Router#
*May 23 06:56:56.348: NAT*: s=10.0.0.10->192.168.1.100, d=13.0.0.1 [56631]
*May 23 06:56:56.348: NAT*: s=13.0.0.1, d=192.168.1.100->10.0.0.10 [56631]
*May 23 06:56:57.350: NAT*: s=10.0.0.10->192.168.1.100, d=13.0.0.1 [56632]
*May 23 06:56:57.350: NAT*: s=13.0.0.1, d=192.168.1.100->10.0.0.10 [56632]
Router#
*May 23 06:57:01.382: NAT*: s=10.0.0.20->192.168.1.101, d=13.0.0.1 [56637]
Router#
*May 23 06:57:03.382: NAT*: s=10.0.0.20->192.168.1.101, d=13.0.0.1 [56638]
*May 23 06:57:03.382: NAT*: s=13.0.0.1, d=192.168.1.101->10.0.0.20 [56638]
*May 23 06:57:04.384: NAT*: s=10.0.0.20->192.168.1.101, d=13.0.0.1 [56639]
*May 23 06:57:04.385: NAT*: s=13.0.0.1, d=192.168.1.101->10.0.0.20 [56639]
Router#
*May 23 06:57:05.387: NAT*: s=10.0.0.20->192.168.1.101, d=13.0.0.1 [56640]
*May 23 06:57:05.387: NAT*: s=13.0.0.1, d=192.168.1.101->10.0.0.20 [56640]
```

Debugging IP nat shows source 10.0.0.10 is translated into 192.168.1.100 to the destination 13.0.0.1. Return packet of Ping also retranslated, as source 13.0.0.1 to destination 192.168.1.100 -> 10.0.0.10. Similarly source 10.0.0.20 is translated into 192.168.1.101 for the destination 13.0.0.1. Return packet of Ping also retranslated, as source 13.0.0.1 to destination 192.168.1.101 -> 10.0.0.20.

```
*May 23 06:57:01.382: NAT*: s=10.0.0.20->192.168.1.101, d=13.0.0.1 [56637]
Router#
*May 23 06:57:03.382: NAT*: s=10.0.0.20->192.168.1.101, d=13.0.0.1 [56638]
*May 23 06:57:03.382: NAT*: s=13.0.0.1, d=192.168.1.101->10.0.0.20 [56638]
*May 23 06:57:04.384: NAT*: s=10.0.0.20->192.168.1.101, d=13.0.0.1 [56639]
*May 23 06:57:04.385: NAT*: s=13.0.0.1, d=192.168.1.101->10.0.0.20 [56639]
Router#
*May 23 06:57:05.387: NAT*: s=10.0.0.20->192.168.1.101, d=13.0.0.1 [56640]
*May 23 06:57:05.387: NAT*: s=13.0.0.1, d=192.168.1.101->10.0.0.20 [56640]
*May 23 06:57:06.389: NAT*: s=10.0.0.20->192.168.1.101, d=13.0.0.1 [56641]
*May 23 06:57:06.390: NAT*: s=13.0.0.1, d=192.168.1.101->10.0.0.20 [56641]
Router#
*May 23 06:57:11.978: NAT*: s=10.0.0.30->192.168.1.102, d=13.0.0.1 [56647]
Router#
*May 23 06:57:13.979: NAT*: s=10.0.0.30->192.168.1.102, d=13.0.0.1 [56648]
*May 23 06:57:13.979: NAT*: s=13.0.0.1, d=192.168.1.102->10.0.0.30 [56648]
*May 23 06:57:14.981: NAT*: s=10.0.0.30->192.168.1.102, d=13.0.0.1 [56649]
*May 23 06:57:14.986: NAT*: s=13.0.0.1, d=192.168.1.102->10.0.0.30 [56649]
Router#
*May 23 06:57:15.987: NAT*: s=10.0.0.30->192.168.1.102, d=13.0.0.1 [56650]
*May 23 06:57:15.988: NAT*: s=13.0.0.1, d=192.168.1.102->10.0.0.30 [56650]
*May 23 06:57:16.989: NAT*: s=10.0.0.30->192.168.1.102, d=13.0.0.1 [56651]
*May 23 06:57:16.989: NAT*: s=13.0.0.1, d=192.168.1.102->10.0.0.30 [56651]
Router#
```

Source 10.0.0.30 is translated into 192.168.1.102 to destination 13.0.0.1. Return packet of Ping also retranslated, as source 13.0.0.1 to destination 192.168.1.100 –> 10.0.0.10.

```
Router#
*May 23 06:57:55.129: NAT: expiring 192.168.1.100 (10.0.0.10) icmp 14045 (14045)
*May 23 06:57:56.155: NAT: expiring 192.168.1.100 (10.0.0.10) icmp 14301 (14301)
Router#
*May 23 06:57:57.180: NAT: expiring 192.168.1.100 (10.0.0.10) icmp 14557 (14557)
*May 23 06:57:57.697: NAT: expiring 192.168.1.100 (10.0.0.10) icmp 14813 (14813)
Router#
*May 23 06:58:01.829: NAT: expiring 192.168.1.101 (10.0.0.20) icmp 15837 (15837)
Router#
*May 23 06:58:03.896: NAT: expiring 192.168.1.101 (10.0.0.20) icmp 16349 (16349)
*May 23 06:58:04.925: NAT: expiring 192.168.1.101 (10.0.0.20) icmp 16605 (16605)
Router#
*May 23 06:58:05.955: NAT: expiring 192.168.1.101 (10.0.0.20) icmp 16861 (16861)
*May 23 06:58:06.984: NAT: expiring 192.168.1.101 (10.0.0.20) icmp 17117 (17117)
Router#
*May 23 06:58:12.663: NAT: expiring 192.168.1.102 (10.0.0.30) icmp 18397 (18397)
Router#
*May 23 06:58:14.725: NAT: expiring 192.168.1.102 (10.0.0.30) icmp 18909 (18909)
*May 23 06:58:15.759: NAT: expiring 192.168.1.102 (10.0.0.30) icmp 19165 (19165)
Router#
*May 23 06:58:16.788: NAT: expiring 192.168.1.102 (10.0.0.30) icmp 19421 (19421)
Router#
*May 23 06:58:17.821: NAT: expiring 192.168.1.102 (10.0.0.30) icmp 19677 (19677)
Router#
```

Assigned Address translations are expired, moving back to pool IPS for reuse.

Router# show ip nat translations

```
R1
Router>
Router>en
Router#show ip nat tra
Router#show ip nat translations
Pro Inside global      Inside local       Outside local     Outside global
icmp 192.168.1.100:46304 10.0.0.10:46304  13.0.0.1:46304    13.0.0.1:46304
icmp 192.168.1.100:46816 10.0.0.10:46816  13.0.0.1:46816    13.0.0.1:46816
icmp 192.168.1.100:47072 10.0.0.10:47072  13.0.0.1:47072    13.0.0.1:47072
icmp 192.168.1.100:47328 10.0.0.10:47328  13.0.0.1:47328    13.0.0.1:47328
icmp 192.168.1.100:47584 10.0.0.10:47584  13.0.0.1:47584    13.0.0.1:47584
--- 192.168.1.100      10.0.0.10          ---               ---
icmp 192.168.1.101:48096 10.0.0.20:48096  13.0.0.1:48096    13.0.0.1:48096
icmp 192.168.1.101:48608 10.0.0.20:48608  13.0.0.1:48608    13.0.0.1:48608
icmp 192.168.1.101:48864 10.0.0.20:48864  13.0.0.1:48864    13.0.0.1:48864
icmp 192.168.1.101:49120 10.0.0.20:49120  13.0.0.1:49120    13.0.0.1:49120
icmp 192.168.1.101:49376 10.0.0.20:49376  13.0.0.1:49376    13.0.0.1:49376
--- 192.168.1.101      10.0.0.20          ---               ---
icmp 192.168.1.102:54496 10.0.0.30:54496  13.0.0.1:54496    13.0.0.1:54496
icmp 192.168.1.102:55008 10.0.0.30:55008  13.0.0.1:55008    13.0.0.1:55008
icmp 192.168.1.102:55264 10.0.0.30:55264  13.0.0.1:55264    13.0.0.1:55264
icmp 192.168.1.102:55520 10.0.0.30:55520  13.0.0.1:55520    13.0.0.1:55520
icmp 192.168.1.102:55776 10.0.0.30:55776  13.0.0.1:55776    13.0.0.1:55776
--- 192.168.1.102      10.0.0.30          ---               ---
Router#
```

Address translations are shown in the output.

Router# show ip nat statistics

```
R1
Router#show ip nat st
Router#show ip nat statistics
Total active translations: 18 (0 static, 18 dynamic; 15 extended)
Peak translations: 18, occurred 00:00:12 ago
Outside interfaces:
  Ethernet0/0
Inside interfaces:
  Ethernet0/1
Hits: 27  Misses: 0
CEF Translated packets: 27, CEF Punted packets: 0
Expired translations: 0
Dynamic mappings:
-- Inside Source
[Id: 1] access-list 10 pool IPS refcount 18
 pool IPS: netmask 255.255.255.0
        start 192.168.1.100 end 192.168.1.110
        type generic, total addresses 11, allocated 3 (27%), misses 0

Total doors: 0
Appl doors: 0
Normal doors: 0
Queued Packets: 0
Router#
Router#
```

Number of translations as well as inside and outside translation interfaces details.

Lab 12-3 : Port Address Translation:

Case Study:

In this Lab, we are troubleshooting the process of Port Address Translation in which number of IP address of an internal network i.e. 10.0.0.0/8 will be translated By PAT (Port Address Translation) into 1.0.0.0 network along with Port numbers.

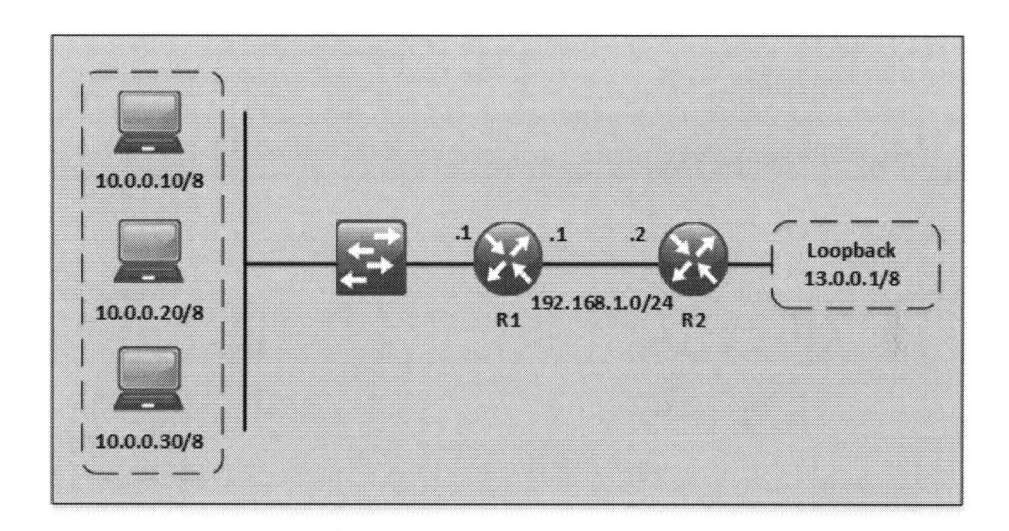

Router 1:

Router(config)#hostname R1

R1(config)#int eth 0/1

R1(config-if)#ip add 10.0.0.1 255.0.0.0

//Assign Correct IP address and Subnet Mask

R1(config-if)#no sh

// Must Turn up the interface

R1(config-if)#ex

*Mar 1 00:00:47.987: %LINK-3-UPDOWN: Interface FastEthernet0/0, changed state to up

*Mar 1 00:00:48.987: %LINEPROTO-5-UPDOWN: Line protocol on Interface FastEthernet0/0, changed state to up

//Interface and Interface Line Protocol, Both are up

R1(config)#int eth 0/0

R1(config-if)#ip add 192.168.1.1 255.255.255.0

//Assign Correct IP address and Subnet Mask

R1(config-if)#no sh

// Must Turn up the interface

R1(config-if)#ex

*Mar 1 00:01:20.571: %LINK-3-UPDOWN: Interface FastEthernet0/1, changed state to up

*Mar 1 00:01:21.571: %LINEPROTO-5-UPDOWN: Line protocol on Interface FastEthernet0/1, changed state to up

//Interface and Interface Line Protocol, Both are up

R1(config)#int eth 0/1

R1(config-if)#ip nat inside

//IP nat inside to the interface connected to the Inside Local Address

//Always configure NAT in correct direction

R1(config)#int eth 0/0

R1(config-if)#ip nat outside

//IP nat Outside to the interface connected translated address will send

//Always configure NAT in correct direction

R1(config)#access-list 10 permit 10.0.0.0 0.0.0.255

//Make sure Access-list number must be the same in NAT Command

R1(config)#ip nat pool IPS 1.0.0.1 1.0.0.255 netmask 255.0.0.0

R1(config)#ip nat inside source list 10 pool IPS overload

// Access list number and Pool Name must be the same

R1(config)#ip route 13.0.0.0 255.0.0.0 192.168.1.2

//Define a static route

Router 2

R2(config)#int eth 0/0

R2(config-if)#ip add 192.168.1.2 255.255.255.0

R2(config-if)#no sh

// Must Turn up the interface

R2(config-if)#ex

*Mar 1 00:06:27.403: %LINK-3-UPDOWN: Interface FastEthernet0/0, changed state to up

*Mar 1 00:06:28.403: %LINEPROTO-5-UPDOWN: Line protocol on Interface FastEthernet0/0, changed state to up

//Interface and Interface Line Protocol, Both are up

R2(config)#int lo 0

*Mar 1 00:06:34.319: %LINEPROTO-5-UPDOWN: Line protocol on Interface Loopback0, changed state to up

R2(config-if)#ip add 13.0.0.01 255.255.255.0

R2(config-if)#no sh

R2(config-if)#ex

Troubleshooting:

Ping from PC 1 to Lo interface 13.0.0.1

```
VPCS> ip 10.0.0.10 255.0.0.0 10.0.0.1
Checking for duplicate address...
PC1 : 10.0.0.10 255.0.0.0 gateway 10.0.0.1

VPCS> ping 13.0.0.1

84 bytes from 13.0.0.1 icmp_seq=1 ttl=254 time=1.204 ms
84 bytes from 13.0.0.1 icmp_seq=2 ttl=254 time=1.364 ms
84 bytes from 13.0.0.1 icmp_seq=3 ttl=254 time=1.349 ms
84 bytes from 13.0.0.1 icmp_seq=4 ttl=254 time=1.193 ms
84 bytes from 13.0.0.1 icmp_seq=5 ttl=254 time=1.385 ms

VPCS>
VPCS>
```

Ping from PC 2 to Lo interface 13.0.0.1

```
VPCS> ip 10.0.0.20 255.0.0.0 10.0.0.1
Checking for duplicate address...
PC1 : 10.0.0.20 255.0.0.0 gateway 10.0.0.1

VPCS> ping 13.0.0.1

13.0.0.1 icmp_seq=1 timeout
84 bytes from 13.0.0.1 icmp_seq=2 ttl=254 time=1.616 ms
84 bytes from 13.0.0.1 icmp_seq=3 ttl=254 time=1.372 ms
84 bytes from 13.0.0.1 icmp_seq=4 ttl=254 time=1.361 ms
84 bytes from 13.0.0.1 icmp_seq=5 ttl=254 time=1.449 ms

VPCS>
VPCS>
```

Ping from PC 3 to Lo interface 13.0.0.1

```
VPCS> ip 10.0.0.30 255.0.0.0 10.0.0.1
Checking for duplicate address...
PC1 : 10.0.0.30 255.0.0.0 gateway 10.0.0.1

VPCS> ping 13.0.0.1

13.0.0.1 icmp_seq=1 timeout
84 bytes from 13.0.0.1 icmp_seq=2 ttl=254 time=1.260 ms
84 bytes from 13.0.0.1 icmp_seq=3 ttl=254 time=1.278 ms
84 bytes from 13.0.0.1 icmp_seq=4 ttl=254 time=1.395 ms
84 bytes from 13.0.0.1 icmp_seq=5 ttl=254 time=1.521 ms

VPCS>
VPCS>
```

Router# show ip nat statistics

```
Router#
Router#show ip nat st
Router#show ip nat statistics
Total active translations: 15 (0 static, 15 dynamic; 15 extended)
Peak translations: 15, occurred 00:03:09 ago
Outside interfaces:
  Ethernet0/0
Inside interfaces:
  Ethernet0/1
Hits: 60  Misses: 0
CEF Translated packets: 60, CEF Punted packets: 0
Expired translations: 15
Dynamic mappings:
-- Inside Source
[Id: 2] access-list 10 pool IPS refcount 15
 pool IPS: netmask 255.0.0.0
        start 1.0.0.1 end 1.0.0.255
        type generic, total addresses 255, allocated 1 (0%), misses 0

Total doors: 0
Appl doors: 0
Normal doors: 0
Queued Packets: 0
Router#
```

Number of translations as well as inside and outside translation interfaces details. Number of Expired Translation details and other information

Router#debug ip nat

```
Router#debug ip nat
IP NAT debugging is on
Router#
*May 23 07:47:51.363: NAT*: s=10.0.0.10->1.0.0.1, d=13.0.0.1 [59687]
*May 23 07:47:51.364: NAT*: s=13.0.0.1, d=1.0.0.1->10.0.0.10 [59687]
*May 23 07:47:52.365: NAT*: s=10.0.0.10->1.0.0.1, d=13.0.0.1 [59688]
*May 23 07:47:52.366: NAT*: s=13.0.0.1, d=1.0.0.1->10.0.0.10 [59688]
Router#
*May 23 07:47:53.368: NAT*: s=10.0.0.10->1.0.0.1, d=13.0.0.1 [59689]
*May 23 07:47:53.368: NAT*: s=13.0.0.1, d=1.0.0.1->10.0.0.10 [59689]
*May 23 07:47:54.082: NAT*: s=10.0.0.20->1.0.0.1, d=13.0.0.1 [59690]
*May 23 07:47:54.082: NAT*: s=13.0.0.1, d=1.0.0.1->10.0.0.20 [59690]
Router#
*May 23 07:47:54.370: NAT*: ICMP id=10985->1024
*May 23 07:47:54.370: NAT*: s=10.0.0.10->1.0.0.1, d=13.0.0.1 [59690]
*May 23 07:47:54.371: NAT*: ICMP id=1024->10985
*May 23 07:47:54.371: NAT*: s=13.0.0.1, d=1.0.0.1->10.0.0.10 [59690]
*May 23 07:47:55.084: NAT*: s=10.0.0.20->1.0.0.1, d=13.0.0.1 [59691]
*May 23 07:47:55.085: NAT*: s=13.0.0.1, d=1.0.0.1->10.0.0.20 [59691]
*May 23 07:47:55.373: NAT*: ICMP id=11241->1025
*May 23 07:47:55.373: NAT*: s=10.0.0.10->1.0.0.1, d=13.0.0.1 [59691]
*May 23 07:47:55.373: NAT*: ICMP id=1025->11241
*May 23 07:47:55.373: NAT*: s=13.0.0.1, d=1.0.0.1->10.0.0.10 [59691]
Router#
*May 23 07:47:56.087: NAT*: s=10.0.0.20->1.0.0.1, d=13.0.0.1 [59692]
*May 23 07:47:56.087: NAT*: s=13.0.0.1, d=1.0.0.1->10.0.0.20 [59692]
*May 23 07:47:56.590: NAT*: ICMP id=11497->1026
*May 23 07:47:56.590: NAT*: s=10.0.0.30->1.0.0.1, d=13.0.0.1 [59692]
*May 23 07:47:56.590: NAT*: ICMP id=1026->11497
*May 23 07:47:56.590: NAT*: s=13.0.0.1, d=1.0.0.1->10.0.0.30 [59692]
*May 23 07:47:57.089: NAT*: s=10.0.0.20->1.0.0.1, d=13.0.0.1 [59693]
*May 23 07:47:57.089: NAT*: s=13.0.0.1, d=1.0.0.1->10.0.0.20 [59693]
Router#
*May 23 07:47:57.592: NAT*: ICMP id=11753->1027
*May 23 07:47:57.592: NAT*: s=10.0.0.30->1.0.0.1, d=13.0.0.1 [59693]
*May 23 07:47:57.593: NAT*: ICMP id=1027->11753
*May 23 07:47:57.593: NAT*: s=13.0.0.1, d=1.0.0.1->10.0.0.30 [59693]
*May 23 07:47:58.091: NAT*: s=10.0.0.20->1.0.0.1, d=13.0.0.1 [59694]
*May 23 07:47:58.092: NAT*: s=13.0.0.1, d=1.0.0.1->10.0.0.20 [59694]
Router#
*May 23 07:47:58.595: NAT*: ICMP id=12009->1028
*May 23 07:47:58.595: NAT*: s=10.0.0.30->1.0.0.1, d=13.0.0.1 [59694]
*May 23 07:47:58.595: NAT*: ICMP id=1028->12009
*May 23 07:47:58.595: NAT*: s=13.0.0.1, d=1.0.0.1->10.0.0.30 [59694]
*May 23 07:47:59.597: NAT*: s=10.0.0.30->1.0.0.1, d=13.0.0.1 [59695]
*May 23 07:47:59.598: NAT*: s=13.0.0.1, d=1.0.0.1->10.0.0.30 [59695]
Router#
*May 23 07:48:00.599: NAT*: s=10.0.0.30->1.0.0.1, d=13.0.0.1 [59696]
```

Source 10.0.0.10 is translated into 1.0.0.1 [59687] and forwarded to the destination 13.0.0.1. Reply from Source 13.0.0.1 to the destination 1.0.0.1 [59687] is translated back to 10.0.0.10. similarly other packets of ping translated for source 10.0.0.10 into 1.0.0.1 [59687], 1.0.0.1 [59688], 1.0.0.1 [59689] and 1.0.0.1 [59690].

Similarly Source 10.0.0.20 is translated into 1.0.0.1 [59691] and forwarded to the destination 13.0.0.1. Reply from Source 13.0.0.1 to the destination 1.0.0.1 [59691] is translated back to 10.0.0.20. similarly other packets of ping translated for source 10.0.0.20 into 1.0.0.1 [59691], 1.0.0.1 [59692], 1.0.0.1 [59693] and 1.0.0.1 [59694].

Same for source 10.0.0.30

```
Router#
*May 23 07:48:52.102: NAT: expiring 1.0.0.1 (10.0.0.10) icmp 10217 (10217)
Router#
*May 23 07:48:53.135: NAT: expiring 1.0.0.1 (10.0.0.10) icmp 10473 (10473)
*May 23 07:48:54.168: NAT: expiring 1.0.0.1 (10.0.0.10) icmp 10729 (10729)
Router#
*May 23 07:48:54.685: NAT: expiring 1.0.0.1 (10.0.0.20) icmp 10985 (10985)
*May 23 07:48:55.202: NAT: expiring 1.0.0.1 (10.0.0.10) icmp 1024 (10985)
Router#
*May 23 07:48:55.719: NAT: expiring 1.0.0.1 (10.0.0.20) icmp 11241 (11241)
*May 23 07:48:55.719: NAT: expiring 1.0.0.1 (10.0.0.10) icmp 1025 (11241)
*May 23 07:48:56.744: NAT: expiring 1.0.0.1 (10.0.0.20) icmp 11497 (11497)
Router#
*May 23 07:48:57.267: NAT: expiring 1.0.0.1 (10.0.0.30) icmp 1026 (11497)
*May 23 07:48:57.785: NAT: expiring 1.0.0.1 (10.0.0.20) icmp 11753 (11753)
Router#
*May 23 07:48:58.302: NAT: expiring 1.0.0.1 (10.0.0.30) icmp 1027 (11753)
*May 23 07:48:58.819: NAT: expiring 1.0.0.1 (10.0.0.20) icmp 12009 (12009)
Router#
*May 23 07:48:59.335: NAT: expiring 1.0.0.1 (10.0.0.30) icmp 1028 (12009)
*May 23 07:49:00.369: NAT: expiring 1.0.0.1 (10.0.0.30) icmp 12265 (12265)
Router#
*May 23 07:49:01.398: NAT: expiring 1.0.0.1 (10.0.0.30) icmp 12521 (12521)
Router#
```

Reserved Translation timeout, Address are assigned back in pool for reuse

Router#show ip nat translations

```
Router#no debug ip nat
IP NAT debugging is off
Router#show ip nat tran
Router#show ip nat translations
Pro Inside global      Inside local       Outside local      Outside global
icmp 1.0.0.1:53993     10.0.0.10:53993    13.0.0.1:53993     13.0.0.1:53993
icmp 1.0.0.1:54249     10.0.0.10:54249    13.0.0.1:54249     13.0.0.1:54249
icmp 1.0.0.1:1024      10.0.0.10:54505    13.0.0.1:54505     13.0.0.1:1024
icmp 1.0.0.1:1026      10.0.0.10:54761    13.0.0.1:54761     13.0.0.1:1026
icmp 1.0.0.1:1028      10.0.0.10:55017    13.0.0.1:55017     13.0.0.1:1028
icmp 1.0.0.1:54505     10.0.0.20:54505    13.0.0.1:54505     13.0.0.1:54505
icmp 1.0.0.1:54761     10.0.0.20:54761    13.0.0.1:54761     13.0.0.1:54761
icmp 1.0.0.1:55017     10.0.0.20:55017    13.0.0.1:55017     13.0.0.1:55017
icmp 1.0.0.1:55273     10.0.0.20:55273    13.0.0.1:55273     13.0.0.1:55273
icmp 1.0.0.1:55529     10.0.0.20:55529    13.0.0.1:55529     13.0.0.1:55529
icmp 1.0.0.1:1025      10.0.0.30:54761    13.0.0.1:54761     13.0.0.1:1025
icmp 1.0.0.1:1027      10.0.0.30:55017    13.0.0.1:55017     13.0.0.1:1027
icmp 1.0.0.1:1029      10.0.0.30:55273    13.0.0.1:55273     13.0.0.1:1029
icmp 1.0.0.1:1030      10.0.0.30:55529    13.0.0.1:55529     13.0.0.1:1030
icmp 1.0.0.1:55785     10.0.0.30:55785    13.0.0.1:55785     13.0.0.1:55785
Router#
Router#
Router#show ip nat st
```

Port address translation entries.

Lab 12-4 : Configuring DHCP Server, Relay and Client.

Case Study:

A company Z added two additional routers (Router_x and End_Client) in their x department and wants to configure DHCP on an old router. Follow given details:

- Make Router (Router_1) DHCP server.
- Create a pool pool_first and Reserve 8 IP addresses from a range 192.168.1.2 to 192.168.1.10 for other IT assets.
- Create a pool pool_R2 and exclude IP addresses from 172.16.10.2 to 172.16.10.51.
- Both pools should be creating on DHCP Router.
- Use IP helper Address command on a router (Router_x), in order to assign IP address to End_Client from a pool_R2
- Use address 1.1.1.1 for DNS server.

Note: You have to use Routing Protocol EIGRP with AS 1 on three routers

Solution:

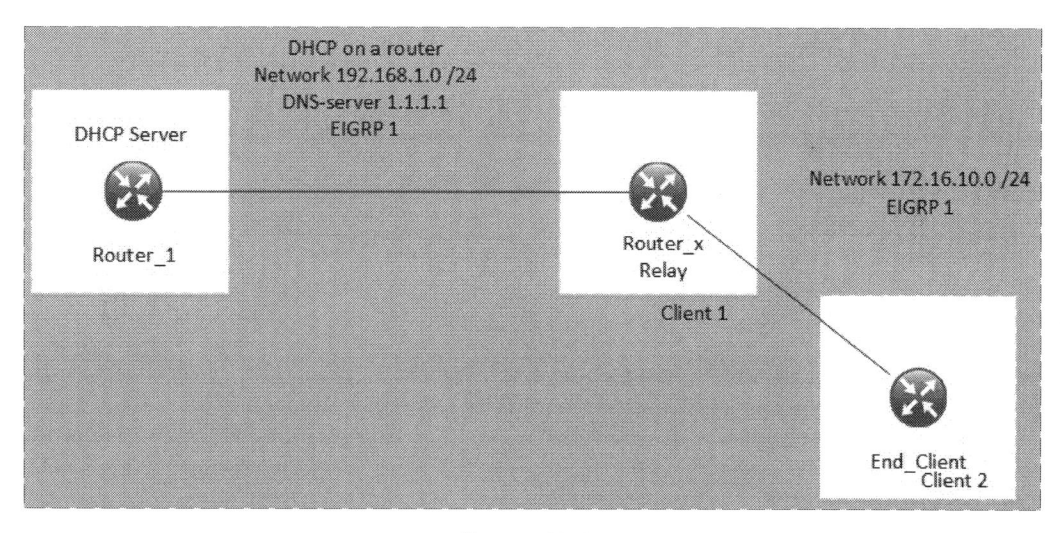

Figure 81 DHCP

DHCP SERVER Configuration:
Router(config)#hostname Router_1
// Configuring Pool for R1

```
Router_1(config)#ip dhcp excluded-address 192.168.1.2 192.168.1.10
Router_1(config)#ip dhcp pool pool_R1
Router_1(dhcp-config)# network 192.168.1.0 255.255.255.0
Router_1(dhcp-config)# default-router 192.168.1.1
Router_1(dhcp-config)# dns-server 1.1.1.1
Router_1(dhcp-config)# lease 60 2 20

// Configuring Pool for R1
Router_1(config)#ip dhcp excluded-address 172.16.10.2 172.16.10.50
Router_1(config)#ip dhcp pool pool_R2
Router_1(dhcp-config)# network 172.16.10.0 255.255.255.0

Router_1(config)#interface Ethernet2/0
Router_1(config-if)# ip address 192.168.1.1 255.255.255.0

Router_1(config)#router eigrp 1
Router_1(config-router)# network 192.168.1.0
Router_1(config-router)#no auto-summary.
```

Note: I used lease for 60 days 2 minutes and 20 seconds, lease has a fixed duration and it expires after it's time, then it will renew IP addresses.

Here, we configure EIGRP protocol to route traffic according to company requirements.

Relay

IP helper-address command forwards DHCP client requests. In our case we are not using it but it can be done with a command on an interface like this

Relay Router Configuration:

```
Router_x(config)#interface ethernet 2/1
Router_x(config-if)#ip address dhcp
Router_x(config-if)#no sh
Router_x(config-if)#
*Mar 10 01:25:52.455: %DHCP-6-ADDRESS_ASSIGN: Interface Ethernet2/1 assigned DHCP
address 192.168.1.11, mask 255.255.255.0, hostname Router_x
```

Note: You can see Clearly, it doesnot assign excluded IP addresses.

```
Router_x(config)#interface ethernet 1/2
Router_x(config-if)#ip address 172.16.10.1 255.255.255.0
Router_x(config-if)#no sh
Router_x(config-if)#ip helper-address 192.168.1.1


Router_x(config)#router eigrp 1
Router_x(config-router)#network 192.168.1.0
*Mar  10  01:30:13.690:  %DUAL-5-NBRCHANGE:  EIGRP-IPv4  1:  Neighbor  192.168.1.1
(Ethernet1/1) i
Router_x(config-router)#network 172.16.10.0
Router_x(config-router)#no auto-summary
```

Client

The client configuration consists of configuring the router or switch as a DHCP client, in our case we used Router with a name Client_1. This is done on a per-interface basis. On each interface, rather than configuring an IP address, execute the following command:

Client Configuration:

```
End_Client(config)#interface ethernet 1/0
End_Client(config-if)#ip address dhcp
End_Client(config-if)#no shutdown
*Mar 10 01:32:15.178: %DHCP-6-ADDRESS_ASSIGN: Interface Ethernet1/0 assigned DHCP
address 172.16.10.51, mask 255.255.255.0, hostname End_Client
$72.16.10.51, mask 255.255.255.0, hostname End_Client
```

Note: You can see clearly it assigned IP address from 172.16.10.51 because we excluded 172.16.10.2 – 172.16.10.50

End_Client(config)#router eigrp 1
End_Client(config-router)#network 172.16.10.0

TFTP, DNS, and gateway options

In the previous sub topic parts, we cover a default gateway and a DNS-Server for DHCP clients and working of a relay router. In order to configure a TFTP server address of like 192.168.2.10, execute the following command at the dhcp pool configuration prompt:

Although in our case we are not using any other server like TFTP but I am going to show you some configurations steps for your understanding:

Router_x(config)#ip dhcp pool 10
Router_x(dhcp-config)#option 100 ip 192.168.2.10

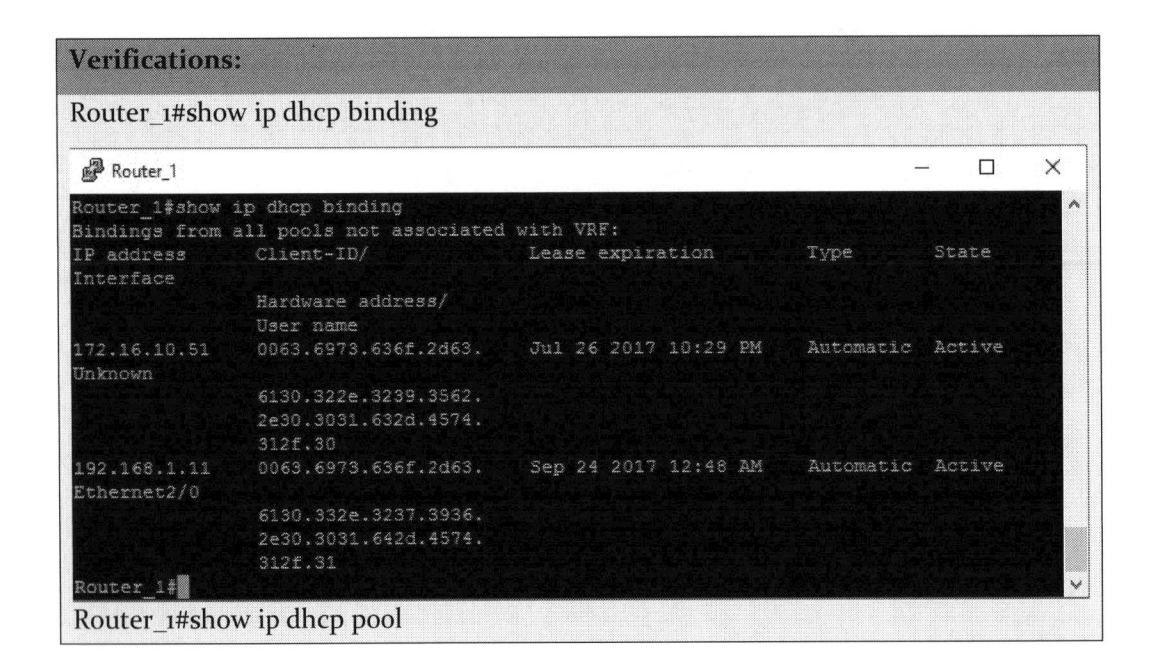

Verifications:

Router_1#show ip dhcp binding

```
Router_1#show ip dhcp binding
Bindings from all pools not associated with VRF:
IP address       Client-ID/              Lease expiration         Type        State
Interface
                 Hardware address/
                 User name
172.16.10.51     0063.6973.636f.2d63.    Jul 26 2017 10:29 PM     Automatic   Active
Unknown
                 6130.322e.3239.3562.
                 2e30.3031.632d.4574.
                 312f.30
192.168.1.11     0063.6973.636f.2d63.    Sep 24 2017 12:48 AM     Automatic   Active
Ethernet2/0
                 6130.332e.3237.3936.
                 2e30.3031.642d.4574.
                 312f.31
Router_1#
```

Router_1#show ip dhcp pool

```
Router_1#show ip dhcp pool

Pool pool_R1 :
 Utilization mark (high/low)    : 100 / 0
 Subnet size (first/next)       : 0 / 0
 Total addresses                : 254
 Leased addresses               : 1
 Excluded addresses             : 9
 Pending event                  : none
 1 subnet is currently in the pool :
  Current index        IP address range                        Leased/Excluded/Total
  192.168.1.12         192.168.1.1      - 192.168.1.254         1     / 9    / 254
Pool pool_R2 :
 Utilization mark (high/low)    : 100 / 0
 Subnet size (first/next)       : 0 / 0
 Total addresses                : 254
 Leased addresses               : 1
 Excluded addresses             : 50
 Pending event                  : none
 1 subnet is currently in the pool :
  Current index        IP address range                        Leased/Excluded/Total
  172.16.10.52         172.16.10.1      - 172.16.10.254         1     / 50   / 254
Router_1#
```

Router_1#ping 172.16.10.51

```
Router_1#ping 172.16.10.51
Type escape sequence to abort.
Sending 5, 100-byte ICMP Echos to 172.16.10.51, timeout is 2 seconds:
!!!!!
Success rate is 100 percent (5/5), round-trip min/avg/max = 28/36/44 ms
Router_1#
```

Note from the Author:

Reviews are gold to authors! If you have enjoyed this book and helped you along certification, would you consider rating it and reviewing it?

Link to Product Page: https://www.amazon.com/dp/B076QN223P

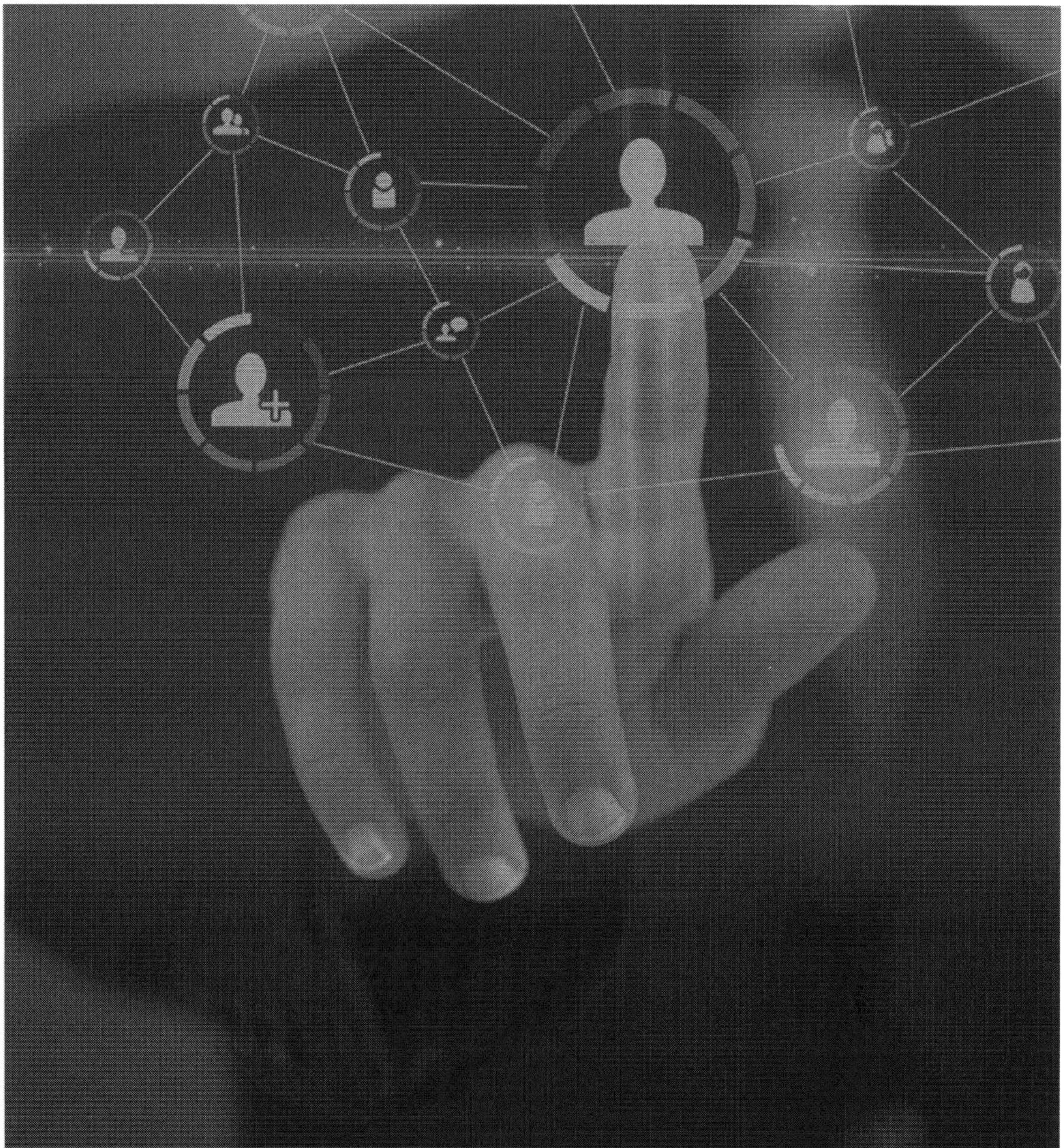

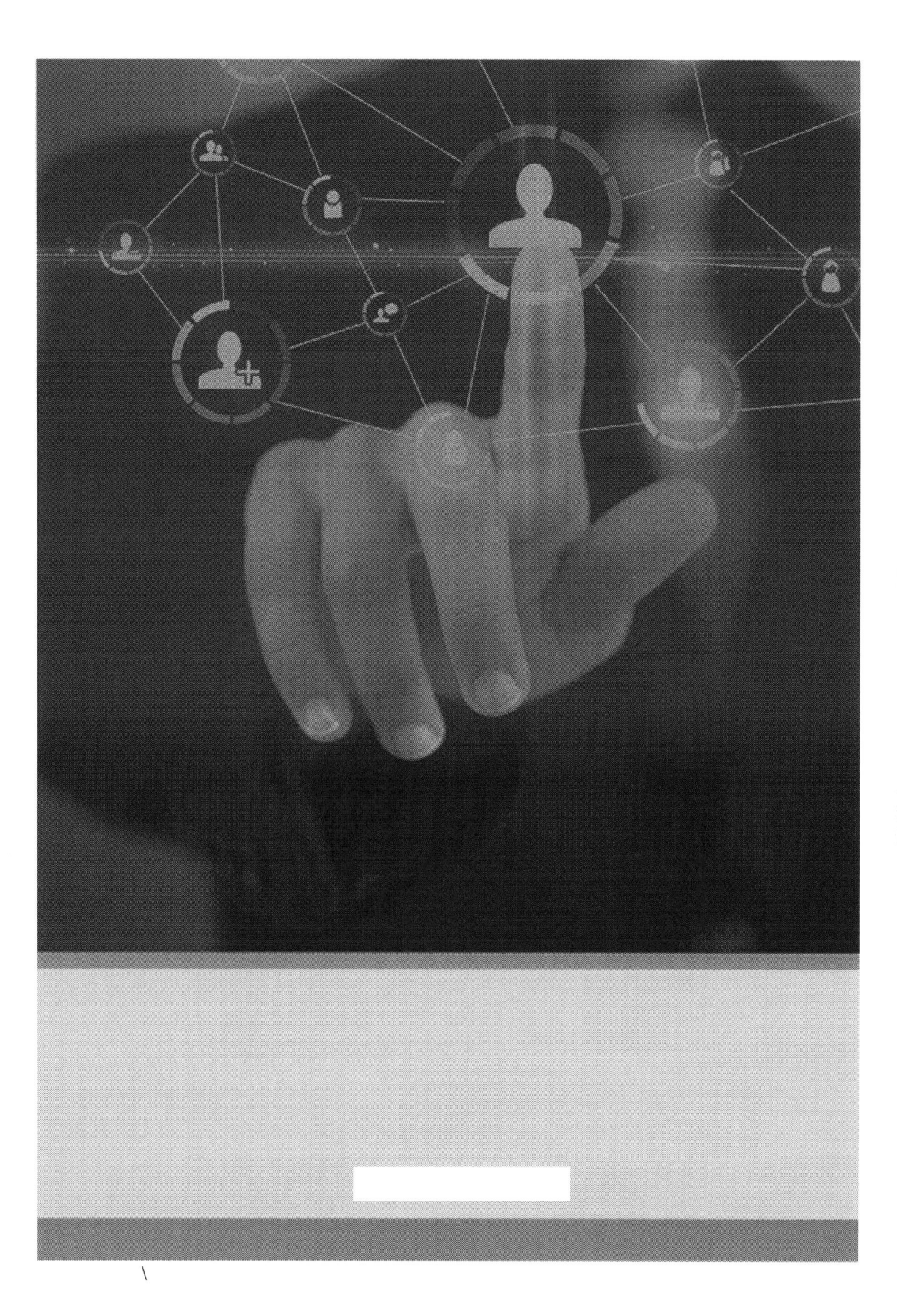

Printed in Germany
by Amazon Distribution
GmbH, Leipzig